HARVARD HISTORICAL STUDIES

Published under the direction of the
Department of History

From the income of
THE PAUL REVERE FROTHINGHAM BEQUEST
VOLUME LXX

Oscar Handlin, Editor

ARGENTINA,
the United States, and
the Inter-American System
1880-1914

THOMAS F. McGANN

HARVARD UNIVERSITY PRESS
CAMBRIDGE, MASSACHUSETTS
1957

Library of Congress Catalog Card Number A57–8626

Printed in Great Britain

Preface

THIS book is an historical analysis of significant years in Argentina's national development—the decades after 1880, when that country emerged as the richest Latin American state and a considerable economic influence in the western world. It is also a study of Argentina's economic, political, and cultural relations with the United States and the Inter-American system. These relations are treated as functions of Argentina's internal development; therefore the structure of Argentine society is examined in some detail, particularly the growth and goals of the dominant class. An elite of landowners and lawyers, merchants and statesmen built twentieth-century Argentina. They called themselves the Generation of Eighty; a later ruler of Argentina described them and their descendants as "oligarchs". Imbued with European ideas and living by European patterns, the aristocrats of the *pampas* dealt with hundreds of thousands of European immigrants, successfully at first; they directed the expansion of the city of Buenos Aires to metropolitan and cosmopolitan rank; they evolved and brilliantly supported a consistently successful foreign policy.

The application of Argentina's foreign policy to relations with the United States and the Inter-American system is closely studied. The first four Pan American Conferences, now known as the Conferences of the Organization of American States, are dealt with—those held in Washington, D.C., 1889–1890, Mexico City, 1901–1902, Rio de Janeiro, 1906, and Buenos Aires, 1910. Argentine reaction to such diverse stimulants as United States protective tariffs, Theodore Roosevelt's "big stick" (and his surprisingly successful later visit to Buenos Aires), and the expansion of United States business interests into

Argentina are traced. Events are set against the backdrop of Argentina's vast agricultural production and the mores of the talented men who, with their British associates, controlled the wealth of the land.

I deeply appreciate the grant from the Woodbury Lowery Fund, given to me by the Harvard History Department and the Harvard Graduate School of Arts and Sciences, which made possible my research in Argentina and in Washington, D.C. I thank the friends who have assisted me: Ann Louise Coffin, James and Chase Duffy, Enrique Gil, Oscar Handlin, Carlos Mayer, Hugh Montgomery, Julius W. Pratt, José Luis Romero, León Shulman, Tomás Sosa Moreira, Guillermo Oriburu Roca, and Milton Vanger. I am indebted to the publishers, editors, and staffs of the Argentine newspapers *La Prensa* and *La Nación*, the former staff of the library of the Jockey Club of Buenos Aires, the staffs of the Sala Groussac of the Biblioteca Nacional, the Archivo Nacional, and the library of the Ministry of Foreign Relation, all in Argentina, and to the persons who assisted me in the National Archives and in the Columbus Memorial Library of the Pan American Union in Washington, D.C. I am especially indebted to the staff of Harvard's Widener Library.

Kirkland House,   Thomas F. McGann
Cambridge, Mass.

Contents

ARGENTINA,

The United States, and the Inter-American System
1880–1914

Buenos Aires, 1880

SEVEN turbulent decades of Argentine history came to an end on September 20, 1880 in the sleepy town of Belgrano when a rump congress established the nearby city of Buenos Aires as the Federal Capital of the republic. This legislative decision took the metropolis from its inhabitants and from the province of which it was the head, and gave it to the entire nation, an act made possible by June's bloody street fighting in the city. At last the conflict for preëminence between *porteños*—the people of Buenos Aires—and provincials that had racked the nation since independence was stilled. No longer would the city rule the nation, and the president of Argentina be merely a "guest" in his temporary capital. An epoch had ended.

The events of 1880 sealed off a bitter era, but the power of Buenos Aires did not die. With the passing years the triumphant federalization of the city became an inverted victory: it was the vanquished porteños who conquered, the victorious provinces that were defeated. Buenos Aires became Argentina, hated or loved by all Argentines, sought by the nations of the world who came to trade, invest, and settle the peaceful pampas. And it was the men of Buenos Aires, native or adopted, who ruled the republic and brought Argentina in one generation from enfeebling fratricide to international influence.

In 1880, Buenos Aires was little marked by the future. Streetcar lines and several railroads crisscrossed the city and the first telephones were being installed, but the general aspect was close to that of the days of the last viceroy in the first years of the century. The population had increased from 44,000 in 1810 to 286,000 in 1880, but the streets, old and new, were no wider than the traditional, shady ten *varas* (about thirty feet) of colonial times.[1] The porteño who ventured beyond the few paved streets in the heart of the city rode—the people of Buenos Aires have never been walkers—through the same dust or mud as had Liniers and Rivadavia and Rosas. Along the main roads leading out of the city to the interior, vast swamps developed in hollows in the pampas after heavy rains, and many a traveler turned back after a ducking in one of these notorious *bañados*, then well out in the countryside, but soon to be deep within the limits of the swelling city.[2]

The streets were flanked by bleak plaster or mud walled houses of one story, their long, barred and shuttered windows close against the narrow strips of dirt that served as sidewalks. Only in the somewhat more prosperous seventies did second stories become common, with the heavily balustraded balconies that still predominate in the older parts of Buenos Aires.[3]

On the crowded sidewalks and in the streets army officers up from the Indian fighting on the southern frontier jostled Spaniards and Italians freshly disembarked from the old countries. Young university students hustled to hear Estrada lecture on constitutional law at the University of Buenos Aires, returning to endless noisy arguments in the Café de Catalanes or the Confitería del Aguila. Along elegant Calle Florida in the late afternoon rolled the luxurious carriages of the elite, bound for pleasure drives in new and fashionable Palermo, from which the memory of The Tyrant's *quinta* had recently been extirpated. At dusk, the carriages would return in ritual procession down Florida between the traditional lines of men waiting on the edges of the sidewalks to ogle the passing women.[4]

In the Río de la Plata, flowing smooth and vast and brown

[1] Luis Cánepa, *El Buenos Aires de antaño, en el cuarto centenario de su fundación, 1536–1936* (Buenos Aires, 1936), p. 74; Nicolás Besio Moreno, *Buenos Aires: puerto del Río de la Plata, capital de la Argentina: estudio crítico de su población, 1536–1936* (Buenos Aires, 1939), p. 430.

[2] Cánepa, *El Buenos Aires*, p. 111; J. Gavira, "Un paisaje urbano," *Revista de Indias*, año II, núm. 5, 1941, p. 45; A. Gallenga, *South America* (2nd ed.; London, 1881), pp. 265–266.

[3] Manuel Bilbao, *Buenos Aires desde su fundación hasta nuestros días* . . . (Buenos Aires, 1902), pp. 24–27; A. Taullard, *Nuestro antiguo Buenos Aires* . . . (Buenos Aires, 1927), pp. 167–184.

[4] Cánepa, *El Buenos Aires*, pp. 207–209, 398–403; Bilbao, *Buenos Aires*, pp. 149–150.

at the foot of the low bank which makes the only distinction between the planes of earth and water that surround Buenos Aires, two spindly piers gave coastal travelers and cargo access to the shore. Overseas vessels, barred by the mud of the shallow estuary from tying up at the *muelle de pasajeros*, discharged their passengers and goods into lighters far out in the river. [5]

In this ragged capital of 1880, men were dreaming mighty dreams of a brilliant, cosmopolitan city of the future—the near future, at that—but upon many of its leaders, as upon the streets and buildings, the past lay heavy in this year of decision. Together with younger men just emerging into prominence stood the old exiles of the thirties and forties who had become the patricians of *la gran aldea*—the great village—in the years after their victory over Rosas in 1852: Mitre and Sarmiento, Eduardo Costa and Vicente Fidel López, and others of familiar name. These were the heirs and executors of Argentina's war for independence from the Spanish monarchy—the Revolution of May. They had suffered persecution and long exile and had returned at last to continue their struggle, no longer against reactionary Rosas, but against the hard economic and political realities of a weak, disorganized nation. Close to these leaders were the landowning gentry, Anchorena, Luro, Unzué, Alzaga and others, owners of great tracts of land and countless livestock—men in search of a market, men who in the difficult years of reconstruction had not yet sacrificed to an intervening hierarchy of management the habit of work and personal supervision of their lands and cattle. Both political leaders and landowners had known hard times. Poverty at the lowest levels and an economy of scarcity up to the top rank of society characterized Argentine life until the 1870's. [6] It was only after 1880, when political conditions had been stabilized, new lands brought under

[5] Taullard, *Nuestro antiguo Buenos Aires*, pp. 28–35.

[6] Emilio Daireaux, "Aristocracia de antaño," *Revista de Derecho, Historia y Letras*, año I, tomo II, nov., 1898, pp. 36–42. An intimate view of the life of these years may be gleaned from a statement by a contemporary reprinted in [*Carlos*] *Pellegrini: Obras, precedidas de un ensayo biográfico por Agustín Rivero Astengo* (5 vols.; Buenos Aires, 1941), I, 167: "I have often visited, as though it were my own, the home of Dr. Valentín Alsina, when he was governor of Buenos Aires. He had all the dignity of an English lord, yet with no more pomp than that provided by his black suit, and the well-ironed collar that rose to his ears. The brick-floored patio, the table lighted by

cultivation, strains of livestock improved, and foreign markets found, that the old, hard days faded.

The effort to develop the country economically, and the continuation of political strife, armed and unarmed, absorbed all energies from 1852 to 1880. The leaven of Sarmiento and Alberdi, prophets of liberalism, was at work, but the results were still isolated: an improved breed of beef cattle, the organization of a railroad company, the establishment of a colony of immigrants—creations that consumed the scant resources of individuals and of the government, despite the slowly mounting inflow of European capital.[7]

Faced with unresolved economic and political issues which more than once in these years threatened to hurl the nation again into civil strife and tyranny, Argentina was little concerned with the outside world. Their land, the frontiers, the Indians, railroads, political factionalism—these causes drained Argentine energies inward as surely as they were absorbing the energy of the men 5,000 miles to the north. Apart from relations with bordering states, and from the issues connected with the slow growth of European capital and immigration, Argentina's international commitments were at a minimum. There was small need, in a nation that did not even have a permanent capital city, to indulge in the luxury of extensive foreign relations. Certain tenets of foreign policy existed, but it was only after 1880 that they became active principles by which the nation advanced its interests.

Political isolation, tending to break down under pressure from within and from Europe, was matched by intellectual isolation, also succumbing to penetration from abroad. The exiles who returned in 1852 to lead their country during another full generation were for the most part men of mature years, informed, sometimes belatedly, in the main currents of European thought. But these men had lived through what they considered

dipped candles, the austere meals (stew and barbecued meat), the poverty, in short, of this magistrate, was all the wealth of those times." There is particular point to this description when we recall that in these years the governor of the province of Buenos Aires was as powerful, and often more powerful, than the president of the republic.

[7] Ysabel Rennie, *The Argentine Republic* (New York, 1945), pp. 90–166.

to be the great national hiatus of the Rosas dictatorship. They regarded themselves as the true continuers of the aborted May Revolution; their eyes were focused on recouping the ground which they believed had been lost after Rosas put an end to the first liberal period in 1828. To accomplish this meant to reëstablish the bases of the republic by endowing it with a constitution and a judicial code, and by making other arduous adjustments to reality. But the leaders tended to cast their thoughts and actions in the mold of the doctrines of earlier days. The *proscriptos* looked back upon the French and American revolutions with a sense of proximity born of their own bitterly deferred revolutionary hopes, and with a fervent idealism reminiscent of the romanticism of their youth. The political liberalism of Guizot and Constant, Bentham's utilitarianism, the social philosophies of Saint Simon and Leroux, and the adaptation of these alien beliefs by such men as Sarmiento and Alberdi—these were materials with which the exiles built.[8] Intensely occupied with the practical problems of their retarded land, they sought to create at last an Argentina new in fact but old in thought—an image of the utopias which they had long ago discerned across the ocean.

Yet this older generation was intensely Argentine. While they controlled the country there was no engulfment of the nation by European ways of life such as occurred after 1880. This does not mean that French and English thought was stifled from 1852 to 1880. Rather it increased, extended by the young men in the schools and universities. There was, for example, Comtean positivism, which was vigorously taught by a French exile named Amedée Jacques to a generation of precocious students in Buenos Aires in the 1860's, a surprising number of whom became men of importance after 1880.[9] But although the younger generation

[8] José Ingenieros, *La evolución de las ideas argentinas* (2 vols.; Buenos Aires, 1918–1920), II, 605–754.
[9] Ricardo Rojas, "Los proscriptos," *La literatura argentina; ensayo filosófico sobre la evolución de la cultura en El Plata* (2nd ed., 8 vols.; Buenos Aires, 1924–25 [from *Obras*, 19 vols.; Buenos Aires, 1922–1930]), XII, 397–428, XIII, 1159–1180; Leopoldo Zea, *Dos etapas del pensamiento en Hispanoamérica: del romanticismo al positivismo* (México, 1949), pp. 267–278; Miguel Cané, *Juvenilia* (1st ed., 1882; Buenos Aires, 1939), pp. 36–59; Aníbal Ponce, *La vejez de Sarmiento; Amadeo Jacques . . .* (2nd ed.; Buenos Aires, 1949), pp. 31–60.

was inculcated with most of Europe's newer doctrines, this intellectual weaning was accomplished in the homeland. The older generation, by choice or necessity, sent their sons to school in Argentina—a pattern which the sons did not usually follow with their own heirs. Saenz Peña, Emilio Mitre, Pellegrini, Alcorta, L. V. López, Dominguito—most of the leaders or potential leaders of the Generation of Eighty attended school and university in Buenos Aires. And not all their training came from foreign texts and the classroom, but, as their fathers expected, could also be gained in the crowded old galleries of the provincial and national congresses in Buenos Aires, where Mitre and Alsina, Vélez Sársfield and Rawson debated.

These were indeed "years of triumphant *criollismo*"[10]—the old, native customs. Del Campo's parody *Fausto* was a best seller at the moment that the barren fields which were later to become Plaza Constitución and Plaza Once de Septiembre were used as assembly points by rough carters and horsemen from the west and south—men who looked suspiciously like Del Campo's *gauchos* Anastasio el Pollo and Laguna. The viaticum was preceded through the streets by a bell-ringer, as in colonial times, and bulky two-wheel wagons of colonial type (*carros de cola*) blocked traffic while dispensing wine in the narrow streets of the nation's largest city.[11] These were years when Indians made as much news as Englishmen.

In 1880, year of denouement, one man summed up the forces, old and new, at work within the nation. Nicolás Avellaneda, a mild, almost feminine man in a society that counted virility at a premium, brought Argentina through its last years of widespread civil strife as effectively as had somber Mitre and raucous Sarmiento in preceding administrations. During his term of office from 1874 to the end of 1880, Avellaneda labored both to suppress civil war and to remove the causes of instability. In 1876 he broke the revolt of Ricardo López Jordán, last of the fighting provincial *caudillos*. In that same year he made a trip by

[10] Paul Groussac, *Los que pasaban: José Manuel Estrada; Pedro Goyena; Nicolás Avellaneda* . . . (2nd ed.; Buenos Aires, 1939), p. 99.

[11] Cánepa, *El Buenos Aires*, pp. 212–213, 301–302, 346; Taullard, *Nuestro antiguo Buenos Aires*, pp. 96–97, 106–107.

railroad, the importance of which, although symbolic, was perhaps equal to that of his victory over López. In 1876, Avellaneda returned to his native city of Tucumán, traveling by rail further than any previous Argentine president, over the weedy pampas and across the salty deserts. This was Argentina's golden spike at Ogden, proclaiming to the world, or better, to western Europe, that another nation stood on the threshold of an era of expansion.

In this same year of accomplishment the first shipment of wheat was exported from Argentina. Avellaneda recognized and described that event for what it was—the most momentous occurrence of his administration.[12] Finally, it was he who initiated the conquest of the desert. Both unsuccessful Alsina and victorious Roca were his Ministers of War; through them he removed a last obstacle to the stability and growth of the nation.

Avellaneda's accomplishments have not been given sufficient recognition by succeeding generations of Argentines. During his tenure ties running deep into the past were severed and strands of the future woven. Appropriately, strong contrasts distinguish his administration. Wealth and population grew during his presidency, yet his government also faced a severe financial crisis of the old sort, the result of internal and foreign wars, mismanaged currency, and the impoverished condition of national revenues. Son of a man whose head had been exposed on a pike in the square of Tucumán by the soldiers of Oribe and Rosas, Avellaneda lived only long enough to witness the first burst of prosperity in the mid-eighties. By his years he belonged to the new generation of the *ochenta*; by his work he was of the age of the organizers, whose achievements he capped. He was forty-eight when he died in 1885. His last important act as president put a dramatic close to the *era criolla*.[13] It was Avellaneda who

---

[12] Nicolás Avellaneda, *Escritos y discursos* . . . (12 vols.; Buenos Aires, 1910), XII, 231.

[13] The date 1880 is a deep chronological crevasse separating the old and the new Argentinas. The apt designation "*era criolla*" is given by José Luis Romero, *Las ideas políticas en Argentina* (México, 1946), p. 63. Ricardo Rojas makes a major division of Argentine history at this point, stating that "after 1880 one may distinguish a new intellectual cycle in the evolution of Argentina." See Ricardo Rojas, "Los modernos," *La literatura argentina; ensayo filosófico sobre la evolución de la cultura en*

signed the legislation on September 21, 1880 that made Buenos
Aires the capital of the republic and ushered in an extraordinary
decade.

El Plata, XIV, 981–982. One of the most profound Argentine thinkers calls 1880
"the year of the death of the gaucho." See Ezequiel Martínez Estrada, *Radiografía
de la pampa* (2 vols.; Buenos Aires, 1942), I, 59. Alberdi, a famed builder of Argentina, recognized the epochal nature of the year 1880 before the year itself had ended.
Writing in the political turmoil of Buenos Aires at the end of 1880, he put it this
way: "Seventy years after the Revolution of May . . . the Republic has been reborn, or rather has just been born as a political structure, on the day when there
ceased to exist the old monarchist institution of the capital-province in which the
colonial regime lived on until 1880." J. B. Alberdi, "La República Argentina consolidada en 1880 con la ciudad de Buenos Aires por capital (1881)," *Obras selectas*
. . . ed. by Joaquín V. González (18 vols.; Buenos Aires, 1920), XII, 5–6.

2

Progress, 1880–1890

THE gathering energies of the nation rushed into unblocked channels of economic activity when the cancer of Buenos Aires was at last healed, and the Indians of the desert south and west had been driven from their lands. Characteristic of this movement was the quick response of congress to the new conditions. Although the civil war had ended only a few weeks before, and congress was still assembled at its place of refuge in Belgrano, where it was engaged in drafting the law of federalization, the senators and deputies found time to turn to economic matters facing the country, and they plunged zestfully into debates over the incorporation of new railroad companies, the establishment of colonies of immigrants, and the building of public works.[1]

This activity reflected national ambitions and coincided with the hopes of Avellaneda, but it was the man who succeeded him as president who set the pace for the decade—indeed, for the generation—ahead. When Julio A. Roca went before congress in May 1881, to deliver his first "state-of-the-union" message, he was already a hero. He was thirty-seven years old, a slim man with a trim goatee, an oval, unlined face, and slightly protruding eyes. He had qualities that many foreigners believe are lacking in a goodly number of Argentine males: he was reserved, not loquacious; subtle, not blustering; and tenacious rather than sporadic in planning and execution. His nationwide nickname was *El Zorro*—"The Fox."[2]

Roca's latest successes had been his greatest. Standing in the

---

[1] Congreso Nacional, *Diario de sesiones de la Cámara de Diputados*, 1880, pp. 130–199.

[2] Leopoldo Lugones, *Roca* (Buenos Aires, 1938); Augusto Marcó del Pont, *Roca y su tiempo* (*cincuenta años de historia argentina*) (Buenos Aires, 1931); Mariano de Vedia, *Roca en el escenario político* (Buenos Aires, 1939). A worthy sketch of Roca is in Octavio R. Amadeo, *Vidas argentinas . . .* (2nd ed.; Buenos Aires, 1934), pp. 17–28.

deep chamber of the senate, before the assembled officials and
the diplomats and plumed ladies in the galleries, he had the
strength of two great victories behind him. He was the Conqueror of the Desert, and the conqueror of Buenos Aires. He was
the man most responsible for placing the nation upon its new
foundation.

Now he had one more victory to win for his country: the
conquest of its wealth. He outlined his achievements to his
audience: ". . . profound peace and the most complete order
and liberty reign in all parts of the republic." And his program:
the nation, he said, is expanding in every direction; there are
great potentialities to be exploited. The government has plans
afoot for the construction of a mighty port at Buenos Aires;
telegraph and rail lines and many other material improvements
will be extended and initiated. Then, significantly, he looked
abroad: "Our credit, both political and economic, is penetrating
all the peoples and markets of Europe and they are at last beginning to believe that we have entered upon an epoch of reason
and maturity." He closed his lucid report with the words which
became the *leitmotiv* of the dawning golden era in Argentina:
the mark of his government, Roca told his eager listeners, was
"peace and administration." [3]

Peace and administration—an elastic phrase, adaptable to
the needs of a single class in the next decades, and productive of
tangible results: railroads, ports, streetcar lines, gas companies,
waterworks, public buildings—even an entire new city, La
Plata, created *ad hoc* as the capital of the province of Buenos
Aires after the decapitation of the city of Buenos Aires. Into
these forms the nation poured its forces, heartened by political
stability and assisted by a most beneficent government.

The world soon heard of Argentine progress. In 1879, the
country had 2,136 kilometers of railroad; in 1889, 6,551. [4] In the
decade 1871–1880, Argentina retained a net of 90,678 immigrants; in 1881–1890, the figure was 648,711; from 1891 to 1910,

---

[3] Heraclio Mabragaña, compiler, *Los Mensajes. Historia del desenvolvimiento de la
Nación Argentina, redactada cronologicamente por sus gobernantes, 1810–1910* (6 vols.;
Buenos Aires, n.d. [?1910]), IV, 1–30.

[4] *Anuario geográfico argentino, 1941* (Buenos Aires, 1941), p. 447.

the number was 1,472,075.[5] In 1876, Argentina exported 21 tons of wheat; in 1890, 327,894 tons; and from 1900 to 1914, an average of 2,285,355 tons each year, not to mention the average yearly corn export of 2,291,551 tons in that same period.[6]

These are some of the intoxicating results of the political and telluric liberation of 1880, but the military and political events culminating in that year are by no means the whole explanation of the surge of productivity which swept Argentina from its isolated and retrograde condition to a position as one of the agricultural powers of the world. Behind this flood of energy was the land—deep, rich earth, deeper than any that the farmers of Europe or New England or even Middle Western United States have ever seen: twelve, fifteen, twenty feet of humus-laden top-soil, and thousands of square miles of level plains without stones or forests. In conjunction with the land, and the men to work it, was the supreme instrument of exploitation—capital, foreign money. European investors were as enthralled as Argentine landowners by the apparently limitless potentialities of the fertile pampas. Banking consortiums in England and to a lesser degree in France, lured on by fast mounting profits, could hardly keep up with the demand for new issues of Argentine bonds. By the mid-eighties investment in a profitable present had become obsessive speculation in a fabulous future. From 1881 through 1885 (Roca was president from 1880 to 1886), Argentine borrowers, public and private, received loans totaling 149,359,000 gold pesos. From 1886 through 1890 (Roca's brother-in-law, Juárez Celman, was president), the figure was a staggering 666,000,000 gold pesos.[7] For ten years the Argentine ruling

[5] *Anuario*, p. 186; Nicolás Besio Moreno, *Buenos Aires: puerto del Río de la Plata, capital de la Argentina: estudio crítico de su población, 1536–1936* (Buenos Aires, 1939), pp. 293–299. The increase of Argentina's population by immigration from 1870 to 1914 was relatively far greater than that of the United States. See Carl Taylor, *Rural Life in Argentina* (Baton Rouge, 1948), p. 57.

[6] *Anuario*, pp. 207, 210; Ernesto Tornquist and Co., Ltd., *The Economic Development of the Argentine Republic in the Last Fifty Years* (Buenos Aires, 1919), pp. 30–31.

[7] John H. Williams, *Argentine International Trade under Inconvertible Paper Money, 1880–1900*, Harvard Economic Studies, XXII (Cambridge, Mass., 1920), pp. 43, 102. The Argentine gold peso equaled United States $0.965; *ibid.*, p. 72, n. 3.

class, followed by the rest of the nation, speculated wildly—and successfully—on the destiny of their land.

At the vortex of the financial whirlpool was the Argentine government, for the government was the instrument of the dominant class in the nation. *Estancieros*—the great landowners and cattlemen—and politicians, speculators, and corporation lawyers were the principal Argentine beneficiaries of the colossal inflation of land values and export prices. Continuation of prosperity for these men in the eighties depended upon their ability to sustain the credit of the Argentine Republic, and that credit paradoxically hinged, not only upon the wealth of the land or the numbers of immigrants, but on the continued flow of foreign money. With credit the soaring imports of foreign machinery, iron, coal, and textiles could be maintained; with these and manifold other articles the nation could continue to exploit its raw materials and expand production, thus closing the magic circle by offering still wider areas for foreign investment.

The Argentine landlords and their associates, immediate owners and distributors of the nation's wealth, were undismayed by the currency inflation that began late in 1884. Already the fortunate legatees of a rise in land values that would have whitened the hair of Henry George, these men also profited by the declining value of the peso. The flow of British pounds and French francs into their bank accounts seemed to insulate them against the harsh reality of the swiftly widening gap between gold and paper. Consequently, the government did nothing to halt inflation, but rather assisted it, even to the point of making secret emissions of paper money in the last desperate days before the bubble burst. [8]

By this extravagant performance in domestic and international finance, the Argentine ruling class bound itself to Europe with chains of gold. In return for these bonds (literal and figurative) the nation paid interest, and also surrendered to foreigners the ownership of its railroads and other utilities, and of vast tracts of land. At the same time, this money enabled the nation to become equipped (in certain regions, at least) with the mechanical trappings of European civilization, and

[8] Ysabel Rennie, *The Argentine Republic* (New York, 1945), pp. 176–181.

permitted some Argentines increasingly to adopt European modes of life.

Forty years before, in *Facundo*, an impassioned attack on the barbaric condition of his country, Sarmiento had called upon the people to defeat their tyrants and join hands with the world in its march of progress under the flags of liberty, science, and education. With that vital sense of reality which marked his career, Sarmiento wrote: "Buenos Aires is so powerful in elements of European civilization that it will end by educating Rosas himself." [9] Sarmiento was nearly correct. Before his death in 1888 Buenos Aires was well on its way to conquering, or reconquering, all of Argentina. And Europe had conquered Buenos Aires.

The scrawny sheep and cattle that had roamed the open range, providing short, greasy wool for the natives and tough, dried meat for Brazil, were rapidly supplanted by pedigreed flocks and herds bred from imported stock and enclosed by tight new wire fences. The Sociedad Rural, a livestock-raisers organization, founded in Buenos Aires in the austere sixties, was by the mid-eighties a power in the province of Buenos Aires and in the national government. [10] The rough and restless gauchos had reached the end of the trail; by 1880 they had been for the most part transformed into sedentary ranch hands—*peones*. It was no coincidence that the first part of *Martín Fierro*, Argentina's spirited "epic" of the vanishing gaucho, was published in 1872, and the last part in 1879.

Political events kept pace with these changes. Burgeoning trade with Europe and the accumulation of wealth by the owners of the estancias, or *latifundios*, of the province of Buenos Aires and adjacent fertile extensions of the humid pampas enabled the landlords to concentrate a preponderance of national authority within their small circle. The interior provinces, important in the days when European trade was small, lost power steadily before the encroachments of the men who controlled

[9] Domingo Faustino Sarmiento, *Facundo: civilización y barbarie en la República Argentina*, Introducción por Joaquín V. González (1st ed., 1845; Buenos Aires, 1915), pp. 33–35, 99.

[10] Emilio Frers, *El progreso agricola de la Nación y la Sociedad Rural Argentina* . . . (Buenos Aires, 1916), pp. 11–101.

the organs of national government in the new capital.[11] The collapse of the Argentine federal structure in fact, if not in theory, dates from this decade. This is particularly surprising in view of the fact that the assumption, or better, the re-assertion, of control over the provinces by the great port city occurred so soon after the defeat in June 1880 of the military forces of Buenos Aires by a coalition of provincial forces led by Avellaneda and Roca. The victory of the provincials over the porteños proved to be a political illusion which dissipated on the realities of economic geography.

The shift of power back to Buenos Aires and the overwhelming role of the great city within the nation must be assessed before the objectives and attitudes of the men who helped to shape Argentine life in the years after 1880 can be understood. This is true because Buenos Aires is in many ways a unique city —whose historical meaning is difficult for even urbanized North Americans to grasp. Buenos Aires has been a big city since 1880. In that year it had 286,700 inhabitants; by 1890, the population had grown to 526,900; in 1900 it was 815,680, and in 1914, 1,553,805.[12] However, this phenomenal growth is equaled in importance by another fact: the remainder of the Argentine nation did not grow proportionately; rather, the great city absorbed the wealth and rights and talents of the provinces until there was created—or intensified, for in some degree this problem has existed from the earliest days in Argentina—a condition of unbalance, of capital against country, of porteño against *provinciano*, that has been one of the decisive factors in the nation's history down to today.

The provincial league that defeated Buenos Aires in 1880 temporarily checked the political authority of the city, but the economic power lodged in the capital and in the province of Buenos Aires undid their efforts. Roca and other hardheaded provincials quickly recognized this fact (if, indeed, they were not already aware of it and sought more to conquer a share in the power of the city rather than to destroy its vigor) and they

---

[11] Ricardo Zorraquín Becú, *El federalismo argentino* (Buenos Aires, 1939), pp. 241–270; Ricardo Rivarola, *Del régimen federativo al unitario; estudio sobre la organización política de la Argentina* (Buenos Aires, 1908), pp. 361–381.

[12] Besio Moreno, *Buenos Aires*, pp. 430–431.

soon succumbed body and soul to the immanent authority of Buenos Aires. But some of the leading figures of the day, men versed in Argentine history and experienced in national affairs, were deceived by the mere legal act of federalization into believing that a rightful equilibrium would thereby be restored to the nation. Most deluded among these federalists was one of the founders of modern Argentina—a principal proponent of the very forces that were at last sweeping parts of the republic to new levels of material achievement. Juan Bautista Alberdi wrote a book in 1880 which he regarded as the sequel to his *Bases*, the study which influenced the formation of the Argentine constitution of 1853. In *La República Argentina consolidada*, Alberdi described the assumed final victory of the provinces over Buenos Aires. Unfortunately for the cause which he upheld, almost everything he so forcefully stated as fact was the reverse of reality. Unerringly he described the elements that made Buenos Aires and its tributary hinterland the giant pivot of the nation —but he insisted that this domination had been nullified by the law splitting the province from its old capital. He understood and wrote that Buenos Aires was the "natural capital" of Argentina, "encompassing all the elements of power in the nation," yet he predicted that, while the recent separation of province from city would give Buenos Aires a "modern and liberal autonomy, [it] will not be the autonomy of the time of Rosas, which was an absorption of the vitality of the nation." He also optimistically demanded an exodus of part of the population of Buenos Aires into the interior, a curb to the growing number of landlords moving into the city to take up residence, and a diminution of the "excessive" number of professional men and foreign businessmen in the city.[13]

Alberdi was an excellent prophet—by opposites. The population of the city of Buenos Aires grew by 84 per cent in the decade from 1880 to 1890; the population of the nation beyond the capital grew by only 29 per cent.[14] The immigrant tide rolling

[13] Juan B. Alberdi, "La República Argentina consolidada en 1880 con la ciudad de Buenos Aires por capital (1881)," *Obras selectas* . . . (18 vols.; Buenos Aires, 1920), XIII, 3, 30, 56, 101–105, 186–189, 194–195.

[14] Author's calculations based on national population figures in *Anuario*, p. 159, and figures for Buenos Aires in Besio Moreno, *Buenos Aires*, p. 430.

onto Argentine shores broke at Buenos Aires; only the lesser part moved on to the pampas encircling the city. Impelled by this influx and by the prevailing faith in automatic progress, the national administration, through a series of laws culminating in 1888, grandly extended the bounds of Buenos Aires. This truly American gesture brought within the new limits of the city distant suburbs and great stretches of open country, and raised the area of the federal capital from fifteen to seventy-eight square miles.[15] In this fashion Argentina was endowed by its optimistic rulers with the outline of a massive head—a potential world capital, capable of serving their most expansive dreams of international commerce. There were no voices raised in those days of feverish accomplishment to inquire if the body—the nation beyond the port—would not be forced to sacrifice its own strength in its effort to support this giant's head.[16]

But Buenos Aires was more than a promise and a haven for Italian and Spanish immigrants, and more than a place for the mansions of the wealthy, who moved into the northern quarter of the city after 1880, the *barrio del norte*, running from the Plaza San Martín out to the Recoleta and beyond. Buenos Aires was primarily an economic power complex, deriving its new dynamism from two factors in addition to its increased population: the port, and the railroad network.

The port of Buenos Aires was dug out of the mud of the Río de la Plata. One hundred and thirty miles from the Atlantic up a silty, shallow estuary, against a low bank offering no natural advantages, the men of the city began in 1882 to create a port to handle their trade. The first section of the harbor (destined within twenty-five years to be second only to the port of New York in this hemisphere in the volume of its shipping) was inaugurated in January 1889. In that year 6,367 steam and sailing ships entered from abroad; in 1880 the number had been 2,201.[17]

[15] H. deMartonne, "Buenos Aires, étude de géographie urbaine," *Annales de géographie*, No. 249, XLIV, 15 Mai 1935, p. 286; Arturo B. Carranza, *La capital de la República, el ensanche de su municipio, 1881 a 1888 (antecedentes, debates parlamentarios, iniciativos, proyectos y leyes)* . . . (Buenos Aires, 1938).

[16] Ezequiel Martínez Estrada, *La cabeza de Goliat; microscopía de Buenos Aires* (2nd ed.; Buenos Aires, 1947), pp. 27–29.

[17] Tornquist, *The Economic Development of the Argentine Republic*, pp. 191–192.

Carlos Pellegrini, vice-president of the nation and, more than that, one of the leaders in the group ruling the land, dedicated the docks in a speech bursting with optimism and a sense of national destiny. Standing tall above the top-hatted dignitaries and the crowds on the piers—he was a husky 6′ 3″, with a handsome head, blue eyes, and flowing, handle-bar moustaches—Pellegrini was just the man to inspire the country with the spirit of the occasion. He described the port in dazzling terms and defined it as "a link with world commerce." Indeed, he said, the Argentine people have come so far and accomplished such wonders in their land that they are "reproducing the genius of the Yankees" (the highest praise of the day in Argentina, so long as it applied to some Argentine economic advance with which the Yankees had absolutely nothing to do). Then Pellegrini rose to the summit of his oration and predicted that the twentieth century "will be the century of America—a future that imposes upon us [Argentines] special duties."[18]

The port of Buenos Aires was indeed a link with the world— a special part of the world. Buenos Aires was a spigot from which poured a torrent of wheat and meat for Europe; it was also a funnel for goods incoming from the other side of the Atlantic. It was a two-way valve, and those who had their hands on the valve controlled the nation. *La tierra adentro*—the land inside— produced; the city bought—and sold. In the city were the quick profits on futures and the surer gains of the shippers. Here the auctioneers swung their hammers on city blocks and leagues of pampas and lots of blooded livestock, posting higher and higher prices every week.[19] Here, in short, Argentine estanciero and speculator and foreign entrepreneur did their business.

The rail system was the other factor upon which Buenos Aires founded its greatness. Customarily, those who have written about Argentina have described the railroads which spread over the nation in the years from 1880 to 1914 as a net of iron cast out upon the country, binding it into unity, bringing progress

[18] Carlos Pellegrini, *Discursos y escritos, 1881–1906, con un prólogo de Enrique de Vedia; recop. por Domingo de Muro* (Buenos Aires, 1910), pp. 51–53.

[19] See the issues of the Buenos Aires daily newspapers, *La Prensa* and *La Nación*, bulging with advertisements of land and livestock sales.

and prosperity to the farthest reaches of the republic. There is
another way of viewing the Argentine railroad system. Look
back down the railroads from the same distant points in the
interior provinces. The effect is the same as peering down the
barrel of a loaded rifle. You are looking back at the mechanism
which decides life or death: Buenos Aires. The city of Buenos
Aires had the first railroad in the country (in 1857), and from
that time to this the province of Buenos Aires has had many
more miles of track than any other province or territory. A map
of Argentine railroads shows a dramatic pattern—most of the
tracks lead to Buenos Aires.[20] Buenos Aires is a magnet attracting the products of the interior. The railroads are not feeders of
the nation; they were laid out and owned and operated as
feeders of Buenos Aires. They drained the land, and Europe was
the catch basin, not only for most of the raw materials shipped
out, but for a good part of the profits. The Argentine people
have never forgotten that foreign capital, principally English,
owned these railroads, although they have sometimes forgotten
what Argentina might have been without them.

These are some of the factors of Argentine progress in the
eighties which make it possible and realistic to speak, as porteños
and Europeans often did in those years, of "Buenos Aires,"
using the name of the city as a faithful synecdoche for the nation.
If we look back on that time, with its English loans and railroads, its English ships and British settlers (for the United Kingdom also exported men to Argentina, livestock breeders, mana-
gers and owners of great *estancias*, grain dealers, and bankers—
all told, a powerful colony of men with two passports); if we
consider the growing trade with France and Germany, and add
to these factors the hypnotic spell cast over Argentine customs
and thought by English and French culture, then we may
identify this remote land as an addition to western Europe's
spreading empire. Specifically, Argentina was an economic
colony of Great Britain ("Take Canada from us, but not

[20] República Argentina, *Dirección de Ferrocarriles Nacionales; estadística de los ferrocarriles en explotación, año 1894* (Buenos Aires, 1896), III, 37, and map at end; *ibid.,
1909*, XXVIII, 42; *Atlas geográfico de la República Argentina* (ediciones Peuser; Buenos
Aires, 1945), Mapa 3.

Argentina," cried one Englishman) and a cultural vassal of France. But Argentina also belonged to the Argentines, or at least to the men who comprised the remarkable Generation of Eighty.

3

The Generation of Eighty: Politics

BEFORE the Argentine revolution of 1810, land was the principal source of wealth and the sanction of social position in the otherwise resourceless Viceroyalty of the Río de la Plata. The revolution for independence did not significantly alter the fundamental social, political, and economic relationships between the masses of the people, the landowners, and the soil. And although the administration of Rivadavia in the 1820's and the dictatorship of Rosas in the next two decades were poles apart in their philosophies of society and government, each bore the same fruit in the further concentration of land in the hands of a relatively few men. After the fall of Rosas and the return of the exiles in 1852, the position of the landed gentry was not changed, despite the work of men like Urquiza, Mitre, and Sarmiento, who applied themselves to the task of awaking Argentina from its long sleep of reaction. These victorious leaders were liberal and pragmatic, but there was no Argentine Homestead Act during their administrations. They accepted the land system as it was and tried to build upon it by spinning out the means of communication and transportation and technical development that would make it workable and by bringing in immigrants to make it fruitful. Aside from the establishment of a few colonies, the methods of land distribution and the laws of land ownership remained essentially unchanged. Indeed, the governments that came after the Rosas regime, needful of revenue and concerned with the white elephant that was the government domain, embarked on much the same types of real estate deals as had the dictator. In one case, in 1857, the government leased 3,000,000 hectares (1 hectare = 2.47 acres) of land to 373 people; in

1867 Mitre's government sold this land on easy terms to its renters.[1]

By 1880 the land pattern of the nation centered on personal holdings which by almost any standard ranged from big (15,000 or 20,000 acres or more) to enormous (200,000 acres and upward). The most valuable land was in the province of Buenos Aires, a sparsely settled region of great estancias, streaked by an increasing number of railroads. Here pasturage was rapidly giving way to tillage and the landowners were making the most of their new position in the expanding national economy. Sheep were replaced by wheat and the Irish herders by Italian farmers; but, Irish or Italian, the men who worked the land did not own it. Some estancias covered entire departments of the province— departments in which there was "neither church nor chapel, the landowners being utterly heedless of the condition of their people."[2] The Department of Maipú, write two Anglo-Argentine observers, "has fine pastures, teeming with flocks and herds, but the poor gauchos are utterly uncared for, the whole country being owned by Alzagas, Acostas, Lastras, Pereyras, and Ramos Mexías. The last-named family has an estate of 400 square miles. The people live in mud huts." Again: "The department [Necochea] was founded in 1865 and is owned by forty large proprietors, the Alzagas, Anchorenas, Casares . . . and others, who take little heed of the condition of their people."[3]

Despite the unbalanced social situation, of which the system of property ownership and tenure was a primary cause, this was an era of marked vitality—the vitality of a frontier region, rich in its soil, chaotic with diverse races and new economic techniques, and possessed of a boundless faith in the future. The fact of surging economic expansion validated the pattern of land ownership. The successful landlords—the *terratenientes*—together with other men who were less well-established but equally far-sighted, were in a mood to indulge in that orgy of land speculation which, lasting for a decade after Roca's conquest of the

---

[1] Jacinto Oddone, *La burguesía terrateniente argentina* (Buenos Aires, 1930), pp. 93–101; Carl C. Taylor, *Rural Life in Argentina* (Baton Rouge, 1948), pp. 174–190.

[2] M. G. and E. T. Mulhall, *Handbook of the River Plate, Comprising the Argentine Republic, Uruguay, and Paraguay* (6th ed.; Buenos Aires, 1892), pp. 99, 346.

[3] Mulhall, *Handbook*, pp. 348–352.

Indian lands in 1879–1880, ended with a few more people (and many of the same people) in possession of still more land. [4]

Many native Argentines who were not lucky enough to be born in or to join the ranks of the terratenientes became tenants or peons, working in fields owned by other men. These *criollos* were frequently no more prosperous than the newest immigrant who wandered out into the countryside to make his fortune. [5] Some there were of both groups, native-born and foreign, who through good fortune and wit and work acquired enough land to warrant inclusion, if not of themselves, at least of their sons and daughters in the upper ranks of society. But for every Basque or Italian or Argentine who went out into the alternately dusty and muddy *pampa central* and struck it rich, there were many who made only a marginal living year in and year out, "playing the crop lottery" on land rented from a *latifundista* whom they never saw.

The masses of foreign immigrants who settled in Argentina in these years—and their numbers diminished in proportion to the distance from Buenos Aires—made possible the nation's mounting prosperity, but they also created problems which affected the social and political fabric of the country. For one thing, the newcomers were curiously hybrid persons before Argentine law. They were under no obligation or compulsion to adopt Argentine citizenship, yet they received the same civil rights of the Argentine constitution as did native-born citizens. They could not vote (legally), but neither were they required to perform military service. An alien could become naturalized by petitioning to that effect after two years of residence, but there was complete official and popular indifference as to whether a man became naturalized or not. Naturalization, in fact, did not offer an immigrant any advantages which he did not already possess, and entailed at least one severe disadvantage—the obligation to do military service. Consequently, most of the immigrants who came to Argentina devoted themselves to the

[4] Oddone, *La burguesía terrateniente argentina*, pp. 215–218; Miguel Angel Cárcano, *Evolución histórica del régimen de la tierra pública* (2nd ed.; Buenos Aires, 1925), pp. 345–357, 394–404.

[5] Mark Jefferson, *Peopling the Argentine Pampa* (New York, 1926), pp. 22–23, 32–36, 84–85.

pursuit of their livelihoods and left their new homeland severely alone.[6] The immigrant could go on with his old citizenship, his old language, his old friends, his old ideas. If Argentina gave him a job, it did not, in the vast majority of cases, offer him land to buy and the chance to play a more stable and responsible role in society and the economy. All too often when land was offered the promise was false, or the colony of which the immigrant became a part failed, or he found that clear title to his land was a mirage concocted by criollo owners who preferred to have tenants and renters rather than competitors. Under such conditions there was little assimilation into the established forms of national life of the tens of thousands of foreigners who descended on Argentina in the eighties.[7] This was painfully clear in that activity which is one of the most objective expressions of a nation's social cohesion—politics.

The native landowning aristocracy was in a commanding political position with respect to the bulk of the population. In the immigrants they found not only laborers but semi-citizens whose failure (or inability, for whatever reasons) to share in the institutionalized activities of the nation assured the criollo minority of the opportunity to continue in control of the machinery of the state. The large number of European immigrants also provided solid reinforcement for the ruling minority's basic policy, which was close collaboration with the principal nations of Europe.

An examination of Argentine politics in the eighties reveals a situation of political corruption organized around the only viable, formal party in the nation, the P.A.N. (Partido Autonomista Nacionalista).[8] The P.A.N. was more than a party; it was for a generation the government of Argentina and a political

[6] Juan A. Alsina, *La inmigración en el primer siglo de la independencia* (Buenos Aires, 1910), p. 11; Frederico Rahola, *Sangre nueva. Impresiones de un viaje a la América del Sud* (Barcelona, 1905), pp. 124–134.

[7] Jefferson, *Peopling the Argentine Pampa*, pp. 164–167; Alsina, *La inmigración*, pp. 42–46.

[8] The following analysis of the Argentine political scene may be verified in differing degree (and not always in accord with the several authors' intents) in almost all the sources for this period. If further verification is needed it may be found in the revolutions of 1890, 1893, and 1905, and in their grandchild, the revolution of 1943.

instrument of the ruling element. Varying with the combinations of men who formed its leadership, it was the core of support for every president from Roca in 1880 to Roque Saenz Peña in 1910.

Roca's military and political authority after he defeated the porteño revolt of 1880 gave the P.A.N. its initial grip on the city and province of Buenos Aires. In a few years the use of national power by the president and his clique and their solicitude for the economic progress of the nation brought about a coalition of the conservative element of the entire country behind the shrewdest leader their class would ever have.

Oficialismo was the order of the day. This is not to say that President Roca or his successor Juárez invented the techniques of federal executive interference in elections and in the operation of the provincial governments. Before the final centralization of the national government in Buenos Aires in 1880, provincial governors had continued to rule their regions with much of the authority and many of the methods of the old-time caudillos. The federal government had rarely been free of a large measure of dependence upon these local chiefs who could marshal their voters and send the right people to the national congress. Roca was a product of the combination of provincial leaders against Buenos Aires, but after assuming the presidency he showed no disposition to subordinate the national executive to the men who had helped him to power. New and relatively great financial and military strength, together with the normal instrument of patronage, lay in his grasp. With consummate political skill he exercised these weapons during the six years of his first administration. No parties of declared principles or broad organization confronted him; there were only *personalista* groups functioning within the practical objective of securing control of the local political machines. Through these cliques

---

Among the few good studies of Argentine political practice, as distinct from histories of political theory, are the following: José Nicolás Matienzo, *El gobierno representativo federal en la República Argentina* (Buenos Aires, 1910), especially pp. 107–119 for a discussion of the fluidity of political parties, and pp. 203–215, which deal with the techniques of presidential domination of provincial governors; Carlos R. Melo, *Los partidos políticos argentinos* (2nd ed.; Córdoba [Argentina], 1945), pp. 5–25; and Carlos R. Melo, *La campaña presidencial de 1885–1886* . . . (Córdoba, 1946).

Roca threaded his way, aided by loyal and efficient agents such as Bernardo de Irigoyen, Juárez, Pellegrini, and Wilde. Elections meant that the P.A.N. was pitted against *ad hoc* groups organized by men of the same fundamental social and political views as their opponents, the chief distinction between the former and the latter being that one was "in" and the other "out." Opposition tickets were fluid in the extreme, to the point of merging with the government forces or disappearing entirely just before an election. The struggle for spoils was characterized by fierce partisanship in press and speech and the engendering of personal antagonisms that are perpetuated to this day among some prominent Argentine families.

A mainstay of the P.A.N. and therefore of the president of the nation, who was the head of the party, was electoral corruption. Every device of political fraud seems to have been known and tried in Argentina in these years. The purchase and falsification of votes was a major occupation of the national and provincial governments. One unnamed contemporary sourly but succinctly described the situation when he wrote: "In the deserted electoral registration offices one could hear nothing but the scratching pens of the government clerks writing imaginary names." [9] The problems of controlling the electorate were simplified for the dominant interests by a limited suffrage, indirect election of the president, and the system of the *lista completa*, by which the entire ticket was elected if its leading candidate won a plurality of votes. As the power of the president grew at the expense of the provincial governors, control of the provinces and their elections became fairly routine. Carlos D'Amico was a living testimony to that fact. D'Amico was a man of distinguished family and personal ability who as governor of the province of Buenos Aires during part of Roca's first term fought against the president's encroachment upon the affairs of the great province. The upshot of this political struggle was unusual in a period when many leaders acquiesced to presidential pressure with more or less profitable results to themselves: D'Amico was forced not only out of political life, but out of the country. In the

[9] [*Carlos*] *Pellegrini: 1846–1906: Obras, precedidas de un ensayo biográfico por Agustín Rivero Astengo* (5 vols.; Buenos Aires, 1941), II, 77.

book which he wrote in his Mexican exile, the former governor
defined the composition of a typical provincial government as
he knew it to be under Roca and Juárez: "A delegate from the
national government, a bookkeeper, a cashier, and the Chief of
Police are all the staff required."[10] When force and corruption
at the provincial level failed to produce the desired results, the
national congress could annul the provincial election, expel
undesired colleagues and hold another election, with closer
attention to a more productive outcome. As D'Amico wrote:
"The only elector in Argentina is the President of the Republic,
who elects the provincial governors, the legislatures, the National
Congress, and his own successor."[11]

As early as the day after Roca's inauguration the great newspaper of Buenos Aires, *La Prensa* (Oct. 13, 1880), foresaw the
continuation of political *caudillismo* in the nation. Of the revolution just ended, which many people interpreted as the signal for
the opening of a long awaited era of purity in Argentine
politics, the newspaper gloomily asked: "Who has triumphed in
the end? No one. Political justice remains unachieved; the
people will continue to suffer their hard lot . . . Their struggle
has not ended; their cause is only latent, and the danger persists
of a series of uninterrupted outbreaks . . ." *La Nación*, also great,
commented on Roca's slogan "peace and administration."
"The country needs peace," said Mitre's paper, "but peace
with justice and liberty."

The outbreaks came, during the next three decades, in the
form of scores of minor blood-lettings in local political struggles,
and in three major revolutionary attempts (1890, 1893, 1905)
to pry loose the grip of the ruling class on the government. But
the ten years from 1880 to 1890 were comparatively halcyon.
Roca's superb political talent and the lavish corruption of the
Juárez government, combined with the diversion of popular
interest into economic activities, served temporarily to dampen
the fires of civil strife. At the same time the dominant interests
in the nation, through their chief representative, the president,

---

[10] Carlos Martínez [Carlos Alfredo D'Amico], *Buenos Aires: su naturaleza, sus costumbres, sus hombres. Observaciones de un viajero desocupado* (México, 1890), pp. 131–132.

[11] Martínez, *Buenos Aires*, pp. 53–58, 123–137.

extended the area of their authority and influence, in part as a
response to Argentina's crying need for greater political centralization and in part as satisfaction of their private aims.[12]

Roca led the nation along these new paths. He was a master
of the possible in politics. His own correspondence is the best
witness to his abilities as a conscious realist in the affairs of men.
He knew his Machiavelli, writing to Juárez, his protégé and
successor, that "Political force lies in knowing how to play the
lion and the fox at the same instant." Again, in a letter to Juárez
dated almost two years before the election of 1880, in which he
discussed his plans for surmounting the considerable obstacles
which lay in his road to the presidency, Roca wrote: "It is
necessary, as you see, to avoid these reefs, and so I shall begin
to maneuver with the skill and prudence of which you know
me capable."[13]

This skill was demonstrated in 1886 when Roca imposed his
successor upon the country. In the years of his first administration, Roca's political power was centered in the interior province
of Córdoba where Juárez was his principal agent. It was from
there that the president brought his wife's brother-in-law, via a
seat in the national congress, to be his heir in the Casa Rosada,[14]
for Roca was bound by the Argentine constitution of 1853
which prescribed that no Argentine president could succeed himself in office.

Roca was neither the first nor the last Argentine ruler to
select his successor and arrange for his accession. There is much
to be said for Roca's administration, despite the rough edges it
may present to those who have the advantage of hindsight.

[12] José Nicolás Matienzo, *La revolución de 1890 en la historia constitucional argentina*
(Buenos Aires, 1926), pp. 6–7, where this leading Argentine authority on the
political history of his country and class writes: "In the decade from 1880 to 1890,
not only did the personal power of the president grow immeasurably, but a deep
political and administrative corruption spread throughout the nation, converting
the government into an instrument for the satisfaction of private interests."

[13] Agustín Rivero Astengo, *Juárez Celman, 1844–1909. Estudio histórico y documental de
una época argentina* (Buenos Aires, 1944), Roca to Juárez, October 26, 1879, p. 144;
Roca to Juárez, July 24, 1878, p. 105.

[14] Roca's influence over Juárez is established by the correspondence between the
two men, which much resembles that of a father and his dutiful, apprentice son.
See Rivero Astengo, *Juárez Celman*, pp. 53–56, 79–150, 297–311, 338–340. Roca and
Juárez married two sisters, Clara and Elisa Funes of Córdoba.

Roca no doubt hoped to perpetuate through Juárez the regime of relative "peace and administration" which he himself had given the country from 1880 to 1886, during which force had been generally supplanted by more subtle political methods. The men of the Generation of Eighty were the sons of murdered or exiled fathers. They had cut their first teeth amidst civil war, turmoil, and hate. In their maturity, particularly after the last war in 1880, they desired surcease from revolution, and peace and prosperity for themselves and their land. Behind the still harsh and vindictive struggle for power in the eighties, there became apparent a spreading acquiescence to the need for mastering the forms, if not the content, of democratic government, in order that the weak but growing national unity might be preserved and the business of building the nation's wealth carried forward.

With the astute grasp of Argentina's destiny which his remarkable career displays, Roca struggled to secure the elements of peace, unity, and progress which the country needed. He was no mere fox, sniffing silently from prey to prey, as his enemies would have him appear. An answer to such charges may also be found, not in his acts alone, but in his correspondence. There is, for example, the letter that he wrote in 1880 when he was under heavy pressure to withdraw his presidential candidacy in the face of the civil war it would almost surely precipitate. "This," wrote Roca, with a depth of understanding which few of his contemporaries possessed, "is no mere election contest, but a question of whether or not we are an organized, united nation, not just one of those 'South American' places upon which the world sneers."[15] It was on this basis—the establishment of a modern Argentina—that Roca fought a revolution and devoted his life to the development of his country's resources and its relations with other nations.

What Roca did, Juárez and his gang very nearly undid. Not that there was any basic difference of program between Roca and Juárez; it was the fact that the latter bolted when the former relaxed his grip on the reins. Juárez gathered his own clique and set out upon a course of exploitation which led to

[15] Rivero Astengo, *Juárez Celman*, Roca to unnamed addressee, n.d. [1880], p. 164.

disaster. A parallel situation might be imagined in United States history if a wiser and stronger Coolidge, conservative yet expansive in economic policies, had been followed in office by a man who combined the political morality and pliability of Harding with the economic and moral tendencies of Jay Gould.

Juárez's attempt to continue the pattern of political control and economic development which Roca had brought to fruition failed through his own defects and through the play of rampant economic forces. With his accustomed acrid truthfulness, the aging Sarmiento lashed out prophetically against Juárez soon after the 1886 election. Said the man who had lived to see the achievement, and the quick perversion, of so many of his plans for Argentina's progress in the way of liberalism: "I am deafened by the roar of crashing institutions. Juárez will be no more than the instrument of the blind forces that are transforming the republic."[16] Sarmiento did not live to see the final collapse of Juárez and his administration in 1890, but he would probably have agreed that the soft-willed president was not wholly responsible for the bloody denouement of his reign. If the forces at work in Argentina were blind, it was the blindness of greed or, to put it more gently, of excessive optimism. Some indication of the state of affairs which Juárez inherited from Roca may be seen in the fact that, as early as 1885, the following distinguished public figures of the day owed the following sums of money to the Bank of the Province of Buenos Aires: President Roca, 1,148,250 pesos; Juárez himself, 120,000 pesos; Pellegrini, cabinet officer, senator, and future vice-president and president, 193,000; Dardo Rocha, candidate for president in 1886 and founder of the city of La Plata, 420,000; and two of Roca's brothers a total of 180,000 pesos.[17] These figures are not necessarily evidence of corruption; they do indicate that these men were engaged in large transactions and that numerous public banking institutions of the nation were most probably wandering in a twilight zone between fulfillment of public

[16] Rivero Astengo, *Juárez Celman*, p. 395.

[17] Rivero Astengo, *Juárez Celman*, pp. 376–377.

On the day of Juárez's inauguration (October 12, 1886), *La Prensa* denounced the prevailing low state of political morals in the government, attributing it to an unchecked pursuit of personal wealth and power.

responsibilities and satisfaction of the personal needs of power-ful politicians. It was Juárez's disgrace that he allowed favoritism to exceed the limits which a more capable man might have imposed.

Juárez's accessibility to his friends was a result of his temperament and his distrust of the popular masses. Where Roca was fond of saying, in French, "Gouverner c'est choisir," and "In politics one ought not to say anything irreparable," Juárez is damningly quoted by his only biographer as having minted this coin: "To consult the people is always an error, since the people have only confused and muddy opinions."[18] This Nietzschean profundity was not in tune with the times in Argentina, and the people proved it to the president by forcing his resignation two years before his term was due to expire. And if Roca talked too little, thereby winning a reputation among his enemies as a taciturn schemer, Juárez talked too much, and Roca told him so.[19] Eduardo Wilde, another leader of the ruling class and close collaborator with Juárez, rendered a mild but revealing judgment upon his president when he said that Juárez was "greater for his heart than for his head." And Juárez painted his own personal and political portrait when he wrote, "I prefer to be deceived than to distrust."[20]

These character traits led to Juárez's expulsion from office—not by his own class, which never really deserted him, maintaining a kind of pact of silence in his defense to the very end—but by the outraged and awakening middle class, led by a few reform-minded men from differing social levels, including the highest, who had not condoned the politico-economic orgy through which the country passed in the eighties.

The tragedy of oficialismo broke with full force upon this nominal president who was the willing tool of interests which profited by his policy of benevolent *laissez faire* and more than benevolent assistance. In the darkening days of May 1890, Juárez rose before the national congress to make humble excuses and to acknowledge indirectly the defrauding of the people

[18] Rivero Astengo, *Juárez Celman*, p. 44.
[19] Rivero Astengo, *Juárez Celman*, Roca to Juárez, September 5, 1872, p. 48.
[20] Rivero Astengo, *Juárez Celman*, pp. 332, 442.

which he and his government had supervised.[21] A few weeks later this unhappy man resigned his office, morally too frail to write his own letter of resignation, a duty he delegated to a friend, the young man whom he had hoped to make the next president of Argentina.[22]

This was Juárez Celman, product of corroding nepotism, representative of the decay of political idealism. And this was Argentine society, set on the shaky foundations of a creole and immigrant mass, capped by a landed gentry indistinguishable in its pursuit of wealth from the emerging tradesman class and the aggressive European speculators who were catalyzing the resources of the nation.

Nonetheless, under the rule of this man and his predecessor, Argentina in the eighties had that peace which Roca advocated in his first message to congress—the internal imposed peace of a dominant minority, yet a not unworthy advance over former conditions. Roca returned to this theme in his exultant final message to that body in 1886: "I successfully conclude my government without having had to inform you during its whole course of civil wars, of bloody interventions, of the rebellions of caudillos, of loans wasted in repressing disorders and suffocating rebellions, of Indian depredations . . . Peace . . . has never before reigned in this land for six consecutive years."[23]

The land was indeed relatively tranquil, but there were some who took a different view of this presidential dispensation of peace. For *La Prensa* (Oct. 12, 1886), it was peaceful simply because, "The parliament is silent, and the Ministers speak only to receive at once the votes of great majorities, attained without effort and without agitation." And to Belín Sarmiento, who inherited some of the vitriolic vigor of his illustrious relative, Argentina was the tragic original of his book—*Una república muerta*. He accused the rulers of the nation of concealing the realities of their regime under myths of a heroic past and dreams of a fantastic future, substituting the promises of their inflated

[21] Heraclio Mabragaña, compiler, *Los mensajes* . . . (6 vols.; Buenos Aires, n.d. [?1910], IV, 343–347.

[22] Juárez's resignation was written for him by Ramón J. Cárcano. See Ramón J. Cárcano, *Mis primeros 80 años* (Buenos Aires, 1943), pp. 166–175.

[23] Mabragaña, *Los mensajes*, IV, 147–148.

oratory for a healthy internal policy.[24] The republic was dead; silence had settled over the field of political liberties which had formerly seen bitter but fruitful contests for freedom. The Argentine army acted as a praetorian guard to support the *status quo*. Even the firemen of Buenos Aires carried rifles.[25] Political passivity was preached by the upper class as a soft name for choking oppression.

Yet Belín's solution to Argentina's distress was typical of the pointless theorizing so common in Argentine political writing. He proposed a revised and strictly enforced suffrage law and the creation of an active elite imbued with honesty and true patriotism, capable of leading the nation to higher and purer levels.[26] He did not indicate how these ends could be accomplished. Roca, not so troubled by these ideals as Belín, wanted peace for a purpose. Peace meant tranquillity, a word much used in Argentina in the next thirty years. Political and social tranquillity were synonyms for the *status quo*—for the chance to develop the nation's pastoral and agricultural potential, obtain foreign loans, build waterworks and railroads. Without this internal peace Argentina would continue to be an outcast in European eyes, merely another South American country, as Roca had put it. In short, a bad risk.

If the slogan "peace and administration" provided respite from generations of conflict, it also was the frame on which were woven patterns of economic exploitation and political reaction. To that formula the word *oligarquía* is inextricably tied.

"The oligarchy" is a term used in the 1880's and after in Argentina by *La Prensa* and by people opposed to the rule of the land by an increasingly tight-knit group. By this opprobrious word was meant the political organization composed of the president and his associates, the provincial governors and their supporters, the national representatives who obeyed the behests

[24] A. Belín Sarmiento, *Una república muerta*. Introducción por Lucio V. López (Buenos Aires, 1892), p. 1.

[25] Belín Sarmiento, *Una república muerta*, pp. 20–21. See also Ezequiel Martínez Estrada, *Radiografía de la Pampa* (2 vols.; Buenos Aires, 1942; 1st ed. 1933), I, 213–216 and II, 118–123 for a masterful analysis of the internal role of the army in Latin America, where external enemies have been nearly non-existent.

[26] Belín Sarmiento, *Una república muerta*, pp. 163–173.

of the executive, whether national or local, and the economic interests, mainly landowners, which allied themselves with these men.[27]

The Argentine oligarchy was described many years ago by José Nicolás Matienzo, a distinguished member and student of the class which he analyzed, in these words:

The governing elements [of the nation] are recruited from a class of citizens which, if it does not properly constitute a caste, nonetheless forms a directing class . . . This class corresponds approximately to the highest social stratum, formed by the members of the traditional families, by the rich, and by the educated ("hombres ilustrados"). The members of this class maintain among themselves more or less tight social and economic relations and, as is natural, share common sentiments and opinions . . . Without this common code there would not exist that interchange of services and favors which they reciprocally lend without distinction of party politics. It is this moral code of the directing class which the citizens designated for the different government positions carry into the public administration, whence they manage the interests of the country.[28]

The ruling class reinforced this conception of the government as its special preserve with an absolutist and centralist doctrine of the executive power.[29] Congress, the banks, the local governors, the party organization, and the formulation of foreign and domestic policies increasingly came under the authority of a small group of leaders, of which the president was the head. These leaders were the active representatives of the aristocratic class and the faithful executors of the common code to which Matienzo refers.

Such a development was inherent, although not necessarily inevitable, in Argentine history. The declaratory act of May 1810, in which the leaders of the Argentine revolution made

[27] A discussion of the origin and meaning of the word in Argentine political history may be found in an article by Rodolfo Rivarola, "La oligarquía según los constituyentes del 53," *Revista de Derecho, Historia y Letras*, año X, tomo 29, marzo de 1908, pp. 492–507. The author states that the word was first applied by the drafters of the constitution of 1853 to cabals of provincial governors.

[28] José Nicolás Matienzo, *El gobierno representativo federal en la República Argentina*, p. 322.

[29] José Luis Romero, *Las ideas políticas en Argentina* (México, 1946), pp. 188–192.

their first attack on the royal government, contained a phrase
to the effect that the governing class of the country should
consist of "la principal y más sana parte del vecindario"—"the
chief and most stable part of the citizenry"—literally, of the list
of neighbors or residents, those who had property and position
in the community. The conservative traditions of Spain, transmitted to her colonies, were retained and reinforced by the
structure of land ownership which persisted after the political
revolution of the first decades of the nineteenth century. The
Argentine landed aristocracy lived within its traditions, not as
with a sere verbal heritage but as a legacy of success—the
success of their victorious struggle for independence, of their
endurance and in many cases increased power under the tyranny
of Rosas, and, finally, of their successful reorganization of the
nation between 1852 and 1880. After 1880, when immigrants
and foreign capital descended on the immense properties of this
class, the efforts of the past were redeemed. New problems also
appeared, but they were for the future; today was for work and
wealth.

The men of the Generation of Eighty embodied the hopes of
their fathers and the teachings of Sarmiento, Alberdi, and other
early Argentine liberals. They had been taught from childhood
that the salvation for their glorious but backward land lay in
adopting European and North American modes of production
and in imitating the cultural pattern of progressive foreign
nations, including their methods of education, customs of work,
and standards of values, all these to be erected upon the basis
of an invigorating European immigration. In these formulations
of liberalism is the source of the positivistic and materialistic
society of Argentina after 1880. Roca, Pellegrini, Juárez, and
their peers were the heirs and executors of the preceding generations. They were men "individualistic, pacific and cosmopolitan."[30] To them fell the task of Europeanizing Argentina. They
fulfilled the dream—and transformed the nation.

[30] Ricardo Rojas, "Los modernos," *La literatura argentina* (2nd ed., 8 vols.; Buenos
Aires, 1924–1925 [from *Obras*, 19 vols.; Buenos Aires, 1922–1930]), XIV, 990.

4

The Generation of Eighty: Wealth and Wisdom

SOME years ago a descendant of General Mitre described the changes which occurred in Argentina after 1880. His words were perhaps more extravagant than those which the old patrician would have used, but the conservative sentiments which they expressed were a clear inheritance from the age of his great-grandfather:

The epoch of prosperity begins with the continuous affluence of foreign capital and the fecund flood of the venal masses. Thus the country was on the march toward its natural predestination, but this happened only at the expense of the nation losing much of its genuine character of primitive virtue, and with deprecation of the sense of historic tradition with its implicit heroic vocation. Youth showed itself indifferent to the examples of the past and prided itself on offering to Progress—the new idol—the homage that was yesterday rendered to Liberty, the ancestral god . . . A dissolute and haughty materialism invaded everything, so much the more dangerous by its very ingenuousness.[1]

Although this is a revealing interpretation of a period of his country's history by a member of a famed family, much of the significance of these sentences lies in what is left unsaid. The author neglects to mention the leading part taken by the Argentine ruling class in this worship at the new shrine of progress. That is a role which the author prefers to assign to the immigrant masses rather than to the established creole aristocracy. Yet a study of the years after 1880 shows that as the time of austerity receded and the era of wealth began, people from all levels of society, from Basque milkman to Castilian estanciero, from English merchant to Argentine lawyer, joined the stampede for money.

[1] Adolfo Mitre, *Mitre, periodista* (Buenos Aires, 1943), p. 219.

The financial fever which consumed Argentina in the eighties followed a classic course: infection with the virus of economic expansion; the delirium of unchecked optimism and speculation; finally, the death rattle of July 1890. In a few years Buenos Aires became a "great gambling house."[2] The patrons came from wealthiest and the meanest homes; the *croupiers'* tables were the Casa Rosada and the Bolsa. During the decade the price of gold climbed wildly until in April 1890 it reached 209 per cent,[3] yet there were few Argentines who desired until too late to halt the upward progress of this fateful figure. In Buenos Aires and in the provinces the same piece of property was bought and sold perhaps a dozen times within a year, at a profit each time; the newspapers were crammed with real estate advertisements; the newest immigrants, men of the oldest families, representatives of foreign corporations, struggled to outdo one another in this inflationary race. The stock exchange was the scene of speculative activity which would have delighted Jim Fiske. The *nouveaux riches* mingled with the established families at the opera and in the *corso* in Palermo. The old aristocracy did not often reward the economic progress of the newcomers with the privileges of social equality. Still, if the fortune were large enough . . .[4]

There were some political leaders and reformers such as Estrada, Goyena, and Del Valle who called vainly for a halt to the savage struggle, but those speculators whom one writer

[2] Ezequiel Martínez Estrada, *Radiografía de la pampa* (2 vols.; Buenos Aires, 1942), I, 200.

[3] John H. Williams, *Argentine International Trade under Inconvertible Paper Money, 1880–1890* (Cambridge, Mass., 1920), p. 115. Juan A. Balestra, *El noventa, una evolución política argentina* (2nd ed.; Buenos Aires, 1935), p. 64, states that gold reached 310 in April 1890, but this figure cannot be accepted in the light of Williams' scholarly study.

[4] There are several contemporaneous Argentine novels which, while esthetically erratic, nonetheless mirror the economic and social scene. Two of these are by Francisco Grandmontagne. The first, titled *Teodoro Foronda* (*Evoluciones de la sociedad argentina*), was published in two volumes in Buenos Aires in 1896. It is a story of the excessive materialism and unstable values of the 1880's. Another book by the same author was published in Buenos Aires in 1898. Called *La maldonada: costumbres criollas*, it is a novel of the corrupt society of Argentina during the Juárez administration.

Perhaps the most important account of this period is *La bolsa* by José Miró [Julián Martel]. This novel first appeared in serial form in *La Nación* in 1890.

aptly called "the new discoverers of Buenos Aires" [5] could not be deterred by speeches from the accumulation of wealth. The new prosperity of the nation fitted too neatly the desires of all classes of society to be curbed by idealism. If the oligarchy's grip on the nation remained unchallenged by other groups until the chaos of 1890 was almost upon the country, it was not only because control by the aristocracy was so complete and the majority of the people so disorganized, but also because the different classes shared this common goal—the acquisition of wealth. The well-being of the nation clearly lay in economic expansion. The upper class derived this conviction not only from the customary human motives, but also from long indoctrination by liberal thinkers who vehemently taught that material progress alone could raise Argentina from barbarism to civilization. The immigrants, among whose motives in coming to America was a desire for economic advancement, fell in step with a political organization and a philosophy which promised to fulfill this ambition. From the merging of these forces—the criollo population dominated by an entrenched aristocracy and the unassimilated immigrant masses, the latter two, at least, bent upon the creation of wealth—may be derived those modes of morality and conduct which have shaped Argentina's recent history. [6]

The eighties were active and elegant, sordid and superficial. Precisely at the time when the crude ways of the past seemed doomed to extinction, a new kind of barbarism appeared, a barbarism unforeseen by the prophets of liberalism. To the primitive and bloody ways of former years, against which Sarmiento had voiced the mighty protest of *Facundo*, was added a new form of social disorganization—the dehumanizing force of a great city, setting man apart from man. The rootless thousands who swarmed into the *barrios* of Buenos Aires in this decade quickly developed social types new to Argentina. These hoodlums and riffraff—*compadritos*, *matones*, *guarangos*—were spawn of transition, caught between the Old World and the

---

[5] Balestra, *El noventa*, p. 9.

[6] Alejandro Korn, *Obras* (3 vols.; La Plata, 1938–40), Vol. III, *Influencias filosóficas en la evolución nacional* (La Plata, 1940), 196, 219–222, 230.

New World, tossed in a confusion both spiritual and physical. They were new gauchos, gauchos of the city. They drifted through Buenos Aires from bar to tango hall, mouthing obscenities, handling women who passed them in the street, spitting on strangers, quick with the knife against the world. [7]

The compadritos were the lower rungs of a shaky social ladder running up to the big speculators in land and railroads. Society was unstable, lacking in values, except the value of money. Yet a yearning to be civilized pervaded the country, or at least the educated and prosperous elements. And Europe was civilization to these Argentines. Europe's inventions and gimcracks were imported and her fads and ideas transmitted by the newspapers to the hungry porteño public. There was eager and unflagging interest in the Argentine press for everything European. The United States, on the other hand, received scant attention. North American coal production and railroad construction or the water system of New York City were matters which the pragmatic porteño occasionally found instructive, but his interest ended there. More to his liking was French literary and theatrical news, mixed with sensational accounts of the latest *crime passionnel*. But the main themes that filled the news columns were always the same—the growth of Argentine commerce, the improvement of land and livestock, the glorious prospects of a nation where nature, government, and people collaborated in the creation of endless wealth.

An aggressively liberal, positivistic spirit pervaded men's minds. Lengthy articles filled the oversized pages of the daily papers advocating reforms in the judicial code, the sanitation code, the penal code—every code but the electoral code (and *La Prensa* and *La Nación* steadily advocated even that reform). And the interest in such reform legislation, modeled on that of Europe, was matched by a cultural attachment of the same proportions. When Victor Hugo died, *Sud América*, the paper of the younger leaders of the upper class, devoted its entire front page to his career. The most important magazine of the mid-

---

[7] Martínez Estrada, *Radiografía*, II, 33–36; Jorge Luis Borges and Sylvina Bullrich Palenque, compilers, *El compadrito: su destino, sus barrios, su música* (Buenos Aires, 1945), pp. 44–51.

eighties, the *Nueva Revista de Buenos Aires*, carried articles on subjects which in most circles in the United States would have been distinctly avant-garde: "La poesía en Austria," "Dostoiewsky," and "A. Daudet." Articles on the United States were as rare in the *Nueva Revista* as in the daily press. When one did appear it was usually a distorted image of an unknown continent. Early in 1883, young Ernesto Quesada, who with his father founded and edited the *Nueva Revista*, published an article which he had written on the remote subject of Ralph Waldo Emerson. He took pains to point out in the opening paragraphs that no one in Argentina knew anything about North American thought or literature except a limited number of students of constitutional law. This did not deter Quesada from plunging into his description of the United States:

Everything in that country is colossal . . . Industry there has had a surprising development; everything is done on a stupendous scale . . . The men don't vegetate; they live as though possessed by an implacable demon—as if electric currents circulated in their veins. They accumulate such fabulous fortunes that it is impossible even to waste them away. . . . It is a country absorbed by the thirst for wealth.[8]

And young Quesada demonstrated the truth of these statements by quoting his source—the *Edinburgh Review*.

La Nación and *La Prensa* did not share these exaggerated views of the United States. And in domestic political affairs, contrasting to the remainder of the press, their position was independently critical. But their pages also were replete with long articles on developments in England and on the continent. It took a presidential election or a disaster in the United States to win an occasional half-column of space, yet nothing European was alien to the newspaper editors and readers of Argentina, whether it was the opening of a hygiene exhibition in such an unlikely place as Naples, an insurrection on the Gold Coast, or the departure of the German Emperor for a hunting trip in Kuchelna. The Franco-Chinese war received more space than did news

[8] Ernesto Quesada, "Ralph Waldo Emerson. Sus doctrinas filosóficas," *Nueva Revista de Buenos Aires*, año II, tomo VI, 1882, entrega de enero [de 1883], pp. 212–213.

from any Latin American nation; the details of Bernhardt's costume were more fully described to the residents of Buenos Aires than were events in the important cities of the Argentine provinces.

One other newspaper of the eighties should be discussed— *La Tribuna Nacional*. This was the newspaper of Roca and, for a time, of Juárez. There is no better place to study the obsessive interest of the decade in material progress and in Europe than in its pages. Founded in 1880, at the beginning of Roca's first administration, *La Tribuna Nacional* expired with revealing timeliness late in 1889 when the economic bubble was on the point of bursting. It was the voice of the *fuerzas vivas* (literally, the "living forces")—the term by which the rulers of the land referred to themselves in order to indicate their "dynamic" leadership of the nation. Every issue of *La Tribuna* was a strident homage to Argentina's felicitous condition. Appropriately enough, from Europe came assurances that Argentina's achievements were much appreciated. *La Tribuna* had what it called an "exclusive commercial telegraph service" from "correspondents" in London, Liverpool, Bordeaux, Paris, Marseilles, Le Havre, Antwerp, Rome, Leipzig, and Madrid. (Was it only a coincidence that in all these places the same government which subsidized *La Tribunal Nacional*[9] maintained diplomatic and consular officers?) To its pages from these cities came the latest quotations and prophecies of the money and commodity markets of Europe, together with words of praise for Argentina's economic and political stability. To repay this encouragement, *La Tribuna* returned to its European readers a biweekly review of the Argentine economy entitled "Review for the Exterior," a persuasive mixture of statistics and optimistic economic predictions. In 1887 (Nov. 7–8) *La Tribuna* assured its public that "The Republic continues unperturbed its prosperous and happy march." In 1888 (July 30), when the Republic was somewhat less happy about its distorted prosperity, the editors cheerfully wrote: "The economic and financial situation constantly improves; not for an instant is there a halt in commercial and

---

[9] *La Tribuna Nacional*, March 29, 1888, admits to having been on the government payroll for an unspecified number of years.

industrial activity, in the progress of the railroads, in the construction of public works, or in the march of all the many elements of the country's wealth and aggrandizement." In early 1889 (Feb. 21) the paper altered its tone, omitted much of its former bold talk about the infallibility of the Argentine economy, and shifted its comments from financial statistics to problems of institutional reform. The most significant word in the oligarchy's vocabulary came into increasing use as the editors of the government press reassured their readers that "the Republic enjoys perfect tranquillity." Many respected citizens of Buenos Aires no doubt agreed with this opinion, but it must have been difficult for the people of the western city of Mendoza to share in it. At the moment that *La Tribuna* printed its official judgment of peace, that province was swept by one of those frequent revolts that marked provincial politics, bringing bloodshed and a severe federal intervention that gave the lie to the government's claims.[10]

La Prensa also shared in the prosperity of the eighties, growing in size and as a powerful voice of truth and justice. On January 1 of each year *La Prensa* published a business supplement that is an interesting indication of the nation's expansion. This special issue combined a detailed statistical review of all phases of Argentine economic activity of the preceding year with an analysis of European market and business conditions. The size of this supplement grew each year during the decade until it reached forty extra-sized pages of small type—a massive testimonial to the national economy and to the greatest newspaper in Latin America.

La Prensa never lacked pride in Argentina's accomplishments, but seldom did her editors relax their cautious judgments of the economic scene. The issue of January 1, 1886, called attention to "the wealth of statistics that marks the economic and social movement of the Republic," but in the same pages the editors castigated the English loan which Pellegrini had recently negotiated in Paris. "This loan contract for 42 million pounds," said

[10] Heraclio Mabragaña, compiler, *Los Mensajes. Historia del desenvolvimiento de la Nación Argentina, redactada cronologicamente por sus gobernantes, 1810–1910* (6 vols.; Buenos Aires, n.d. [?1910]), IV, 262.

La Prensa, "which is the most vast credit arrangement made to this date by a Latin American nation, demonstrates an advanced grade of decadence on the part of the government." Not content with this courageous attack upon the sacred cow of English credit, the editors followed their warning with a call for liberty, basing their appeal on the very fact of Argentine prosperity: "A people that is master of such wealth merit all the benefits of free institutions."

But even *La Prensa* gave ground before the apparently irresistible prosperity which was sweeping the land. The last annual economic review which the paper published before the crash of 1890 was a thirty-six-page issue that contained a few warnings against economic malpractice and political corruption but which on the whole viewed with complacence and even with optimism the colossal bubble that was about to burst on the nation.

This is another way of saying that *La Prensa* could not disassociate itself from the philosophy that dominated the country. Whatever we call it—liberalism, positivism, or a Spanish equivalent, *cientificismo*—the doctrines which came into full practice in Argentina in the eighties were stamped with a European trademark, adopted by Argentine leaders, and sanctified by success. The history of Argentine liberalism extends from the radical leaders of the 1810 revolution through Rivadavia and his University of Buenos Aires with its preaching of utilitarianism to Urquiza, Mitre, and Sarmiento, who took the refounded nation in hand after 1852.[11] The victory of liberalism was complete by 1880. The nation for the first time could gather in abundance the slowly matured harvest of the past. But the years had worked profound if little understood alterations in the old doctrine. In conformity with the rapid economic and social changes which were twisting the nation into a new shape, liberalism took on restricted and special meanings.

Roca, Juárez, and the governing class which they represented knew with Victorian certitude what this new liberalism meant.

[11] Alejandro Korn, *Influencias filosóficas*, pp. 191–219, 317–318; Leopoldo Zea, *Dos etapas del pensamiento en Hispano-américa: del romanticismo al positivismo* (México, 1949), pp. 267–282.

It meant peace—Roca's peace—"the resolute elimination of any fair struggle for power, a struggle that could be dangerous for the country, which was in a process of transformation, and even more dangerous for their own class [the oligarchy]." And liberalism meant administration—Roca's administration—"the fulfillment of the . . . ideals of progress and enrichment."[12] In achieving these objectives the oligarchy was far from being a consciously selfish minority intent upon choking back the rights of other groups. There can be little doubt that the Argentine rulers believed in the rectitude of their program. The bloody sacrifices which had been made before 1881 in the name of internal peace and liberty, together with the tangible benefits accruing to the nation during the years following the federalization of Buenos Aires, were sufficient warrant for the continued application of the liberal creed. History had placed the Argentine landowner—and the city of Buenos Aires—in a position midway between the rich pampas and Europe. It was fitting that the men of property should derive the principal benefits from that coincidence. But the double impact of European capital and immigration on the liberal Argentine ruling class transformed a hitherto somewhat paternal creole aristocracy into an elite increasingly isolated from the mass of the people. The new liberalism was no longer a radical doctrine but a shield for the privileges of an aristocracy.[13]

A restricted and inflexible form of liberalism, a "sectarian liberalism," came to the fore in Argentina after 1880. Although historians have demonstrated that the zenith of liberalism in England had been passed by the 1880's, it would be a rewarding study in social dynamics to show that the lag between Argentina and Europe was such that the Argentines did not yet perceive that they too had lost the old liberal *élan* and had begun to retrench on the practice, if not on the theory, of liberalism. Certainly for Argentina, just emerging on the world scene, liberalism seemed to be an inexhaustible guide to the perfect society, as it had been the touchstone of success for the most powerful nation on earth. The Argentine aristocracy found

[12] José Luis Romero, *Las ideas políticas en argentina* (México, 1946), p. 186.
[13] Romero, *Las ideas*, pp. 167–208.

economic collaboration with England an admirable complement to ideologic imitation.

However, beneath the surface uniformities of sectarian liberalism (under the liberal spell men even trimmed their moustaches in the "liberal" style[14]) there were grave problems such as that involving freedom of the press. Why did an oligarchic government which maintained itself through rigged elections and federal interventions permit the existence of a bitterly hostile and usually free press? One of the answers to this question seems to be that the oligarchy believed that it could counter the opposition press with its own newspapers. Another is that in the view of the ruling class a free press could accomplish little so long as the instruments of political control remained in the proper hands. There is a further consideration: the free press— and this comes down to *La Prensa* and *La Nación*—was, after all, part of the heritage of the ruling class, and the owners and editors of these papers were members of that class. Freedom of the press was a necessary condition of the intense personal struggle for power among the members of the oligarchy; it was part of their liberal doctrine and it was an escape valve for pressures within the elite, as well as a means of battling the enemies of the moment.[15] Furthermore, the independent press made up for the disservices it did to the men in power by its services as the medium of ideas, as the purveyor of the economic doctrines of the oligarchy, and as the chief link with European thought and economic activity. Finally, the opposition press could be, and sometimes was, silenced by the government. Argentine liberalism was autocratic; it provided freedom for the press to print anything that might contribute to the material growth of the community, but not the freedom to report the simple fact that the administration-controlled congress had met in secret session.[16]

[14] Carlos Martínez [Carlos Alfredo D'Amico], *Buenos Aires: su naturaleza, sus costumbres, sus hombres. Observaciones de un viajero desocupado* (México, 1890), pp. 35–36.

[15] For instance, *Sud América*, the cruelly partisan paper of the Juárez interests, nonetheless advocated the maintenance of unlimited freedom of the press for all groups, despite what the editors called the "scandals of license" in which their opponents indulged. See *Sud América*, February 25, 1885.

[16] In 1881 the Chamber of Deputies on its own authority jailed the editors of several papers who had reported the holding of a secret session. See Congreso Nacional, *Diario de sesiones de la Cámara de Diputados*, October 3, 1881, pp. 1–3.

Such peculiarities of sectarian liberalism reflected the concepts of liberty, order, and progress held by the ruling elements. In practice these good words seem to have meant liberty for the governing class, order ("tranquillity") for the rest of the people, and progress for the individual who could make the most of the economic free-for-all. Political ideas, however, were not the only European concepts which the oligarchy imported for its own use. Social Darwinism also made its appearance, providing support for the dominant group and a ready reference for reasons as to why the economic and political bounds of the people should be restricted. Principal spokesmen of the aristocracy such as Pellegrini insisted that the untutored masses were unfit to assume the burdens of liberty. The time for all that would come, of course, but for the present anarchy would be the only result of an extension of popular freedom. The people should be content with the guidance of the enlightened elements in the nation. A definition that fits the Argentine aristocrat of this era may be found in the observation that "only the nineteenth-century liberal could combine contempt for the common man with faith in democracy."[17] In economic matters, despite preachments of equality of opportunity, the common man had to run fast to keep up with those on the inside. The national government was Janus-like in its economic policies. On one side the president and congress employed their wide authority to facilitate and subsidize "public works," a series of projects which served public interest and private profit. On the other, when it served its interests the policy of the government was a most chaste laissez faire—no tariffs that might interfere with the flow of trade, no labor unions to interfere with the "natural movement" of business, and no taxes to reduce the possession of wealth.

Railroads, the most important exploitive agency in Argentina, provide a particularly interesting example of the economic philosophy of the day. This philosophy might be called one of active laissez faire, so active that a principal concern of the administration was to divest the government of the railroads it

[17] Crane Brinton, "The New History Twenty-Five Years After," *Journal of Social Philosophy*, 1:145 (January, 1936).

owned. In earlier, less profitable times the national government and the provinces had built and operated many of the railroads needed to open up the country; the Juárez regime, faithful to its liberal creed, sold these one by one to private interests. One of the last to go was the important Ferrocarril Oeste, the most profitable railroad in Argentina, and perhaps in the world. In 1889, congress voted to sell this line to a British company. There was some opposition in the legislature, but not much, and resistance was overcome by the government ministers who appeared before the legislature to argue that a properly functioning government should not interfere in economic matters, particularly to the extent of running a railroad. In support of this position the chief government spokesman turned to contemporary European liberal thought, buttressing his position with the names and arguments of Spencer, Buckle, and Leroy-Beaulieu.[18]

There were many other achievements for liberalism in this decade. Political administrative practice was formalized, at least in theory; sanitation and penal codes were evolved and promulgated with some excellent results; civil life was relatively stabilized. Argentina even had its own *Kulturkampf* at this time, when, despite intense Catholic opposition, the officially Catholic presidents Roca and Juárez pushed through a thoroughgoing secularization of many ecclesiastical functions. And the nation was endowed with the capital plant that would one day make it one of the world's greatest exporters.

Not only in the ideology of liberalism but in the whole realm of the intellect the oligarchy was deeply in Europe's debt. Culturally, the ruling class lived in an iron lung. Its members looked first to France, but they did not neglect the values of England, Germany, or Italy. Dr. Eduardo Wilde (and in this rare case the title actually signified M.D.), Roca's Minister of Justice and Public Instruction and long-time ambassador to Spain and Belgium, was a student of French and English literature. Politician, diplomat, deft humorist of the oligarchy, he was happiest living where he died—in Europe. Pellegrini

---

[18] Raúl Scalabrini Ortiz, *Historia de los ferrocarriles argentinos* (Buenos Aires, 1940), pp. 48–51.

delighted in British parliamentary history and in later years was almost as often in Paris or London as in Buenos Aires. Martín García Merou, who was Roca's personal secretary in 1885 and 1886 and later for many years ambassador to the United States, wrote a history of North American diplomacy, but the bulk of his literary work was European travel impressions and literary criticism. Even writers and part-time statesmen, such as Lucio V. Mansilla, who remained faithful in their major works to Argentine themes, worshipped in the cult of French letters.

Among the men of the Argentine upper class who combined public life with the pursuit of letters, Miguel Cané was outstanding. A gentleman and scholar, considered by his peers to be their most accomplished writer, he was a man whose grand manner and distinguished appearance proclaimed the very model of the Argentine aristocrat. His career was typical of his class. Born in Montevideo in 1851 during his father's exile, he returned to Buenos Aires and studied at the Colegio Nacional, later taking his law degree from the University. He contributed to the newspapers, was elected deputy at the age of twenty-four, and was appointed postal and telegraph director in Roca's first administration. For the rest of his life he was successively minister to Colombia, Austria, Germany, Spain, and France. Between embassies he held two key cabinet posts—one as Minister of the Interior, the other briefly as Foreign Minister in the crisis of 1893. During these years he lectured frequently at the University, published several gracious collections of travel impressions and essays on European literature, including a translation of *Henry IV*, and held a seat in the senate. He died in Buenos Aires in 1905 and was buried in the only place where he could properly have been laid to rest—the cemetery of the oligarchy called the Recoleta.[19]

[19] Biographical data for these pages are taken from Enrique Udaonda, *Diccionario biográfico argentino* (Buenos Aires, 1938), and from cited books and essays. For Cané, see Ricardo Sáenz Hayes, *Miguel Cané y su Tiempo (1851–1905)* (Buenos Aires, 1955), Belisario J. Montero, *Miguel Cané. Impresiones y recuerdos (de mi diario)* (Buenos Aires, 1928), and Aníbal Ponce, *La vejez de Sarmiento. Amadeo Jacques . . . Miguel Cané* (2nd ed.; Buenos Aires, 1949), pp. 195–207. On p. 195, Ponce says of Cané: "During many years Buenos Aires saw in him its expression and its pride; the expression and pride of a liberal *bourgeoisie* that handled the affairs of the country as though they were family matters."

Cané's career contains that close relationship between politics and letters which marked the liberal aristocrats of this era and may still be found in Latin America to a delightful degree— that easy movement from one's library to the national congress and from diplomatic receptions in Paris to the university lecture platform. But with the Argentines of this generation the link between the pen and the power of the state was not a matter of dabbling in alternate hobbies. It was a serious business, as Cané himself demonstrated in 1902. In that year, a Law of Residence of Foreigners was passed by congress and signed by President Roca. The law in practice severely limited freedom in Argentina. It was aimed primarily at anarchists, but it was also a stern step taken by the ruling class to repress growing opposition among the people, who were restless under the suppression and perversion of their civil rights. The man who prepared the original draft of this *Ley de residencia,* which hacked deeply at that pillar of the Argentine constitution which was a main source of the growth of the nation—the unfettered freedom of foreigners to live in Argentina—was the author of the pleasant schoolday memories of *Juvenilia* and the urbane critic of the latest French poetry—Miguel Cané. [20]

Under the influence of the cultural orientation toward Europe, more and more of the young men of good families were sent abroad for schooling. Few of these boys had to write home for money: their fathers were often no farther away than Rotten Row or the Bois. And, if their sisters did not make the trip to Europe, they sat at home in Buenos Aires in a dim *salon* amid potted palms and heavy tapestries, reading Georges Sand, Musset, or the *Revue des Deux Mondes,* and gossiping over Parisian fashions. [21]

Even the horses in Buenos Aires were affected by the passion for things European. Vehicular traffic in Argentina moved on the right-hand side of the street until 1889. In that year it was

[20] See Romero, *Las ideas,* pp. 196–197, and *Diputados,* session of November 22, 1902, pp. 345–364, and session of November 27, 1902, pp. 414–416.

[21] Elvira Aldao de Díaz, *Reminiscencias sobre Aristóbulo del Valle* (Buenos Aires, 1928), pp. 13–35, 46–51, 219–220.

decreed that traffic should proceed on the left, in the European manner.[22]

Despite such enthusiasm for civilization's benefits, Argentina in the last two decades of the past century did not have a defined intellectual class. Literature and the professions were in the hands of the aristocracy. Artists, writers, and teachers who supported themselves by those activities were nearly non-existent or, if they existed, were almost unknown. The times were not propitious for earning one's living by one's art alone; the creative person was submerged or swept along in the tidal wave of the almighty peso.[23] The nearest approach to what may be called a professional intellectual group was formed by the man who worked on the important periodicals. It is perhaps significant that it was Rubén Darío, a foreigner working for *La Nación* in the early nineties, who became the center of one of Argentina's first non-aristocratic intellectual groups. Another literary figure of this decade who also was connected with a periodical was José Alvarez ("Fray Mocho"). In 1898, Alvarez founded *Caras y Caretas*, the Argentine *Punch* of long and amusing life; in addition, he gained fame with his witty stories of the native scene. And in this same period Juan A. García and Agustín Alvarez began their sharp attacks on the imperfections of Argentine society, a warning of the intense social criticism which would later emerge as the most important activity of Argentine intellectuals. But this would come only after the turn of the century. Meanwhile, the authors of the Generation of Eighty continued to write their gentle essays, typified by the fragile work of Wilde and Cané, men who were loyal to the code of peace and progress which their class upheld.

The world of the oligarchs grew calmer in the eighties as the storms of the past diminished. As the directing class became

[22] Luis Cánepa, *El Buenos Aires de antaño, en el cuarto centenario de su fundación, 1536–1936* (Buenos Aires, 1936), p. 112.

It is no small indication of the nationalistic revolution which Argentina underwent between the 1880's and the 1940's (and of the gearing of Argentina to the American auto) that, in 1945, General Perón, who was in effective power, restored to Argentina's avenues and alleys the old pattern of traffic.

[23] Estanislao S. Zeballos, "La crisis del gobierno y del país," *Revista de Derecho, Historia y Letras*, año II, tomo 5, Jan. 1900, p. 450.

more and more successful, characteristics of a closed elite began
to appear. There were still rough edges to society in this hectic
decade, but the lords of the pampas and of Buenos Aires had
begun that imitative process which would in a few years make
them strikingly similar to their cherished model, the English
aristocracy.

The education of the youths of the upper class was a continuation of already close relationships sprung from the inter-
marriage of a small number of families. Childhood playmates
continued as schoolmates in Buenos Aires. Then came the
university. Some of the young men stayed at home, others went
abroad, to English or German universities, or studied under
French tutors. Then, and on the numerous European trips of
later life, these men traveled on the same ships, stayed at the
best hotels, joined good clubs, and stopped at the same fashionable spas. At home they imposed a pattern of town and country
life on their common heritage of political leadership and landed
wealth. Their town houses had mansard roofs and handsome
iron fences and sweeping marble stairways; their estancia houses
had gables, half-timbering, and swan-dotted ponds.

The Argentine aristocrats were bound together by blood and
history and by the circumscribed lives they led. The same gentlemen who in the morning nodded through a *Te Deum*, seated in
their red plush chairs ranged in facing rows along the central
aisle of the cathedral, and who exchanged grave bows from
their passing carriages in the afternoon at Palermo, dined and
wined together elegantly that evening at the Jockey Club,
and continued their discussions next morning on the floor of
one of their other two clubs—the national congress or the stock
exchange.

The death of one of their number brought them together with
magnetic certainty in a black-clad huddle at the graveside in
the Recoleta. Always in the Recoleta. Here, in this city of tombs,
generations of aristocrats have taken up residence in mausoleums
magnificently adorned, built on lots no less fashionably located
than the ones their owners enjoyed in life. By the bier of the
hero—for each of the fallen became briefly a hero in the
Recoleta—the living gathered, and manly tears were wept as

the ringing tones of eulogies broke the quiet air under the cypresses, looking out across the wide gleaming river.

These Argentines had an Old World Spanish emotionalism and a formidable ritual of death, but they were New World and American in other matters. The men of the Generation of Eighty not only changed the direction of traffic in Buenos Aires —they began to rebuild the city. Under the vigorous intendant, Torcuato de Alvear, scion of one of the important families, the Avenida de Mayo was driven through the heart of the city in the last years of the decade. The Avenida was tree-lined and possessed a novelty in sidewalks wide enough for whole families. Shaped in the style of the Champs Elysées and the Boulevard des Italiens, this stately street nevertheless met with the customary public resistance to civic improvements. "Who ever heard," the good citizens said when Alvear's workmen began the record-breaking demolition of the ill-smelling Recova Vieja, half of the historic Cabildo, and another twenty blocks of buildings—"Who ever heard of making a street where buildings are?" But the Argentines who ran the country had a *yanqui* haste about them and the avenue was laid out and other public projects undertaken with a breadth of planning and a speed which destroyed worthwhile landmarks but gave to Buenos Aires the fine prospects it possesses today.

The public life of the upper class took on new dignities commensurate with the growth of their wealth and their city. On the appointed days of national celebration, the president led his cabinet, the diplomatic corps, and all the other leaders of the nation in a short but solemn procession from the Casa Rosada to the cathedral on an adjoining side of the Plaza de Mayo, where each top-hatted dignitary could give thanks for his own blessings and the prosperity of the nation. Another event of significance was the running of the annual Gran Premio at Palermo's Hipódromo—which was opened in 1883, the year after the founding of the Jockey Club. This event called forth some of the spirit and many of the costumes appropriate to Derby Day—not a surprising similarity, since the decision to found the Jockey Club in Buenos Aires was made by Pellegrini, Cané, and one or two others as they dined together in Paris after attending the Derby at Chantilly.[24] But of all the solemn occasions which in these years attained the importance of national rituals the one uniquely Argentine was the day when the president and his entourage appeared at the fair grounds in Palermo to inaugurate the annual livestock exposition of the Sociedad Rural. Here the wealth and power of the nation paid tribute to the animals that sustained them; here each year the upper class studied the steadily rising barometer of success in the prices paid for its prize sheep, cattle, and horses.

Occasionally some member of society broke through the bounds of class good conduct. Such a man was Fabián Gómez y Anchorena, heir of vast wealth and intimate of Alfonso XII of Spain, who created him Count of Castaña. This Argentine nobleman could not endure the weight of his palace in Buenos Aires, with its hoard of Gobelins, masterworks of art, and gold-encrusted fountain; his life was bizarre beyond sanity and ended in impecuniosity on a small family stipend. This was a fate probably not shared by one of his lawyers, to whom Gómez graciously gave as a fee for legal services the deed to his favorite estancia, "La Pampita," eight square leagues (approximately seventy-five square miles) of land near Mar del Plata.[25]

Gómez may have been one of a type within the upper class, but his qualities were not those which his peers held in esteem. The authority of the oligarchy centered in shrewd, hard-driving men like Roca, Pellegrini, and Bernardo de Irigoyen. Pellegrini was in many ways the most interesting of this trio. To his friends and to the public he was "El Gringo." His English blood (he was the grandnephew of John Bright) overcame his French and Italian parentage and was borne out in his blue eyes, craggy face, and unusual height. He was more robust in spirit, as he was in body, than many of his reserved porteño colleagues. He dressed as handsomely as they and shared their proclivity for pinching pretty girls, but he could also deliver a jolting slap on the back to some unsuspecting friend, which was distinctly *not* a customary local gesture.

[24] [Carlos] *Pellegrini: Obras, precedidas de un ensayo biográfico por Agustin Rivero Astengo* (5 vols.; Buenos Aires, 1941), II, 343.

[25] Pilar de Lusarreta, *Cinco dandys* [sic] *porteños* (Buenos Aires, 1943), pp. 100–101, 104.

In 1876–77, Pellegrini made the first of many trips to Europe. When he returned he plunged into the political maneuvers of the "Conciliation," emerging with the friendship and admiration of Avellaneda and Roca. Minister of War and the Navy in Avellaneda's Belgrano government in 1880, he had a decisive part in that rump government's triumph over the revolutionary forces of Buenos Aires. National senator from 1881 to 1883, his first action was the introduction of a bill to found a national bank; his second measure was a bill to create a legislative committee to investigate the financial condition of the republic.[26]

In 1885, Roca sent Pellegrini to the bankers of London and Paris to convince them—perhaps "guarantee" is a more accurate word—that Argentina was good security for additional loans. The forty-two million pound Baring Brothers' loan of that year is testimony both to the qualities of Argentina and of its engaging Anglo-Franco-Italian emissary. Upon his return from Europe, Pellegrini was appointed Minister of War by President Roca. In 1886 he emerged as vice-president of the nation from a closely controlled election which must have reinforced the already high confidence of the London money market in its Argentine creditor. But, although he was vice-president under Juárez throughout the years of the great speculation which followed, Pellegrini had too keen a knowledge of men and money to become enmeshed in the conspiracy of corruption that ultimately brought on the revolution of 1890.[27]

This did not mean that Pellegrini was favorably disposed to the political party which was organized in 1890 under the meaningful name Unión Cívica. This party was formed by popular leaders such as Alem, whose political strength lay in the crowded barrios of Buenos Aires and with the growing middle class, and by dissident older leaders such as Mitre, who were disgusted with the political reaction and corruption practised by the *unicato*—the single-party Juárez rule. That there was a profound difference between these two merging elements, the old and the new, was proved by their early split, but at the

[26] Pellegrini, *Obras*, II, 26–27.

[27] Paul Groussac, *Los que pasaban: José Manuel Estrada, Pedro Goyena, Nicolás Avellaneda, Carlos Pellegrini, Roque Sáenz Peña* (2nd ed.; Buenos Aires, 1939), pp. 306–308.

3

outset they agreed on the need for implementing Argentina's democratic constitution and enfranchising those whose right to vote had been long denied or perverted. Vice-president Pellegrini took a different view of matters. He could not stomach the ruin of the national credit which the Juárez clique was consummating, but beyond that his political philosophy was cut from the same cloth as that of the majority of the class to which he belonged.

In November 1889, shortly after the first meeting of the future Unión Cívica, Pellegrini said, "This Unión Cívica de la Juventud is a summons to disorder and anarchy—formidable and indestructible factors in our history. It will cause us trouble." On other occasions he stated that he did not believe that the Argentine people were ready for free suffrage; that to give them electoral liberty would be like placing a firearm in the hands of a child and that therefore the existing tutelary regime must be continued. In Pellegrini's opinion, the best way to reform Argentine politics—he did have to admit that reform was needed—was to select good provincial governors who would in turn send worthy men to the national congress.[28] Good would thus automatically supplant bad, although the electoral process was left considerably befogged by this prescription.

The modest reforms advocated by Pellegrini and the passivity of the views which he expressed were characteristic of the oligarchy's conservative political philosophy. Apparently as firm in control of the government as they were of the resources of the nation, the Generation of Eighty accepted and used the "affluence of foreign capital and the fecund flood of the venal masses." Progress was also their god. In pursuing wealth, in imitating Europe's ways, the Argentine aristocrats were themselves prime forces in reshaping their past and creating modern Argentina.

[28] Groussac, *Los que pasaban*, pp. 311, 349; Aldao de Díaz, *Reminiscencias*, pp. 100–102.

5

The Generation of Eighty: Pride and Optimism

DESPITE the influence which Europe exercised upon them, the Argentine aristocrats seldom faltered in their devotion to their own country. Many immigrants to Argentina also fell under the curious spell which the land exercises. Perhaps this spirit has been best expressed in a novel of the period—Grandmontagne's *Los inmigrantes prósperos*. Don Gabino is sailing back to visit his native Spain, whence he had emigrated many years before; he is returning in wealth to the little village he left in poverty. Gabino's life has been dedicated to the accumulation of pesos; other values have had little meaning for him. But, as he stands by the rail of the ship pulling away from the great white expanse of Buenos Aires, he voices in a moment of emotion the hidden feeling of the years: "Tira mucho esa tierra"—"How strongly that land draws one back."

What is the origin of this patriotic and sentimental attachment shared alike by new and old Argentines? The answer seems to lie in the powerful pride and optimism which has long possessed the Argentine people. These qualities in part arise from certain historical and physical facts; in part from less assessable but perhaps no less important considerations of temperament and social myth. The psychological constitution of the Argentine people is not a subject to be dealt with here, although it is impossible not to wonder to what extent it is the sensitive and recalcitrant Spanish temperament, reinforced by Italian emotionalism, which accounts for the strong solution of aggressive pride which Argentines have been distilling for years. On the side of history, however, one may suggest that events at the beginning of the nineteenth century had such an impact on Argentine thought that a prideful national myth was established, to be amplified through the traditions learned by successive generations.

The first of these events was the defeat in 1806 of a strong British attempt to seize Buenos Aires and the colony of which it was the head. Unexpectedly, the ragged troops and angry people of the city expelled the numerous, battle-hardened invaders. Bitter at their defeat in this coveted temperate land, the British returned to Buenos Aires in 1807 with a powerful fleet and an army of 11,000 regulars. This attack also was smashed by the aroused citizens of the weak Spanish vice-royalty. Two victories over mighty Britain! What proof to these colonials of their valor and glorious destiny! Three years later the Argentine war for independence began in Buenos Aires, to lead eventually to the expulsion of Spain from the countries of the Río de la Plata. Little wonder that Mariano Moreno, the Sam Adams of the Argentine revolution and a confirmed Rousseauist, cried out: "Since nature has created us for great things, we have begun to do them." From this time on "a new consciousness, overladen with self-esteem, motivated the criolla minority and masses."[1]

The particular circumstances of their revolution gave impetus to legitimate national pride. The great Argentine leader San Martín not only won independence for his own country but, by his famous crossing of the Andes and subsequent battles, made possible the liberation of Chile and Peru. Thus was established an historic thesis which has grown with the years: that Argentina had liberated the greatest part of the Spanish continent and had created the basis for a united America. Two generations later this theme found expression in the first issue of *Sud América* (May 5, 1884), the Juárez newspaper. In an editorial declaration of faith written, in all probability, by Saenz Peña and Pellegrini, these leaders of the Generation of Eighty voiced their Argentine doctrine of Americanism:

The men of May cast the Argentine revolution in an essentially American form; it was the idea of America that agitated Buenos

---

[1] José Luis Romero, *Las ideas políticas en Argentina* (México, 1946), p. 68. See also Ricardo Levene, ed., *El pensamiento vivo de Mariano Moreno presentado por Ricardo Levene* (Buenos Aires, 1942), p. 54.

Aires, Santiago, Lima, Caracas, Bogotá, and México; there was a South American policy proclaimed by the revolution . . . When our fathers invoked their nationality, the name American was the first they employed to distinguish themselves from Europe . . . This is the principle that we come to uphold, yet without forgetting constantly to safeguard the interests which the Argentine Republic must defend on its own soil and beyond in the broad scene of the South American nations.

This expression of American internationalism—and, incidentally, of Argentine leadership—was to be more closely defined five years later at the First Pan American Conference, where one of the delegates of the Juárez-Pellegrini administration was Roque Saenz Peña.

The glorious revolution of May was followed by years of internal turmoil and the hiatus of the Rosas regime. After the fall of the dictator the nation resumed its struggle toward the goal which its founders had set: the development of the economic resources of the land under a liberal government. Argentine statesmen and historians turned back to praise the country's early achievements and to foretell a brilliant future. This burgeoning pride was founded not only on the increasing wealth of the nation but also on what were to the Argentines obvious advantages of geography and population. By 1880, Argentina thought of itself as the only great white nation of South America. Chile was far away across the Andes (far away from Buenos Aires, at least), and in reality was no more of a threat to Argentina, despite her "Prussian" reputation, than were the Indian lands to Argentina's north—Bolivia and Paraguay. Uruguay was a miniature nation; some Argentines persisted in referring to it as a lost province of Argentina. Brazil—Brazil was beyond the jungles and the seas, and besides—think of the colors of her people! Thus the Argentine upper class conceived a splendid isolation, based not only on its wealth but also on the popular doctrine of the superiority of the white race.

A sign of Argentina's increasing national pride was the resistance which developed in the eighties to the use—or misuse—of "South American," words which many Argentines took to be a European deprecation by which all the barbarians of the Latin

American republics were disdainfully lumped together. Argentina wished to avoid even a verbal merger with the smaller and darker countries. She wanted desperately to be a nation. It was in a spirit of challenge that the young leaders of the Argentine aristocracy deliberately selected the name for the newspaper that they founded—*Sud América*—and in its first issue proudly proclaimed that conservatism and good credit would open the road to peace and order.

Other words were used: "race," "the place we deserve," "honor," and "Europe." The years after 1880 were good to this class and these words meant much. The Argentine leaders began to believe that they had passed beyond the dark period of revolutions. Proud as they were of their past, they began to take even greater pride in their present achievements. *Sud América's* editors complained (March 7, 1885) that if there was a revolution in Bogotá, Europeans thought that Buenos Aires was on the verge of civil war. Such a misconception grieved the men who were at last convinced that progress was indeed perpetual —and that Argentina was due for its share. An aggressive note entered into the expressions of national pride which flowed faster and faster from the lips and pens of the leaders of the republic. The eighteenth century had given to their grandfathers its doctrine of indefinite progress; [2] from their fathers the Generation of Eighty inherited not only this belief, but evidence of its truth. From Buenos Aires the rulers of the land looked outward, seeing poorer neighboring nations across the backs of herds of fat cattle and flocks of sheep and across widening fields of golden grain. And beyond the sea they saw rich markets. In the shimmering perspectives of pampas, broad Plata, and ocean, everything lost size and importance except the nearest objects, the products of their soil and of their labor. From this mood of prosperity and expansion grew an idea often expressed from the eighties onward: the future of mankind would be settled in the New World. Ernesto Quesada in his *Nueva Revista de Buenos Aires* expressed the attitude of his generation when he wrote: "The attention of thinking men throughout the whole world is

[2] Juan A. García, *La ciudad indiana.* (*Buenos Aires desde 1600 hasta mediados del siglo XVIII*) (5th ed.; Buenos Aires, n.d. [1900]), pp. 220–221.

fixed here [on America], for here the destinies of humanity are being worked out."[3] And two more sober commentators on the Argentine scene—both of them soon to be important figures in the government of the country—expressed a similar opinion. In an article written in 1888, Norberto Piñero and Eduardo L. Bidau wrote: "The Argentine Republic now counts among the number of civilized nations. Europe and the United States are observing with curiosity and interest the advances which we are making in varied directions."[4]

The implication in such utterances was not a new one. Argentines have long known that they have a rendezvous with destiny. This knowledge is born of what one scholar called "that formidable optimism which has been at once the force and the opiate of the Argentine people."[5] So important a witness as President Avellaneda has testified to the obstinacy of this vision. "Our people," he wrote, "were born possessed of the opinion of their greatness, whether because of an infantile hallucination of pride, or because of some revelation of their destinies."[6] (The president was not so unpolitic and so un-Argentine as to omit the latter possibility.) And Juan A. García, one of the most severe critics of his generation, wrote that, "As a basis of pride and self-love . . . there was the sentiment of the grandness of the country."[7]

More recent critics, holding provocative if sometimes uncertain theories of social psychology, have found a serious basis for the idea which Avellaneda no doubt expressed jokingly: that the

---

[3] Ernesto Quesada, "El Congreso Literario Latino-Americano y el americanismo," *Nueva Revista de Buenos Aires*, 3:303 (March 1882).

[4] Norberto Piñero and Eduardo L. Bidau, "Historia de la Universidad de Buenos Aires," *Anales de la Universidad de Buenos Aires*, I (1888), 5.

[5] Octavio R. Amadeo in his prologue to Leopoldo Lugones, *Roca* (Buenos Aires, 1938), p. 29.

[6] Octavio R. Amadeo, *Vidas argentinas* . . . (2nd ed.; Buenos Aires, 1934), p. 139.

[7] García, *La ciudad indiana*, p. 218.

Agustín Alvarez, in a book which he revealingly entitled, in English, *South America*, lashed at the false system of education which prevailed in Argentina in the eighties and nineties, by which successive generations of students were instilled with a shallow but exaggerated belief in the glory and destiny of their country and indoctrinated with an excessive sense of personal and national honor. See Agustín Alvarez, *South America. Ensayo de psicología política* (Buenos Aires, 1918; first published 1894), pp. 59–61.

Argentine people have truly been the victims of a hallucination. These writers maintain that there is a connection between the vast optimism which undeniably characterizes the people and the equally vast distances that stretch before them, distances which throughout the country's history have induced the scanty populace to exercise a limitless imagination upon the glorious individual and national destinies lying beyond the horizon.

Beyond that hazy line where the purple pampas waver with the heat up into the blue sky (Argentines insist that *their* sky is a different blue from any other, and so, indeed, it seems to be), the first settlers believed that golden cities lay, whose conquest would bring to the victors long-dreamed-of wealth and fame. The City of the Caesars was Argentina's El Dorado, a mirage beckoning in a land of disappointment where there was no gold, no silver, no Indian masses. It was a dream of distances—distances never really explored until after the middle of the last century when the narrowly encompassing Indian frontier was at last driven back and obliterated. Suddenly the dream was made real. Gold was found on every side, on every square league of fertile soil. The vision became fact. The urge for aggrandizement, the desire for wealth and power so long deferred, could now be satisfied by the conquest of land and animals. [8] Argentina would count for something in the world. So too would Buenos Aires. When colonial Lima and Mexico City had been regal capitals, Buenos Aires had been a dirty hamlet. The image of hidden wealth and the faith that it would be discovered had helped to keep alive the dream of a Buenos Aires that would one day surpass in size and in luxury all the cities of Latin America.

North Americans may recognize something of themselves in these historic Argentine traits. There are obvious geographic and social resemblances between the two nations; consequently, some of their attitudes seem similar. Inhabitants of the United States are not the only people who have had, and perhaps still have, a manifest destiny, just as the United States is not the only country to possess a great west—a west so rich and wide that

[8] Ezequiel Martínez Estrada, *Radiografía de la pampa* (2 vols.; Buenos Aires, 1942), I, 9-31, 194-197.

trains rolling across the endless plains had to lower their cow catchers to smash through slow-moving herds of animals—bison in the United States, sheep and cattle in Argentina.

The two countries grew at roughly the same time and in much the same way. But the United States was more advanced than Argentina and therefore served as a model to some Argentine leaders. A few of the leaders of the generation of Caseros borrowed directly from North America—Alberdi in constitutional law, for example, and Sarmiento in educational method. After 1880, however, Argentines were busy with the practical application of these past borrowings and with their own expanding frontiers and trade. Their attitude toward the United States changed from awe for the republican giant of the New World to a bold assertion that Argentina would someday be just as rich and busy as the land of the Yankees. Even Sarmiento's attitude changed. Where once he had been the goad of his people, urging them to imitate the United States, his message now became a strident challenge—a promise that the goal was in sight. His last written words (1888) were: "We shall reach the level of the United States. We shall be America as the sea is the ocean. We shall be the United States." [9] By 1890, in a prize essay sponsored by the Sociedad Rural, the assembled estancieros were assured that Argentina possessed material conditions superior to those of the United States, and would someday be greater. [10]

La Prensa, cosmopolitan and traditional, took a somewhat less challenging stand which blended the old respect for the republican virtues of the United States with a desire to duplicate that nation's stunning economic growth. In a lengthy editorial in 1886, *La Prensa* utilized the United States as a club with which to beat the oligarchy. Under the title "El Gran Modelo" the editors wrote: "We [Argentines] take pride in the triumph of the free institutions of North America, but we forget to study the secret of victory, which is none other than liberty . . . The Argentine Republic ought to aspire to grow like the United

[9] D. F. Sarmiento, *Obras de D. F. Sarmiento*, ed. by A. Belín Sarmiento. Tomos XXXVII and XXXVIII: *Conflictos y armonías de las razas en América* (Buenos Aires, 1900), XXXVIII, 421.

[10] Alois E. Fliess, *El presente y el porvenir Argentina* . . . (Buenos Aires, 1890), pp. 7–10, 61-69.

States, and not in the manner, and with the elements, of France, England, and Germany."[11]

Argentina in the eighties seemed to have good grounds for this hope of matching the United States. Argentina was big, her soil was fertile, and immigrants were pouring into the country at a rate relatively greater than that of the United States. The constitution urged the men of the whole world to come to live in Argentina. Of coal and oil and minerals not much had yet been discovered, but what Argentine could doubt that his towering Andes would soon surrender their wealth to the relentless progress of the nation? Why should Argentina be deprived of that which lesser lands such as Bolivia and Peru possessed in abundance?

These were the dreams of the eighties. Despite *La Prensa*, the United States was no longer an overpowering model of political virtues which had to be mimicked, nor was it yet a giant whose own growth would perpetually outdistance that of the smaller southern land. The United States was merely a distant challenge.

Foreign travelers to Argentina in these years were unanimous in relating the feverish activity and conspicuous materialism which marked this "coming" land. There was Theodore Child, for instance, an American visitor of 1890, who took a rather critical view (perhaps remembering that foreign eyes had but recently found the United States wanting in the graces of civilization). Yet Child's shafts were blunted. To him the streets of Buenos Aires were unutterably noisy and congested—but full of energetic people getting things done. The hotels and restaurants of the city were disappointing after all that one had heard about this progressive capital—one must have recourse to the really large establishments before one finds a suitable cuisine and accommodations. The country is wealthy—no doubt of that: "the jewellers of Paris and of London do not make a more brilliant display of costly jewels than their colleagues of the Calle Florida." But Child came closest to an accurate description

[11] September 12, 1886. This editorial ended with the customary Cassandra-like warning of economic collapse. If the government continues to borrow at the present rate, wrote the editors, "before the end of the century all its income will not suffice to pay the interest on the debt." *La Prensa* overestimated the government's solvency by ten years.

of braggart, bustling Buenos Aires when he pronounced his decision: "So much luxury and so little real comfort."[12]

An English traveler named Turner, whose account of Argentina in the years from 1885 to 1890 might cause a reader to think that the author had lost a considerable sum of money in the crash of the latter year, is even more unflattering. The Argentine male, he reports,

. . . is taught to believe that he is born to be a ruler in a great and mighty land to which the nations shall by and by play the part of the sun, the moon and the stars . . . In reality only half civilized, the Argentine aspires to be considered the peer of the modern Parisian . . . He is a copyist, an imitator of all that is showy and shallow, a Frenchman without the thrift or talent of the Frenchman. Distinct nationality he has none; if he had he would still be wearing his *poncho* and eating *puchero* [stew]. He studies engineering and his plans are unsafe unless revised by a foreigner. He studies law and frames acts which plunge the country into turmoil. He studies finance, sweeps the banks away, and sacks the treasuries.

This English writer damns the city as well as its citizen: "Buenos Aires, with its rank materialism, sordid avarice and gross sensuality; its ungodly, unsociable, hybrid population; its showy finery and superficial veneer of civilization."[13]

Another attitude was struck by William E. Curtis, an American who was later to play a part in Pan American affairs. After a whirlwind tour of Latin America in 1884, which included a day in Buenos Aires, Curtis wrote a large book in which he declared: "Buenos Ayres . . . is the most enterprising, prosperous and wealthy city in South America—a regular Chicago— the only place in the whole continent where people seem to be in a hurry." Curtis summed up his observations in a phrase which must have rung pleasantly in Argentine ears: "The

[12] Theodore Child, *The Spanish American Republics* (New York, 1891), pp. 261–264, 278.
[13] Thomas A. Turner, *Argentina and the Argentines: Notes and Impressions of a Five Years' Sojourn in the Argentine Republic, 1885–90* (London, 1892), pp. vii–viii, 147. The Argentine male has long been a source of considerable wonder to the men of other lands. For a biting attack on his own sex, see Martínez Estrada, *Radiografía*, II, 124–128.

Argentine Republic will some day become a formidable rival of the United States."[14]

Here again was the challenge of the United States, this time echoed by a foreigner, and a North American at that. How impressive seemed the course of the nation when to such sentiments were added the measured words of one of France's most distinguished economic geographers, Vavasseur, who wrote: "The Argentine Republic, which occupies in the temperate zone of South America a position analogous to that of the United States in North America, may dream, if not of equal power, at least of a similar future."[15]

Travelers' accounts of Argentina were reinforced by imposing geographies published in these years. The most extensive were Daireaux's two volumes, *Vida y costumbres en El Plata* (Buenos Aires, 1888), and Latzina's *Géographie*. The former was more than a physical geography: it was a social, political, historical, economic survey calculated to make the heart of any Argentine—and perhaps of any European investor—beat faster. The two most powerful men in the nation, Roca and Mitre, placed their *imprimatur* on these volumes, apparently pleased with such chapters as "Public Credit and Private Wealth" and "Virgin Lands and Cattle." Latzina's appraisal was more formal, more scientific. There one may find a multitude of statistics, ranging from those pertaining to railroads to an impossibly exact enumeration of all the foundlings cared for by Buenos Aires institutions since 1779.

The turbulent decade of the eighties was filled with the confusion of good taste and the grotesque which marks a young, fast-growing nation. The well-to-do had not yet had time to develop a suitable watering place in their own country, but toward the end of the decade they began to make a fashionable resort out of the rocky beaches and bare hills of Mar del Plata on the Atlantic. As late as 1892, the new bathing resort was still "a straggling place, dangerous for bathing and possessing hardly

[14] William E. Curtis, *The Capitals of Spanish America* (New York, 1888), pp. 549, 579.

[15] Francisco Latzina, *Géographie de la République Argentine*. Avec une introduction par M. E. Vavasseur (2nd ed.; Buenos Aires, 1890), p. xxvi.

any attraction." Even the British had not yet established themselves. Hurlingham, later to become *the* British suburb of Buenos Aires, with golf courses and polo fields and estates, was still merely "a favorite rendezvous on holidays for races, athletic sports, etc.," where "several Englishmen have built cottages."[16] At the same time, in the Boca, the Buenos Aires waterfront slum where many of the immigrants ended up, fires, floods, and epidemics were regular occurrences, little heeded by a government and people with their eyes set on the future. How could one be interested in the Boca when great things were being accomplished daily a few miles away in the town of Quilmes, where, at the Highland Scot Canning Company, "five hundred horned cattle can be killed, cut up and tinned in $2\frac{1}{2}$ hours, and at the close not a vestige is left of the operation"?[17] And although the wine cellars of the Jockey Club were being filled with the French vintages that would one day make them perhaps the best in the world, the exterior of the building succumbed to the uncertain electrical taste of the era; the entire façade was outlined by rows of naked electric light bulbs—an object of admiration and a lesson in luxury, but hardly a tribute to the taste of the distinguished gentlemen who entered the brass-bound portals and trod the crimson carpets.

If this decade were not a golden age, it seemed to the Argentine aristocrats to be its dawn. Provincial yet cosmopolitan; proud of their land and themselves yet quick to imitate the ways of other lands and other men; eager for internal peace yet on the verge of a bloody revolution; liberal in economic matters but conservative in politics; sensitive to the nuances of European culture yet adolescent in its domestic application; proud of their history, but prouder of their future—such were the men of the remarkable Generation of Eighty who brought Argentina onto the stage of world affairs.

[16] M. G. and E. T. Mulhall, *Handbook of the River Plate, Comprising the Argentine Republic* . . . (6th ed.; Buenos Aires, 1892), pp. 86, 98–99.
[17] Mulhall, *Handbook*, p. 95.

6

Argentina in Latin America, 1880–1889

THE men who ruled Argentine society, controlled the economy, and made and unmade governments were also the masters of the nation's foreign policy. The management of foreign relations was administratively, morally, and for material reasons the oligarchy's possession. Administratively, because the aristocracy alone had the capacity for the practice of diplomacy according to Europe's weighty tradition of statecraft. Morally, because neither the criollo masses nor the swarms of immigrants conceived of Argentina in international terms. After 1880 it was only the topmost social class that saw the republic's growing international importance. And in material terms because the nation lived by foreign trade. Trade was in the hands of the oligarchy; so too were relations with the trading nations.

Europe and commerce became synonymous in Argentina as the nineteenth century entered its last decades. Economic ties between the other states of Latin America and Argentina were insignificant relative to the volume of European trade.[1] It is the growth of this unbalanced trade that is a condition for understanding Argentina's political attitude toward the rest of Latin America during the years after independence. Argentina had ample opportunity to participate in political activities with the other Latin American states, but chose to follow its own course. So, when the United States appeared on the scene in the eighties, hauling the chariot of a revived Pan Americanism,[2]

[1] Francisco Latzina, *La Argentina considerada en sus aspectos físico, social y económico* (2 vols.; Buenos Aires, 1902), II, 512–513.

[2] There are two Pan American movements. The first was that of the middle years of the nineteenth century, launched by Bolívar in the Congress of Panama in 1826. Bolívar's romantic scheme is treated in James B. Lockey, *Pan Americanism, Its Beginnings* (New York, 1920).

the rulers of Argentina were ready to meet the apparent challenge with a set of principles and practices developed in dealing with Latin America and Europe.

Despite the claims which Argentines make for their efforts in the struggle to create inter-American unity—an idea which they maintain originated in its true form with Monteagudo, Moreno, and San Martín [3]—an examination of the chief occasions of cooperation between the Latin American states during most of the nineteenth century shows that the Argentine record is one of absenteeism and opposition. This attitude was founded on a cautious appraisal of the uncertainties of South American political life, and nourished by a desire to preserve unimpaired the nation's hard-won sovereignty.

The porteños—for it was they who controlled the foreign affairs of the state from its inception—displayed in 1823 the emerging Argentine policy toward the other states of the continent. In that year Argentina signed a treaty of friendship and defense with Colombia. The Colombian government wished to extend the treaty into a sort of collective security arrangement embracing other parts of America; Rivadavia, the Argentine Minister of Foreign Affairs, refused to go beyond specific commitments to Colombia alone. He regarded a wider agreement as impractical in view of the disturbed conditions prevailing in many parts of South America. The Argentine government also mistrusted the possible hegemony of Bolívar and his Gran Colombia, an apparently powerful state composed of what are now the republics of Colombia, Venezuela, and Ecuador. [4]

Argentina was soon offered a more tangible opportunity to assist in constructing a Spanish American political union. This

[3] *La política internacional de la Nación Argentina. Absoluta identidad de su tradición y sus principios con los sustentados en el Acto de Chapultepec, la Declaración de México, la Declaración de las Naciones Unidas y la Carta del Atlántico.* República Argentina. Ministerio del Interior. Subsecretaría de Informaciones. Comp. and ed. by Carlos Alberto Silva (Buenos Aires, 1946), pp. vii–xi, 5, 10–16; Ricardo Levene, ed., *Historia de la Nación Argentina (desde los orígenes hasta la organización definitiva en 1862)* (10 vols. in 15; Buenos Aires, 1936–50), VI (third part, second section), 599–600 (chapter by Humberto A. Mandelli); Robert N. Burr and Roland D. Hussey, eds., *Documents on Inter-American Cooperation* (2 vols.; Philadelphia, 1955), I, 42–47.

[4] *Política internacional,* p. 21; Víctor Andrés Belaúnde, *Bolívar and the Political Thought of the Spanish American Revolution* (Baltimore, 1938), pp. 261–262.

was Bolívar's Congress of Panama of 1826, called by the Libera-
tor to establish a council of American states. Argentina was not
represented at this first Pan American meeting. The Argentine
chief executive faintly endorsed the dispatch of a delegation to
the congress, on grounds of expediency, but the legislature let
the matter die.[5] Here again the shaky domestic situation and
fear of foreign entanglements prevented participation by the
most powerful state of southern South America in a visionary
attempt to build a common political structure out of a common
heritage.

The next significant congress of the first, and more idealistic,
Pan American movement took place in Lima in 1847. Although
overly optimistic and ultimately unproductive, this conference
had a clear purpose: to devise means of repelling existing and
threatening foreign aggressions. Chile, Peru, Ecuador, Bolivia,
and New Granada (Colombia) attended. Argentina was invited
but did not attend. The excuse given by the Rosas government
was paradoxical: "The extraordinary circumstances in which
the republic finds itself . . . do not permit it to occupy itself
with this matter, which for its magnitude and importance
demands serious and profound meditation and calm."[6] The
"extraordinary circumstances" consisted of the armed intervention of England and France in the affairs of Argentina, a precise
example of the reason behind the calling of the conference which
Argentina refused to attend.

Nine years later the idea of an American confederation was
again revived. In 1856 the Continental Treaty was signed by representatives of Chile, Peru, and Ecuador, and later by Bolivia,
Costa Rica, Nicaragua, Honduras, Mexico, and Paraguay.

[5] *Política, internacional,* pp. 22–23; Levene, *Historia,* VI (third part, second section),
599–602.
There is similarity between the records of the United States and Argentina in the
matter of non-participation in the Panama Congress. Both governments were more
concerned with domestic and European affairs than with Bolívar's plans. Consequently, while both appointed plenipotentiaries to the assembly, not one of them
arrived at the meeting. One of the United States representatives died en route, the
other arrived after the congress had adjourned. The Argentine delegate did not
depart from Buenos Aires.
[6] *Congresos americanos de Lima.* Recop. de documentos . . . prólogo por Alberto
Ulloa (2 vols.; Lima, 1938), I, 181–182.

By this treaty the signatories agreed to respect the integrity of their territories, to refrain from hostile acts until the means of pacific settlement of their disputes were exhausted, and to establish uniform procedures with regard to their mutual trade, the application of private law, and the exercise of the professions. [7] When Argentina was asked to sign the treaty, Urquiza, head of the government, refused. He stated that the cause of peace would be more effectively served by bilateral treaties, and implied that the Continental Treaty was ill-conceived in the light of the isolation of the South American states. [8] Thus, Urquiza lengthened the precedent of Moreno, Rivadavia, and Las Heras, who had all pointed to the practical limitations on Spanish American idealism.

Argentina is a land whose history is marked by numerous periods of crisis or development followed by abrupt denouements. 1862 was such a moment. In that year the relatively strong administration of General Mitre took office, and Buenos Aires reassumed a dominant role in the nation after a long struggle with the provinces. It was also the year when the question of inter-American cooperation turned up again in Buenos Aires to confront the government. In July the Peruvian minister to Argentina invited that government to reconsider its refusal to sign the Continental Treaty. France had invaded Mexico, Spain had annexed Santo Domingo, the independence of the American states seemed threatened by resurgent European intervention. The minister of Peru appealed for Argentine cooperation in reanimating the Continental Treaty as a collective security pact. [9]

After four months Seoane received a lengthy reply from the Argentine foreign minister, Rufino de Elizalde. The Argentine spokesman stated his government's attitude toward European intervention in no uncertain terms:

The Argentine government has no cause to admit the existence of that threat. A league [against America] could not be formed by the

---

[7] J. M. Torres Caicedo, *Unión Latino-Americano: pensamiento de Bolívar para formar una liga Americana* . . . (Paris, 1865), pp. 241–250; Burr and Hussey, I, 135–138, 146–147.   [8] *Política internacional*, pp. 24–25.

[9] Seoane to Costa, July 18, 1862, *Registro oficial de la República Argentina* . . . (Vol. I—, Buenos Aires, 1879—), IV (1857–1862) (Buenos Aires, 1883), 534.

material and commercial interests of Europe because those interests are in harmony with those of the American nations . . . The Argentine Republic has never feared the threat of a European combination, nor of any one of the nations . . . The action of Europe in the Argentine Republic has always been protective and civilizing . . . Bound to Europe by the ties of the blood of thousands of persons . . . receiving from Europe the capital which our industry requires, and given the existence of an interchange of products, the Republic, one may say, is identified with Europe as much as is possible . . . It is clear that there are more links, more interest, more harmony between the American republics and certain European nations than between themselves.

The Argentine foreign minister next considered the formation of an American union through a congress of American states as envisaged in the Seoane proposal:

America, containing independent nations, with their own means and needs of government, cannot ever form a single political entity . . . The Congress of Plenipotentiaries is completely sterile and improper . . . A political body with the sole object of intervening in cases of war by the contracting parties, or to hinder their freedom in acts which they may judge proper, is in no way acceptable to the Argentine government.[10]

This important definition of Argentine policy may have seemed hardheaded to the men of Buenos Aires, who discerned that their future lay with Europe's rich markets and not with the impoverished American states, but it must have seemed merely hardhearted and, in the light of the future, myopic, to the other American states. Within three years Argentina was involved in another inter-American congress, called to repel yet another European attack on South America.

In 1864, Spain occupied the valuable Chincha Islands off the coast of Peru. A conference assembled in Lima to meet this threat. Sarmiento was named by the Argentine government as an observer at the meeting, but a delay in receiving an official invitation caused the Mitre administration to refuse to empower

---

[10] Elizalde to Seoane, November 10, 1862, *Registro*, IV, pp. 534–538. The note was published by the Argentine government immediately after its dispatch to Seoane. See *Congresos americanos de Lima*, I, cii; Burr and Hussey, I, 150–153.

him to act as a delegate. The volcanic Sarmiento went ahead on his own, a possibility that his government had foreseen and which had contributed to the decision to limit his power to act in the assembly. He joined in a formal denunciation of the Spanish government "in his name and that of the Argentine people." His part in the congress was disavowed by the administration in Buenos Aires. Later, President Mitre succinctly stated Argentine policy. "Argentina above all," he said, then adding, "but the government will not cease to be American and a good neighbor."[11]

The Lima conference seemed to be the last gasp of Bolivarian Americanism. After 1865 the vision of a united America faded for a time. Argentina, by the independent course it had pursued in America, was a factor in dissipating the hopes for a political utopia. Starting with a justifiable suspicion of the possibility of cooperation in the midst of chaos, Argentina gradually formulated its own American policy. One part of this policy was composed of intense nationalism, characterized by fear of any commitments that might limit sovereignty, and a touchy pride that added a realistic if sour note to the diplomatic melody played by the Latin American states. The other, positive side of Argentine foreign policy was the development of close relations with Europe after the fall of Rosas, together with the advocacy of bilateral treaties to solve specific problems in America.

Fifteen years elapsed before there was another attempt to form an organization of American states.[12] Then, in 1880, Colombia invited the Latin American countries to assemble in Panama to draw up a treaty that would bring peace to the continent through a permanent system of arbitration. The noble dream aroused America again; almost all the nations accepted the invitation. Argentina, although she did not accept, did not refuse.

[11] *Política internacional*, pp. 28–29; *Congresos americanos*, I, 344–356.

[12] A congress had been held in Lima in 1877 for the purpose of making uniform certain parts of the international private law of the participating nations. Peru, Chile, Ecuador, and Cuba sent delegates, as did Argentina—the latter having decided that this assembly's objective was worthwhile. The congress petered out aimlessly after the outbreak of the War of the Pacific, staged by two of the principal participants. The United States was invited but refused. *Congresos americanos*, II, 122, 134–135.

The time as well as the content of the Argentine reply is critical. The battle of Buenos Aires had scarcely ended and President Roca had been in office only a few weeks. The civil war was over and its cause uprooted. The Generation of Eighty stood on the threshold of a decade of opportunity. It was in this atmosphere that Bernardo de Irigoyen, Roca's foreign minister, drafted his reply to the Colombian government.

It was fitting that one not of the younger generation should have voiced traditional Argentine doctrines in a commanding tone appropriate to the widening perspectives of the nation. Irigoyen was Catholic and conservative, an estanciero and a politician—and not far from being a statesman. In his youth he defended federalism and wrote poems to "La Niña," Manuelita, daughter of Rosas. Now he served at Roca's side as minister of foreign affairs and later as minister of the interior. It was he who actually founded the Argentine foreign office, and his tough supervision of domestic politics through his ministry and the P.A.N. did much to consolidate the oligarchy's political position. To the people of Buenos Aires who passed his mansion on Calle Florida he was Don Bernardo—with emphasis on the "Don."[13]

In the note of December 1880, Irigoyen first referred to Argentina's profound American sentiments and her record of arbitration. Then he turned to a subject unrelated to the Colombian invitation, but of much concern to the group governing Argentina:

Europe no longer harbors thoughts of conquest or the chimera of reprisals . . . The demands of civilization, the great interests of commerce . . . and the liberality with which America surrenders its riches to men born in all the latitudes of the globe, are the beneficent influences that suppress the antagonisms of both worlds.

Next he expressed sympathy with the Colombian arbitration proposal—and poked holes in it from the practical side, calling

[13] F. A. Barroetaveña, *Don Bernardo de Irigoyen, perfiles biográficos* (?Buenos Aires, ?1907); José Bianco, *Don Bernardo de Irigoyen, estadista y pioneer (1822–1906)* (Buenos Aires, 1927); Joaquín de Vedia, *Como los vi yo: semblanzas de Mitre, Roca . . . Irigoyen . . .* (Buenos Aires, 1922), pp. 145–161; Carlos Martínez [Carlos D'Amico], *Buenos Aires: su naturaleza, sus costumbres, sus hombres . . .* (México, 1890), pp. 35–43.

attention to the War of the Pacific, at that moment raging between states with arbitral agreements. Declarations in favor of
arbitration are meaningless, he wrote, without observing the
vital American tradition of the independence and sovereignty
of states. This led him to conclude that:

It is necessary to disclaim explicitly the attempts at violent . . .
conquests which would raise permanent obstacles to future stability.
The areas taken by force of arms . . . would be in America a sense-
less aggression against the fraternity of nations . . . The Argentine
government does not consider the isolated stipulation of arbitration
as an efficacious means of eliminating international discord . . . In
my opinion we could arrive at this result only by incorporating into
American public law the principles here stated . . . which . . . will
be, in the present and in the future, the true guarantees of peace.[14]

Irigoyen had Chile in mind when he spoke out against forcible annexations, but the doctrine of peace which he advocated
was becoming a foremost tenet of the Argentine Generation of
Eighty. Peace at home and abroad meant the chance to develop
national resources, win European capital, and attract immigration. This was "future stability." The possibility was more than
remote that Argentina herself might engage in war for territorial reasons—she had an abundance of land begging for
exploitation.[15] Irigoyen also put the American hope for continental peace through arbitration in clearer perspective. Above
arbitration were "the true guarantees of peace"—absolute
respect for national sovereignty in all its forms. Yet the obverse
of the Roca-Irigoyen foreign policy coin was friendliness to
Europe—without any tremors about intervention.

This significant statement of Argentine foreign policy, quite
unsolicited by the government of Colombia, indicated that
Argentina anticipated playing a larger part in American affairs.
Irigoyen was talking about American issues and giving his
solutions, not presenting excuses. Although Europe was clearly
first in Argentine thinking, Irigoyen went on to state that his

---

[14] Irigoyen to the minister of foreign relations of Colombia, December 30, 1880,
Memoria de relaciones exterióres presentada al honorable Congreso Nacional (1880–1905,
1910–1914, Buenos Aires, 1881–1906, 1911–1915 [not published for period 1906–
1909, inclusive], Buenos Aires, 1881), pp. 84–89.
[15] Ricardo Zorraquín Becú, *El federalismo argentino* (Buenos Aires, 1939), p. 267.

government wished to participate in an inter-American congress, but on its own terms, which would give to the new meeting "a wider scope than that proposed."[16]

How the Colombian government might have reconciled its proposed conference and Argentine insistence on a meeting with quite distinct objectives, it is impossible to say. Argentina did not get a chance to present its opinions on national sovereignty and non-intervention. Continued fighting between Chile and Peru prevented the meeting.

The issue of American policy was briefly stirred in 1884 when Foreign Minister Victorino de la Plaza, who was destined to become president thirty years later, caused one of the officials of his ministry to publish a paper on the reasons for the failure of inter-American congresses. This document fulsomely reviewed the hopes for American fraternal union born in the revolution, criticized the selfishness and inactivity of the American states that had blocked the application of the elevated principles of international law, and defended Argentina's record in America. As for Europe, this spokesman wrote: "It is most reasonable that we should not seek to antagonize Europe, but on the contrary should assimilate all its advances in the sciences, art, industry, and even the practices of its administrative institutions."[17]

Despite the orientation toward Europe so often expressed, Argentina had not forgotten South America. Moreno, Rivadavia, Urquiza, Mitre, and Roca had not dashed off to every American conference that had been called, but they had never wavered in verbal support for realistic Spanish American cooperation that took into account essential national interests. Now, increasing Argentine political stability and prosperity provided the Generation of Eighty with the opportunity and incentive to step to the front in American affairs.

In 1888, Argentina and Uruguay united in summoning an American congress that exemplified the Argentine concept of the proper approach to continental union. All the South American nations were invited to the South American Congress of International Private Law to meet in Montevideo in August

---

[16] *Memoria*, 1881, pp. 88–89.
[17] *Política internacional*, pp. 36–38.

1888.[18] Behind this title lay the desire to improve relations between the American states by agreement on the mutual rights and responsibilities of their citizens.

The conference was attended by Brazil, Bolivia, Peru, Paraguay, and Chile, as well as Argentina and Uruguay. Among the delegates who assembled, none were destined to take a more commanding part in the conference and none to be greater leaders in their own countries in the years ahead than the two representatives from Buenos Aires. Within a year this same pair would sit down to another conference table at the First Pan American Conference in Washington. In 1888 they stood together, as they would in Washington—two men from the same class, with similar training, like careers, and equal gifts of intellect and talents of statesmanship.

Manuel Quintana was fifty-three. He had the appearance and manner of an idealized Spanish grandee. Born in Buenos Aires, he died there in 1906 in his second year as president of the republic. A fine orator in the style of the day, Quintana held almost every high position in the land during his lifetime. A student of international law, a veteran of national political struggles, this haughty man is one of a memorable group of Argentine aristocrats.[19]

Roque Saenz Peña belongs to that group for the same reasons of birth and good breeding, and because he represented the whole nation with intelligence and understanding. Saenz Peña was heavy, unhurried—and always dressed in grey. He not only was an aristocrat; he looked like one. A porteño, born in 1851, he received his law degree at the University in 1875. He was at once elected to the chamber of deputies of the provincial legislature of Buenos Aires, as a member of the Autonomist Party. In those days the legislature of the province was at least the equal of the national congress in prestige and power. Among Saenz Peña's colleagues were his father, then president of the senate,

---

[18] *International American Conference, 1889-1890. Reports of Committees and Discussions Thereon* (4 vols.; Washington, D.C., 1892; hereafter cited as *IAC, Reports*), IV, 282–283.

[19] Enrique Udaonda, *Diccionario biográfico argentino* (Buenos Aires, 1938), pp. 567–568; Vedia, *Como los vi yo*, pp. 202–219; Pilar de Lusaretta, *Cinco dandys* [sic] *porteños* (Buenos Aires, 1943), pp. 17–37.

and a good share of the rising generation—L. V. López, Eduardo Wilde, Miguel Cané, J. M. Estrada, Quirno Costa, Irigoyen, Roca, Alzaga, Bengolea, and Casare.[20]

The smooth-running escalator of his class was carrying Saenz Peña rapidly upward through the lower levels of a promising political career when he suddenly jumped off. In 1879 he left Argentina and joined the Peruvian Army to fight against Chile. This was not primarily a gesture of "solidarity" with Peru; Saenz Peña left Buenos in the dark mood of an unrequited love affair.[21] Even so, he got his share of fighting. He took part in the bloody battle of Arica and when his superior officers had been killed around him, he assumed command of the shattered Peruvian division. He was captured in the victory charge of the Chileans and briefly imprisoned.[22]

Late in 1880, after his return from Chile, Saenz Peña was appointed sub-secretary of the ministry of foreign relations, under Irigoyen. Then came the inevitable trip to Europe, shared with Ezequiel Ramos Mejía, Paul Groussac, and Pellegrini. Back home, he helped to found *Sud América* in the following year. He mixed in politics for a while, then withdrew from public activity, but in 1887 he accepted appointment as minister to Uruguay, where he was joined by Quintana in 1888 to make up the Argentine delegation to the Montevideo Congress.

The Argentine foreign minister, Quirno Costa, spoke to the assembly on the first day. He recalled the internal struggles which had long isolated the Latin American nations from one another. This state of affairs, he said, was now happily ended through the beneficent influence "of our liberal institutions . . . [and] the immense riches of our far-flung territories." He went on to foretell ever closer commercial and political relations among these states, but he did not neglect to remind his

[20] Roque Saenz Peña, *Escritos y discursos*. Compilados por Ricardo Olivera (3 vols.; Buenos Aires, 1914, 1915, 1935), III, 315–319; Felipe Barreda Laos, *Roque Saenz Peña* (Buenos Aires, 1954). Contrary to the practice of others, Saenz Peña did not employ an accent mark on his paternal name.

[21] Paul Groussac, *Los que pasaban: José Manuel Estrada . . . Roque Sáenz Peña* (2nd ed.; Buenos Aires, 1939), p. 369; Octavio R. Amadeo, *Vidas argentinas: Rivadavia . . . Sáenz Peña* (2nd ed.; Buenos Aires, 1934), pp. 110–111.

[22] Saenz Peña, *Escritos*, III, 189–191, 334–343.

audience of the need "to tighten relations with Europe, which must be more intimate and more fraternal with each day."[23]

On this note the delegates got to work. Some years later the United States State Department described the meeting as one which "by its nature and for all purposes and effects was exclusively South American."[24] This was more true of the spirit than of the ultimate results of the Montevideo Congress. The assembly produced treaties on international civil and commercial law, literary and artistic property (copyright), trademarks, patents, penal and procedural law, and a convention on the practice of the liberal professions. These pacts were ratified by the governments whose representatives prepared them. Between 1896 and 1900, France, Spain, and Italy became parties to the treaty on copyright.[25]

More significant than this impressive record of accomplishment was the implication of the words "exclusively South American." A new Pan American movement, under United States auspices, had just been launched, and invitations to the First Pan American Conference had recently been sent out from Washington for a meeting in 1889. But in Montevideo the Argentine delegates were sketching the first lines of quite a different picture of international harmony, one which foreshadowed a strong Latin America, independent of foreign domination, solving its own problems in its own way. The exclusion of states of non-Iberic, or of non-Latin, descent was implicit in the purpose of the meeting: the matters of law which were proposed and resolved emanated exclusively from the heritage of Roman jurisprudence shared by the participants. Conflict with Anglo-Saxon law did not concern the delegates. Their job was to form a *corpus* of private law to be used among the Latin American states. Progress in this direction implied the possibility of progress toward eventual political collaboration.

[23] República Oriental del Uruguay, *Actas y tratados celebrados por el Congreso Internacional Sud-Americano de Montevideo* (Montevideo, 1911), pp. 6–9.

[24] The Pan American Union. The Columbus Memorial Library. Third International Conference of the American States. Confidential memorandum for the use of the delegates of the United States of America, p. 22.

[25] Confidential Memorandum, p. 23. Chile did not ratify the treaty on international civil law.

Quirno Costa and Saenz Peña had gone over the question of inviting non-South American states to Montevideo and had decided against it. In March 1888 the foreign minister had written to his minister in Uruguay that it had been determined (in conjunction with Uruguay),

. . . to invite [only] the South American states, having in mind their close bonds of political and commercial interest and even of neighborliness. The other states of North and Central America either would not come or would come late, and perhaps one of them would assume a disturbing role of supremacy . . . . If the congress were for all sections of the continent [hemisphere], we would naturally have to call it an "American Congress," and I fear the possibility of failure, thus destroying an idea which, if realized among the South American states, could later be accepted by other nations.[26]

The Argentine delegates were no less effective because they did not arrogate to themselves a dominant role in the assembly. In a superb extemporized speech, Quintana hammered home the Argentine conviction of the primary importance of guarding national independence. "All are equally independent; all are equally sovereign," he said, but went on to claim that Argentina had always been among the first and would continue to be among the first states to bring her laws into line with international law, in this way contributing to harmony and progress among peoples.[27] In whatever debates they intervened, Quintana and Saenz Peña were perceptive and persistent in driving through the interpretations which fitted their legal and political doctrines. They repeatedly emphasized that Argentine sovereignty should not, and indeed, could not, be impaired by any action taken by the assembly. Their speeches and shrewd parliamentary tactics exposed weaknesses in opposing positions; they were insistent and successful in keeping the congress within the procedural limits which they deemed effective.[28]

The final meeting of the Montevideo Congress was attended by the president of Argentina. This was the first occasion upon which an Argentine president had left his country for such a

[26] Quirno Costa to Saenz Peña, March 13, 1888, in Saenz Peña, *Escritos*, III, 359.
[27] *Actas*, pp. 230–235.
[28] *Actas*, pp. 189–190, 252–253, 269–272, 283–284.

purpose. In Montevideo, Juárez Celman heard his foreign
minister speak again to the delegates. Quirno Costa praised the
efforts of the assembly toward "the closer binding of the South
American countries," but it was the Old World, rather than the
New, which interested the Argentine spokesman, "the Old
World, which not only sends us capital and machinery, but also
the . . . works of its great thinkers [and] . . . with which we exchange our products and divide our riches." He reviewed the
American dream of Monteagudo, San Martín, and Bolívar, and
the fear of Europe which had spurred the weak new nations of
America to hope for a strength-giving union. But now, he con-
tinued,

Those perils have passed, and the South American nations abide
in the midst of peace and progress, with which they will dismiss the
nineteenth century, to become great and powerful in the twentieth,
which, it has been said, will be the century of America. With abiding
faith in the great destinies awaiting each one of the South American
nations, all enjoying close relations with the Old World . . . each
will be the architect of its own fortune, but all are united in interest
in the future of South America, whose sons desire that it shall always
be said of the states forming it: "All for one and one for all." [29]

In his message at the opening of the Argentine legislative
season in the following May (the conference in Montevideo
lasted from August 1888 to February 1889), President Juárez
expressed his satisfaction with the assembly and with the work
of the two Argentine delegates. [30] Such satisfaction was merited.
The Montevideo meeting was an Argentine triumph. By this
assembly Argentina in effect served notice on Latin America—
and on any other nation aware of South American developments—that she had come of age in continental affairs. Backed
by a thriving economy and apparent political stability, the
Argentine government had spoken with authority in the convocation and conduct of the assembly. The leaders of the nation
were displaying a positive interest in Latin America, interest

[29] *IAC, Reports*, IV, 286–287.
[30] Heraclio Mabragaña, compiler, *Los mensajes. Historia del desenvolvimiento de la
Nación Argentina, redactada cronologicamente por sus gobernantes, 1810–1910* (6 vols.;
Buenos Aires, n.d.), IV, 295–296.

greater than any shown since the victorious days of San Martín. And coming as it did in the shadow of the impending First Pan American Conference, the Montevideo congress demonstrated that there might be more than one way of defining Americanism.

The work of the two Argentine delegates deserved the praise of their government. Saenz Peña and Quintana had displayed considerable talent. They also gained experience in handling the problems of a multi-national conference; and they had successfully emphasized their country's policy without being aggressive or anti-United States.

One of the premises of that policy—the one around which much of Argentina's foreign relations had revolved from independence onward—was national sovereignty. Untarnished national independence had been the concern of a long line of statesmen from Moreno to Mitre. If these statesmen had been blind to threats from Europe, they had also been deaf to appeals for cooperation from other American states.[31]

A modification of this attitude toward America was implied in Argentine participation in the Montevideo meeting. Europe was more vital than ever to the rulers of the nation, but they seemed also to have a renewed interest in what happened in Latin America. Devotion to the dogma of sovereignty was well founded on the circumstances of the nation's struggle for freedom, both during the revolt against Spain and later. It may also be related to that collective pride which characterizes the Argentine people. Argentines were proud of their past and present. And they were fiercely proud of their future, especially after 1880. This is a factor which goes far toward explaining both the zeal for national sovereignty and the awakening interest in the New World. The Generation of Eighty was to carry on

[31] A curious demonstration of willingness to forgive Europe its sins was made by Foreign Minister Elizalde in his correspondence with Seoane in 1862. The latter, in pleading for Argentine cooperation against European intervention, recalled Argentina's harsh experiences with English and French intervention during the government of Rosas. In his reply Elizalde showed that he remembered Rosas quite clearly, but he couldn't seem to recall any trouble with Europe, a circumstance natural to one whose enemy's enemies were friends: "In the long span of the dictatorship of the barbarous elements that lay in the nation's bosom as a consequence of colonialism and civil war, the European powers rendered Argentina decided services." Elizalde to Seoane, November 10, 1862, *Registro*, IV, 535.

and strengthen devotion to the concept of sovereignty. At the same time, the Argentine leaders saw a widening field for national influence, commercial and, perhaps, political. It was the idea of foreign political intervention which dismayed them, not economic. Foreign business activity was welcomed. An expanding function of the foreign policy of the oligarchy was to see to it that nothing interfered with relations with Europe. This accounts, as has been indicated, for the emphasis placed upon peace in this decade. Peace was so essential to trade that the Argentine government in its relations with neighboring states advocated and practised a policy of arbitration of boundary disputes, faithfully accepting even adverse awards.[32] However, it should be appreciated that the areas that were arbitrated by Argentina were not regions supporting, or capable of supporting, livestock or cereals.

When the United States turned toward Latin America in the eighties, it was confronted by Argentina, rich and peaceful, with close ties to Europe, a strong sense of its own national destiny, and an awakening American conscience.

[32] Two United States presidents and the United States minister in Buenos Aires had a hand in Argentine boundary arbitrations. See Gordon Ireland, *Boundaries, Possessions, and Conflicts in South America* (Cambridge, 1938), pp. 27–34 (Argentina-Paraguay; Hayes award in the Chaco Central, 1878); pp. 10–17 (Argentina-Brazil; Cleveland award in Misiones, 1895); pp. 17–20 (Argentina-Chile, Los Andes demarcation; U.S. Minister Buchanan one of three commissioners, 1899). On Argentina's record of arbitration from 1810 to 1920, see also *Política internacional*, pp. 173–271.

7

The United States and Argentina: Trade

THE United States made a good start toward winning Argentine friendship by quickly showing interest in the new nation struggling to emerge from the revolution of May 1810. Defective communications did not hinder the administration in Washington from seeking out the *junta* of independence in Buenos Aires. On August 27, 1810 the Secretary of State of the United States instructed Joel R. Poinsett to proceed to Buenos Aires as a special agent. Poinsett was assigned two main objectives: to explain to the authorities in Argentina the "mutual advantages of commerce with the United States," and to promote the good will suitable to inhabitants of the same hemisphere, "having all a common interest."[1] Thus, somewhat optimistically, were Argentina and the United States first linked.

Nine months after Poinsett's instructions had been drafted, the Argentine government recognized W. G. Miller, a Philadelphian, as United States vice-consul in Buenos Aires—the first official representative of a foreign state to be recognized by the Argentine authorities.[2] And, although there ensued a period during which the United States rebuffed Argentine efforts to

[1] R. Smith to Poinsett, June 28, 1810, in William R. Manning, ed., *Diplomatic Correspondence of the United States Concerning the Independence of the Latin American Nations* (3 vols.; New York, 1925), I, 6–7.

The date June 28 seems incorrect. According to J. Fred Rippy, *Joel R. Poinsett, Versatile American* (Durham, N.C., 1935), p. 50, n. 3, the date on the original document is August 27, 1810. Poinsett's instructions read as though they were drawn up in anticipation of an approaching revolt in Buenos Aires; only if we assume this to have been the case can the date June 28 be accepted, since approximately fifty days were needed for a sailing ship to voyage from Buenos Aires to the United States. It is likely that the instructions were drafted in August, after Washington learned of the outbreak of revolution in the Viceroyalty of the Río de la Plata.

[2] Ministerio de Relaciones Exteriores y Culto. *Catálogo de la biblioteca, mapoteca y archivo* . . . (Buenos Aires, 1910), p. 920.

obtain its assistance in the war against Spain, the United States government gave full recognition to the new nation on May 17, 1823, when Caesar Augustus Rodney became the first minister and diplomatic representative accredited to Argentina by a non-South American country. [3]

Seven years of friendly, if slim, relations followed these propitious early ties, [4] only to be interrupted in 1831 by a dispute over the part taken by the United States in the seizure of the Malvinas, or Falkland, Islands by Great Britain. Although diplomatic relations were interrupted for eleven years as a result of this affair, the two governments maintained correspondence through the United States consul in Buenos Aires and the Falklands issue dropped from sight—if not from memory—when relations were resumed in 1843. [5]

Two years later, menaced by the prospect of European intervention—that same intervention whose existence Foreign Minister Elizalde refused to admit twenty years later [6]—the Argentine government appealed to the United States to take a clear stand against the aggressors. Washington replied that it was impossible for the United States to take any action against the European powers, but Secretary of State Buchanan offered cordial moral support to the Buenos Aires government. [7] The intervention crisis passed, no doubt leaving a sense of disillusionment with "la gran república" in the minds of Argentine leaders. But in this case, as in the Falklands affair, it should be emphasized that Argentina's animosity was directed principally against the chief offenders, Britain, and Britain and France together, and not against the United States.

[3] J. Q. Adams to Rodney, May 17, 1823, Manning, *Independence*, I, 186–192. Argentina appointed a minister to Washington on December 28 of that year. See *Catálogo de la biblioteca*, pp. 879, 922.

[4] Manning, *Independence*, I, 235–237, 267–268, 292–293, 616–665. During the period 1823–1830 the State Department sent three instructions to the United States legation in Buenos Aires.

[5] William R. Manning, ed., *Diplomatic Correspondence of the United States, Inter-American Affairs, 1831–1860* (10 vols.; Washington, D.C., 1932–39), I, 3–23, 65 ff.; Julius Goebel, Jr., *The Struggle for the Falkland Islands; A Study in Legal and Diplomatic History* (New Haven, 1927), pp. 439–462.   [6] See, above, p. 80, n. 31.

[7] Carlos María de Alvear to James Buchanan, November 1, 1845, Manning, *Inter-American Affairs*, I, 300–302; Buchanan to Harris, March 30, 1846, *ibid.*, pp. 29–32.

With the exception of these minor disturbances, the United States and Argentina got along well together during the pre-Civil War era. After the defeat of the dictator Rosas, two treaties were quickly signed between the successor Urquiza government and Washington. One was a Treaty for the Free Navigation of the Rivers Paraná and Uruguay (July 10, 1853), the other a Treaty of Friendship, Navigation, and Commerce (July 27, 1853), containing a conditional most-favored-nation clause.[8] Under the patronage of these treaties and with the good will of the liberal government of the Argentine Confederation, trade between the two countries increased slowly but steadily. The yearly average value of commerce between the nations from 1854 to 1860, inclusive, was nearly $4,000,000. Of this amount, more than two-thirds was in the form of Argentine exports to the United States.[9] The Civil War had a disastrous effect on United States exports to Argentina, but after the war trade with Buenos Aires increased rather impressively until 1873, mainly in Argentine exports to this country. Then it fell off, during the remaining years of the decade, to levels well below those of 1865–1873.[10]

The reasons for this decline are not hard to find. Argentina after 1861 and the United States after 1865 entered new phases of economic development. The former found that Europe was able and willing to act both as a profitable market and as a supplier of goods and money. The latter was occupied with internal expansion; its merchant marine was a derelict drifting on the oceans of the world; protection against foreign products was the gospel of the market place.

[8] David Hunter Miller, ed., *Treaties and Other International Acts of the United States of America* (8 vols.; Washington, 1931–1948), VI, 211–280.

[9] The yearly average value of Argentine exports to the United States, 1854–1860, was $2,716,872; of imports from the United States, $1,157,601. *Report on the Commercial Relations of the United States with All Foreign Nations* (Vol. I–, Washington, 1856–, Washington, 1866), p. 595.

[10] From 1865 to 1878, inclusive, the yearly average value of Argentine exports to the United States was $5,629,497, and of imports from the United States, $2,057,140. After 1873 the total value of imports and exports each year ran from $2,000,000 to $4,000,000 less than the average of the preceding eight years. United States Treasury Department, Bureau of Statistics, *Statistical Abstract of the United States, First Number, 1878* (Washington, 1879), p. 33. The computations are by the author from annual figures.

The United States Wool and Woollens Act of 1867 had a specific unfavorable effect in Argentina. The act contained a provision raising duties on unwashed wool, which was the principal Argentine export to the United States. The adverse effect of the clause upon Argentine wool producers led to a proposal in 1869 by that government for the United States to enter into an agreement for the reciprocal reduction of duties. This suggestion was strongly rejected by Secretary of State Hamilton Fish.[11]

By the end of the seventies there was neither sufficient trade nor any vital political relationship to give promise of sustaining for long a positive friendship between Argentina and the United States.[12] Yet in the 1880's a significant change occurred in Argentine-United States trade. The volume of commerce rose, but equally important was the shift in direction which occurred. Since 1850, commerce between the two countries had been heavily in favor of Argentina. As late as 1881 the value of the goods which Argentina sent to the United States was more than two and one-half times the value of United States products imported by Argentina. After that date, the movement of trade altered decidedly (Table 1). As in former years, Argentina continued to send the United States hides and some wool, adding to these products in the eighties important quantities of linseed and *quebracho*—a hard wood from which tannic acid is derived. The United States sent Argentina lumber, cotton cloth, rice, and flour, but in this decade new items began to

[11] República Argentina, Ministerio de Relaciones Exteriores, *Reciprocidad Comercial: Negociones entre Estados Unidos y la República Argentina* (Buenos Aires, April 1892), pp. 30–31. Fish's note is given on p. 31. The *Foreign Relations* papers have not been published for 1869.

[12] National Archives, Records of the Department of State, American States, Argentina, Diplomatic Instructions, 1801–1906, Vol. 16, January 6, 1872 to the end of 1879. There was little for the State Department to instruct its representatives in Buenos Aires to do in these years. Almost all of the instructions—and the despatches, too—were concerned with post administration, mainly how the minister was going to get on leave and how much of his leave would be paid for. The only political events of this decade were the protracted case against the Argentine government of an aggrieved American citizen named William Hale, and the arbitration award made in 1878 by President Hayes in the Middle Chaco boundary dispute. For the latter, see John Bassett Moore, *History and Digest of the International Arbitrations to Which the United States Has Been a Party* (6 vols.; Washington, 1898) II, 1923–1943.

4

appear on the manifests of ships unloading American goods in Buenos Aires: petroleum products, agricultural implements, industrial machinery.[13] The competitive nature of the economies of Argentina and the United States in raw materials, which was a root cause of the declining trade between them up to the

TABLE I. Value of Argentine trade with the United States (dollars): 1882-1890.

Year	Argentine Imports	Argentine Exports
1882	2,727,917	5,234,914
1883	3,357,670	6,192,111
1884	4,825,813	4,110,038
1885	4,676,501	4,328,510
1886	4,333,770	5,022,346
1887	5,671,729	4,100,192
1888	6,099,411	5,902,159
1889	8,376,077	5,454,618
1890	8,322,627	5,401,697

Source: *Statistical Abstract, Eleventh Number, 1888* (Washington, 1889), p. 57; *ibid., Fourteenth Number, 1891* (Washington, 1892), p. 69.

eighties, had not been seriously altered. What had changed was the industrial capacity of the United States. The Yankees were beginning to export manufactured goods. However, they still did not need much in the way of raw materials, at least from Argentina. Under these changing circumstances, relations between the two countries altered.

The reawakening of United States interest in Latin America, typified in these Argentine trade figures, was not wholly material. The Civil War had been followed by the growth of a friendly sentiment in the United States toward the other republics of the hemisphere. This warm attitude was based in part on the chastening effect which the civil conflict had on the United States, a country that had formerly believed itself immune from

[13] The shift in the balance of trade described here is treated in general terms by Paul de Witt, "The Commercial Relations Between the United States and Argentina," *The Southwestern Political and Social Science Quarterly*, 11:163-165 (September 1930).

the internal disturbances so frequent in Latin America, and in part on the common sense of relief following the expulsion of the French from Mexico.[14] The post-Civil War generation in the United States stood midway between the era of manifest destiny of the forties and fifties and the "imperialism" of the century's end. It was during this time of vague good will toward Latin America that men in the United States began to assess the value of developing closer ties with the nations to the south.

James G. Blaine was the first prominent American to grasp the fact that his country might benefit from a larger export market and that Latin America might be the market. Taking advantage of the favorable political attitude toward the United States existing in most of Latin America, Secretary of State Blaine in November 1881 invited the American states to a Peace Congress. This meeting he described in the invitation as solely for the "purpose of considering . . . the methods of preventing war between the nations of America." Blaine also stated: "It is far from the intent of this government to appear before the congress as in any sense the protector of its neighbors or the predestined and necessary arbitrator of their disputes. The United States will enter into the deliberations of the congress on the same footing as the other powers represented . . . [that is] as a single member among many co-ordinate and co-equal states."[15]

Blaine's idea was stillborn. After Garfield's assassination, Blaine was replaced by Freylinghuysen, who, for domestic political reasons, cancelled the proposed congress.[16] Some of the Latin American states had already accepted the invitation; others, including Argentina, had not replied. After the cancellation, four nations, not including Argentina, expressed regret that the meeting would not be held.[17]

[14] See John Bassett Moore, *The Principles of American Diplomacy* (New York and London, 1918), pp. 383–386, and J. B. Lockey, "James G. Blaine," *The American Secretaries of State and Their Diplomacy*, S. F. Bemis, ed. (Vols. VII, VIII; New York, 1928), VII, 273–274.

[15] International American Conference, 1889–1890, *Reports of the Committees and Discussions Thereon* (4 vols.; Washington, D.C., 1890), IV, 256–257.

[16] Circular of August 9, 1882, *Reports of the Committees*, IV, 272–273; D. S. Muzzey, *James G. Blaine, A Political Idol of Other Days* (New York, 1934), pp. 214–218.

[17] *IAC, Reports*, IV, 273–277.

Blaine was not the sort of man to take rebuff. When he learned that the conference would be scuttled he wrote an angry open letter to President Arthur. Somewhat forgetful of the proclaimed purpose of the meeting, he called it "a friendly and auspicious beginning in a large field which we have hitherto neglected, and which has been practically monopolized by our commercial rivals in Europe."[18] Although his efforts for this conference were unavailing, Blaine's interest in Latin America helped to touch off a chain of Pan American proposals in the United States Congress which were to culminate six years later in the issuance of invitations to another inter-American meeting—the First Pan American Conference.

Blaine was correct in stating that Europe had a stranglehold on Latin American trade. Argentina was the principal—and willing—victim of this economic invasion. As the eighties went on and Argentina's internal wealth and foreign trade soared, the share of the United States in this market also grew, but what that nation got were only crumbs from Europe's table.

It was not because of any lack of information as to the potentialities of the Argentine situation that the United States lost out in the rush for the Argentine market. Throughout the eighties there was an American consul in Buenos Aires whose reports to his government were more complete than those turned in by any other of our consular officials in any part of the world. In detailed and well-informed letters to Washington, Consul Edward Baker tried every device—facts, cajolery, pleas—to open the eyes of United States businessmen to the vast opportunities in Argentina. His first report of the decade hit at a defect of American foreign trade which he iterated and reiterated throughout the next ten years—the decayed condition of United States shipping, which left the port of Buenos Aires almost empty of American vessels.[19] That same year he sent in

[18] James G. Blaine, *Political Discussions, Legislative, Diplomatic and Popular, 1856–1886* (Norwich, Conn., 1887), p. 410.

[19] Baker's report of June 2, 1880, *Reports from the Consuls of the United States on the Commerce, Manufactures, etc., of Their Consular Districts. Commercial Relations of the United States* (No. 1–, October 1880–, Washington, D.C., 1880–) (Title became *United States Consular Reports* with Report No. 37, January 1884, and has since undergone other alterations. It is cited hereafter as *Consular Reports*), No. 1, October 1880, pp. 73–74.

another report analyzing the Argentine market in general and specific terms. The great bulk of the imports of manufactures, he wrote, still belongs to the countries of Europe. What else could be expected, he asked, when United States businessmen paid no attention to the local demands, disregarded "the usages

TABLE 2. Argentine imports from and exports to various countries through the port of Buenos Aires for 1882 (dollars).

Country	Imports	Exports
England	15,650,644	12,870,797
France	10,640,919	14,355,550
Germany	4,384,000	4,520,120
United States	2,727,917	5,234,914

Source: Report of January 20, 1883, *Consular Reports*, No. 30, April 1883, p. 543. The figures for the United States have been taken from *Statistical Abstract, 1888*, p. 57; Baker's figures for United States Commerce in 1882 are unaccountably incorrect. He himself contradicts them on p. 546 of this same report.

and customs of the market," and sent goods so carelessly packed that they were usually in a ruinous state upon arrival? United States merchants, he went on, "must consult the styles and tastes which are in vogue here . . . The Argentine people are exceedingly fastidious in their tastes and in their surroundings . . . and they affect in a wonderful degree whatever the fashions of Paris approve." But to get this trade, Baker asserted, the United States had to make up severe deficiencies. There should be direct United States agents, or better yet, branch offices. There should be American steamships capable of competing with those of the European powers—not antiquated sailing vessels which formed the bulk of our shipping. Only by such steps, he said, can we establish the "secret, silent influences of a closer and more intimate intercourse," and thus win Argentina to our side "in the race of empire."[20]

[20] *Consular Reports*, No. 3, January 1881, pp. 60–64.

In his report for 1881, Baker showed who was winning the race. Argentine foreign trade for that year amounted to about 100,000,000 pesos, of which imports totaled 44,000,000 and exports 56,000,000. Europe controlled 80,000,000 pesos of the total trade—34,000,000 of imports, 46,000,000 of exports. United States trade was about 8 per cent of the total. The European merchants and governments, Baker wrote, have worked hard to get this business. "They have laid the foundations of a fixed and permanent trade" on three main factors. First was regular steam communication—twenty- to thirty-day service from England and western Europe, which meant smaller inventories and quick ordering for European houses; in contrast, orders from the United States usually required fifty or sixty days of shipment in sail. Second, Europe had branch houses or direct agents. And third, Europe had its own banks in Argentina, doing a most lucrative business.[21] Baker followed this letter with another of the same date in which he described the desperate need for a United States bank in Buenos Aires. He wrote mournfully that "There is scarcely a hide or a pound of wool

---

[21] Report of January 16, 1882, *Consular Reports*, No. 17, March 1882, pp. 315–318. Baker's trade figures are in gold pesos, which were worth about $.96 US. His figures were obtained for the most part from the Argentine government—and are for the most part inaccurate. This is a fact which neither Baker, nor any student of the subject, can remedy, since it is a result of the Argentine practice of that time of attributing imports and exports to the country from which or to which the goods were actually shipped, and not to the country of origin or ultimate destination. Baker himself acknowledged the inaccuracy of Argentine commercial data in his report of December 22, 1889, *ibid.*, No. 115, April 1890, pp. 597–598. Curiously, such error as was introduced into Argentine data by this method affected the United States as much or more than any other country because some part of the American goods imported into Argentina went from the United States to England and then came to Buenos Aires on British ships.

Another grave but irreparable defect of Argentine trade data of this period results from the method then used for computing the value of goods. This method was that of the "aforos medios," whereby a more or less theoretical value was assigned to an imported or exported product—a value derived from the cost of freight, insurance, and other charges, as well as the worth assigned to the item. No effort was made to assign products their actual market value where produced. On this point, see the report of H. Jacobson which forms part of the following document: The Pan American Union. The Columbus Library. "Fourth International Conference of the American Republics, Buenos Aires, July 1910. Memoranda Submitted by the Pan-American Committee of the United States for the Use of the Delegates from the United States." Confidential. Typescript. No date.

shipped from here to the United States the invoice of which, except in the case of special purchases, is not made out to Baring Brothers and Co., or to Brown Bros. and Co., or to some other English banking house." In this same letter Baker delicately suggested that a modification of the United States wool tariff would improve trade between the two countries.[22]

Baker's report for 1882 (Table 2) gave figures on the trade of the port of Buenos Aires with various countries in that year.[23] He concluded that this unworthy showing by the United States would be appreciably altered only when Americans established the bases for a sound trade—banks, branch houses, and steamship lines.[24] A few days later he attacked the United States-Argentine economic relationship from another angle. In a comprehensive report on Argentina's mighty advance in agricultural productivity he foretold the goal toward which Argentines were working—the day when they would supplant the United States as a principal supplier of food to England and Europe.[25]

Time after time Baker drove home the opportunities and needs confronting the United States in Argentina. In October 1883 he again argued for steamers, banks, and branch houses or direct agents. Twice in the next year he urged attention to these same matters.[26] By 1885 he was in despair over the United States carrying trade. In that year there were 1,153 English steamer arrivals and departures in Buenos Aires, 1,126 French, 117 German—and, for the United States flag, none. Argentina's foreign trade in that year totaled 176,101,069 gold pesos, of which England had 48,191,969, France 37,710,024, Germany 15,775,442, and the United States 10,570,560.[27]

---

[22] Report of Jan. 16, 1882, *Consular Reports*, No. 17, March 1882, pp. 318–319.

[23] Trade records for this period from Argentine ports other than Buenos Aires are almost totally lacking, but this is not a serious deficiency in reckoning Argentine trade since probably more than nine-tenths of the country's commerce passed through the metropolis. See *Consular Reports*, No. 30, April 1883, pp. 543–544.

[24] *Consular Reports*, No. 30, pp. 547–551.

[25] Report of Jan. 23, 1883, *Consular Reports*, No. 32, August 1883, pp. 309–332.

[26] Reports of Oct. 1, 1883, *Consular Reports*, No. 35, November 1883, pp. 42–43; March 13, 1884, *ibid.*, No. 41, May 1884, pp. 359–360; Sept. 30, 1884, *ibid.*, No. 47, November 1884, pp. 354–359, 388–389.

[27] Report of Dec. 17, 1886, *Consular Reports*, No. 82, August 1887, pp. 319, 322.

The feeble standing of the United States was not caused by any lack of Argentine interest in a larger trade. The Argentine government had a long-standing offer to provide a partial operating subsidy for any American steamship line running between Buenos Aires and the United States, and both President Avellaneda and President Roca had told our ministers in Argentina on several occasions that their government desired a greater commerce with the United States.[28] But after a few attempts by United States shipping men to organize a line, all of which failed to secure adequate backing in the United States, American businessmen in Buenos Aires had only "the siren song" of steamer service to their homeland.[29]

Meanwhile, in the five years from 1880 to 1885 England had tripled her exports to Argentina.[30] The time could be foreseen when Great Britain would take much of her meat and grain from the pampas, rather than from the United States. The number of cattle almost doubled in Argentina from 1881 to 1888.[31] Sheep were forced farther and farther south and west. Agriculture was expanding primarily as a result of mounting cattle production, with estancieros renting to colonists on alfalfa contracts. The area of cultivated land rose from a scant 580,008 hectares in 1872 to 2,459,120 hectares in 1888.[32] The organization of the meat export industry began after 1880.[33] In 1885, 590 long tons of frozen meat were shipped out. In 1888 the figure was 3,869 long tons.[34] *Sud América* (July 5–7, 1884)

[28] T. Osborn to W. Evarts, Sept. 22, 1880, *Foreign Relations, 1880,* pp. 33–34; B. Hanna to T. Bayard, Jan. 1, 1887, *ibid., 1887,* pp. 6–7; Hanna to Bayard, Nov. 20, 1887, *ibid., 1888* (Part I), pp. 2–4; Report of Hanna, Sept. 25, 1886, *Consular Reports,* No. 72, December 1886, pp. 448–455. There is only one brief reference by our State Department during this decade to the desirability of improving communications between the United States and Argentina. See Blaine to Osborn, Oct. 5, 1881, National Archives, Records of the Department of State, American States, Argentina, Diplomatic Instructions, Vol. 16, No. 151.

[29] Baker's report of Dec. 17, 1886, *Consular Reports,* No. 82, August 1887, p. 320.

[30] *Consular Reports,* p. 338.

[31] Simon G. Hanson, *Argentine Meat and the British Market: Chapters in the History of the Argentine Meat Industry* (Stanford, California, 1938), p. 99.

[32] Ernesto Tornquist and Co., Ltd., *The Economic Development of the Argentine Republic in the Last Fifty Years* (Buenos Aires, 1919), p. 26.

[33] Hanson, *Argentine Meat,* pp. 48–51, 115.

[34] Baker's report of Dec. 22, 1889, *Consular Reports,* No. 115, April 1890, p. 589.

expressed the belief that, while the United States produced more meat, and probably better meat, Argentina had climatic advantages and a steadily improving stock, and in the long run would drive New Zealand, Australia, and the United States out of the English market. Grain shipments boomed. The twenty-one tons of wheat exported in 1876 grew to 237,866 tons in 1887. The figures for corn exports for the same years: 8,058 tons and 361,844 tons.[35] Wool had long been a prime export commodity and it became even more important in this decade. But while the United States tariff laws in effect discriminated against Argentine wool, which was dirtier, greasier, and therefore heavier than wool from other parts of the world,[36] France readily bought this staple, in return finding a good market in Argentina for jewelry, wearing apparel, luxury foods, and other special products.[37]

However, the efforts of Blaine and of Baker were not in vain, despite their initial failures to stir up interest in Latin America. Under an act of July 7, 1884, President Arthur appointed a three-man commission to go to South America "to ascertain the best mode of securing more intimate international and commercial relations between the United States and the several countries of Central and South America."[38] Secretary of State Freylinghuysen gave his instructions to the trade commissioners on August 27 with the comment that, "at no time since the foundation of this government has there been a deeper conviction of the advisability of knitting closely the relations of the United States to the large family of independent nations which has grown up on the American continent." Despite the scarcely

---

[35] Tornquist, *Economic Development*, pp. 30, 77.

[36] See the objection of the Argentine minister in Washington to our wool duty, which he claimed to be "100 per cent" as compared to the free entry of our goods into Argentina, or entry after paying a moderate 5 or 10 per cent duty. Domínguez to Freylinghuysen, Sept. 29, 1883, Records of the Department of State, American States, Argentina, Notes, Vol. 2.

[37] Baker's report of Dec. 17, 1886, *Consular Reports*, No. 82, August 1887, p. 336.

[38] *Reports of the Commission Appointed Under an Act of Congress Approved July 7, 1884 "To Ascertain and Report Upon the Best Modes of Securing More Intimate International and Commercial Relations Between the United States and the Several Countries of Central and South America."* (Separate of House of Representatives, 49th Congress. 1st Session, Ex. Doc. No. 50) (Washington, 1886), p. 3.

concealed surprise of the Secretary of State at finding that Latin America had come of age, he was able to point out to the commissioners, somewhat paradoxically, that their primary duty was to stimulate inter-American commerce, "and to convince our neighbors . . . if need be, that our aims are devoid of all ulterior purpose of material or political aggrandizement [and] that we hold out to them the hand of good fellowship and not that of controlling power." The methods for developing trade suggested by Freylinghuysen sounded remarkably like a latter-day Point Four program, and included reciprocity, the internal development of the Latin American states through the introduction of American capital and technical skill, and improved ocean transportation. [39]

The Secretary then paid his debt to Blaine, and took a long look at the future. The act of July 7, he stated, resulted from the original (Blaine) proposal to convene a Pan American conference. The report of the commission "will necessarily have an important influence in the determination of the expediency of holding such a conference . . . [and] this government might even be prepared to consider the practicability of instituting a consultative council of representatives from the several states of the continental family, whose views as to international questions among them might have respectful heed." [40]

Thus, hesitantly, was the idea of the present inter-American system, embodied in the Organization of American States and the Pan American Union, first presented by the government of the United States.

[39] *Reports of the Commission*, pp. 5–8.
[40] *Reports of the Commission*, p. 11.

8

Growing Conflict

As the three American trade commissioners started on their long journey through Latin America late in 1884, the attitude toward the United States prevailing among the leaders of the Argentine upper class was a mixture of admiration and mounting suspicion.

Although in the seventies the old but tenuous tradition of Argentine respect for the United States had become weaker than ever before, it had by no means vanished. The eighties opened on a promising note, with a successful mediation by the United States minister in Buenos Aires in an Argentine-Chilean boundary dispute.[1] And a modest but pleasant symbol of a long friendship was preserved until 1888 by the Argentine Chamber of Deputies, which followed the custom of holding a brief session on each July Fourth and then adjourning in honor of "la nación americana," as the United States was distinctively termed.

But the gaps which appeared between the two countries as the decade went on could not be concealed by a local mediation or by such devices as parliamentary adjournments. There was a fundamental Argentine attitude toward the United States which at first ran parallel to, and then against, the tradition of friendship, and which ended by dissipating the once strong current of sympathy that had flowed from the Argentine people toward "la gran república del norte."

Not all the leaders of Argentina shared Sarmiento's utopian vision of the United States. When at mid-century the American eagle screamed "Manifest Destiny," the faraway Argentines

[1] *Papers Relating to the Foreign Relations of the United States* (Washington, D.C., 1862–), report for 1881, pp. 3–13, 15–17.

shuddered, despite their respect for the moral and material accomplishments of the Yankees. One of those who viewed the United States with mixed emotions was Juan Bautista Alberdi, the man who, perhaps more than any of his fellow-countrymen, had placed his nation in a position of almost filial respect for that country. He had accomplished this through the influence of his ideas upon the writing of the Argentine constitution of 1853—a durable document, closely patterned upon that of the United States, which influenced Argentine juridical and political ideals and practices along the lines followed in the northern republic.

For more than a quarter of a century the Argentine people drew much from the United States, as from an experienced, wise parent, but around 1880 a reaction set in against this youthful compliance. Some of the best minds in the nation—Francisco Ramos Mejía, J. V. González, Del Valle—began to move in the direction of a mild intellectual revolt, aiming at nationalizing the juridical structure of Argentina, diminishing American influence, and providing a more realistic foundation upon which to build solutions to Argentina's new needs.[2] This emphasis could not, of course, be admitted by Alberdi, who in domestic matters remained an advocate of American socio-juridical methods. Yet in another field, where United States influence was also soon to be opposed by Argentina, it was Alberdi who was the most formidable opponent of the Yankees.

This field was Pan Americanism. In Argentine minds Alberdi shares with the *próceres*—the initiators—of Argentine independence the credit for creating the idea of American union. But Alberdi's Americanism did not include the United States. It was not Pan Americanism but Hispano-Americanism, tied tightly, if paradoxically, to Europe.

In 1844, Alberdi published his *Memoria sobre . . . un Congreso General Americano*. In it he states the conditions and objectives of an "American union," including the peaceful settlement of political disputes, the establishment of a common coinage, and

[2] Leo S. Rowe, *The Federal System of the Argentine Republic* (Washington, D.C., 1921), pp. v–vii.

the elimination of trade barriers. [3] The *Memoria* has been upheld by successive generations of Alberdi's compatriots as the inspiration for the modern Pan American movement and the source of Blaine's Pan American ideas and of the program of the First Pan American Conference of 1889-90. [4] And, indeed, there is a surprising, if not unnatural, similarity between the ideals of the *Memoria* and the ideal agenda of the first great Pan American conference.

Alberdi feared the United States. His antagonism was directed principally against the Monroe Doctrine. The Spanish American states, he wrote in a later work, "ought to lean upon commercial treaties with Europe, so as to defend themselves against Brazil and the United States. Their peril is in America; their safeguard in Europe." [5] To his mind the Monroe Doctrine was a cloak hiding United States intervention in Latin America. Accusingly he asked: "What is the doctrine of Monroe?" Bitterly he answered his own question: "The doctrine of an egoism." [6] He asserted that the Monroe Doctrine was not even a domestic product of the United States—Canning was its creator. And Europe, with her markets, her immigrants, her capital, was the hope and strength of Latin America. [7]

The anti-United States attitude of which Alberdi was the most prominent spokesman might have gone unheeded but for the reappearance of the United States on the South American

[3] Juan Bautista Alberdi, *Memoria sobre la conveniencia i objetos de un Congreso General Americano* (Santiago [Chile], 1844), especially pp. 22–27; Burr and Hussey, *Documents*, I, 88–97.

[4] Isidoro Ruíz Moreno (h), *El pensamiento internacional de Alberdi* (Buenos Aires, 1945), p. 81. Joaquín V. González in 1910 claimed that there was "a complete coincidence in the detailed points of both programs [Alberdi's *Memoria* and the agenda of the First Pan American Conference], authorizing the presumption that the plan [Alberdi's] was not unknown." This comment by González was cited with satisfaction a generation later by the Socialist leader Alfredo Palacios in his biography of Alberdi. See Alfredo L. Palacios, *Alberdi, constructor en el desierto* (Buenos Aires, 1944), p. 91. Matienzo also believed that Alberdi anticipated the program of the First Pan American Conference. See José N. Matienzo, "La política americana de Alberdi," *Revista Argentina de Ciencias Políticas*, I, No. 1, Oct. 12, 1910, pp. 1–42.

[5] Juan Bautista Alberdi, "Política exterior de la República Argentina," *Escritos póstumos* (16 vols.; Buenos Aires, 1895–1901), III (1896), 7–8.

[6] Juan Bautista Alberdi, "America," *Escritos póstumos*, VII (1899), 123.

[7] W. W. Pierson, "Alberdi's views on Europe and the United States," *Hispanic American Historical Review*, 3:368–369, 371–372 (August 1920). See also Ruíz Moreno, *El pensamiento internacional de Alberdi*, pp. 91–98.

scene in the eighties. Blaine's Peace Congress proposal of 1881 attracted no attention in Argentina, but his interposition in west coast affairs after the War of the Pacific revived Argentine curiosity as to the intentions of the awakening "Anglo-Saxon" giant. And a little later a new note crept in, as on July 4, 1884, when *Sud América* published a friendly anniversary greeting to the United States in its editorial column, but displayed a slight uneasiness by warning that, in the relations between the two nations, "the traditional sentiment has suffered somewhat with the material preponderance" of the United States. On August 7 of that year *Sud América*—actually either Saenz Peña or Pellegrini—attacked United States meddling on the west coast. But a month later the newspaper, which spoke for the oligarchy, took a different view of the United States, or at least of United States capital. A few North Americans had come to Buenos Aires to look into the possibility of establishing the long-awaited steamship line. *Sud América* (Sept. 12, 1884) greeted them warmly, personified the group with the revealing noun "customer," and pointed to the importance of American capital and "know-how."

Despite the warnings from the past about the dangers lurking within the Monroe Doctrine, despite their traditional touchiness to the least hint of political intervention, these Argentines of the booming eighties were ripe for economic collaboration with the Yankees. It was at this moment that the United States trade mission arrived in Buenos Aires.

The report on Argentina which the commissioners later presented to the United States Congress was dated "Buenos Aires, June 13, 1885." It was not particularly surprising, or unlike the methods of such traveling delegations, that this report retraces the ground already laboriously covered by the man on the scene, in this case Consul Baker. The commissioners began by proudly proclaiming something that the Argentines already firmly believed. "The Argentine Republic," they announced, "is the United States of South America."[8] Then

---

[8] "The Special Report on the Argentine Republic" covers pp. 386–460 of *Reports of the Commission Appointed . . . to . . . Report Upon the . . . Commercial Relations Between the United States and the Several Countries of Central and South America* (Separate of House of Representatives, 49th Congress, 1st session, Ex. Doc. No. 50) (Washington, 1886). The quoted phrase may be found on p. 386.

they proceeded to the conclusions that American ships were sadly lacking in Argentine waters, and American trade was pitifully small. [9]

The report of the commission is valuable chiefly because of written answers made by leading American merchants in Buenos Aires to questionnaires sent out by the special agents. Edward A. Hopkins, a man long connected with business ventures in South America, told his countrymen that British control of the Atlantic carrying trade gave them the whip hand over the United States in Argentina. The British, he wrote, ship out American goods from England, "obliterate our marks," sell the goods as English, and pocket the profit. American mercantile houses in Argentina have actually decreased in number from ante-steamship days, he said. They have been more than re-placed by English and European houses which "take good care to order nothing from us save such products as cannot be gotten elsewhere." The good will of the Argentine people for the United States, Hopkins told the commissioners, so strong before and after the Civil War, has been sacrificed by our ignorance and neglect. [10]

Other American businessmen in Buenos Aires—Samuel B. Hale, C. S. Bowers, Dwight Love—added their opinions to those of Hopkins. All advocated United States business expansion in Argentina. One of them, Russell B. Pealer, an agent of American railroad interests, had emphatic, if belated, ideas on that subject. "English companies," he wrote to the commission, "have all amassed immense fortunes out of these railway enterprises and government guarantees. Now is the time for the American people to get a foothold and with their capital control and monopolize the public works of this great valley [the Río de la Plata] . . . The greatest enemies and

[9] *Reports of the Commission*, pp. 386, 394–395.

[10] *Reports of the Commission*, pp. 408–417. According to another American in Argentina, the English not only put their marks on quality American goods which they bought for sale in Argentina, but they were also known to place inferior fabrics of their manufacture on the market with a United States label. Hanna to Bayard, July 25, 1888, *Foreign Relations, 1888*, p. 13; William E. Curtis, *Trade and Transportation Between the United States and Spanish America* (Washington, 1889), pp. 288–290.

competitors the Americans have to contend with out here are the English."[11]

Among these merchants only Hopkins pointed out that the United States tariff had practically destroyed the American market for Argentine wool. Another man called attention to the bad effect of sloppy American business methods. And only Richard Pearson noted that the most important deterrent to trade between the two countries was the complementary nature of their economies.[12]

The trade commissioners talked to President Roca and Foreign Minister Ortiz. According to the commissioners these officials gave their "hearty approval" to the idea of holding a conference of American states. The commissioners also reported ingenuously that "a reciprocity treaty would be willingly formed, if a basis for it could be found"—a view which President Roca no doubt shared. Both Argentine officials told the Americans that the United States wool tariff and the lack of steamship communication with the United States were detriments to trade, and that "if the United States thoroughly comprehended the vastness of undeveloped wealth of this region, its money and sons would flow hither in streams, with profit to each side."[13]

The final reports[14] of the trade commission were published in October 1885. The commissioners told Congress that the Latin American republics believed "that our country heretofore has given them too little thought and that in its greatness and introspection it has failed to take a warm interest in the trials and struggles of [their] peoples." An inter-American conference, they claimed, would be just the thing to bring these countries closer to the United States. Specifically, either in or out of such a meeting, the agents recommended the attention of the United

[11] *Reports of the Commission*, pp. 419–420.

[12] *Reports of the Commission*, pp. 410, 441–442, 450.

[13] *Reports of the Commission*, pp. 396–397.

[14] One of the commissioners, T. C. Reynolds, returned to the United States ahead of the others. His report, dated June 27, 1885, is in *Reports of the Commission*, pp. 38–56. The report of William E. Curtis and Solon O. Thacher is in *ibid.*, pp. 21–33. The three agents were in general agreement on the main issues, although Reynolds was more cautious and critical of political and economic conditions in Latin America.

States to: (1) the need for regular and direct steam communication, (2) the need for reciprocal trade agreements, "with actual and equivalent reciprocal concessions in tariff duties," (3) the need in Latin America for simplified customs schedules, (4) the need for an expanded and improved United States consular service, (5) the need for an increased number of American business firms in Latin America, (6) the need for a better knowledge of the wants of the Latin Americans, and (7) the need for American banks.[15]

The commissioners omitted to mention in their generally admirable report one fact of great significance to one of the Latin American countries. The fact was that the two commissioners who visited Argentina spent exactly twelve hours in that country. They arrived in Buenos Aires on the night boat from Montevideo on the morning of June 13; they left on the return trip at six o'clock that evening. They saw the president and foreign minister: who else they may have seen is a question, and one that the Argentines did not feel flattered to ask themselves. Of all Latin Americans the Argentines were perhaps least likely to appreciate such a whirlwind inspection. Yet it was precisely in Argentina, and precisely at this opportune time, that the United States could have made the best use of a carefully managed official visit. The proud porteños did not forget this scant treatment. A few years later a prominent figure of the ruling class, Vicente G. Quesada, ambassador to the United States from 1885 to 1890, wrote a book in which he savagely attacked the "norteamericanos." Under the *nom de plume* Domingo de Pantoja, Quesada recalled the trade commission's brief appearance in Buenos Aires: "That commission was in the Argentine Republic for a matter of hours only, and its reports are not the result of study, but are purely fantastic mirages."[16] Quesada's son, Ernesto, carried the memory of the visit down through thirty years of teaching and writing. In 1919 he referred to it, and incidentally gave one reason for the brevity of the stay in Argentina: the commission's "tour through the countries of

---

[15] *Reports of the Commission*, pp. 23, 55.

[16] Domingo de Pantoja [V. G. Quesada], *Los Estados Unidos y la América del Sur: Los yankees pintados por sí mismos* (Buenos Aires, 1893), pp. 88–89.

the Plate was disgracefully full-tilt because in the interval [between departure from and return to the United States] the presidential election had taken place in North America, the Democratic party had triumphed, and the mission had as a consequence been terminated."[17]

Whether the fault was Democratic or Republican the Argentines did not know or care. Foreign Minister Ortiz reported the visit to the Argentine congress. The United States mission, he wrote, departed as soon as it arrived. President Roca and he had conferred with the Americans and had agreed that trade between their countries should be increased. But, said the foreign minister, "I explicitly stated the bad effect that the protectionist tariff of 1867 had produced on our economy." He had gone on to urge "the suppression of those tariffs and the return to liberal principles."

Ortiz then gave the opinion of the Roca government toward the American idea of holding a conference on peace and trade:

The idea of an International Conference with such aims cannot be less than auspicious for peace and material and moral progress in general . . . Once the moment has arrived for discussing [these proposals], the Argentine government will place no obstacle in the way of their acceptance, provided always that they are not opposed to the treaties and obligations existing with other nations, or to the elevated ideas of universal confraternity that forms the basis of our institutions.[18]

Although the First Pan American Conference was at this moment only a plan being toyed with in Washington, the new interest of the United States in their affairs had literally been brought home to Latin America by this traveling trade commission. If the mission had been handled properly, if the commissioners had been able to give to the Argentines the attention they deserved, something might have been accomplished to shift the delicately balanced views of the leaders of the Generation of Eighty in a direction more favorable to the economic interests

---

[17] Ernesto Quesada, "La evolución del panamericanismo," *Revista de la Universidad de Buenos Aires*, XVI (1919), 326.

[18] *Memoria de relaciones exteriores presentada al honorable Congreso Nacional, 1885* (Buenos Aires, 1886), pp. 49–51.

of both countries. Europe was far ahead in the contest for Argentine trade, but it was exactly this economic gap which the Argentines were willing to see closed by aggressive Yankee businessmen. The United States made a grave mistake in Argentina in 1885 by failing to talk business; we made a graver mistake, in this vital decade, by talking politics. The vision of some kind of inter-American political and economic *union* which was beginning, as we shall see, to fascinate government and business leaders in the United States, was too much for the Argentines to take. This explains Foreign Minister Ortiz's suspicious hedging on future commitments, and this from the same administration that had a standing offer to subsidize a Yankee steamship line.

The issue of an inter-American political organization thus unfortunately preceded, in Argentina, any effective steps to improve trade. And the Argentines have never been people to fail to note which way the wind is blowing. The nation which had the closest ties with Europe, and which was evolving a more substantial relationship with the other Latin American states, leading to the Montevideo Congress in 1888, was deeply concerned with the benefits or the detriment that might follow from a vague council of American states led by the most powerful nation in the hemisphere. Interest in the intentions of the United States suddenly intensified.

From university doctoral theses to the most important periodicals in the country the question of an "American Union" became a timely subject. One dissertation for the University of Buenos Aires took the stand that any "Unión Americana" must exclude the United States, since Yankee aims and ambitions were alien to those of the Latin American nations.[19] The main controversy, however, centered around a book by Alejandro Calvo, Argentina's leading authority on international law.

Calvo's *Política americana*[20] was acclaimed by many Argentines, including Mitre and Adolfo E. Dávila, as an outstanding contribution to international political thought. Perhaps this was

---

[19] Francisco B. Astigueta, *Solidaridad americana*, Facultad de Derecho y Ciencias Sociales. Tesis . . . (Buenos Aires, n.d. [?1885]).

[20] Alejandro Calvo, *Política americana* (Buenos Aires, 1886).

because the book was full of the idealism which Mitre and other leaders advocated in international affairs. Calvo appealed to universal, not national or sectarian, aspirations. He called for the development of a genuine internationalism based on friendship and commerce with all the world, but particularly with the United States. He rejected the idea then gaining ground in Argentina that racial superiority—albeit a temporary superiority—was the reason for the Anglo-Saxon margin of achievement over the people of Spanish descent. He even accepted the Monroe doctrine, which, he wrote, is and should be the slogan of a common cause. [21] Calvo closed by urging his countrymen to imitate the United States in political and economic matters and to enter a political alliance with the great republic, with the aim of generalizing the Monroe Doctrine in order to eliminate all danger of intervention in the New World.

Calvo's ideas were in the tradition of Sarmiento and the mid-century school of Argentine constitutionalists, men who had learned much from the United States and who wanted Argentina to pursue a forthright international policy embracing both Europe and America. But the weakness of the United States in Latin America, especially in South America, had given the mature European states a clear path to the markets and minds of these people. By 1886 the race seemed to have been lost for good by the United States, and there were capable Argentine defenders of the European victors who had no desire to see the Yankees emerge again as contestants in the struggle.

Two formidable defenders of the pro-European policies of the Generation of Eighty promptly demonstrated that a pro-United States policy did not fit the realities of Argentina's greatest decade. The two were Bernardo de Irigoyen and Ernesto Quesada.

In November 1886 the former foreign minister published an article in the new *Revista Nacional*, the most authoritative magazine then appearing in the country. Using Calvo's own title,

[21] Regarding the failure of the United States to implement the Monroe Doctrine in the Malvinas affair of the 1830's, Calvo was forced to admit that "The United States, especially its representatives in El Plata, showed themselves unjust and cruel." *Política americana*, p. 16.

"Política americana," Irigoyen appraised the international record of the United States and found it wanting. He berated United States interventionism, which in his opinion stemmed from the misdirection of the Monroe Doctrine. He maintained that United States leaders, including Blaine, had expressed dangerous expansionist ideas under the guise of manifest destiny. Irigoyen saw no need for any nation to become associated with the Monroe Doctrine—it was enough always to combat intervention from wherever it came. On that subject Argentina would not compromise. Non-intervention is, and should be, he concluded, one of the strongest principles of Argentine foreign policy.[22]

Irigoyen's declarations were followed in two months by an article by Quesada entitled "La política americana y las tendencias yankees." Although it did not carry the weight of the pronouncements by Irigoyen, who was one of the small group actually directing the nation, the attack by the son of the ambassador to the United States went deeply and bitterly into the problem of relations with that country:

> Friendliness with the North Americans has been a tradition with us, based not only on admiration for that nation's astounding progress, but also upon the fact that, having in great part modeled our organization upon that of the United States, we used to consider them our natural teachers . . . However, the United States today is trying to inaugurate a policy with a continental character, above all in the sphere of commerce.[23]

The economic future of Argentina, Quesada continued, is deeply involved in the search for markets which the United States has undertaken. There is particular cause for alarm because Latin Americans are amenable to the appeal of ideals and calls to brotherhood, while the North Americans are realistic, practical, and work only for their national interest.

Quesada went on to attack, as totally unproductive, former efforts at inter-American cooperation, "all of which have gyrated

in the gilded spheres of pure theory."[24] But times have changed.
The United States has come on the scene with practical objectives and practical methods, sheltered by the Monroe Doctrine
which, "applied *latu sensu* [*sic*], will hereafter serve to second in
a most efficacious manner the new tendencies of Yankee policy."
Now, he wrote, because of the great progress of recent years,

All eyes are turning to this poor and deprecated South America,
the home of perpetual revolutions, ungovernable peoples, and
general decay. Ah! today one speaks only of the Confederation of the
Three Americas . . . today there is no praise sufficient for those who
yesterday were merely—*South Americans!*[25]

Quesada was by no means finished with the United States.
His charges were the most timely, serious, and persuasive of any
made against the *norteamericanos* up to that moment in Argentina. Three years later his ideas, almost in his words, would be
thrown as a challenge by two of his countrymen at a startled
United States delegation to the First Pan American Conference.
In a second article in the same magazine, published a month
later, the young Argentine publicist attacked a proposal then
beginning to receive considerable attention in the United States
—the idea of establishing some kind of customs union with
Latin America. In Quesada's opinion this plan showed the
Yankees to be the Prussians of the western hemisphere. He
warned that the North Americans were seeking to establish an
American Zollverein, in order "to make Latin America economically tributary to the United States, converting it into a vast
confederation, [which is a] project sufficiently serious that the
statesmen of Latin America will think twice before accepting
such a Greek gift."[26] Then he went on to reveal the reasons for
his fear of the plan for a customs union:

Even without attributing importance to the political part of this
project, the enormity of the commercial monopoly toward which its
economic section tends is so great that, should it be accomplished,

[24] Quesada, "Política americana," Jan. 1, pp. 131–132, 134.
[25] Quesada, "Política americana," Jan. 1, pp. 137–138, 143. The words "South
America" and "South Americans" are in English in the original.
[26] Ernesto Quesada, "Política americana y las tendencias yankees," *Revista
Nacional*, año I, tomo II, no. 10, Feb. 1, 1887, p. 197.

the Latin American states would find themselves isolated from Europe, to whom they owe their life, populated as they are by its immigrants, and made fecund by its capital, and they would also face the loss of markets for raw materials and the loss of generous loans.[27]

Quesada told his readers that, behind the expansionist plans of the Yankees, hidden from the sentimental Latin Americans by the cloak of a magic "Americanism," stood powerful trade groups who were also ultra-protectionist. In the face of the impending economic intervention of the United States in Latin America, it may be necessary for Argentina,

. . . to attend the Conference of Delegates [the First Pan American Conference] and to adopt a definite line of conduct respecting Yankee commercial policy . . . The most vital interests of Europe and America are beginning to meet in open battle on this terrain, and without doubt one side or the other will employ every available means to remain master of the field . . . The Argentine Republic must proceed with great skill and caution . . . and its statesmen must remember that sentimentality was never a realistic counsellor in practical politics . . . This country is destined to be a giant within a short time: why, then, compromise this future by international conventions that can do us grave harm?[28]

Calvo, whose book had precipitated these opinions, published a defence of his position in April 1887, but his idealism made a weak showing against the advocates of an Argentine *realpolitik*. His generalizations about "the harmonious communion which is implanted by the republican spirit" among all the Americas might have appealed to an earlier generation, but it had little meaning for the Generation of Eighty.[29]

In short, the leaders of that generation were beginning to develop their own ideas about foreign policy, under mounting pressures from within, from Europe, and from the United States. A sort of "open-door policy" was making its appearance: the open door for Europe, but for the United States a door held cautiously ajar.

[27] Quesada, "Política americana," Feb. 1, p. 197.
[28] Quesada, "Política americana," Feb. 1, pp. 207–210.
[29] Alejandro Calvo, "Política americana," *Revista Nacional*, año I, tomo II, no. 12, April 1, 1887, p. 331.

It was undeniable that the Yankees were on the move to the south. The United States Congress devoted more time to Latin America after 1880 than ever before. Hinton Rowan Helper initiated the procession of bills and resolutions which passed through congressional hands in this decade. In 1880 he had a friend introduce a bill into the Senate providing for the construction of a vast intercontinental railroad to unite the Americas and thereby stimulate commerce.[30] Then followed a spate of bills, petitions, and joint resolutions in connection with Blaine's abortive Peace Congress.[31] These had been succeeded by other legislative steps leading up to the appointment of the trade commission of 1884–1885.[32] Finally, the favorable report of that commission cleared the way for another series of bills in the period from 1885 to 1888, each branch of the congress attempting to outdo the other in finding the most attractive method of promoting political and economic relations with the Latin American republics. Proposals of all sorts were tossed back and forth; some wanted a customs union, others a convention on a common monetary standard, others an inter-American assembly on the means of achieving peace and prosperity. Although some Democrats had a hand in concocting the Pan American prescription which was offered in 1888, the national leaders of the Republican Party, McKinley, Sherman, and Frye of Maine were chiefly responsible for the ultimate legislative product.[33]

Curiously, while these plans were being evolved in Washington, and while the Argentines were being told of the evil days ahead, there was only one other incident that ruffled political relations between the two countries—and that was brought on, or revived, by the Argentines themselves. No sooner had Ambassador Quesada arrived in Washington in 1885 than he raised the fifty-year-old issue of the Malvinas or Falkland Islands. Perhaps encouraged by the increasing stature of his country in world affairs, the Argentine representative requested the United

[30] International American Conference, 1889–1890, *Reports of Committees and Discussions Thereon* (4 vols.; Washington, 1890), IV, 293–294.

[31] A. C. Wilgus, "James G. Blaine and the Pan American Movement," *Hispanic American Historical Review*, 5:677–678 (November 1922).

[32] IAC, *Reports*, IV, 295–309.

[33] IAC, *Reports*, IV, pp. 309–375.

States government to pay an indemnity for its part in the affair that had led to the loss of the islands. He was promptly and bluntly—too bluntly—put in his place by President Cleveland. In his message to Congress in December 1885 the President described the condition in which the United States had found the Falklands in 1831 as "derelict," and rejected the Argentine claim as "wholly groundless." [34]

Meanwhile, our representatives in Buenos Aires were doing their best to encourage trade and to smooth the way for the inter-American conference which would eventually be called by the United States. As sometimes happens, these representatives tended to see matters from the point of view of the people to whom they were accredited. There were difficulties to overcome in forwarding United States business interests in Argentina: even the establishment of a submarine cable connection between the two countries was attended by "much delay caused by the friends of the European line and a portion of the press." [35] Yet at the same time that the United States was coming under attack for planning economic intervention in Argentina to monopolize its trade and drive out Europe, the American minister was sending a soul-searching despatch to Washington in which he blamed the low state of United States trade on our own high tariff. There was wisdom for the future in Minister Hanna's last sentences: "Whether the United States shall care practically to cultivate close relations is exclusively a question for its people and government. But if it is attempted, I doubt whether we can shut our ports against its chief product and succeed." [36]

A diplomatic gesture toward strengthening relations with Argentina was made by the United States in the early part of 1887, when the post of minister was elevated to that of envoy

[34] J. D. Richardson, *et al.*, compilers, *A Compilation of the Messages and Papers of the Presidents, with Additions . . . to 1922* (20 vols.; New York, n.d. [copyright 1897–1923]), X, 4910; Vicente G. Quesada, *Recuerdos de mi vida diplomática: misión en Estados Unidos, 1885–1892* (Buenos Aires, 1904), pp. 155 ff. The official view of the Argentine government is expressed in *Memoria de relaciones exteriores presentada al honorable Congreso Nacional, 1886* (Buenos Aires, 1887), pp. 44–46. See also Julius Goebel, Jr., *The Struggle for the Falkland Islands: A Study in Legal and Diplomatic History* (New Haven, 1927), pp. 463–464.

[35] Osborn to Bayard, July 16, 1885, *Foreign Relations, 1885*, p. 5.

[36] Hanna to Bayard, Feb. 23, 1887, *Foreign Relations, 1887*, pp. 10–11.

extraordinary and minister plenipotentiary. This was much grander sounding than it was in fact. The United States envoy extraordinary and minister plenipotentiary was all alone at his post in Buenos Aires until 1888. In that year a secretary of legation was finally appointed, at a salary of $1,500 a year.[37] Our feeble diplomatic representation was matched by the paltry physical property of our legation, which consisted of a single "office-room, 13 by 17 feet, lighted only through a glazed door, and situated in the back corridor of a residential building, with bedrooms on either side."[38]

Despite such difficulties, Minister Hanna presented the facts as he saw them to the Democratic administration at home. Late in 1887 he informed his government of the termination of export duties by Argentina, and pointed out that it was time for the United States to reduce its import duties, especially those bearing on wool. Our duty on unwashed wool he described in strong language as a "palpable and unjust discrimination against a sister republic struggling against many hindrances to follow in the footsteps of the United States."[39] In 1888 he again decried the exclusion of wool, and predicted that Argentina would rival the United States in cereal production. "It is idle to hope," he added, "that Argentine industry, now attracting such wide attention as a commercial factor, will have anything to do with us on any other than a reciprocal basis. If they cannot trade with us by exchange they will look elsewhere and act independently, and what is still more serious, in direct conflict with us."[40] A little later Hanna warned that even Canada was beating us out in Argentina: a special Canadian trade commissioner had arrived in Buenos Aires; he told Hanna that a Canadian steamship line was soon to be inaugurated.[41]

[37] Rivas to Vilas, Oct. 17, 1888, National Archives, Dept. of State Records, American Affairs, Argentina, Diplomatic Instructions.

[38] Wharton to Vilas, No. 118, Aug. 28, 1889, Dept. of State Records.

[39] Hanna to Bayard, Nov. 19, 1887, National Archives, Dept. of State Records, American Affairs, Argentina, Diplomatic Despatches, Vol. 26 [No. 93]. This despatch was published in *Foreign Relations*, report for 1887, pp. 1–2; the words "palpable and unjust" were excised.

[40] Hanna to Bayard, No. 143, March 22, 1888, Dept. of State Records, p. 10.

[41] Hanna to Bayard, No. 150, May 3, 1888, Dept. of State Records, p. 12.
As did other visitors, the Canadian trade commissioner succumbed to the

A few weeks later Minister Hanna had more news for the State Department. He reported the substance of a despatch which had just been received at the Argentine Foreign Ministry from Ambassador Quesada in Washington. Quesada condemned the Republican Party protectionists who, "when talking of America and of this continent merely mean the United States, and overlook Argentine trade and Argentine interests." The ambassador went on:

. . . to call the special attention of the Argentine government to these loud utterances of the Republican Party of the United States, and to the fact that these very Republicans are the first to applaud the sanction of a Convention of Delegates of American states to report on the best means of increasing commercial relations . . . The people in the United States are willing to take, but not to give; the Republicans want our consuming power, but will not budge an inch to make reciprocal concessions.[42]

The United States was waking up to Latin America, but the Argentine leaders were waking up to the Yankees.

excitement of Argentina in the eighties. In his official report he described Buenos Aires as "one of the busiest cities I have ever seen," and the country as a whole as one where "there seems no practical limits to a steady growth . . . for a great many years to come." The public transportation system was excellent, the quantity of shipping amazing, the soil "rich beyond anything that has ever come under my observation," and the government "very progressive." See Simeon Jones, *Report of Simeon Jones, Esq., Commissioner to South America with Respect to the Argentine Republic, Uruguay and Brazil* (Ottawa, 1888), pp. 2-3.

[42] Hanna to Bayard, July 31, 1888, National Archives, Department of State Records, American Affairs, Argentina, Diplomatic Despatches, Vol. 26.

9

The Triangle

In Richmond, on the Thames a few miles from London, Lieutenant General Julio A. Roca was guest of honor at a banquet on the evening of July 9, 1887. As the sun set over the lovely countryside, the great and near great of the English financial world gathered in a flag-decked dining hall in the Star and Garter Hotel in tribute to a man whose name had been unknown to most of them less than ten years before. There were three hundred covers; the invitation, under the shield of the Argentine Republic, came from Messrs. Baring Brothers and Co., C. de Murrieta and Co., Morton Rose and Co., J. S. Morgan and Co., the London and River Plate Bank, the Central Argentine Railway, the Buenos Aires Great Southern Railway, the City of Buenos Aires Tramways, and ten other railroads and public utilities. The distinguished ladies and gentlemen of the party lacked nothing for their pleasure: the evening was lovely, the drive from London just long enough to develop an appetite for the *medaillons de foi gras en Belle-vue*, the *zephyrs de volaille à la Monglas*, and the nine types of wine that added their sparkle and color to the long menu.

As one of the Argentine guests, who called himself "Traveller," described the occasion in his report to Roca's own newspaper in Buenos Aires, this was truly a great event of the world of "high-life." "They say," the reporter continued,

. . . that never before, in a number so large and select, have the leading bankers and merchants of London offered such a demonstration of esteem to a foreign leader, nor made such eulogies to a new country as those that they rendered to the Argentine Republic. Nor is there the slightest exaggeration in this opinion. It is enough to run down the list of those present at Richmond, among whom are the most powerful, circumspect and honorable capitalists of this great mercantile metropolis . . . [These are] men who know our country, applaud the policies followed by General Roca during his administration, and appreciate the influence that he has had in the prodigious unfolding of our riches and our credit.[1]

When the time for speeches came Lord Revelstoke (Baring) stood and proposed a toast to the Queen, which was enthusiastically received. Lord Revelstoke, "Traveller" instructed his Argentine readers,

. . . is the present head of the House of Baring, and represents all that is highest and most respected in English commerce. The firm of Baring Brothers, one of the most powerful in the entire world, enjoys a spotless reputation, for never in its long history has it been involved in a doubtful operation . . . No one with any sense could fail to recognize the firm's credit, nor would anyone dare to cast suspicion upon its word of honor.[2]

It was with like confidence that the banqueters settled back to hear Revelstoke's introductory remarks. He spoke at length on the historic association of Argentina and England, ending with a businesslike and somewhat parental word for the future:

The unalterable maintenance of these relations, resting, as is natural, on the credit of the nation [Argentina], forms a financial link between us. I can say truthfully that we have confidence that the pride with which the Argentine Republic has up to now preserved its irreproachable good name and credit will always be one of the principal aims of its government.[3]

To these thoughts the Argentine minister to England replied, tracing his country's long-standing debt—both literal and figurative—to England. He was followed by Frank Parish, son

[1] This description is taken from the letters by "Traveller" which appeared in *La Tribuna Nacional* on July 30 and August 12, 1887. Roca's paper printed not only full accounts of proceedings, but also the menu, the program of music, and a diagram showing the guest seatings. The event was sufficiently important in Argentine eyes to warrant the separate publication of the account of the banquet under the title *El Teniente General Julio A. Roca y el comercio inglés. El gran banquete en Londres* (Buenos Aires, 1887) (by "Traveller" and hereafter cited under that pseudonym). The quoted phrases are from "Traveller," pp. 5–6.

[2] "Traveller," p. 21.

[3] "Traveller," p. 24.

of Woodbine Parish, first British representative in Argentina (in the 1820's), and one of the most important Anglo-Argentine businessmen. It was Parish's pleasant task to present the guest of honor to the gathering, but first he had a few words of his own to say. He described Roca as the man who had brought peace and prosperity to Argentina. Then Parish also cast a cautious glance at the future:

> May God will that President Juárez complete his mission, and that he follow the same path of peace and industry; and that his government, as the repository of the confidence of us all, continue lending its support to the foreign enterprises and to the capitalists who have put their faith in his administration. [4]

Mr. Parish, too, had parental words for his Argentine listeners:

> I am happy that our guest has arrived in our country at such a felicitous time, when he could see the English nation in its highest epoch, celebrating the jubilee of our beloved sovereign. The majestic spectacle that we have been able to offer to General Roca and to his compatriots must be interesting for them, giving them, as it does, an example of what fifty years of good government can produce in the conduct and in the heart of a people. [5]

Finally, Roca rose to acknowledge his and his country's obligations. He praised English character and English commercial brilliance; he promised that Argentina would be faithful to her financial responsibilities. Then he closed the evening with a toast:

> To the Argentine Republic, gentlemen, that will someday be a great nation, because it has the ambition, the faith, and all the necessary conditions of climate, laws, and space! Argentina will never forget that the condition of progress and prosperity in which it finds itself at this moment is owed in great measure to English capital . . . I toast the friendly and cordial relations that now exist between England and the Argentine Republic. May they never be interrupted! [6]

Truly, as "Traveller" wrote, "The City has its great and penetrating eyes upon us, following the outlines of its mountains

---

[4] "Traveller," p. 34.   [5] "Traveller," p. 35.   [6] "Traveller," pp. 36–41.

of gold." [7] Fortunately for the distinguished company at the Star and Garter, their gaze could not penetrate three years into the future, to see the streets of Buenos Aires stained with blood, and the doors of the House of Baring closed.

The City had had its eyes on Argentina since the 1820's, when another Parish and earlier representatives of Baring Brothers had established political and financial relations with the unpromising young republic. The first English loan to Argentina was made by Baring in 1824 and amounted to one million pounds. Only about one-half of that sum reached Argentina; the English deducted in advance their interest and amortization up to 1827, not an unwise precaution in view of the unsettled conditions along the Río de la Plata. [8]

From that daring beginning, British investments in Argentina expanded slowly until the magnificent burst of new investment beginning in 1880. In that decade, which opened auspiciously with the visit of two English princes to Buenos Aires, the high point of British investments in this region in the nineteenth century was reached. In 1890 the total nominal value of British capital in all Latin America was above 422,000,000 pounds. Of this amount, Argentina alone had 154,338,000 pounds—more than twice the value of British capital in Brazil or in Mexico, the next most important areas of Britain's Latin American investment. In Argentine railroads alone the British had almost 66,000,000 pounds; in other fields, such as public utilities and banks, British capital in Argentina far surpassed that in similar enterprises in any other Latin American nation. [9]

Rare was the voice raised against the domination of the Argentine economy by British money. Aside from the repeated general warnings in La Prensa and La Nación of the danger of overexpanding the country's financial structure, only one prominent figure of this period protested on principle against

---

[7] "Traveller," in La Tribuna Nacional, August 12, 1887.

[8] Ricardo Levene, ed., Historia de la República Argentina (desde los orígenes hasta la organización definitiva en 1862) (10 vols. in 15; Buenos Aires, 1936–1950), VI (second section), 378–384, 552–567; Ysabel F. Rennie, The Argentine Republic (New York, 1945), p. 32.

[9] Based on J. Fred Rippy, "The British Investment 'Boom' of the 1880's in Latin America," The Hispanic American Historical Review, 29:281–283 (May 1949).

British money control—and that man was a political exile. Carlos D'Amico, governor of the province of Buenos Aires until he was ousted by the Roca-Irigoyen machine, writing from his Mexican refuge, attacked the English for making Argentina a slave of the pound sterling and the Argentines for accepting their chains so willingly. D'Amico also ran counter to the policies of his former colleagues at home when he protested against the government's practice of unrestricted sale of land in huge blocks to foreigners. D'Amico wanted Argentina to follow the example of the United States and divide its superbly rich "frontier" lands into small holdings for sale to citizens and immigrants.[10]

These were counsels of perfection under the circumstances. Argentina—Buenos Aires—had come to depend on Europe for almost everything: money, people, technology, fashions, news. The list could be drawn endlessly through each level of the country's life. Even in that activity which was rapidly becoming their forte, the Argentines still looked to Europe; the best-blooded rams and bulls were brought in from England and France to continue the slow build-up of native stock.

Roca's trip to England and the continent followed quickly upon the end of his term as president of Argentina.[11] In a sense it was a voyage of reparation—certainly of gratitude. Although the journey did not reach on the continent the heights attained during the visit to England, it was marked by the same mixture of pride and thankfulness with which a heavy debtor at last tells his creditor that he can repay his loan, with interest. The old grim days of civil war and Indian fighting and pastoral impoverishment were forgotten: it was Roca in mufti, Roca the president of the most progressive nation in Latin America who toured Europe while his intimate associates Juárez Celman and Carlos Pellegrini took up the burdens of the presidency and vice-presidency in Buenos Aires.

French investments in Argentina in the eighties were second in size only to those of the British. Banks and railroads were also

[10] Carlos Martínez [Carlos Alfredo D'Amico], *Buenos Aires: su naturaleza, sus costumbres, sus hombres. Observaciones de un viajero desocupado* (México, 1890), pp. 173–175.

[11] The receptions accorded to Roca in Europe were reported in detail in *La Tribuna Nacional*, June–September 1887.

heavily favored by French capitalists.[12] Less strong than the British economically, the French surpassed their rivals in cultural domination over the eager Argentines. One Franco-Argentine author pointed out that France had not only great economic interests to guard, but that ten thousand Frenchmen lived in Argentina. Argentina, this observer reported, "is a *simpático* land, even more French, more subject to French ideas, than the very colonies that have belonged to France for centuries."[13]

As if to parallel the symbolism of Julio Roca's visit to England in 1887, when that country celebrated its imperial glory, Vice President Pellegrini was in attendance in Paris in 1889, when France commemorated her great achievements in the Universal Exposition. But Argentina was more than a witness to another's accomplishments. The Argentines had a large, even impressive, exhibit at the exposition. The leaders of the Generation of Eighty were proud of the progress that they had made in ten short years and they wanted the world to know about it. They were determined to show, at the hub of civilization, not only that a place called Argentina existed, but that the best products of their kind had been made to spring from fruitful soil that only yesterday seemed eternally barren. To Paris they sent their finest wools and hides, samples of their choicest grains, and even a shipment of meat, frozen for the long trip across the ocean and kept so for display to the curious visitors. And among the foreigners who toured the Exposition not the least numerous were the Argentines themselves, attracted by the double opportunity of seeing both France and Argentina on parade.[14]

---

[12] J. Fred Rippy, "French Investments in Latin America," *Inter-American Economic Affairs*, II, No. 2, 1948, p. 54.

[13] Emilio Daireaux, *Vida y costumbres en El Plata* (2 vols.; Buenos Aires, 1888), I, vii. This work was also published in French in Paris in the same year under the title *La vie et les moeurs á La Plata*.

[14] The excitement of being in Paris at exposition time was enough to overcome old personal animosities. Pellegrini wrote that when he and his formidable political adversary Dardo Rocha sighted each other in the street they embraced spontaneously. See [Carlos Pellegrini] *Pellegrini, 1846–1906: Obras, precedidas de un ensayo biográfico por Agustin Rivero Astengo* (5 vols.; Buenos Aires, 1941), II, 212. On Argentina's share in the exposition see Santiago Alcorta, *La República Argentina en la Exposición Universal de París de 1889* (2 vols.; Paris, 1890).

One reason that Pellegrini was in Paris was to oversee his government's display, and to act as the spokesman for his country. No better representative could have been sent than this tall, handsome gentleman who was as much at home in Rome, London, and Paris as in Buenos Aires. The vice-president was delighted with the Argentine products that he saw handsomely displayed to the astonishment of visitors who would have been hard put to point to Buenos Aires on a globe. But there was one product of Argentina which did not please Pellegrini. He described it in a letter to his brother:

Twenty of our soldiers have arrived to act as an honor guard for the pavilion. They are good sorts, but they are all *chinos* [the Argentine equivalent to *mestizo*]. The esthetic has been sacrified to the truth, because this is the true type of our soldiery. But here people are repelled, and they ask us how it is that we are all white, yet the soldiers are mulattos. But in spite of everything, the soldiers have been noted for their bearing and martial air.[15]

Pellegrini had more to do in France than put forward his country's best face. He was also sounding out the European money market—and what he heard was not pleasant. By July 1889, Argentina had reached the crest of its boom. The wave was about to break. The vice-president, who was the most experienced Argentine official in matters of international finance, could detect the reefs ahead:

Over here the market for Argentine offerings is beginning to weaken. Just a few days ago the *Financial News* said: "Nothing to report in the market: the only sensational news is that it has been *two days* since an Argentine loan was floated!" Now comes the announcement of a loan of forty million [pounds] for the national government and twenty-five million for Córdoba! Furthermore, part of the guaranteed railroad offering has not yet been put up, and there are the provincial loans. Uriburu and Sanford want to float 5,500,000 pounds for the proposed docks in La Plata. Baring Bros. still have in their pocket the greater part of the fifty million for the public works: the Land Companies are asking for cash, in short, for the ocean; gold is at 172, the *cédulas* are flat on the ground, and the brokers helpless.[16]

[15] *Pellegrini*, pp. 213–214.   [16] *Pellegrini*, p. 216.

Even Pellegrini did not appreciate the fact that the country was confronting a catastrophe. In the next sentence of this letter he wrote almost blithely: "A little imprudence will bring about a repetition of the situation created in the days of Romero and Plaza, which cost me so many headaches to untangle."[17] To compare the "recession" of a few years before to the crisis at hand showed a misunderstanding of the realities of Argentina's exploding economy. Yet Pellegrini was correct on one score: when the crisis did envelop the nation in 1890, it was once again upon his shoulders that the task of meeting it devolved.

Pellegrini and the other Euro-Argentines who ruled the land from Buenos Aires could not be expected voluntarily to redirect their thoughts and actions to strictly national political and economic needs. Indeed, for them there were no strictly national needs; Argentina was too closely tied to Europe to permit separation. The newspaper *La Nación*, despite the fact that it opposed all the extravagances of the government, voiced the country's pride in the past decade of achievement, of which the Paris exposition was the ultimate proof. With perhaps a thought for the Pan American Conference that had opened in Washington four weeks before, and certainly with deep faith in Argentina and in Europe, Mitre, or his editor, wrote on October 30, 1889: "The Argentine Republic now has an established personality in the civilized world. From this moment forward one may say that Argentina will be highly esteemed, because we have made known the rich products of our soil, of our industry, and of our intelligence."

In the United States, Argentina was coming into higher esteem. After 1885, American businessmen and politicians began to display interest in getting a larger share of the Argentine and Latin American markets. Plans for holding some kind of inter-American meeting were considered in congress. The mail of legislators responsible for formulating the approach to the other American states grew heavy with proposals, petitions, ideas and complaints from individual businessmen, trade groups, and organizations with special interests to advance. Prominent

[17] *Pellegrini*, p. 216.

mercantile and financial leaders supplied the State Department, either by request, or voluntarily, with their views on what they believed needed to be done to increase trade with Latin America, and described the ways to do it.[18]

By 1888 the multitude of schemes and suggestions had been sifted by the State Department and by the several committees of congress that had a hand in planning the course to be followed. Early that year a bill was drafted, passed by both houses of congress and sent to the White House. On May 28, 1888 the bill became law without the signature of President Cleveland.[19]

Under the provisions of this law the President was authorized to invite all the governments of Latin America to meet in Washington, D.C. in the following year. The essential portion of the law's preamble states that the nations are invited to assemble:

... for the purpose of discussing and recommending for adoption to their respective governments some plan of arbitration ... and to consider questions relating to the improvement of business intercourse and means of direct communication between said countries, and to encourage such reciprocal commercial relations as will be beneficial to all and secure more extensive markets for the products of each of said countries.

The specific topics composing the meeting's agenda were then enumerated:

... (1) Measures that shall tend to preserve the peace and promote the prosperity of the several American states. (2) Measures toward the formation of an American customs union ... (3) The establishment of frequent communication between the ports of the several American states ... (4) The establishment of a uniform system of customs regulations ... and port dues ... (5) The adoption of a uniform system of weights and measures ... (6) The adoption of a common silver coin ... (7) An agreement upon ... a definite plan of arbitration ... (8) And to consider such other subjects relating

[18] An interesting study could be made of the growth of business interest in the Pan American idea in the eighties, based on correspondence from individuals and associations available in the United States National Archives, Records Relating to International Conferences, Department of State Accession 161, Nos. 32 and 34.

[19] International American Conference, 1889–1890. *Reports of Committees and Discussions Thereon* (4 vols.; Washington, D.C., 1890), IV, 375.

to the welfare of the several states represented as may be presented by any of the said states.

The law authorized the President to appoint as many as ten United States delegates to the conference, and stated that the other nations might send as many delegates as they wished, but that each state would be entitled to only one vote.[20]

On July 13, 1888, Secretary of State Bayard, acting under the law, extended his government's invitation to the other Americas. The Secretary repeated the terms of the law, adding:

> I have to call your particular attention to the scope and object of the conference suggested, which, as will be observed, is consultative and recommendatory only. The proposed conference will be wholly without power to bind any of the parties thereto . . . The topics for discussion are manifestly of profound importance, and it is believed that a friendly and frank exchange of views in relation to these subjects will be of practical use . . . Certain topics are suggested as proper subjects for a comparison of views, but the field is expressly left open to any participant state to bring before the conference such other subjects as may appear important to the welfare of the several states represented.[21]

The Pan American idea was nearing realization. In the United States interest and activity mounted. Here the work of one man deserves particular attention. William Eleroy Curtis was neither businessman nor elected public official. He was a more typically American product than either merchant or politician. He was a promoter—a sincere, energetic promoter. Curtis had found a cause, and a good part of his life's work, in Pan Americanism. He was born in Ohio in 1850 and as a young man began working as a newspaper reporter. While employed in that capacity in 1885, he received an appointment as the secretary of the special commission on trade with Latin America. When one of the commissioners resigned, Curtis was appointed to succeed him. Thus, by the time of the commission's return to the United States, Curtis was something of an expert in inter-

[20] *Statutes at Large of the United States of America* (Boston, 1845–1873; Washington, 1874–), XXV, 155.
[21] Bayard circular, July 13, 1888, *Foreign Relations, 1888*, pp. 1658–1659.

American affairs. He wrote a book, *The Capitals of Spanish America*, published in 1887. It has the merit of exuberance, and a good deal of accurate description; it also has the overriding defect of superficiality in its grasp of Latin America.

But Curtis' book increased his reputation. Henceforth he became a self-appointed, one-man lobby for Pan Americanism. His ideas were pondered by senators; he corresponded with big and little businessmen throughout the East and Midwest. In 1889 he published another book, called *Trade and Transportation Between the United States and Spanish America*, a curious official-unofficial work, printed by the Government Printing Office and composed largely of government statistics and reports on Latin America, yet ostensibly the individual and private effort of Curtis.

Trade and Transportation is a detailed and quite admirable combination of a history of commerce and a persuasive business prospectus, calculated, it would seem, to give not only facts but also incentive to American traders and manufacturers. The author painted a somewhat rosy picture of the potentialities of commerce with the other Americas by implying that the same conditions of wealth and energy that characterized Argentina held true for the rest of Latin America, but his sections on specific countries and problems were sound. With regard to Argentina, Curtis pointed vehemently to its "enormous foreign commerce," growing population, and mounting cereal exports. He referred to the unfavorable impact on Argentina of the United States tariff on wool, but he carefully avoided committing himself on this ticklish point by quoting at length a report from Consul Baker. Curtis employed the same device in describing the accomplishments of the Argentine meat industry, apparently agreeing with Baker that it did not represent "any great competition" for American meat producers. The rapidly increasing trade of Germany with Argentina was noted and attributed to the wise employment by the Germans of the very methods which the United States had so long ignored: the introduction of regular steamship service, the opening of branch offices, and the establishment of banks. Curtis ended his section on Argentina by quoting from an interview with an Argentine official which clearly showed the attitude of the Buenos Aires government. Adolfo G. Calvo, Argentine consul-general in New York stated: "We want the United States to take its present heavy tariff duties off our wool." Calvo also said that Argentina welcomed United States trade, but that little could be hoped for without adequate transportation, and that here the United States government was to be blamed for failure to back a shipping line after the Argentine government had voted a subsidy for that purpose. The consul-general also revealed a facet of the Argentine mind that deserved as much thought as his other statements. "American goods," he said redundantly, "are not too good for the Argentine market, because the people of the Argentine Republic, like the people of the United States, are rich and want to get good things, even though they have to pay good prices for them."[22]

If Curtis' book was needed ammunition in the hands of those pushing Pan Americanism in the United States, *Export and Finance* was an even more important weapon in the trade offensive. This newspaper was founded in New York City in June 1889, just five months before the opening of the conference. It was probably the first periodical in the United States devoted to commerce with Latin America and its files afford an insight into the forces behind Yankee Pan Americanism.

Chief among these forces was the Republican Party, which in 1889, the year of the First Pan American Conference, seemed to be entering an apogee under the leadership of President Harrison and James G. Blaine. Actually it is more accurate to speak of certain sections of eastern Republicanism as the principal sponsors of the new policy toward the other Americas. The desire of the commercial East to increase foreign exports, and the need of the manufacturing East for cheap foreign raw materials contributed to this policy, but these ambitions ran headlong into the ever more rigid party dogma of protection. The result was a wobbly stand on specific issues raised in the drive for the Latin American market. *Export and Finance*'s policies resemble the vacillating course of a salesman who is chasing

---

[22] William E. Curtis, *Trade and Transportation Between the United States and Spanish America* (Washington, 1889), pp. 4–8, 65–69.

an elusive new customer but frequently doubles back to see that no one is underselling his old customers.

In its second issue, *Export and Finance* (June 29, 1889) came out with a loyal and strong plea for protection. Without tampering with its tariff structure, the paper claimed, the United States could increase business with Latin America by a closer study of that market, a great selling effort, a merchant marine revived by federal subsidies, and the granting of long-term credits to Latin American buyers, instead of the suspicious cash or short-term credit methods presently being used by United States merchants.

A few weeks later (July 20, 1889) the paper gave the Argentines a chance to tell Yankee businessmen what they should do to build up trade with their great land. In an interview with John A. King, who was "Director of the Information Bureau of the Argentine Republic in the United States," the readers of the paper were told that Argentine entrepreneurs wanted American banks in Buenos Aires, direct and cheap steamer service subsidized by the United States and Argentina, and reduction of United States duties on raw materials such as wool and flaxseed. King saved himself just in time from the precipice by hastening to add: "I do not mean this in a free trade sense, but in the sense of such a reduction as would give our merchants a chance to compete with those of other nations." An editorial in the same issue echoed these opinions. Trade with Latin America can be and must be built up, wrote the editors, and steps such as the establishment of banks and the subsidization of steamship lines must be taken to achieve the goal. But the editors made it clear that "the tariff, high or low, is not a question that enters materially into our trade with Spanish America."

After a few more weeks *Export and Finance* grew bolder. On August 31, 1889 an editorial was published calling for free wool, and some hard things were said about "the wool growers of Ohio." Yet on September 21 the paper swung back to placating the wool growers and indicated willingness to forget all about tariff reductions.

But the periodical soon returned to its free wool position and stuck to it throughout the Pan American Conference and up to its own expiration. *Export and Finance* was also aggressively optimistic about the potential achievements of the conference, and high in its praise of Blaine and W. E. Curtis. In an editorial on November 2, 1889 the editors denied that the conference, which was just getting under way, had any ends of political domination over Latin America. What we want, they wrote, is "that trade which by right of contiguity, affinity, and mutual interests belongs to us."

Who were meant by "us"? To judge by the names of the paper's advertisers and of the men whose opinions entered into its columns, "us" meant the large importers and exporters of New York and the eastern seaboard and the manufacturers of wool and other products who were interested in obtaining foreign raw materials and overseas markets. "Us" could have meant W. R. Grace, who, in an interview with a reporter from *Export and Finance* (March 1, 1890), demanded free wool, free copper, and free sugar as the first conditions for improving trade with Latin America. Only such a combination of manufacturing and commercial interests can explain the paradoxical editorial of January 18, 1890 in which *Export and Finance* proclaimed that it was fighting for "protection and reform"—and defined those terms to mean government subsidies, abolition of the wool tariff, an improved consular service, and the founding of American branch banks in Latin America. Only that association of interests can give meaning to the editorial of February 1, 1890, entitled "The True Protective Theory," in which the editors tried to ride at the same time the two horses of protection and the free admission of such raw materials as wool, ending in between both mounts with the safe statement: "We are prepared to view with equanimity the piling of duties on foreign *manufactures* as high as the Eifel [*sic*] Tower."

The views of the eastern capitalists whose voice was *Export and Finance* were similar to the beliefs of the Argentine leaders with whom they hoped to improve relations in the imminent Pan American Conference. Both groups drew their strength from sectarian liberalism; both preached *laissez faire*, but on their own behalf advocated and practiced government intervention. Continuing economic health, or its facsimile, was, naturally enough, the chief concern of the aristocrats of Buenos Aires and of the rugged individualists of New York, and this accounts for the faithful reproduction in *Export and Finance* of the glowing reports of Argentina's economic well-being which emanated from Buenos Aires at the moment when that world capital began to weaken from financial fever. It was hard for American businessmen to believe, now that they had awakened to Argentina's wealth, that it might be snatched away from them, not by Europe, but by the Argentines themselves.

As 1889 merged with 1890 and the crisis in Argentina deepened, American businessmen interested in Latin America refused to believe that there was a crisis. Had not *Export and Finance* on January 18, 1890 published a letter from a correspondent in Buenos Aires, written in December 1889, which brought the bracing news that "The country is experiencing the prosperity that comes from wisely extending public aid to private enterprise"? (It was five months since Pellegrini had found the London and Paris money markets sinking under the weight of Argentine securities.) Had not Consul General Calvo assured the publishers (Feb. 8, 1890) that the Argentine government was solving its temporary difficulties by the sale of 24,000 square leagues of land for good European gold, and that "the land is being sold today and the money is going into the treasury" and that "colonists are settling themselves on the land at a rate and in numbers not equalled before this"? (How could the readers of this authoritative journal, which had printed so much exciting information about Argentina, know that Calvo's claim merely reproduced the wishful thinking of the desperate government of President Juárez Celman?) Did not a correspondent in Buenos Aires—right on the scene—report in February 1890 that "The situation here would indeed be inexplicably bad if, fortunately for the country at this venture, its magnificent resources did not come to the rescue"?[23] (The final collapse was still five months away.) Was not the fall of the Argentine cabinet on April 12 a mere shift in administrative personnel, "without any political significance"?[24] (The new cabinet that Juárez appointed was

[23] *Export and Finance*, March 22, 1890.   [24] *Export and Finance*, April 26, 1890.

to be his last.) Finally, did not *Export and Finance* assure its readers on June 7, 1890 that "the worst is over" in Buenos Aires, and a week later claim that the rumor that a revolution threatened in Argentina was only a "silly-billy story"?[25] That day *Export and Finance* ceased publication. Next month the revolution came in Buenos Aires.

But this was still in the future. In 1888 the call had gone out for a conference and the acceptances, including Argentina's, were coming in.[26] In January 1889, Secretary Bayard sent a special emissary to visit Latin America to assuage any suspicions that might be harbored there as to the intentions of the United States,[27] but this mission seems to have been unnecessary: each of the Latin American states, whatever its motives, apparently believed that it was in its best interest to attend the first truly pan-American conference.[28]

The United States delegates to the conference had been selected by mid-1889 and each had written to the new Secretary of State, Blaine, informing him of his agreement with the program that had been laid down in the law of May 1888.[29] Argentina, it was clear, would be an important factor with which the United States delegates would be working; how important was brought out in the Argentine trade figures for the

[25] *Export and Finance*, June 14, 1890. In earlier issues the editors made an attempt to picture chronic Latin American revolutions as merely "a bit of rioting" or "public protest meetings." See *ibid.*, April 5 and May 3, 1890.

[26] IAC, *Reports*, I, 15–16 for Argentina's acceptance dated October 10, 1888.

[27] Bayard selected John G. Walker, the secretary of legation at Bogotá, as special commissioner to tour Latin America to meet possible objections to the conference. Walker was instructed to visit Peru, Chile, Argentina, Uruguay, Paraguay, Brazil, and Venezuela, but to give particular attention to Argentina, Brazil, and Chile, "whose cooperation is believed to be peculiarly important and less assured than that of some other countries." Bayard to Walker, Jan. 18, 1889, National Archives, Department of State, American States, Diplomatic Instructions, Argentina, Vol. 16.

[28] The only nation that did not attend the conference was Santo Domingo. In the light of future events the reason was revealing: the United States had failed to ratify a reciprocal trade treaty which it had made with the Dominican government in 1884. IAC, *Reports*, I, 25–27.

In her acceptance Chile reserved the right to exclude arbitration from the topics which she would treat at the meeting. This was a result of the unsettled territorial questions which had come out of the War of the Pacific. *Ibid.*, I, 20–21.

[29] The National Archives, Records Relating to International Conferences, Department of State Accession 161, No. 34, Envelope 14.

first half of 1889, which reached Washington the month before
the opening of the conference. These showed that in the first
six months of that year, Argentina's total foreign trade amounted
to a staggering 166,119,780 gold pesos, of which England had
approximately one-third, France more than one-fifth, Germany
more than one-tenth, and the United States only one-twelfth.[30]
But the United States delegates were confident that the door
to Latin America would swing open as soon as the key of Pan
Americanism was placed in the lock. One of our delegates
summarized in practical terms his views and those of his
colleagues toward the serious domestic and foreign issues which
were presented by the assembly agenda. Andrew Carnegie
wrote Blaine from Stockholm on July 22, 1889, "The act inviting
a conference makes six definite propositions, all of which, in
my opinion, are admirably calculated to promote the end in
view." The most important of these in Carnegie's mind was the
proposal regarding the establishment of a customs union among
the American states, which would, of course, involve our own
tariff structure. But, he wrote, "The advantages sure to flow
from a customs union are so great as to justify considerable dis-
turbance of our present system." He warned that during the
conference the United States delegates should avoid "an attitude of undue prominence." He endorsed without reserve the
establishment of a vast net of steamship lines subsidized by the
government. And he closed with the pugnacious warning: "Let
the country be told it will cost money, but that the time has
arrived when the republic must fight for [sic] secure the greater
portion of the trade of its southern neighbors."[31]
Two days after this letter was written the President of
Argentina handed his instructions to the Argentine delegates.
With regard to the customs union proposal the instructions read:

[30] Baker's report, Aug. 23, 1889, United States *Consular Reports*, No. 108, September 1889, p. 166.

Argentina's foreign trade for 1888 was 228,524,013 gold pesos. Baker's report,
Dec. 22, 1889, *ibid.*, No. 115, April 1890, pp. 589, 594. My figures for the percentage
of foreign trade taken by the United States, England, France, and Germany in the
first half of 1889 are based on the percentages given here by Baker for 1888.

[31] The National Archives, Records Relating to International Conferences,
Department of State Accession 161, No. 34, Envelope 14.

The formation of an American customs league clearly involves the proposition of excluding Europe from the advantages accorded to its commerce . . . Such a thought cannot be agreeable to the Argentine government . . . [which] by no means wants to see the debilitation of its commercial relations with that part of the world to which we send our products and whence we receive capital and strong arms . . . The present convocation has as its object the erection of an American Zollverein, but since the laws of the United States in these matters are based on principles opposed to our own laws, it will be impossible to accept any proposition tending toward the amplification in America of the protectionist system of the United States, which would imply restrictions on our commerce with Europe.[32]

On the proposal to establish shipping lines, the delegates were instructed to support the plan, although there was little to be gained. No real benefit could accrue to Argentina by the establishment of ship connections with the United States until that government altered its tariff structure.

The Argentine delegates were further instructed that the plan to unify tariff schedules in the Americas "must be rejected as an unconstitutional limitation imposed on the sovereignty of the states in matters that are in the domain of private legislation."

The final point upon which the Argentine representatives received instructions was the proposal to adopt a fixed plan of arbitration. "That idea," wrote the president, "involves the most serious danger to the independence of sovereign states."[33]

Early in August 1899, two Argentine delegates sailed for Europe, en route to Washington for the First Pan American Conference.

[32] Roque Saenz Peña, *Escritos y discursos*, ed. by Ricardo Olivera (3 vols.; Buenos Aires, 1914, 1915, 1934), III, 369.
[33] Saenz Peña, *Escritos*, III, pp. 369–371.

10

The First Pan American Conference: I

THE Argentine delegation was originally composed of three men—Roque Saenz Peña, Manuel Quintana, and Vicente G. Quesada. From his post in Washington, Quesada wrote to his son in Buenos Aires a few months before the meeting: "I have requested and insisted [to the Argentine government] that three delegates be named, considering that the United States has named ten, so that it may be possible, with the other Latin American delegations, to equalize the influence of the North Americans."[1] But when his government, in agreement with this opinion, named as delegates Quesada himself, and the other two men, the Argentine minister requested permission to return home on leave during the sitting of the conference. He later gave as his reason for this action his realization that the role he would have to play at the assembly would seriously impair his usefulness as minister in Washington after the conference had ended.[2] In other words, Quesada did a bit of diplomatic crystal gazing and acted accordingly. He did not neglect, however, to place his knowledge of the United States at the disposal of Quintana and Saenz Peña. He met the two active delegates in Paris while they were en route to Washington and the three men concerted their ideas to the point of unanimity on all the issues to be discussed at the conference.[3]

The ten United States delegates to the First Pan American Conference were headed by John B. Henderson—of "Henderson's Castle" on Sixteenth Street in Washington—a wealthy

[1] Vicente G. Quesada, *Recuerdos de mi vida diplomática: misión en Estados Unidos (1885–1892)* (Buenos Aires, 1904), p. 119.

[2] Quesada, *Recuerdos,* p. 118.

[3] Ernesto Quesada, *Primera Conferencia Panamericana* (Buenos Aires, 1919), p. 4.

lawyer, former senator, and president of the Republican national convention in 1884, who, although he held no public position at the time of the conference, was a man of considerable influence in the national capital. Henderson had no experience as a diplomat, nor had he any knowledge of Spanish.[4] The only man in the delegation who met both criteria to some degree was William Henry Trescot, a State Department officer who had been sent by Blaine on an ill-fated mission to South America in 1881. One other delegate knew a little Spanish: Charles Flint was a Maine woods moose hunting companion of Thomas Baring, a member of the firm of W. R. Grace, and a person of other considerable business interests in Latin America.[5] Another delegate was Cornelius N. Bliss, owner of textile mills, former chairman of the Republican committee of New York State, and for many years president of the Protective Tariff League.[6] Two delegates whose names are perhaps most familiar today were Andrew Carnegie, a "John Stuart Mill protectionist," and Clement Studebaker, an active Republican. Then there was Morris Estee, a California lawyer, chairman of the Republican committee for his state, and chairman of the convention that nominated Harrison in 1888. Another important man was Henry Gassaway Davis, banker, coal mine operator, railroad owner, and ex-senator. The remaining members of the United States delegation were John F. Hanson, a cotton textile manufacturer who played a very minor part in the conference, and Thomas Jefferson Coolidge, distinguished New England textile manufacturer and banker.

The fitness of this otherwise powerful delegation for the task at hand was delicately described a few months after the close of the conference by Matías Romero, Mexican minister and

[4] Biographical data on the members of the United States delegation to the conference are drawn from the *Dictionary of American Biography*, various eds. (21 vols.; New York, 1928–1944), and the *National Cyclopaedia of American Biography* (Vol. I–, New York, 1893–), except where other sources are cited.

[5] Charles R. Flint, *Memories of an Active Life: Men, and Ships, and Sealing Wax* (New York and London, 1923), pp. 9, 43–46.

[6] President McKinley many times urged Bliss, who was his close friend, adviser, and former Secretary of the Interior, to run with him as vice-president in 1900. Bliss did not like the relative monotony of public administration and steadfastly refused the offer, thus leaving the position to Theodore Roosevelt.

dean of the diplomatic corps in Washington and head of the
Mexican delegation to the conference, who wrote, "It is entirely useless, as far as the Latin American nations are concerned, to enquire whether the [United States] government
could have selected gentlemen better fitted for the work, because if those appointed had not the necessary qualifications, the
United States was the principal sufferer from any embarrass-
ment that resulted."[7] Romero himself spoke and wrote flawless
English, and it was his tactful mediation, together with the dis-
cretion and parliamentary skill of James G. Blaine, which combined on several occasions to save the conference from collapse.

Roque Saenz Peña and Manuel Quintana disembarked in
New York on September 28 after a forty-day journey from
Buenos Aires. They proceeded at once to Washington. There, at
noon on October 2, 1889 in the "diplomatic room" of the State
Department, the representatives of Latin America and the
United States gathered for the opening session of the First Pan
American Conference. [8]

But not the two Argentine delegates. They boycotted the
meeting. Their reason for this action was characteristically both
practical and principled. Diplomatic custom provided that a
member of the inviting delegation be chosen to preside over the
conference. However, the unusual nature of the meeting, which
was, perhaps, the first in history at which such a number of
nations had come together to discuss matters not sprung from
war; the fact that there was no outstanding diplomat among the
United States delegates; and the great personal interest which
had long been displayed in Latin American affairs by Mr. Blaine,
who, by a turn of political fate was once again Secretary of
State, nine years after his original proposal of a Pan American
meeting—all these circumstances seem to have persuaded a

[7] Matías Romero, "The Pan American Conference," *North American Review*,
151:358 (September 1890).

[8] International American Conference, 1889–1890, *Minutes of the Conference*
(Washington, 1890), pp. 9–14.

Properly speaking, the First Pan American Conference was the First International American Conference, just as the Pan American Union was for many years
known formally as the International Bureau of American Republics. The term
Pan American came into early general use to designate these bodies.

majority of the conference delegates a few days before the first session to agree to elect the United States Secretary of State as the permanent president of the assembly at the opening meeting. Quintana and Saenz Peña refused to agree to this procedure, insisting that a man not accredited as a delegate was *ipso facto* barred from holding office as president of the conference.[9] Carnegie, Henderson, and Bliss attempted to find a solution to the impasse that would satisfy the men from Buenos Aires but as the time for the opening of the conference neared and no progress had been made they appealed to their fellow-delegate Charles Flint to find the answer. "We don't understand them [the Argentines]," they told Flint, depending on his experience with these strange Latin Americans to find the solution. Flint went to Saenz Peña and Quintana and said that he would resign his seat in order to allow Blaine to take his place, thus fulfilling their requirements for the Secretary's election to the chair.[10] Faced by this specific proposal, the Argentines compromised. They told Flint that such a step was unnecessary: they were not attempting to disrupt the United States delegation, nor were they opposed to Blaine personally, but they could not sacrifice the principle involved. Therefore, they said, they would withdraw their objection to Blaine's election, but they would not attend the first session at which that election was to be formalized.[11]

Conciliation by the Argentines extended only to a point, however. When the day and hour of the opening session came, Quintana and Saenz Peña did not conceal themselves in their hotel rooms, and plead the usual diplomatic "illness." They donned top hats and cutaways and rode through the streets of Washington, in an open carriage, so that the public could have no doubt as to their real motives.[12]

[9] Saenz Peña and Quintana to Zeballos, Oct. 11, 1889, *Memoria de Relaciones Exteriores presentada al honorable Congreso Nacional, 1890–1891* (Buenos Aires, 1892), p. 10.
[10] Flint, *Memories*, pp. 148–151. There is the implication in these pages that the two Argentine delegates were willing to see the presidency of the conference go to William Trescot, who was a Southerner and (presumably) a Democrat, and that Flint saved the day for Blaine and his party.
[11] *Memoria, 1890–1891*, p. 11.
[12] Ernesto Quesada, *Primera Conferencia*, p. 7.

In reporting their opposition to Blaine to their chief, Foreign Minister E. S. Zeballos, the Argentine delegates put down the real reason behind their conduct. "We were not disposed," they wrote, "that the international conference at which we were present should be administratively directed by the government of the United States."[13]

To the news of "l'affaire Blaine," the Argentine foreign minister replied with expressions of pleasure at the manner in which Quintana and Saenz Peña had handled the "delicate" matter. Zeballos also warned the two Argentine representatives that the efforts of the United States delegates during the conference would be largely directed to an attempt to "recuperate the advantages lost by the isolation of our markets with respect to theirs."[14]

Whatever the rights of the two nations involved in this dispute, it is fair to conclude that Argentina was fighting Pan Americanism before Pan Americanism existed. But that Argentina had not correctly assessed the actualities of the political balance within the Latin American delegations at the conference may be deduced from her failure, despite this bold step, to obtain support from any one of them. Further, the failure of the two Argentine delegates to withdraw from an assembly whose permanent president they had declared not qualified to hold office laid these gentlemen open to the suspicion that they realized there was more to be gained by wintering in Washington than by summering in Buenos Aires.

When the conference got under way on October 2, it succeeded only in voting itself into a lengthy hiatus. After listening to Blaine's welcoming address, hearty in its appeal for a future made strong and peaceful through Pan American cooperation, the delegates adjourned, not to reconvene until November 18. The reason for this long suspension of conference work was a 6,000-mile "de luxe" railroad excursion, arranged, paid for, and conducted by the United States government to impress the Latin American visitors with the economic might of the United

---

[13] *Memoria, 1890–1891*, p. 12.
[14] Zeballos to Quintana and Saenz Peña, Nov. 28, 1889, *Memoria, 1890–1891*, pp. 14–15.

States. A special train whose opulence "would have aroused the greed of a prince of the 1001 nights"[15] whisked the delegates from Boston to Buffalo, from Chicago to Collinsville, and from Altoona to Omaha. Every city of any size had its reception committee ready, manned by public-spirited citizens, including those whose business interests or hopes lay in Latin America. There were visits to textile mills, paper mills, furniture factories, a stockyard, and the Garfield Monument. Gaiety and elegance abounded at every stopping place. So did speechmakers—some with long speeches, some with very long speeches, and all ebullient, proud, and implacably devoted to The American Way. Fortunately the Latin American guests, alternately deluged with praise and ignored in these speeches, were able to fight off the gathering weariness of the long weeks of travel well enough to equal the score with some astounding feats of oratory.[16]

This extensive publicity effort was wasted as far as Manuel Quintana and Roque Saenz Peña were concerned. Neither of them went on the trip. Alone among the seventy-three delegates and their subordinates comprising the conference personnel, the gentlemen from Argentina declined the opportunity to view the material prosperity of the United States.

If the two Argentine delegates, resting in Washington and perfecting their plans for the forthcoming business sessions of the conference, could have seen their hometown newspapers for October and November, they would have found little about Pan Americanism, but a great deal about the rocketing cost of gold in Argentina, the Paris exposition, and the revolution in Brazil. On October 19, *Sud América* gave its readers in Buenos Aires a factual report on the aims of the conference, and pointed out that a statement by William E. Curtis that the United States delegation was made up of five Republicans and five Democrats was untrue—the proportion was eight to two. A little later

[15] Charles A. O'Rourke, *Congreso Internacional Americano. Paseo de los delegados. Objeto del Congreso* (New York, 1890), p. 12.

[16] International American Conference, 1889–1890, *Reports of Committees and Discussions Thereon* (4 vols.; Washington, 1890), Vol. III: *Excursion Appendix: Narrative of the Tour of the Delegates Through the United States: Together with Descriptions of Places Visited, and Reports of Addresses Delivered.*

(October 30), the same official paper took a favorable view of the possibility of beneficial economic cooperation with the United States. Latins and Saxons, the paper concluded, may one day struggle over the vastnesses of the new world, but to talk of such a struggle now is premature. Meanwhile, the *yanquis* could be of great help in strengthening Argentina as a new, vital center of civilization.

The most popular evening paper, *El Diario*, took a similar stand, writing (August 14, 1889) that the forthcoming congress should not be viewed as an attempt by the United States to apply the Monroe Doctrine in a political sense, but as a great opportunity for Latin America to make commercial gains out of the new Yankee industrial strength.

A more sober journal, *El Nacional*, on October 4 commented on Argentina's safe geographic position with regard to the United States, that "eagle whose talons tender to us the sarcastic offering of reciprocal free trade." On October 31 this famous old Argentine paper commented on the grave fears felt in Europe that the Pan American Conference might succeed in implementing its program. "The eternal pretension of the United States," wrote the editors, "is to give economic significance to the Monroe Doctrine, with a view to making the nation's astounding productivity dominant, in the guise of continental leagues."

La Prensa had little to say about the conference in its first weeks, but that little was a sweeping item published on October 5 under the line "Bulletin-Washington: It seems that the Congress has turned out to be a fiasco since it has not lived up to public expectations nor succeeded in awakening the least interest."

The most serious attack against the conference was made by *La Nación*, which began publishing in November a series of long articles by its correspondent in the United States. The correspondent was José Martí, Cuban revolutionary and prolific publicist. His reports were shrewd, detailed, and powerfully written, their complex and allusive style a delight to Argentine readers. In the first of these articles, printed in the November 8 edition of Mitre's paper, Martí described the grand tour of the delegates, the purpose of which, he said, is to implant in the minds of the Latin American representatives "the desirability of having their people buy in the east and not elsewhere."

The cry against the conference was strong in the two most important foreign language newspapers in Buenos Aires, the *Standard* and *Le Courrier de La Plata*. On November 29 the voice of the English colony predicted that the conference would be a complete failure because of the selfish tariff barriers erected by the various countries participating, especially the United States. *Le Courrier* was also accusatory. On October 3 its readers were told, "The famous Monroe Doctrine will be enlarged; it is not a question of the non-intervention of Europe in the affairs of the American continent, but of the preponderance . . . of the United States."

Meanwhile the exhausted excursionists had returned to Washington and the Pan American Conference started up again on November 18. There followed weeks of wrangling over rules and procedures, during which the Argentine and United States delegations clashed repeatedly. This prolonged conflict lasted from November 18 to January 15 and fostered ill will between the two delegations, which flared out later over the major issues of the meeting.

The language barrier was an early and persisting complication in the assembly, and one on which the Argentine delegates, both of whom claimed to know no English, were not disposed to compromise. On the first day of the resumed sessions Quintana made the issue clear to the North Americans. Unaccountably, no preparation had been made for interpretation at this meeting. The minutes of the October 2 session having been read in English, Blaine moved the next business, but before he could get any further Quintana made a very positive request that the journal be read in Spanish. Blaine was obliged to ask Matías Romero to assist the United States by undertaking this task. As soon as the Mexican minister had finished playing the part of secretary, Quintana submitted a resolution calling upon the conference "to elect . . . two secretaries who speak both the English and Spanish languages

correctly."[17] There was a double motive behind this resolution:
not only did Quintana intend to establish the parity of the two
languages within the assembly, but he was also aiming to
eliminate from the conference the man whom Blaine had named
as its chief secretary and who had done much of the organizational work—William E. Curtis. Curtis was distinctly *persona non
grata* to many of the Latin American delegates. By the terms of
Quintana's successful motion, Curtis, who spoke no Spanish,
was automatically excluded from the chief administrative
position of the conference. Blaine, however, circumvented
Quintana's action by immediately reappointing Curtis as
"executive officer" of the assembly, a euphemism which could
hardly have improved the opinion of Curtis held by the
Argentine and other Latin American delegates.

It was becoming apparent that the Argentine delegates had
clear ideas of the proper conduct of international assemblies.
At this same session of November 18, while they were busy establishing the equality of Spanish and English, United States
delegates Bliss and Flint were equally busy introducing petitions
and invitations from various private parties outside the conference, calling upon that body to take actions or to attend
functions that seemed desirable to the petitioners. Quintana
put an abrupt end to this practice by proposing and seeing
passed a resolution stating that "these invitations . . . should be
understood to be addressed to the delegates individually . . .
and not to the conference, which cannot take action upon
subjects not comprised in the act of congress providing for its
meeting."[18] This was the first appearance of a principle later
effectively applied by the Argentines to other problems—that
of restricting the functions of the conference precisely to the
agenda.

In this somewhat tense atmosphere the delegates settled
down to the business of devising a set of rules to govern the

[17] IAC, *Minutes*, p. 18.
There is scattered evidence in the journals of the conference that the two
Argentine delegates had a more than passable knowledge of spoken and written
English. See, for example, Saenz Peña's comments in IAC, *Reports*, I, 162.
[18] IAC, *Minutes*, pp. 19–20.

conference. In the key matter of internal organization a divergence between Argentina and the United States became apparent which affected the entire course of the conference. The Argentine representatives sought from the outset to construct and define a set of rules that would limit freedom of discussion. This was in opposition to the broad interpretation of the scope of the assembly advocated by the United States in the interest of a free and cooperative exchange of opinion among the many assembled states. The arguments eventually pivoted on the interpretation of the convening act written by the United States Congress, which was the basic law of the conference. The Argentines claimed that only the specified topics enumerated in the convening act were allowable subjects for discussion. Their stand was well-taken, cogently argued, and ultimately victorious. The Argentine effort to bind the conference to limits may be attributed to a fear that the restless power of the United States would influence the other delegates to exceed the bounds which had been indicated, and that thus the United States would emerge from the conference claiming the role of arbiter of the western hemisphere.

An example will illustrate the tenor of Argentine opposition in these organizational conflicts. A primary obstacle to the formulation of a set of rules, and one to which by its nature the Argentines did not care to cede, was the disparity between Anglo-Saxon and Latin parliamentary procedures. The chairman of the rules committee was a Chilean delegate, but Quintana, a member of the committee, soon took over leadership of the discussions. One of the first clashes came on November 27 when conference chairman Blaine rather naïvely proposed that the fixing of the sequence in which speakers should have a right to the floor throughout the conference should be left in every case to the courtesy of the delegates themselves. Quintana and Saenz Peña took the floor successively to inform Blaine that "International congresses do not ordinarily make rules . . . [but that] when rules are made, they adopt rules . . . to fix the order of speaking to avoid having to decide it in each case." Blaine withdrew his optimistic motion and by unanimous vote the conference established the rule that the sequence of delegates on the

floor should be the order in which the floor was requested.[19]
This checked the Secretary of State's effort to create a·climate
of open, easy discussion and precluded the possibility that the
United States delegates might obtain an advantage over less
numerous and influential delegations by monopolizing the floor
through the "courtesy" of their own or other friendly representatives.

Time after time Saenz Peña and Quintana arose to protest,
to limit, to bind the power of the delegates into narrow paths
hedged by parliamentary controls. When the United States
moved to allow the private secretaries of the delegates to attend
sessions, Quintana opposed and the proposal was voted down,
on the grounds that "private secretaries have no official character."[20] Since the conference was not public, Quintana had
justification. Perhaps his aim was to eliminate a potential source
of "leaks."

The upshot of the struggle over the rules of the conference
was the adoption, virtually unaltered, of the original report of
the committee on rules, six of whose seven members were Latin
Americans, including Quintana. The rules followed almost
exactly those adopted at another assembly in which Quintana
and Saenz Peña had prominent parts—the Montevideo Congress of the previous year.[21]

The rules at last agreed upon, the Conference began to work
on the agenda. One of the most important issues before it was
that of the "common silver coin." This question was turned over
to the "committee on the monetary convention," composed of
seven delegates, five of whom were Latin Americans, but none
Argentine, and two North Americans, Estee and Coolidge. After
lengthy study this committee submitted its recommendations,
but not in a single report. Three separate reports were put
forward. The five Latin American delegates united in the

[19] IAC, *Minutes*, pp. 36–37; IAC, *Reports*, I, 56, Art. VIII.

[20] IAC, *Minutes*, pp. 50–51.

[21] The rules were adopted piecemeal at the sessions of November 21, 27 and 29,
and December 2 and 4. See IAC, *Minutes*, pp. 27–30, 35–41, 42–48, 49–52, and
53–59, respectively. The rules governing the Montevideo Congress may be found
in República Oriental del Uruguay, *Actas y tratados celebrados por el Congreso Internacional Sud-Americano de Montevideo* (Montevideo, 1911), pp. 19–23.

majority statement, recommending that the Conference propose to the constituent governments the formation of a commission which would do exactly what the convening act of the conference specified—establish, after technical study, an "international silver coin." The two United States delegates on this committee each managed to produce a minority report.[22] The complexities of the coinage arguments to which each of these gentlemen devoted himself does not concern us. However, the awkward division in the United States delegation was to prove unfortunate for the proposition of a common silver coin, and for the prestige of the United States within the conference.

The Argentine delegates capitalized on the split in Yankee ranks. Their attack followed two lines. First, they seized on the basic procedural dilemma created by the dissension between the Americans; second, they attacked the use of silver as the standard in the projected coinage, although silver was the metal specified in the convening act of the conference, in the majority report of the committee which handled the question, and had been partially supported by both Estee and Coolidge, despite their disagreement as to details.

The long exchange of speeches between fellow-delegates Estee and Coolidge which marked the opening of the coinage debates in the plenary session on March 26 was not interrupted by the Argentine delegates for several hours. The Americans needed no help in displaying their weakness. Finally, however, the situation seemed ripe. Quintana stood up and spoke:

The United States delegation lacks official instructions from its government upon this vital subject . . . The attitude maintained by the United States delegation confirms this fully . . . A delegate only represents one nation—a nation has but one vote—and in the presence of these facts I ask myself: How can a single delegation advance two opinions, two ideas, two plans so entirely distinct that they contradict each other openly? . . . Is this a conference of private individuals speaking for themselves, or is it a diplomatic conference in which each delegate represents the idea of his government?

This conference owes its birth to a law of the United States; the delegates have presented their respective credentials; these

[22] IAC, *Reports*, II, 624–668.

credentials have been ratified in the bosom of the assembly—but the delegate who speaks in his own name speaks without full power; and I say further that if he is not able to interpret his credentials he has no right to present his private opinions to representatives of foreign governments . . . This being the case . . . the Argentine delegation, in harmony with the ideas expressed by it from the first day, insists that it cannot take these opinions into consideration, nor continue negotiations upon this basis. It will have the greatest pleasure in remaining here to the close and in treating all the subjects for which the conference was convened, but these must be treated officially, and by those who hold an official character and speak in the name of their government.[23]

This blunt accusation threw the United States delegates into a frantic defense of their exposed position. While the other nations sat silent, Henderson, Coolidge, and Estee argued bitterly against the two Argentines through the sessions of March 26, 27, 29, and 31, and April 1, 2, and 7. Estee defended the obvious fact that the United States delegation had no instructions by claiming the protection of Article IX of the conference rules, which states that each delegate might submit to the gathering his written opinion upon a matter in debate. Coolidge contributed the thought that if the Argentine delegation wanted to know the opinion of the American delegation on any given topic, all they had to do was call for a vote and they would get the American opinion.[24] He did not indicate how long it might take the ten United States representatives to unite their diverse views.

Saenz Peña straightway demolished this rebuttal. He pointed out that, although the North American delegates seemed proud of the fact that they were uninstructed, all the other delegates *had* been instructed; that in diplomatic practice acts ratified by instructed delegates morally bound the governments represented, whereas uninstructed delegates bound no one by their individual opinions; that Article IX, referred to by Mr. Estee, had not been conceived to apply to the various members within a single delegation, but to each delegate speaking for his deputation as a unit. "I will not vacillate in saying," Saenz Peña

[23] IAC, *Reports*, II, 713–716.   [24] IAC, *Reports*, II, 718.

continued, "that if the delegation of the United States does not hold the opinion of its government, the Argentine delegation will refuse to give its opinion on this subject [the monetary resolution]."[25] Henderson hastily moved the adjournment of the session.

On the following day mediatory efforts were made by the Mexican and Colombian delegates, and some of the other Latin American representatives talked over practical phases of the proposed international coinage. This had little effect on the two Argentines. They reported that they were ill, and did not attend.[26]

On March 29 the United States delegation retreated. Henderson submitted a signed amendment to be attached to the majority report of the monetary committee in lieu of the previous double minority report. This new amendment was identical in meaning, if not in wording, with the report of the majority of the committee. The division in the United States delegation seemed to have been healed overnight, and a slight flavor of independence had been salvaged from the wreckage as a token to the idea of free discussion within the conference. The gentlemen from Argentina were still ill.[27]

Quintana was in his seat at the next session, on March 31. The North Americans soon learned that the coinage question could not be disposed of on the basis of Henderson's compromise as quickly and quietly as they wished. The Argentine statesman was conciliatory—at first. There was no need, he said, of performing the unpleasant task of replying to Mr. Estee's speeches of March 26. "Why," he asked quietly, "discuss the contradictory plans of Messrs. Coolidge and Estee if they represented nothing more than their personal ideas, and must in the end be replaced, as they have been, by a plan proposed by the United States delegation, which, I must suppose, is the faithful expression of the ideas of its government?" This whole disagreeable incident having been cleared away, Quintana continued, it remained only to analyze the committee report and the United

[25] IAC, *Reports*, II, 721–723.
[26] IAC, *Reports*, II, 737–738, 741–748; IAC, *Minutes*, pp. 556–560.
[27] IAC, *Reports*, II, 750–756; IAC, *Minutes*, pp. 523, 556–558, 561.

States amendment thereto, and to vote upon them according of their merits, for, while the nations had been called together to discuss adoption of a common silver coin, it was quite proper to regard the use of silver as unacceptable, if such happened to be the opinion of any nation. Argentina was willing to talk over a common coin, but why choose silver and exclude gold?

This was too much for Estee, who jumped up to protest that the United States, having already ceded to Argentina the disputed point of each delegate's right to an opinion, now had to see the monetary plan itself attacked. Unperturbed, the Argentine replied by introducing his own plan, which omitted any mention of the type of metal to be utilized in the projected coinage. [28]

The session of April 1 was devoted to arguments for and against the use of silver and for and against sending the whole matter back to committee. At last it was moved to return the issue to the reporting committee. The vote was taken and the motion approved, eleven to four. Costa Rica, Haiti, and Nicaragua voted with the United States. [29] The result of this step was foregone. On April 2 a new resolution came from the committee, recommending the creation of a commission that would meet at a future date to discuss the establishment of an international coin and determine of what metal the coin should consist. Silver was not mentioned. This resolution was voted: fifteen in favor, one—Guatemala—opposed. [30] Argentina and the United States thus voted on the same side, or, more correctly, the other Latin American nations voted with Argentina, and the United States voted with the majority.

The battle of the silver coin was a defeat for the United States. The Argentines had driven the Americans into retreat over the conduct of their own delegation; the Argentines had led the movement which resulted in a departure from the act of congress under which the conference met. The representatives from

[28] IAC, *Reports*, II, 763–766, 773–782.

[29] IAC, *Reports*, II, 800–815.

[30] IAC, *Reports*, II, 815–816. Quintana would not vote for this resolution, though it was the result of his own efforts, until he received assurances from the committee that there was not even an implication in the resolution that silver was the most desirable metal for the future coin. See *ibid.*, p. 819, April 2. IAC, *Minutes*, p. 595.

the Argentine Republic had succeeded in getting the assembly to substitute their plan for the original American project and they had revealed the United States delegates to be uninstructed, divided among themselves, and unable to resist the attack of a Latin American delegation.

Another major issue before the Pan American Conference was the establishment of a hemispheric system of arbitration. Here the struggle between Argentina and the United States was again the pivot of all discussions, but under unusual circumstances. Neither country wished to abandon leadership in the creation of an arbitral plan. The two nations were allied in the same cause, but hostile allies seeking to gain the advantage of one another.

When the Conference turned its attention to arbitration, the first plan proposed for committee consideration was submitted jointly by the Argentine and Brazilian delegates. This was done on January 15. On January 20, Quintana and Saenz Peña cabled to the Argentine foreign minister the motives which underlay their action. The Argentines and Brazilians, they told Zeballos, had agreed to present together a plan of arbitration so as to demonstrate their "bi-lateral solidarity." By submitting its plan ahead of any other, the Argentines continued, the Argentine delegation had weakened those who sought permanent arbitration tribunals or even compulsory arbitration—projects which must be avoided because they do not take into account "the danger to which sovereignty is [thereby] exposed."[31]

The United States delegates of course did not know of this Argentine attitude toward arbitration. They had the easy belief that a compulsory system could be approved within the conference and perfected in practice as soon as the proper machinery had been set up. Their disillusionment began when Quintana arose on the afternoon of April 14—the first delegate to ask to speak on the final committee plan of arbitration, which had just been presented to the assembly after weeks of study. The plan did not authorize the establishment of compulsory

[31] IAC, *Minutes*, pp. 106–108; Quintana and Saenz Peña to Zeballos, Jan. 20, 1890, *Memoria, 1890–1891*, pp. 17–19.

arbitral machinery, but Quintana wished to make clear his country's views despite the mildness of the suggested system:

> In the eyes of international American law there are on these continents neither great nor small nations. All are equally sovereign and independent, all equally worthy of consideration and respect. The arbitration proposed is not, consequently, a compact of abdication, of vassalage, or of submission. Before as well as after its conclusion, all and each of the nations of America will preserve the exclusive direction of their political destinies, absolutely without interference by the others . . . Such, gentlemen, is the clear letter of the proposed treaty, such has been the predominant idea of the committee, which has constantly eliminated all suggestions tending to attribute to its stipulations a compulsory character, even though it be purely moral . . . I need hardly add, were it otherwise, that the Argentine delegation would not hesitate to withdraw its support . . . The Argentine delegation will also congratulate itself for this explanation of its ideas respecting the project of arbitration. Perhaps this will serve to prevent, in the future, interpretations as unauthorized as they are repugnant to the sincerity of some, the dignity of others, and the cordiality of all.

MR. SAENZ PEÑA: I desire to endorse in full the opinions expressed by my honorable colleague, Dr. Quintana.[32]

This opened the floodgates. Henderson and Quintana, the heads of their respective delegations, had been at odds during most of the lengthy conference, and Quintana's last words were aimed at the chief of the American deputation. Throughout the debates that ensued the Argentine insisted that the final resolution must preserve what we may call the "point of independence"—that is, the right of any state to exclude from arbitration any matter which it deemed involved its own independence. This Henderson opposed, advocating instead that arbitration "be applied to the settlement of [all] such questions as may arise."[33]

But Quintana would not be put off. The debates became confused skirmishes in semantics, further complicated by the difficulty of making clear translations into both English and Spanish

[32] IAC, *Reports*, II, 961–964.
[33] IAC, *Reports*, II, 1011, 1037.

of the numerous changes in wording which the Argentines introduced as the sessions dragged on. In one meeting Quintana and
Senator Henderson battled over the preamble of the plan, the
latter denouncing it as empty rhetoric, the former upholding
its noble sentiments; in another session Quintana engaged Blaine
in a squabble over procedure. [34] On another occasion, when
there seemed to be a division of opinion in the United States
delegation similar to that which had occurred over silver,
Quintana insisted that each delegate on the floor must support
the views of any fellow delegate who had served on a committee
and signed the committee report. Blaine carefully told the
Argentine that the chair did not recognize such a practice as
the parliamentary law of the conference. "There is no reason
why," said the Secretary of State tartly, "when there is free
speech, every delegate should be absolutely compelled to proceed in the same way." [35] But when at last, on April 18, the
whole arbitration plan had become thoroughly muddled over
one of its many technicalities and the session had turned dan-
gerously acrimonious, Carnegie asked for a recess. After several
hours of mediation between the Argentines and his own delegation, Blaine returned to the conference hall, not to the chair,
but to the floor, to present personally the amendment upon
which he had obtained agreement. [36]

This was the turning point in the debates. The Argentines,
who had shown an obdurate intention of voting back to committee each article of the lengthy arbitration plan, ceded this
particular detail to Blaine's personal authority, but their position had been upheld so consistently by the other Latin American
representatives during these discussions that the United States
was finally forced to admit its isolation. On the next to the last
day of this conference, which had already lasted more than six
months, the weary delegates voted unanimously to recommend
to their governments the amended arbitral plan containing the
"point of independence."

On that day José Martí wrote a voluminous letter (printed

[34] IAC, *Reports*, II, 1040–1042, 1056–1059.
[35] IAC, *Reports*, II, 1068.
[36] IAC, *Reports*, II, 1135–1147.

May 31) to *La Nación*, describing the struggle over arbitration. His story was loose and unreliable, full of quoted phrases which were in fact mainly his own ideas of what the United States delegates were thinking, but the moral that he drew was clear: the Argentines had defeated an American scheme to erect a system of compulsory arbitration with a permanent tribunal obedient to the dictates of Washington. He likened the entire conference to a Chinese puzzle-box—box within box until at last the mystery is solved: the Yankee arbitration plan, by which the United States would emerge to dominate Latin America.

Martí would have had just as powerful a message for the readers of *La Nación* if he had described what the Argentines actually achieved in this phase of the First Pan American Conference. They had pointed out to the other Latin American states what they saw as the danger in trusting "great" nations who sought a condition of "vassalage" for their smaller neighbors. They had fought successfully for the equality of states, the principle of nonintervention, and the preservation of sovereignty. They had upheld the doctrine of arbitration as a vital force in international relations. And, Martí might have added, the Argentines not only brought the United States to accept, for the sake of a façade of uniformity, their interpretation of arbitration, but had caused the Secretary of State of the United States to descend to playing the role of delegate in a conference that he had summoned into existence.

11

The First Pan American Conference: II

In addition to the conflict between Argentina and the United States over the monetary union and arbitration, not to mention the struggle with the rules of the conference, one other major topic caused dispute—the customs union. But before taking up that major issue, the work of the conference with regard to the lesser topics on the agenda will be traced.

Here too the United States ran up against the alert Argentines. An example is the case of item five of the convening act— the "adoption of a uniform system of weights and measures." The report of the committee on weights and measures was delivered to the assembly on January 15, 1890. It recommended the adoption of the metric system by all the American states. The report was signed by one Latin American and one United States delegate.[1] Since the United States was the only major American nation not already using the metric system, the proposal affected her most drastically; yet when the subject came up for debate on the floor, the United States delegates demonstrated every interest in the practical advantages of the recommendation and indicated their intention of voting in favor of the plan.[2] The other delegates restricted their supporting comments to the improvement of the multilingual text of the resolution. There was one exception—Argentina.

It was paradoxical to find that nation, herself a user of the metric system, opposed to the resolution on weights and measures. The Argentine delegate, Mr. Saenz Peña, did not, however, argue his case on the merits or defects of the system. His purpose lay farther afield, as his speech shows:

[1] International American Conference, 1889–1890, *Reports of Committees and Discussions Thereon* (4 vols.; Washington, 1890), I, 77–80.
[2] IAC, *Reports*, I, 81–92.

I think that anything relative to the domestic affairs of a country is a subject for its own legislation, and that it is beyond the province of this conference to dictate in such matters. The conference must limit its efforts to determining the form in which international commercial relations are to be maintained, but it is in the interest of each state to make its internal policy uniform with its international relations.[3]

Despite the foggy meaning of the last sentence, Saenz Peña's idea is clear. Here was a representative of the country which had sought repeatedly to restrict debate to the points named in the convening statute of the assembly attempting to deny that body's right to consider one of those topics. Here was the label "compulsion" applied to the acts of a conference which was in fact, as the Argentines had doubtless observed before accepting their invitation, purely recommendatory. Saenz Peña's admonition to his listeners to preserve their freedom of action was nonetheless significant. This was the first session of the conference devoted to debate on the agenda, and the Argentines may have wanted to make clear from the outset the restrictive view which they held of the assembly's powers, despite the fact that in this instance they were ultimately bound to give an affirmative vote. To do otherwise would have been to deny their own country's system of weights and measures.

Another question considered by the assembly was that of making port dues uniform. On March 5, 1890 a committee of the United States, Venezuela, and Chile recommended to the conference that port charges in all the American nations should be combined into one nominal levy. The committee added that had the law of the conference so authorized, they would have recommended the abolition of port dues in the interest of stimulating inter-American shipping and commerce.[4]

The committee's recommendation was discussed during part of five sessions. Before these discussions ended, the gentlemen from Argentina succeeded in returning the original report to committee, succeeded in adding Argentina and two other nations to the original committee, and managed to reverse the initial report, substituting for it their own recommendation,

---

[3] IAC, *Reports*, I, 86–87.   [4] IAC, *Reports*, I, 412–414.

which preserved to each nation the right to levy whatever port charges it desired.

All this was accomplished by appealing to the wording of the convening act. As Quintana put it: "There exists an erroneous impression that the committee was instructed to *reduce* dues . . . To make port dues uniform is one thing; to reduce them, another." It was not, he continued, within the competence of the assembly to contemplate such an unauthorized intervention in the internal affairs of Argentina and his country would in no way support such a recommendation. [5]

The pleas of the North American delegates on behalf of the mutual benefits to be derived from a reduction of port dues fell on very deaf ears. The claim by the United States representatives that the original report should be accepted for the good of all concerned met only the icy Argentine retort: "If the reports have to be accepted by all the delegates as obligatory, then there is no reason for the existence of the conference." [6] Argentina insisted that her amendment to the first report—which in effect destroyed the latter by permitting each nation to fix the amount, if not the number, of the dues it would charge—be put to a vote. When this was done, the United States emerged alone in the negative, against fourteen votes favoring the amendment. Even Venezuela and Chile, co-signers of the first recommendation, had come to see things the Argentine way. [7]

The report on the table having been upset, it was necessary to return it to committee for restatement. To coordinate the committee more closely with the opinions which had been voiced on the floor, four new members, including Quintana, were added to that body. On April 10 discussion of the revised recommendation of the revised committee was begun, and on the following day the new, or Argentine, resolution was unanimously approved by the assembly. [8] Port charges remained unaltered, as did the power of each nation to change them. The United States had again given way before Argentina, a nation possessing a large foreign commerce but no merchant marine, and dependent upon port charges for a good part of her revenue.

[5] IAC, *Reports*, I, 462–465. [6] IAC, *Reports*, I, 463.
[7] IAC, *Reports*, I, 477. [8] IAC, *Reports*, I, 482–488, 494–502.

Another maritime problem, and one of long-standing interest to both Argentina and the United States, was that of steamer connections in the Atlantic. The committee on communication in the Atlantic reported out a proposal for the establishment of a line of freight and passenger vessels to run between New York, Rio, Montevideo, and Buenos Aires, the enterprise to be subsidized in the following ratio by the governments concerned: The United States, 60 per cent; Argentina and Brazil, $12\frac{1}{2}$ per cent each; Uruguay, 5 per cent.[9] Argentina, it may be presumed, stood to make as much proportionate commercial gain as any of the nations concerned, not to speak of other benefits which might flow from strengthened inter-American ties. But any assumption that the Argentine delegation would raise no objection to this plan was not substantiated in the debate following the committee's report. On the contrary, the Argentine representative, who, together with his North American opponent provided all the discussion on the topic, made a reservation which was a conditional withdrawal from the plan.

By the reservation which he introduced, Saenz Peña in effect withdrew before the plenary session the support which he had given in committee. He was motivated by his country's alarm over United States tariff policy. He had apparently learned of a portion of the new tariff law (the future McKinley Bill) then under study in the United States Congress, by the terms of which the import duty on wool was to be increased and a duty placed on raw hides, hitherto on the free list. With this in mind, Saenz Peña addressed the Conference:

We have been called to encourage American commercial relations, but when we return to our country to give an account of our laborious mission we shall be forced to say: We went to Washington with a product on the free list, and we have obtained a law which burdens it with a duty; another product was taxed at six, but when the conference was over we found it taxed at seven . . . Therefore the Argentine delegates give their vote in favor of the plan under discussion, but they will recommend to their government not to approve it if the United States tariff should be altered to the injury of Argentine products. This vote is the result of a formal agreement

[9] IAC, *Reports*, I, 265–267.

with my honorable colleague [Quintana] and should be inserted in full in the minutes with all explanatory remarks.[10]

And so the matter stood.

The disputes over weights and measures, port dues, and communications appear mild compared to the encounter between Argentina and the United States over the customs union question.[11]

The convening act of the United States government and the invitation from the State Department which followed, emphasized the possibility of enlarging inter-American trade by a broad and free discussion of pertinent measures, specifically the creation of a customs union. There was no concealment of the economic interest which motivated the United States in calling together the American states, nor, on the other hand, was there any hint that such trade plans were one-sided or oppressive to the interests of the other nations. Some practical commercial resolution might have been reasonably expected to result from this first meeting of the great majority of western hemisphere states. Such, indeed, was the result, but it was only after a hard and unsuccessful struggle with Argentina that the United States

[10] IAC, *Reports*, I, 271–273.

[11] Argentines and Yankees did agree on a few matters at the conference. These and the remaining items on the agenda are reviewed here. A resolution on communication on the Pacific was unanimously passed. Argentina naturally took no part in the discussion. See IAC, *Reports*, I, 276–311. A resolution on communication on the Caribbean was unanimously approved. Argentina displayed no interest in this topic. See *ibid.*, pp. 312–342. A resolution was unanimously approved recommending adherence to the treaties on international private law adopted at the Montevideo Congress in 1888. This success for Latin law was also a victory for Quintana over Henderson. See *ibid.*, pp. 876–932. The conference voted fourteen to one (Chile) to recommend adoption of the Montevideo extradition code. Saenz Peña and Quintana had been the principal authors of that code. The United States delegation did not participate in the discussion. See *ibid.*, pp. 570–623. A resolution on patents and trademarks was unanimously approved without discussion, with the Montevideo treaties on these subjects recommended as models for the action of the other American states. See *ibid.*, pp. 555–569. A resolution on sanitary regulations was approved thirteen to two (Chile and Mexico). There was no dispute between Argentina and the United States on this subject. See *ibid.*, pp. 505–553. The same was true of the resolution on the inter-continental railroad. See *ibid.*, pp. 93–102. The International Union of the American Republics (the "Pan American Union") was established by unanimous vote of the conference on April 14, 1890. The United States, but not Argentina, participated in the brief discussion. See *ibid.*, pp. 681–689.

was able to complete a resolution that partially fulfilled the expectations of the convening act.

The idea of a customs union did not endure its first test. The proposition was rejected by the committee formed to consider it, a group comprising Henderson, Saenz Peña, and six other Latin Americans. The reasoning behind the rejection was sound and was concurred in by the United States delegate. The committee pointed out the utopian nature of the plan and the practical obstacles lying in the way of an attempt to combine suddenly many nations and distinct economies into a single international body. However, the committee, or rather the majority of the committee, did not shut the door to the possibility of improving inter-American trade. Instead, the committee majority submitted to the conference their own proposal, that the assembled delegations should resolve to recommend to their governments the desirability of concluding bilateral or multilateral reciprocity treaties which, if written in sufficient number and scope, would someday make possible the area of free trade envisaged in the original customs union proposal. The representatives of Brazil, Nicaragua, Venezuela, Colombia, Mexico, and the United States signed this report.[12]

Two members of the committee did not sign it. Argentina and Chile submitted a minority report—a document outstanding for its brevity. This read: "Resolved, That the proposition of a customs union between the nations of America be rejected."[13]

It is certain that Argentina alone did not defeat the idea of a customs union which the United States had inserted in the convening act. That suggestion had already been defeated by the committee formed to consider it. But the interesting and revealing fact is the intransigent attitude of the Argentine leaders who, not content with the elimination of the union, now launched a prolonged attack, inactively seconded by Chile, against the alternative project of reciprocal treaties. The persistent attempt by the men from Buenos Aires to prevent even the consideration by the Conference of the majority resolution involved the United States delegates in day after day of angry

[12] IAC, *Minutes*, pp. 293–296.   [13] IAC, *Minutes*, p. 296.

debate with their formidable colleagues Saenz Peña and Quintana, chiefly the former, who delivered sixteen speeches on the
reciprocity project, as compared to seven speeches apiece by
Henderson and Estee.

Debate on the two committee reports before the Conference
began on March 15, with both Henderson and Saenz Peña
demanding the floor. The two men dominated the ensuing sessions—the latter calm and cogent, the former forceful and hot-
tempered. Saenz Peña spoke first, and his statement deserves
extended examination as one of the most important declarations
of Argentina's position in the world after 1880. The future
foreign minister and president began by saying:

> We, the Argentine delegates, have attended the discussion of this
> matter free from prejudice and exempt from reservations . . . We
> are not animated by any unreasonable sentiments of self-defense . . .
> The truth is that our knowledge of each other is limited . . . The
> republics of the north have lived without holding communication
> with those of the south . . . [and] they have failed to cultivate with
> us closer and more intimate relations. In this fragmentary and auto-
> nomic development of the three zones of America, the United States
> have forced themselves upon the attention of the world by their
> conspicuous greatness and their wise example. The nations which
> have not reached such eminence are the subject of misrepresenta-
> tions, perhaps involuntary, such as those which caused a senator of
> this country [the United States] to say: "The Spanish American
> states will commence by surrending the key of their commerce, and
> end by forgetting that of their politics."
> I begin by declaring that I do not know the key to Argentine
> markets—perhaps because none exists, since they lack any statutes
> of exclusion, or any machinery whatsoever of publication or
> monopoly.[14]

Without pausing to note that the Pan American Conference
was meeting to consider means of overcoming the deficient inter-
American relations which he described, Saenz Peña went on to
praise the Argentine free market and the principle of free trade.
A free flow of commerce already existed, he pointed out, between certain American states and Europe, a sound exchange

[14] IAC, *Minutes*, pp. 297-298.

between raw material areas and manufacturing centers. But, he said emphatically, "to attempt to assure free trade between non-interchanging markets would be a utopian luxury and an illustration of sterility."[15] The United States, he said, have failed because of their tariff system to support inter-continental commerce to the degree needed by the Latin American nations.

The ample statistics and arguments which Saenz Peña introduced at this point in his speech need not detain us, but it is interesting to note the contradiction in which the speaker involved himself, that of having first attributed the small volume of trade between Argentina and the United States (for it was of that "republic of the north" that he spoke) to the non-complementary nature of their economies, and next declaring the United States tariff the root of the evil. The fact of the matter seems to be that during this reciprocity debate the Argentines were concerned with their European trade first, trade with the United States second, and hemispheric reciprocity last. This explains why Saenz Peña attacked the United States tariff as discriminatory, but also berated the idea of a preferential Pan American trade bloc, which might cut out European commerce.

During this and subsequent speeches Saenz Peña was, in effect, arguing that Argentina should have the pie of an unprotected United States market,[16] while eating Europe's richly frosted cake. Any attempt to set up an American free trade area, he said,

... would be a war of one continent against another—eighteen sovereignties allied to exclude from the life of commerce that same Europe which extends to us her hand, sends us her strong arms, and complements our economic existence, after apportioning to us her civilization.[17]

[15] IAC, *Minutes*, p. 303.

[16] Only a few weeks earlier the United States minister in Buenos Aires had cabled Blaine to tell him that the Argentine government was ready to cooperate fully with the United States in developing their trade. Foreign Minister Zeballos had told the minister so, although he had at the same time expressed grave apprehension over the fact that our actions with regard to foreign commerce fell short of our professions. Pitkin to Blaine, No. 25, Jan. 10, 1890, *Papers Relating to the Foreign Relations of the United States* (Washington, D.C., 1862–), *1890*, p. 1.

[17] IAC, *Minutes*, p. 317.

Saenz Peña was belaboring a corpse. The customs union plan had been defeated before he had begun to speak. His aim was to lay the ghost of reciprocity which now loomed above the corpse. Yet it was obvious that, having praised free trade, Argentina could not successfully deride the proposal to negotiate reciprocal treaties among the American states. Other grounds of attack were needed.

The Argentines found such premises in their frequently used stratagem, which was to declare that the members of the committee on the customs union had exceeded the powers and limits assigned to the conference by its convening law. Undeniably the second point of the act of Congress of May 1888 had specified that the conference should consider the formation of a customs union. But, said Saenz Peña, the committee's reciprocity proposal is not the union which the conference was supposed to study. The meeting has strayed far afield, and Argentina does not intend to join in officious, substitute declarations.[18]

Saenz Peña closed his long oration with a challenge that was immediately picked up and echoed as a rallying cry by Argentines in the decades ahead:

I have terminated my official declaration. Permit me now to make a most personal statement. Let no one see in what I have said anything but fraternal affection for all the nations and governments of this continent . . . I do not lack affection or love for America, but I lack ingratitude or distrust toward Europe. I do not forget that Spain, our mother, is there, and that she watches with earnest rejoicing the development of her ancient domains . . . I do not forget that Italy, our friend, and France, our sister . . . who has just called the world together on the Champs de Mars, are also there.

The nineteenth century has put us in possession of our political rights, and affirmed those which her elder sister brought with her . . . Let the twentieth century, already called by many the century of America, behold our trade with all the nations of the earth free, witnessing the noble duel of untrammeled labor, of which it has been

---

[18] IAC, *Minutes*, pp. 318–320. Saenz Peña also made the perceptive and prophetic comment that reciprocity could also be interpreted to mean not tariff reduction but tariff retaliation. See *ibid.*, p. 322, and Chapter 12, below.

truly said, God measures the ground, equalizes the weapons, and apportions the light.

Let America be for humanity.[19]

Thus did the slogan "America for the Americans," so often imputed to the Yankees, meet its match in the more embracing call, "America for humanity."

The outlook for the success of the Conference was not good, even in the eyes of the optimistic editors of *Export and Finance*, who on February 1 could foresee only indirect commercial benefits from the meeting, and who by March 8 were calling the assembly "disappointing." In Buenos Aires the attitude of the press was more definite. *El Diario* (April 10, 1890) wrote that Europe's fears of the North American customs plan were groundless—Latin America had repudiated the scheme.

Early in the conference, *La Prensa* (Dec. 7, 1889) had said the same thing, going so far as to give to the Argentine delegates the historically inaccurate advice that "they should imitate the conduct of the North Americans at the Panama Congress: attend, but take no part in the deliberations." After this, lofty *La Prensa* ignored the Pan American Conference until its issue of May 29, 1890, when it printed verbatim and without comment Roque Saenz Peña's "America for humanity" speech.

It was *La Nación* that carried on the most important campaign against the Conference and the United States, through the dazzling letters of Martí. On December 19, 1889 the Cuban exile warned the porteños that the independence of Latin America would have to be declared a second time, this time to save it from the United States.

The next day Martí told his Argentine audience that the United States was absolutely in the power of economic corruption; that the North Americans were avid to seize Santo Domingo and Cuba; and that the conference was an outright struggle between the forces of good and evil. Martí also relayed to Buenos Aires anecdotes about the Argentine delegates. One of these concerned a conversation between Henderson and Quintana, in which the former censured the latter for his absence from the opening session of the conference. To this

---

[19] IAC, *Minutes*, pp. 323–324.

Quintana replied coldly: "I have been where my duty ordered me, and where it appeared to me better to be." Another story involved a Colombian delegate who did not know whether the acts of the conference should be called "agreements" or "decisions." Quintana settled the matter: "It is all the same if they are called 'agreements,' 'decisions,' 'opinions,' or 'semblances' —none of them obligate the delegations that dissent from them." And there was Blaine's compliment to Quintana: "In Boston, Mr. Delegate, people would judge by your appearance that you were the president of a university"—and the reply: "In my country, Mr. Secretary, everyone has the same appearance."[20]

On May 22, 1890 the editors picked up Saenz Peña's cry "America for humanity," praising it as "the concise and graphic slogan of a genuine policy for our America." Blaine, said Mitre's paper, was the puppet of a big, wealthy party, and only the Argentine delegation had preserved the true spirit of Pan Americanism by saving the conference from entering on the economic road mapped out for it. A week later *La Nación* summarized its views on the new order in the hemisphere. Genuine Pan Americanism meant the carrying out of the principles of 1810. Argentina is a nation with a mission—"disinterested Americanism"; it is a country with no Texas in its record— rather there is the renunciation in Paraguay. The term "Pan Americanism" is offensive; it implies protection: the proper word to use is Americanism. And "the Argentine Republic emerges as the principal focus of radiation of Americanism, just as it was the most intense focus of its initiation."[21]

[20] *La Nación*, Jan. 24, 1890.

The writer has been told by a grandson of Quintana that when Mr. Blaine mentioned admiringly a pearl stickpin that the Argentine delegate was wearing, Don Manuel removed it and presented it to the Secretary of State.

[21] *La Nación*, May 29, 1890.

The foreign language papers in Buenos Aires took a dim view of the proceedings in Washington. The *Standard* wrote on March 20, 1890 that "British capital constitutes the foundation of almost the entire trade and industry in the Spanish American republics, and it is preposterous to dream of dethroning for many years to come the influence thereby acquired by Great Britain." The Argentine delegates to the conference were advised that "the sooner they returned to their own country, the better."

Le Courrier (Jan. 26, 1890) concluded bilingually that "L'impression qui se dégage du Congres de Washington: 'Much ado about nothing.' "

But in Washington, Saenz Peña still had work to do to free the Conference from the American reciprocity plan. By his speech he had cast reciprocity into a limbo with the customs union, beyond consideration by Argentina. He had shown his country with its face turned resolutely, devotedly, to Europe. But no one else had spoken.

Henderson obtained the floor. The oratorical waters rose to new heights. Estee and Flint seconded their leader, while Quintana gave Saenz Peña an occasional respite. Each delegation attacked the arguments, the parliamentary tactics, even the veracity of the statistics employed by the other delegation.[22] Each nation proved to its satisfaction that the other maintained discriminatory tariffs. The debates became increasingly personal. Finally Henderson recalled to the obdurate Argentines the specific statement in the preamble of the convening act to the effect that one of the aims of the assembly was to "encourage reciprocal commercial relations." After reviewing the broad and friendly wording of the United States invitation, the chief of the American delegation bluntly demanded a more courteous phrasing of the terse minority report that Argentina and Chile had submitted.[23]

Saenz Peña answered by rejecting the assertion that the preamble of the act, or the invitation, held any authority over the discussions in the conference. His disclaimer was categorical. "The preamble," he said, "loses all its importance when I quote to the honorable delegates the article in which are clearly set down the subjects which the government of the United States submits to the consideration of this conference." But he terminated his speech by announcing that the Argentine and Chilean delegations had agreed to modify the wording of their report. The minority resolution, he announced, had been altered from, "Resolved, That the proposition of a customs union between the nations of America be rejected," to,

[22] At one point Saenz Peña remarked: "I did not hear without a start the statement by Mr. Henderson when he told us that my figures were mistaken. The honorable delegate has not proved his assertion. This may have been due to his magnanimity, but I am inclined to believe that it was owing to my own accuracy!" See IAC, *Reports*, I, 193.

[23] IAC, *Reports*, I, 158–160.

"Resolved, That the American customs union is considered impracticable." [24]

This did not greatly advance the cause of reciprocity. Henderson returned to the attack, with Romero trying to help him bridge the gap. But Saenz Peña had the best of all comers with his incisive criticisms of United States arguments and his frosty references to positions adopted by several of the American delegates in the heat of the debates. [25]

The conflict over reciprocity was threatening to disrupt the assembly. On April 7 the United States moved to break the deadlock. Mr. Estee presented a motion that the majority report of the committee on the customs union should be put to an immediate vote, since "the discussion now seems to be upon the question which is the better country, Argentina or the United States." [26] The vote was taken on April 10. Twelve nations, including the United States, voted in favor of the recommendation to work for inter-American reciprocity treaties. Argentina, Chile, and Bolivia voted against the proposal. [27]

The dispute was not ended by this vote. No sooner had the majority resolution been voted than Saenz Peña requested a vote on the minority report. It was a clever move. The Argentine representative stated that his reason for demanding this action was the fact that *only* the minority report expressed the views of the conference on the topic assigned to its consideration—the customs union. The majority report, he maintained tenaciously, was invalid because it made an unauthorized recommendation. [28]

The situation was crucial for the United States delegation. To deny that the assembly could lawfully vote on the minority report would only serve to martyr the Argentine delegation and

[24] IAC, *Reports*, I, 160; IAC, *Minutes*, p. 342.

[25] IAC, *Reports*, I, 174, 195–197, 200–205.

[26] IAC, *Reports*, I, 231–232.

[27] The roll call on the vote was as follows: in favor of the reciprocity report: the United States, Nicaragua, Peru, Guatemala, Colombia, Costa Rica, Brazil, Honduras, Mexico, Venezuela, Salvador, and Ecuador; opposed: Argentina, Chile, Bolivia. Paraguay abstained. The delegate from Uruguay had withdrawn from the conference on February 10. The minutes do not account for Haiti's absence from this session. See IAC, *Minutes*, p. 653.

[28] IAC, *Reports*, I, 246–247.

its two associates by denying that freedom of action which the United States had attempted to uphold during the conference. To allow a vote might imperil the small gain toward improving inter-American trade which the United States had so far salvaged from the meeting. To permit a vote on the minority report would not only be equivalent to admitting the Argentine claim that the majority report was invalid, but might possibly lead to an overthrow of the vote just taken.

Blaine attempted to avert another vote by stating that the wish of the minority delegates could best be made evident in the journal by allowing the chair to record them as having voted a minority report, without taking a vote of the conference on the report itself. This by no means satisfied Saenz Peña, whose persistence in demanding a roll call provoked Blaine into the sharply voiced ruling: "The Chair aimed to protect the rights of the minority, but in no deliberative body can the minority coerce the majority. The motion is out of order." To this the Argentine diplomat replied:

It appears to me that when the minority demands a vote of the conference, it makes use of an indisputable right. It has the right to know the opinion of the conference upon those subjects which are confided to it for study, and without reference to the members of the majority or to the nations which they represent. This is a right of . . . equality, which places us all on a level . . . I think, therefore, that there is no objection to the conference expressing an opinion upon the subject of customs union. This is a right of the minority, which has studied the question and desires to know the form in which the conference accepts or rejects it.

I therefore insist that the minority report be voted upon.[29]

This time Blaine acceded to Saenz Peña's demand, perhaps agreeing with his argument, perhaps because he wished to avoid prolonging the stalemate.[30] The voting began on the

[29] IAC, *Reports*, I, 247, 251–253.

[30] Before the roll call began, Henderson and Estee argued against the absurdity of voting on two mutually exclusive resolutions, but the only result was that these gentlemen became further frustrated by the Argentine tactics. Henderson ended up voting against one of his own motions, and Estee commented querulously, "I think we are either all right or all wrong, and I appeal to my colleagues here as to whether we have been talking about something or about nothing for the past month. We have made a tremendous mistake some way." IAC, *Reports*, I, 254–259.

motion to authorize the minority report to be voted upon; this was defeated, eleven to five. Voting this time with Argentina were Chile, Paraguay, Bolivia, and Costa Rica.[31] As a result, the minority report was never brought to the table. The long, angry struggle over reciprocity thus ended in a numerical victory for the United States, but it was a distinctly partial victory for the idea of hemispheric economic cooperation which had been the prime motive behind the conference.

The Conference came to an end on April 19, 1890 with a brief speech by Blaine in which he told the departing delegates, "The extent and value of all that has been worthily achieved by your conference cannot be measured today. Time will define and heighten the estimate of your work; experience will confirm our present faith; final results will be your vindication and your triumph."[32]

Argentina emerged from the First Pan American Conference into a new decade, during which her beliefs and strength were to be severely tested. But in the decade that had just ended, and in the assembly that marked its close, the rulers of Argentina—the Generation of Eighty—had responded to serious challenges, internal and external. They had made their land strong, establishing peace and plenty where they found fratricidal strife and impoverishment. They had developed a foreign policy centered upon close relations with Europe at every level of national life, and they successfully defended this policy in Washington against the first assertion by the United States of its own primacy in inter-American affairs—so successfully that in 1890 Argentina, and not the United States, stood as the

[31] IAC, *Reports* I, 261.
[32] IAC, *Minutes*, pp. 856–857, April 19, 1890.

Blaine also invited the delegates, in the name of President Harrison, to embark upon a trip through the Southern states similar to their excursion through the East and Midwest. According to José Martí the trip was a failure, only two out of eighteen delegations starting out from Washington. The excursion train was called back from Richmond. See *La Nación*, June 19, 1890. Martí also told his readers in Buenos Aires that after the conference had ended the Latin American delegates gathered in the Shoreham to toast "the heroes of the day," Quintana and Saenz Peña—"unflinching defenders of the rights of the oppressed." To this Quintana supposedly replied, "We of America are but a single people." See *ibid.*, June 15, 1890.

champion of "America"—indeed, of all mankind—in the eyes of Latin Americans. [33] The Argentine leaders made the form of the Pan American Union not a bloc, but an axis. The western hemisphere had a south as well as a north pole.

The primitive land and its capital city by the great river that Poinsett and Rodney had visited seventy-five years earlier had traveled far on the paths of progress and liberalism—farthest of all in the ten short years beginning in that bloody June of 1880. Now their land and their trade, their blood and their untarnished sovereignty told the people of Argentina that what they had always believed was in fact true—God, and the future, were Argentine.

[33] See Saenz Peña's proud report to the Argentine foreign minister in which he writes: "Argentine policy needs no more defense than its revelation." Saenz Peña to José María Astigueta, June 25, 1890, *Memoria, 1890–1891*, p. 23.

12

The Not-So-Gay Nineties

As the Pan American Conference ended in Washington, events in Buenos Aires were moving speedily toward disaster. Ten years of speculation and political "peace" had aroused and united against the government old heroes such as Mitre and Bernardo de Irigoyen and new spokesmen of the growing middle class such as Del Valle and Alem. Students and merchants, lawyers and laborers found common cause against the Juárez regime as it struggled to bail out the ship of state by opening wider the inflationary intakes. The price of gold soared. European credit dried up. On April 13, Juárez's cabinet resigned; that same day a group called the Unión Cívica was organized to win honest elections. The economic position of the administration was so desperate that it requested the government of the United States to discuss a silver loan and a "metallic alliance." [1] On July 26 fighting began in the streets of Buenos Aires. Juárez resigned on August 6.

The king was dead, but it was a case of "long live the king." The oligarchy, led by Roca and Pellegrini, rallied and defeated the revolutionists militarily, but these leaders decided that it was necessary to replace Juárez. Vice President Pellegrini assumed the executive power. His first act was to face the English bankers. From Argentina's financial wreckage Pellegrini ferreted every peso, and he sent them all to England to service Argentina's debts. Pellegrini's acts during his time in office from August 1890 to October 1892 did not immediately restore prosperity to Argentina, nor save the partnership of Baring Brothers and

---

[1] Pitkin to Blaine, July 13, 1890, National Archives, Dept. of State, American States, U.S. Legation, Argentina, Diplomatic Despatches, Vol. 28, unnumbered confidential cipher telegram.

Company which succumbed to financial asphyxiation, choked to death by Argentine bonds, but he salvaged some regard in Europe for Argentina's credit. A syndicate supported by the Bank of England arranged a consolidated three-year moratorium loan to Argentina. Security for payment of the new bonds was to derive from a lien upon Argentine customs revenues—a stipulation little spoken of at the time, or since, in Argentina. Even Pellegrini momentarily backed away from this deep commitment and did something which showed the strain he was under. He too turned to the United States for help. In June 1891, after a year during which the economy had worsened rather than improved, the president spoke privately to the United States minister in Argentina about interesting American financiers in establishing a bank in Buenos Aires. Minister Pitkin reported to Washington that "European and especially English capitalists were ready to give succor, but the President preferred to treat with our capitalists and to employ silver."

Pellegrini appeared to be serious about this proposal: the Argentine government paid for the United States minister's cable! Pitkin was excited. There is money to be made in Argentina, he pointed out; American "capitalists may command their own terms" should the plan go through. The "people are alienated from England to a notable degree" and look to the "Great Republic," he continued. The Department of State's current efforts to expand trade with Latin America would be served, Pitkin cabled, and a bank would also be a "staunchion" [*sic*] for a United States steamship line. [2] But these opportunities, for what they may have been worth, did not materialize. Argentina struggled through its difficulties with sterling rather than with dollars. [3]

A more drastic threat of foreign economic intervention than a customs lien may have hovered over Argentina. Miguel Cané wrote to Roque Saenz Peña from Paris in October 1891 (a letter which he immediately turned over to Foreign Minister Zeballos), warning that the British government was considering

---

[2] Pitkin to Blaine, June 3, 1891, Despatches, Vol. 29, No. 132.
[3] Harold E. Peters, *The Foreign Debt of the Argentine Republic* (Baltimore, 1934), pp. 42–47.

the creation of a financial commission to take charge of Argentina's revenues. This bitter end to Argentine sovereignty could be averted, Cané wrote with passion, only if Argentina met all its obligations, even though to do so meant to sink the nation in poverty. Cané's fears also proved groundless, for, as Zeballos tactfully expressed it many years later when he published his friend's letter in his important periodical, the *Revista de Derecho, Historia y Letras*, "the government adopted the opportune diplomatic and financial means to pacify the aroused creditors of Argentina."[4]

Creditors were not the only persons disturbed by the economic hurricane sweeping over the nation. There were plenty of customers for the free steamship passages which the Brazilian government offered to those who would emigrate from Argentina to Brazil.[5] Over a period of several years Argentina's net immigration barely equaled emigration. All public works projects except construction of the port of Buenos Aires were canceled, as were government-backed railroad and land-colonization concessions. The country lay paralyzed. At the height of the boom in 1889 total foreign trade had amounted to 254,719,239 gold pesos; in 1891 it fell to 170,426,780 gold pesos.[6]

But crops were sown; and they grew; and Europe bought. As the nineties wore on, whether because of measures of retrenchment, or fidelity to debt payments so far as was possible, or the momentum provided by Europe's demand for food, Argentina slowly moved onto steadier ground. The annual average value of trade for 1892–1897 was 205 million gold pesos. In 1898 trade was valued at 241,258,358 gold pesos. By 1899 another era of prosperity seemed at hand: total foreign trade was valued at 301,768,202 gold pesos.[7]

Of this trade, the amount exchanged between Argentina and the United States was as follows: 1889, $14,748,474; 1891,

---

[4] *Revista de Derecho, Historia y Letras*, año VIII, tomo 22, Oct. 1905, 519–521.

[5] Baker's report, Nov. 17, 1890, *U.S. Consular Reports*, No. 124, January 1891, p. 40.

[6] Baker's reports form perhaps the best account available in English of the great Argentine depression. See *U.S. Consular Reports*, No. 124, January 1891, pp. 37–85; No. 138, March 1892, pp. 385–390, 427–432; No. 151, April 1893, pp. 481–562.

[7] Ernesto Tornquist and Co., Ltd., *The Economic Development of the Argentine Republic in the Last Fifty Years* (Buenos Aires, 1919), p. 140.

$8,796,579; yearly average, 1892–1897, $11,905,221; 1898 $12,344,949; 1899, $14,676,071.[8] Among the products exported to the United States were hides, wool, and quebracho, a wood from which tannic acid is derived; the United States sent Argentina principally agricultural machinery, lumber, and kerosene.

Trade between the two nations in the nineties was thus relatively modest—relative to Great Britain and Europe—as it had been in the eighties, although absolutely somewhat greater. The fact was that Argentina and the United States continued to have larger interests elsewhere. Yet they did not neglect each other. Stimulated by the richness of the other's market, a vision which the new Pan American movement had at least done nothing to discourage, a commercial and political sparring match took place in this decade which mirrored the economic attitudes of the two nations and added the next chapter to the lengthening history of their often uneasy relationship.

Reciprocity was the issue—reciprocity, wool, and the tariff of the United States. In the nineties in the United States it happened that wool was a key or test commodity in the struggle over tariff legislation. It happened also that wool was the chief export of the Argentine Republic, but not to the United States.

Reciprocity was the other side of the coin of protection, but it was a side that few Republican leaders cared to look on. Blaine was aware of this long before most Americans, just as he had been concerned in the previous decade with Pan Americanism as a way to larger markets for United States products. In the early nineties he sought to combine these factors in a curious manner into an economic foreign policy, attempting to secure a measure of free trade through a protective tariff bill.

The time was ripe. Blaine was fresh from the Pan American Conference; congress was debating new tariff legislation. Had not the majority report of the Pan American Conference committee on the customs union urged the gradual extension of free trade through reciprocity treaties? Blaine put the two together. In a letter to President Harrison on June 4, 1890, accompanying his report on the International American Conference just ended, the secretary of state emphasized the debility

[8] *Statistical Abstract of the United States, 1906* (Washington, 1907), p. 217.

of our trade and shipping with Latin America. He urged the president to recommend to congress a system of reciprocity which amounted to a free exchange of the principal exports of the United States and Latin America. Blaine also took pains to single out in this letter the fact that Argentina had not joined the other American states at the conference in recommending the negotiation of reciprocity treaties, "for the reason that the attitude of our Congress at that time was not such as to encourage them to expect favorable concessions from the United States." [9]

Harrison endorsed Blaine's ideas in a modified form in his message to congress, adding the claim that except for wool, every important article exported from Latin America to the United States entered duty free. [10]

Blaine had a fight on his hands now, but he received support from some old associates in the Pan American cause. Early in August, Charles Flint wrote to William E. Curtis, recently appointed Director of the Bureau of American Republics, describing the publicity which he and other New York merchants were undertaking on behalf of reciprocity, Flint alone having sent out more than 2,000 letters. [11] A surge of requests for Latin American trade information swept into the State Department. [12] At the same time, congress was being made aware of another aspect of Latin America through a bill for the incorporation of an International American Bank, an idea that had also stemmed from the First Pan American Conference, and from a letter of Blaine's to Harrison on May 27, 1890 in which the secretary pointed out that England and Europe controlled the financial transactions of the United States in Latin America.

Congress took no action on the bank (of which all the United States delegates to the First Pan American Conference were to

[9] United States Tariff Commission, *Reciprocity and Commercial Treaties* (Washington D.C., 1919), p. 145.

[10] *Reciprocity*, p. 146.

[11] National Archives, Records Relating to International Conferences, Dept. of State Accession No. 161, First International American Conference, No. 32, Envelope No. 2.

[12] Records Relating to International Conferences, Envelopes numbered 2, 3, 4, 5, 10, 15.

become concessionaires),[13] but Blaine did succeed in persuading congress to incorporate reciprocity into the McKinley Tariff Act. This was no small achievement if one considers that, when "Czar" Reed, powerful speaker of the house, was questioned about his views on reciprocity, he growled, "Reciprocity? What in hell is reciprocity?"[14]

Blaine's reciprocity was of a peculiar type; it was retaliatory. Under the McKinley Act, foreign tariff concessions on United States goods were to be gained, it was hoped, by threatening to impose duties on Argentine shipments to the United States. This was not true of all products, for under the "tropical reciprocity" provision of the act certain items entered duty free— sugar, coffee, tea, hides, and molasses. Argentina's largest export to the United States was hides. As it had been for twenty years, this product continued untaxed. Wool was Argentina's second largest export to the United States. The McKinley Act raised the duty on wool to new levels, despite the fact that carpet wool, the principal type of Argentina's greasy wool, was not grown in the United States.[15]

Treaties were negotiated under the retaliatory provisions of the act with several Latin American states, including Brazil. On January 3, 1891, Blaine invited Argentine Minister Quesada's attention to the subject of reciprocity. Nothing was heard from the Argentine representative, but not because he did not hear from his government. In May he was instructed by his foreign office that "the attitude of the government is not favorably inclined to that reciprocity which it appears [the United States] seeks so eagerly." Quesada was told to call the attention of the United States government to the freedom of

[13] The House Committee on Banking and Currency reported favorably on the bank on June 26, 1890, but the bill did not come to a vote on the floor. House of Representatives, 51st Congress, 1st Session, *Report No. 2561*, Ser. No. 2814. Introduced in the next Congress, the bill again disappeared. House of Representatives, 52nd Congress, 1st Session, Report No. 985, Ser. No. 3045.

[14] Charles R. Flint, *Memories of an Active Life: Men, and Ships, and Sealing-Wax* (London, 1923), p. 177.

[15] Chester W. Wright, *Wool-Growing and the Tariff; a Study in the Economic History of the United States* (Cambridge, Mass., 1910), pp. 97, n. 2, 104–105, 217–222; F. W. Taussig, *The Tariff History of the United States* (7th ed.; New York and London, 1923), pp. 258–259.

access of United States products into Argentina compared to the prohibitory United States duties on such Argentine goods as wool.[16]

By August 1891 the Department of State was impatient. The United States minister in Buenos Aires was informed that the time was approaching when the president must impose duties upon imports from countries which had no reciprocal trade agreement with the United States. In the case of Argentina the situation was clear, the instruction continued, because so many of Argentina's products entered the United States duty free. The Department added, perhaps to coat the pill, that the United States government proposed to extend liberal encouragement to the establishment of a line of first-class steamers between New York and Buenos Aires.[17]

Minister Pitkin went to the foreign office and applied the stick of a threatened one and one-half cent per pound duty on Argentine hides entering the United States, and he dangled the carrot of the steamers. Foreign Minister Costa told him that Argentina's main objection to a reciprocity agreement with the United States was fear of reprisal by European nations under the most-favored-nation clauses of their treaties with Argentina. There the matter stood.[18]

Whatever the outlook for United States commercial aspirations in Argentina, it was further dimmed when Estanislao S. Zeballos succeeded Costa as foreign minister in October 1891. Zeballos liked the United States, especially in his later years, and knew more about the northern republic than most of his countrymen. But he loved Argentina. He possessed perhaps the sharpest and most active pen and the hottest temper in a land where these traits are not uncommon. He also spoke with double authority; he was president of the powerful Sociedad Rural at the same time that he was foreign minister.

---

[16] *Memoria de Relaciones Exteriores presentada al honorable Congreso Nacional, 1890–1891* (Buenos Aires, 1891), pp. 209–219.

[17] Wharton to Pitkin, Aug. 3, 1891, National Archives, Dept. of State, American States, Argentina, Diplomatic Instructions, Vol. 16.

[18] República Argentina, Ministerio de Relaciones Exteriores, *Reciprocidad comercial: negociaciones entre Estados Unidos y la República Argentina* (Buenos Aires, 1892), pp. 3–5, 9; Pitkin to Blaine, Oct. 7, 1891, Despatches, Vol. 29, No. 156.

Zeballos set about putting the United States aright on reciprocity. First he let Pitkin know that fear of estranging Europe was the reason why Argentina was "moving slowly" on reciprocity.[19] Then he dispatched a masterful note to the United States government in which he reviewed historic and current difficulties in the economic relations of the two nations. The political and economic drawing apart of Argentina and the United States began in 1867, the foreign minister wrote, with the sanction of the system of protection by the latter. He accused Americans of being "heedless" of the Argentine market. Then came his counters to the retaliation threat: Argentina might tax lumber imports from the United States or go further and denounce the friendship and commerce treaties of 1853. However, Zeballos continued more softly, Argentina might make concessions on United States imports if the United States retained hides on the free list and removed the duty on Argentine wool.[20]

In conversations with the United States minister, Zeballos went about again on the European tack. He showed Pitkin "confidential diplomatic correspondence" demonstrating that England and Germany had proposed to France intervention to appropriate Argentine customs revenues, and he said that such action might be taken should Argentina sign a reciprocity treaty with the United States.[21] He assured Pitkin that he and the Argentine president favored reciprocity but that the problem had to be handled carefully because of "the restive sense among Argentines that the United States had exhibited an indisposition for intercourse with them." Following another line, the foreign minister told the United States representative that "France, Germany, and England have taken financial possession of the Republic" and that Argentina wished to use the United States to "free herself from Europe."[22] As if to give evidence of his friendship, although in another connection, Zeballos a few days later, in response to hints from Blaine, offered the United States moral support in the latter's difficulties

---

[19] Pitkin to Blaine, Dec. 5, 1891, Despatches, Vol. 29, No. 164.
[20] *Reciprocidad comercial*, pp. 30, 37–39.
[21] Pitkin to Blaine, Jan. 17, 1892, Despatches, Vol. 29.
[22] Pitkin to Blaine, Jan. 20, 1892, Despatches, Vol. 29, No. 177.

with Chile, making a categorical promise to supply cattle and other goods to the United States at Antofagasta in six days, presumably meaning in the event of war between the northern and southern republics.[23]

Chile was one affair, trade with the United States another. Wool was the key to the dispute and Zeballos did not vary from his insistence that the United States remove its wool duty as a step toward reciprocity. He finally stated flatly to the United States emissary that the issue would be carried no further until the Americans did something about wool.[24]

The dispute grew bitter. The United States minister reported to Washington that his efforts for reciprocity were quickly made known to the English, French, German, and Italian ministers by the foreign office, and that these gentlemen were employing "threats" to combat the negotiation. The Argentine government stated that it would not permit extradition of a United States fugitive if that country's attitude toward reciprocity did not change. Blaine again repeated his warning that the United States would retaliate against Argentine hides. Meanwhile, France had no difficulty securing a favorable trade agreement with Argentina.[25]

In the end the United States obtained no new trade agreement with the recalcitrant Argentines. Nor were penalties invoked against Argentina, although retaliation was applied to other Latin American nations under the McKinley Tariff. Perhaps the reason was that later stated by a spokesman of the administration when he explained at a congressional hearing in Washington, that the president did not believe Argentine duties on United States goods were unreasonable.[26]

[23] Blaine to Pitkin, Nov. 4, 1891, Instructions, Vol. 16; Pitkin to Blaine, Jan. 30, 1892, Despatches, Vol. 29; Blaine to Pitkin, Feb. 1, 1892, Instructions, Vol. 17.

[24] *Reciprocidad comercial*, pp. 41–57, 59; Pitkin to Blaine, Feb. 20, 1892, Despatches, Vol. 30, No. 183.

[25] Pitkin to Blaine, May 30, 1892, Despatches, Vol. 30, No. 199; Pitkin to Zeballos, May 30, 1892, Despatches, Vol. 30; Fishback to Foster, Aug. 23, 1892, Despatches, Vol. 30, No. 211; Blaine to Pitkin, March 30, 1892, Instructions, Vol. 17, No. 176; Blaine to Pitkin, April 17, 1892, Instructions, Vol. 17, No. 179.

[26] House of Representatives, 54th Congress, 1st Session, Report No. 2263, Vol. 10, *Report of the Committee on Ways and Means Concerning Reciprocity and Commerce*, Appendix B, "Trade with the Argentine Republic and Uruguay," p. 79.

The estancieros who provided Argentina's wool and hides—
and foreign ministers—continued to watch with interest the
changing fortunes of the political parties in the United States.
When the new Cleveland administration took office, the Argentine minister was quick to mention the blessing free wool would
be for the commerce of both lands, since it would also encourage
Argentina to lower her duties. [27] (Consul Baker had long since
pointed out that free Argentine wool in the United States would
not necessarily mean a United States trade bonanza in Argentina. England, he noted, purchased little Argentine wool, yet
dominated the latter's imports. [28])

As the Democratic tariff bill, the Wilson Bill, moved through
congress in 1894, the Argentine foreign minister called on
United States Minister William Buchanan in Buenos Aires to
express the satisfaction of President Luis Saenz Peña and his
administration over the passage of free wool by the United
States Senate, and to state Argentina's willingness to make concessions in return. [29] (President Saenz Peña's son had proclaimed
at the First Pan American Conference that he "did not know
the key to Argentina's commerce.")

The Tariff Act of 1894 put an end to reciprocity and removed
the wool duty. Prior to the passage of the act the State Department failed to undertake the negotiation of trade concessions
with Argentina. After the act passed the United States received
none. [30] Subsequent overtures for tariff reductions were met by
the Argentine foreign minister's "coolly" informing the American minister that the Argentine government did not consider
itself under any obligation to the United States because of the

[27] *Report of the Committee on Ways and Means,* p. 79.

[28] Baker's report, Dec. 22, 1889, *U.S. Consular Reports,* No. 115, April 1890,
pp. 587–588.

[29] Buchanan to Gresham, June 20, 1894, *Foreign Relations, 1894,* No. 28, pp. 4–5;
Zeballos to Gresham, July 30, 1894, *Foreign Relations, 1894,* pp. 5–6.

[30] While the Wilson Bill was in congress, Argentine Foreign Minister Zeballos
stated in a diplomatic paper that crude petroleum imports had been placed on the
Argentine free list because the House Ways and Means Committee had approved
free wool. See Zeballos to Gresham, Jan. 30, 1894, *Foreign Relations, 1894,* pp. 3–4.
When the United States minister in Buenos Aires learned of this statement he
termed it a false concession. No United States crude petroleum had entered Argentina in the past or was likely to enter in the future. See Buchanan to Gresham,
Oct. 1, 1894, *Foreign Relations, 1894,* No. 59, pp. 12–13.

removal of the wool duty.[31] The Argentine attitude may have been based on the belief that United States goods were already generously treated, and the fact that 75 per cent of the government's revenues derived from customs duties.[32]

Argentine exports to the United States benefited under the 1894 act. Their value increased from $3,499,030 in 1894 to $7,675,270 in 1895, largely because of heavier wool purchases by the United States, which imported 6,129 tons from Argentina in 1894 and 12,187 tons the following year.[33] United States trade, on the other hand, made no great strides in Argentina. That country's total imports in 1894 were worth $89,478,660. Of this amount 38 per cent came from Great Britain, 22 per cent from France, 12 per cent from Germany, 8 per cent from Belgium, and less than 6 per cent from the United States. Furthermore, Argentina was becoming a strong competitor of the United States in Europe's grain markets.[34]

Once more, however, the cold winds of protection returned to chill the Argentine representatives in Washington even before the Republican victory of 1896, but their protests were of no avail either before or after McKinley's victory.[35] The Tariff Act of 1897—the Dingley Tariff—not only reimposed duties on wool but raised them to new heights, and placed hides under the tariff, dutiable for the first time in twenty-five years. Reciprocity provisions were also written into the law.

As a result of the new tariff, and just at the time when the United States minister had come to believe that his country was getting a firmer foothold in the Argentine economy, a spirit of retaliation invaded the Argentine commercial community and

[31] *Report of the Committee on Ways and Means*, p. 80; Buchanan to Gresham, Oct. 5, 1894, *Foreign Relations, 1894*, No. 63, pp. 14–17; Buchanan to Gresham, Nov. 19, 1894, *Foreign Relations, 1895*, Part I, pp. 3–4.

[32] Buchanan to Gresham, Aug. 13, 1894, *Foreign Relations, 1894*, No. 49, pp. 7–8.

[33] Buchanan's report, June 15, 1897, *U.S. Consular Reports*, No. 206, November 1897, p. 413.

[34] *Report of the Committee on Ways and Means*, pp. 84–86.

[35] *Memoria de Relaciones Exteriores, 1895–96*, pp. 10–15; *Report of the Committee on Ways and Means*, pp. 91–94; Domínguez to Olney, Dec. 26, 1895, *Foreign Relations, 1895*, Part I, No. 19, pp. 4–5; Martín García Merou to Sherman, May 1, 1897, National Archives, Dept. of State Records, American Affairs, Diplomatic Notes Exchanged Between the Argentine and United States Governments, Vol. 4.

was reflected in congress. The Sociedad Rural, perhaps the most influential body in the country after the government itself, and staunchly free trade at home and abroad, protested officially to the Argentine government against the United States tariff duties as they affected Argentine exports. The government in turn protested to the United States.[36] Higher duties on goods such as lumber and agricultural machinery which were imported principally from the United States were prepared for the Argentine congress by the Uriburu administration. The popular United States Minister Buchanan worked hard with— or on—friendly cabinet officers and key congressmen to minimize the new schedules.[37]

An issue of wider implication was raised by the tariff controversy. Leading Argentine writers on economic matters began to question the traditional free trade position of the liberal oligarchy. Much criticism was directed at the United States for impairing the flow of commerce; a remedy was seen in abandonment of the most-favored-nation clause in Argentina's trade pacts.[38] In the senate a speech in support of such a motion touched on what was to become for a later generation the most important issue in Argentina. "Reading these treaties," said the senator, "one sees that the Argentine Republic plays the role of a neutralized nation, completely neutralized, so that foreign nations dispute their interests within our territory." Argentina was strong now, the speaker said, and must slip off her handcuffs in order to compete more effectively for Europe's grain and meat markets.[39]

The question of Argentina's economic sovereignty was not brought to decision at this time, but the tariff controversy led to another attempt at a reciprocity agreement between Argen-

[36] Emilio Frers, *Cuestiones agrarias* (2 vols.; Buenos Aires, 1918), II, 119–122; Buchanan to Sherman, Sept. 15, 1897, Despatches, Vol. 35, No. 394.

[37] Buchana to Sherman, Jan. 8, 1898, Despatches, Vol. 35, No. 434.

[38] Alejandro Guesalaga, *Estudio de los tratados de comercio de la República Argentina* (Sucre, Bolivia, 1898), pp. 71–79; Ricardo Pillado, *Política comercial argentina. Contribución a su estudio* (Buenos Aires, 1906), pp. 152–225 (material published earlier); Francisco Seeber, "Supresión de las aduanas," *La Biblioteca: Historia, Ciencias, Letras*, II, Sept. 1896, pp. 39–52.

[39] Congreso Nacional, *Diario de sesiones de la Cámara de Senadores*, Sept. 19, 1896, pp. 39–52.

tina and the United States. The United States had trumps to play with Argentine wool and hides under duty; the Americans also believed that their own products were suffering from high Argentine duties. Each country thought it was being hurt economically.

Trade talks began and lasted more than one year, the Argentines proceeding slowly because of the opposition of manufacturing interest, fear of loss of revenue, and the danger of European retaliation. Finally a treaty was worked out that provided for a 20 per cent reduction of the Dingley rates on sugar (a new Argentine export), wool, and hides, in return for Argentine reductions on a number of products imported from the United States, and modification of the *aforo*, an inadequate system of customs values based on the final sale price of an imported article.[40]

The agreement, one of the series known as the Kasson Treaties, was signed in Buenos Aires in July 1899 by Minister Buchanan and Foreign Minister Alcorta. It went to the United States Senate Committee on Foreign Relations. In May 1901 a supplementary convention was signed extending the period for ratification of the treaty an additional eighteen months. The Argentine government at first balked at the extension, unhappy over the delay. They would have been more unhappy had they known that Secretary of State John Hay, conscious of the power of American wool growers, had told the United States representative in Buenos Aires that the treaty would have to be held up in Washington pending a more favorable response in the United States.[41] That response never came. When it became known in Argentina that the committee on foreign relations had repeatedly failed to report out the agreement, the reaction was one of distaste but not of surprise.[42] The Argentines had long anticipated such inaction. Nothing more was heard of the treaty.

[40] *Reciprocity and Commercial Treaties*, p. 219; J. L. Laughlin and H. P. Willis, *Reciprocity* (New York, 1903), p. 313, n. 1; Buchanan to Hay, Dec. 27, 1898, Despatches, Vol. 35, No. 592; Buchanan to Hay, Jan. 18, 1899, Despatches, Vol. 35, No. 614.

[41] Lord to Hay, March 3, 1900, Despatches, Vol. 39, No. 4; Hay to Lord, March 26, 1900, Instructions, Vol. 17, unnumbered, confidential.

[42] Lord to Hay, May 3, 1902, Despatches, Vol. 40, No. 182.

Free hides were not to appear again in the United States until 1909, free wool not until 1915.

If United States economic diplomacy in dealing with Argentina in the nineties proved ineffective or worse, our private business methods were also less than adequate. Consul Baker was no longer a voice alone; all our representatives in Argentina joined in telling of United States neglect of the richest market in Latin America. The secretary of the legation testified in Washington that the United States was losing business by insisting on cash in New York whereas German and English houses extended six to nine months' credit. Our agents, usually not United States citizens, were unable to compete with English and German representatives backed by their banks and branches. The attitude of the Argentine people toward the United States is one of indifference, this observer continued, because we have been indifferent to them, not even packing our goods properly. [43]

Consul Baker maintained his barrage of reports until 1897, when a fatal accident ended his quarter-century of service. His refrain was unaltered: the United States must match Europe's facilities—banks, branches, steamers—and institute a more generous tariff. Germany's trade had multiplied fourfold between 1880 and 1894, he claimed, because she had developed these instruments.

There was light in Baker's gloom. In 1893 three steamship lines opened a modest service between New York and Buenos Aires. They were all English lines, but they did provide direct communication. In 1896 a group of businessmen representing the National Association of Manufacturers visited Argentina and was cordially entertained by Argentine leaders. Baker regarded this as a potential reward for his years of appeals for attention to Argentina. In an article published in 1897, Argentina's best-known economist called for the development of United States shipping and banks in his country, while García Merou, the pro-United States representative of Argentina in Washington, surveyed for his government the impediments to trade between the two countries and came up with the same old

[43] *Report of the Committee on Ways and Means*, pp. 95–101.

list, emphasizing also the competitive nature of the economies and the harm done by protectionism. [44]

Less realistic and perhaps therefore more optimistic than either Baker or García Merou was the United States consul in Córdoba, six hundred miles inland from Buenos Aires, who had vision and, possibly, a taste for puns. Wrote Consul Thorne: "The capitalists of the United States could easily control the commerce and friendship of all South America by taking in hand the completion of the few thousand miles of railway still needed to join New York and Buenos Aires. The ports at present are hopelessly given over to the Europeans, but this inside track would be exclusively our own." [45] Thorne clearly had not heard of the Pan American Railway Commission, then attempting precisely this feat.

The consul in the growing city of Rosario, up-river from Buenos Aires and destined one day to be the greatest grain-shipping port in the world, also pointed out what United States businessmen must do to get ahead. Their ignorance of and assumed superiority over the Argentines would have to be modified. The Germans were model businessmen; they were thorough in satisfying their customers, worked for a moderate profit, and gave long credit. The consul did note, however, that there was an increasing acceptance of such United States products as tools and cotton goods. [46]

Minister Buchanan added a new note by complaining that excessive freight rates, resulting from monopolistic rate-fixing by the shipping companies operating between New York and

[44] Baker's reports, *U.S. Consular Reports*, Nov. 17, 1890, No. 124, January 1891, p. 70; *ibid.*, Dec. 26, 1892, No. 151, April 1893, pp. 541–542; *ibid.*, Jan. 24, 1896, No. 197, April 1896, p. 494; *ibid.*, No. 185, February 1896, pp. 255–256; *ibid.*, Aug. 18, 1896, No. 194, November 1896, pp. 465–467; *Special Consular Reports* (Nos. 1–71, Washington, 1890–1915), Vol. VI, *1891–1892*, Nov. 26, 1890, pp. 18–20; *Report on the Commercial Relations of the United States with All Foreign Nations* (Washington, 1856–), *1894–1895*, I, Dec. 29, 1894, pp. 435–436; *ibid.*, *1895–1896*, I, pp. 624–625; Buchanan to Olney, Oct. 30, 1895, Despatches, Vol. 32, No. 68; García Merou to Olney, Sept. 22, 1896, *Foreign Relations*, p. 1; Carlos Lix Klett, *Estudios sobre producción, comercio, finanzas é intereses generales de la República Argentina* (2 vols.; Buenos Aires, 1900), II, 778; *Memoria de Relaciones Exteriores, 1897*, note, pp. 250–330.

[45] Thorne report, Oct. 1, 1897, *Commerical Relations, 1896–1897*, I, 786.

[46] *Commercial Relations, 1897*, March 1897, p. 98; report by J. M. Ayres, Nov. 1, 1901, *ibid.*, 1901, pp. 605–607.

Buenos Aires (Lamport and Holt, Norton, and Knott's Prince Line), prevented a larger trade. He urged establishment of a United States merchant marine. But in a less public place Buchanan pointed to the lack of adequate return cargos to the United States as an explanation of high freight rates.[47]

Buchanan also took heart as the century drew to a close. The British were complaining a bit about United States competition. So too were the Germans. The volume of exports in the last year of the decade was encouraging.[48] Perhaps the United States was beginning to improve its economic position despite itself.

Issues other than commercial marked the relations of Argentina and the United States in the years between the First Pan American Conference and the Second in 1901. Two of these issues grew out of the first conference, which, despite its failures, set up a feeble framework for the future and committed the nations of the hemisphere to act together, or at least to talk about acting together.

One project was the Inter-American Railroad, considered by Blaine to be the most important act of material promise taken by the conference. In accordance with the conference resolution an Inter-Continental Railroad Commission was organized, surveys run, volumes published, meetings held—and after thirty-three years of gradually diminishing activity the commission faded away, its task of uniting Argentina and the United States by rail unaccomplished, as it remains today.[49]

But the idea was strong at the outset when the commission assembled for the first time in Washington in December 1890. Blaine was on hand to receive the delegates of nine Latin American states. No Argentine representative was present, Minister Quesada having begged off from appointment by his

[47] *Revista de Derecho, Historia y Letras,* año I, t. 3, June 1899, pp. 491–494; Buchanan report, Jan. 18, 1899, *U.S. Consular Reports,* No. 224, May 1899, pp. 141–143.

[48] Buchanan reports, *U.S. Consular Reports,* No. 227, August 1899, p. 758; May 6, 1899, *ibid.,* No. 228, September 1899, pp. 21–26; *ibid.,* No. 230, November 1899, p. 507.

[49] Blaine to Pitkin, March 25, 1890, Instructions, Vol. 16, No. 516; J. A. Caruso, "The Pan American Railway," *The Hispanic American Historical Review,* 31:608–639 (November 1951).

government in order to depart for his other post in Mexico, where he took his mission to be the formation of a Latin American bulwark against the "pressure of a powerful neighbor."[50]

At the eighth meeting of the commission two Argentine delegates appeared. At the ninth meeting they informed the other members that they would abstain from voting for any appointments to the commission's staff, "the instructions of their government being not to involve the Argentine Republic in any expense." Nevertheless, the Argentines continued to participate in the meetings. They told the assembly that the railroad was planned for the wrong place—it should serve the Atlantic coast and Buenos Aires. They pointed out that Argentina already possessed a good railroad system; consequently, it would "not be equitable that the Argentine Republic contribute toward the expenses of the survey, this country having done its part." After expressing the wish that the noble ideal of the railway might be converted into a splendid reality, Argentina ceased to have anything further to do with the Pan American railway. The fact that the United States also had a good railroad network did not prevent its congress from paying the bill for $120,000 for the expenses of the commission for 1891–1892.[51]

There can be no doubt that the Argentine government was in financial straits after the "crac" of 1890. Perhaps this fact accounts for Argentina's reaction to another and more important outgrowth of the First Pan American Conference,

[50] Vicente G. Quesada, *Recuerdos de mi vida diplomática; misión en México (1891)* (Buenos Aires, 1904), p. 7.

[51] *Intercontinental Railway Commission* . . . (3 vols. in 4; Washington, D.C., 1895–1898), I, 31–34, 37–40, 65–66, 87–90. A more abortive product of the First Pan American Conference than the Railroad Commission was the Inter-American Monetary Commission which convened in Washington in January 1891 under a conference resolution. This body, whose purpose was to establish an international monetary union, was doomed from the outset by financial realities. The Argentine delegates joined in voting the permanent dissolution of the commission in April 1891. See *Minutes of the International American Monetary Commission. Actas de la Comisión Monetaria Internacional Americana* (Washington, 1891). Thomas Jefferson Coolidge, who had been one of the delegates to the First Pan American Conference, apparently remembered that meeting when he was asked by the secretary of state to be chairman of the monetary conference. He wrote: "knowing that it would come to nothing, I respectfully declined getting involved again in a silver argument." T. Jefferson Coolidge, *Autobiography* . . . (Boston, 1902), p. 149.

7

the permanent organization then known as the Bureau of the American Republics, from which has descended today's Pan American Union. The multi-national Bureau was designed to serve as a clearinghouse for commercial information among the Americas. It was placed under the supervision of the secretary of state. The first director of the Bureau was the well-known man-about-Latin America, W. E. Curtis. The Bureau was allowed $36,000 for expenses of the first year, the sum to be pro-rated among the Pan American nations on the population basis, but to be advanced by the United States.[52]

When Argentina's share of the expenses for the first year was not forthcoming, the Department of State instructed the United States minister in Buenos Aires to determine the reason for the default. The answer he received from the foreign office was clear: the Argentine congress had appropriated no funds for the purpose. The United States representative enlarged upon this statement in somewhat inverted English. He reported to Washington that "scant national revenues had been orally made known to this Legation, but in no particular appears a desire to be in active touch with us."[53]

Some years later, Zeballos, who had been foreign minister at the time of the first default, wrote that he had "prevented the participation of the Argentine Republic [in the Bureau] because maintenance of that office brought us nothing, and by mixing our country in the economic policy of the United States aroused suspicions in our relations with . . . Europe."[54]

The United States viewed matters differently. Each year thereafter the subject of Argentina's nonpayment of obligations was raised by the Department of State with the Argentine government on behalf of the Bureau of American Republics. The United States expected Argentina to pay its share of the operating costs of the international organization. For example, Argentina owed $1,462.50 for 1893. (Bolivia, Paraguay,

[52] *International Bureau of the American Republics* (Washington, 1906), p. 9.

[53] Quesada to Blaine, March 1, 1892, Notes, Vol. 4; Pitkin to Foster, Jan. 16, 1893, Despatches, Vol. 30, No. 232.

[54] Estanislao S. Zeballos, "El Congreso Pan-Americano," *Revista de Derecho, Historia y Letras,* año IV, t. 11, Nov. 1901, p. 143.

Nicaragua, and Peru owed lesser amounts, befitting their popula-
tions.) When Argentina failed to pay, the United States government assumed the Argentine debt. But the United States had no
intention of accepting Argentina's default as equivalent to
withdrawal from the Pan American organization. Twelve
months' notice had not been given as called for under the
chartering document. Yet Argentina had no intention of paying.
The Argentine foreign minister stated that, by decree of January 7, 1892, Argentina's subvention to the Bureau had terminated, and he said that the United States knew it. Furthermore,
Alcorta stated, the resolutions taken at the First Pan American
Conference were not binding, and Argentina did not think
highly of the manner in which the Bureau was operating, the
nations comprising it not having control over its organization,
procedures, or publications.[55]

The same requests and the same replies, when there were
replies, continued for two more years. Then John Hay and the
well-disposed Argentine minister, García Merou, conferred.
Argentina returned to the official Pan American fold, agreeing
to resume payments as of July 1, 1898.[56] She had lost nothing
politically or financially. The Bureau was reorganized at this
time, no longer to be, it was hoped, "seemingly an adjunct of
the State Department," as our minister in Argentina put it. A
permanent executive committee composed of the representatives in Washington of five American states, with the Secretary
of State always ex officio one of the five, was created to supervise
the director's operation of the Bureau. The word International
was placed first in the Bureau's name. And in what may have
been one of the earliest demonstrations of United States gratitude to a foreign state which had disowned its freely assumed
obligations, the State Department waived the claims which it

[55] Bureau of the American Republics, *Annual Reports, 1891–* (Washington, D.C.,
1892–), report for 1893, p. 24; Buchanan to Olney, Sept. 2, 1896, Encl. 1, Alcorta
to Buchanan, Aug, 26, 1896, Despatches, Vol. 33, No. 261; Buchanan to Gresham,
Oct. 29, 1894, Despatches, Vol. 31, No. 68; Buchanan to Olney, March 14, 1896,
Despatches, Vol. 31, No. 210; Buchanan to Olney, April 29, 1896, enclosing note
of Alcorta to Buchanan, April 29, 1896, Despatches, Vol. 33, No. 222.

[56] Buchanan to Sherman, May 28, 1897, Despatches, Vol. 33, No. 352; Jones to
Sherman, Feb. 2, 1898, enclosures, Despatches, Vol. 35, No. 453.

had assumed against Argentina for the unpaid subventions that the Treasury of the United States had made good.[57]

Something of the attitude of the leaders of Argentina toward the Pan American system may have been revealed in their treatment of the Bureau of the American Republics; other aspects of their position were shown in the two international incidents which occurred in the hemisphere in this decade. The first was the Venezuelan affair of 1895, in which that country and Great Britain disputed the boundary of British Guiana, and the United States government, in an excess of politics or of nationalism, or both, introduced its hand not only to twist the lion's tail but to pull his teeth. Although the heated verbal tussle between the United States and Britain revolved around an issue—intervention—in which Argentina always professed concern, the Argentines were in general disinterested. Perhaps this was because England was an old and prosperous business associate, or because the Argentines were busy repairing their economic damage, or simply because British Guiana was unimportant and remote. Paul Groussac, the Frenchman who had lived thirty years in Argentina and who had another thirty years of literary leadership before him, found harsh things to say about both England and the United States in his esteemed review, *La Biblioteca*, as one might expect of a man who was at once an Argentine and a Frenchman. *La Nación* (Dec. 19, 20, 1895), as usual friendly toward the United States, tried to smooth over the incident as a proper action under the Monroe Doctrine. *La Prensa* (Dec. 18, 1895) called on Argentines to support Cleveland, reporting an interview with Acting President Roca in which that leader expressed the same opinion and added his view that "unless this attitude is adopted, the time may come when the European nations seek to treat South America as they are treating Africa." But *La Prensa* balanced these sentiments by rejecting, in the same issue, the idea of a Pan American conference which, the Argentine thunderer muttered, might

[57] Buchanan to Hay, Dec. 19, 1898, No. 590, and following letter from Director Frederic Emery of the Bureau of the American Republics to Assistant Secretary of State A. A. Adee, Despatches, Vol. 37; The Archives of the Pan American Union, *Minutes of the Executive Committee of the International Bureau of the American Republics*, I, note facing p. 1; II, p. 117; *International Bureau of American Republics*, pp. 3, 13–16.

degenerate into commercial reciprocity treaties. "Europe respects us," wrote the editors, "because our relations with her are based on fundamental, reciprocal interests."

Even Zeballos, now Argentine minister in Washington, considered the United States stand on Venezuela friendly and reasonable, without tending toward a protectorate;[58] but a yet more influential person, Carlos Pellegrini, expressed fear of the domination of the United States over Latin America (*El Diario*, Dec. 22, 1895).

The second issue of the decade, the Spanish-American War, did not go off quite so quietly in Argentina, nor with such an even division of sentiment. There were more people of Spanish descent in Argentina than in any country in the world outside of Spain. Judging from their reaction, each one was firmly and loudly an enemy of the United States. On the other hand, there were few expressions among the oligarchy of hostility to the United States, or of fondness for Spanish rule in Cuba. Perhaps this was in part due to memories of Argentina's own role in freeing much of South America from Spanish control only two long generations earlier.

There were two prominent figures, however, Roque Saenz Peña and Paul Groussac, who linked love of Spain and hatred of the United States. At a Spanish patriotic rally in Buenos Aires the two men pulled out all the stops of Latin American oratory. Saenz Peña's classic "America for humanity" speech was the keynote. There were allusions to the "gross and greedy screech of Monroe." The United States was pictured as alcoholic and materialistic, Spain as noble and lyric. Furthermore, a third speaker claimed, Americans have ice in their veins, while Spaniards—to them "love lifted the toast of beautiful women, brunette and passionate."

Saenz Peña's own speech was more sober and more significant. The United States, he said, seeks to destroy not only Spanish authority in Cuba, but all native authority. Looking at the Pan American movement he voiced approval of "the failure of the continental bloc aimed at European commerce." With perspicacity he stated that "the doctrine of Monroe pronounced

[58] *Memoria de Relacions Exteriores, 1895*, pp. 84–87.

against intervention, but this pronouncement was made with mental reservations . . . reserving *de facto* American intervention."[59]

The two principal dailies of Buenos Aires were largely silent on the war, perhaps for the reason given by *La Nación* on April 6, 1898, which saw opinion divided, one part going to Spain, one part to Cuba, and one to the United States. On April 22, *La Prensa* cast a fervent vote for the mother country, and on the following day *La Nación* agreed that the United States had imposed war upon Spain. Then Mitre's "tribute of doctrine" returned to working both sides of the street, with a pro-United States article on May 3 by Guglielmo Ferrero and an anti-United States article on May 30 by Max Nordau. The big evening paper *El Diario* was more outspoken. After all, said the editors on August 13, "the Monroe Doctrine is a very respectable thing when applied by the artillerymen of Sampson, and Dewey." But what may have most concerned Argentina about the war, and accounted for much silence and backing and filling of opinion, was shown by *El Economista* (April 27, 1898) in the statement that the business interests of Argentina wanted nothing to do with any war.

The young chargé of the United States legation kept the wires to Washington humming with reports of Spanish activity and Argentine attitudes. It was his opinion that the Argentine government favored the independence of Cuba and abstained from making its position public only because of national political considerations and "jealousy" of the United States.[60] When the United States minister returned to his post he reported some fear among Argentine leaders over United States expansion. But he also reported that the minister of foreign affairs had informed him that the Spanish minister had been requested to restrain the public demonstrations of his compatriots in Argentina. Buchanan also reported that Roca had told him that war would have had to come sooner or later and that in the end

[59] Roque Saenz Peña, Paul Groussac, and José Tarnassi, *España y Estados Unidos, función dada en el Teatro de la Victoria el 2 de Mayo de 1898* . . . (Buenos Aires, 1898).

[60] Jones to Sherman, April 20, 1898, unnumbered telegram, and same to same. April 21, 1898, No. 483, Despatches, Vol. 35.

"Cuba and Puerto Rico would very probably become part of our own country by the logic of events, even against our own wishes."[61]

That the leaders of the oligarchy spoke differently among themselves is brought out by a letter of Pellegrini to Cané, written from Paris. "You have seen now how the United States has treated Spain," the former president wrote. "What fellows! The day when their power exceeds England's, if there is no reaction in the United States, they will end in some madness. A [United States] senator has just said that the Yankee empire will have as its bounds the *aurora borealis* in the north, the equator in the south, the rising sun in the east, and the immensity of the west. Lucky for us they are stopping for the present at the equator."[62]

[61] Buchanan to Day, July 14, 1898, Despatches, Vol. 35, No. 536.
[62] Ltr. of Dec. 18, 1898, *Pellegrini: 1846–1906: Obras* (5 vols.; Buenos Aires, 1941), II, 512.

13

Novecientos and the Second Conference

AT the turn of the century the Argentine oligarchy was confident. Roca was president again (1898–1904), as he had been twenty years earlier. The decade past had been economically troubled, and relations with Chile over the boundary with Argentina were inflamed, but in 1900 the nation was at peace and richer than at any previous time in its history. From 1890 onward, with the exception of 1893, the country exported more than it imported, a reversal of the trade pattern of the past. After 1895 new investment entered, mainly in new fields such as tramways, gas and electric power, and warehouses. Together with that of England, German, French, and Belgian capital played a larger role. At the end of the decade the conversion law was passed, placing the currency on a sound basis. This was one of Pellegrini's contributions to the financial health of the nation, just as another of his creations, the Banco de la Nación Argentina, had brought strength to the banking system eight years earlier, in 1891. By 1901 complete service on the foreign debt had been resumed and Argentina's international credit stood higher than ever before.[1]

But improving economic conditions were accompanied by a deteriorating political situation. The revolution of 1890, for wider political rights and in protest against the economic collapse of the nation, had been defeated by a combination of two factors—the military victory of the government, in which

[1] Ernesto Tornquist and Co., Ltd., *The Economic Development of the Argentine Republic in the Last Fifty Years* (Buenos Aires, 1919), p. 140; John H. Williams, *Argentine International Trade Under Inconvertible Paper Money* (Cambridge, Mass., 1920), pp. 149–152; Harold E. Peters, *The Foreign Debt of the Argentine Republic* (Baltimore, 1934), pp. 33–34; Sixto Bayer, "Pellegrini en las finanzas," *Revista de Ciencias Jurídicas y Sociales*, año XII, 3a. época, núm. 50–51, 1947, pp. 140–163.

Pellegrini and Roca played leading parts, and a series of opposing political moves by the oligarchy which stripped the opposition of the half-success it had gained from the oligarchy's decision (again mainly the work of Roca and Pellegrini) to dispense with the further services of President Juárez.[2] With President Pellegrini standing staunch against any political reform, Roca and Mitre (the latter still supposedly an opposition leader) agreed to arrange for a conservative president for the period 1892–1898. In one of the more subtle political maneuvers of any campaign, the two experienced politicians eliminated what they considered to be the dangerous candidacy of Roque Saenz Peña by thrusting the office upon his aging father, Luis. The son, in filial duty, withdrew from politics. Unfortunately for the oligarchy's hopes for political tranquillity, the Unión Radical staged a violent if unsuccessful revolt in 1893 which, along with the nation's persistent economic malaise, proved too much of a strain upon the capabilities of the elder Saenz Peña and upon the loyalty of his class. He resigned in 1895 and his term was completed by José E. Uriburu, who in turn was succeeded in 1898 by his relative by marriage, the great stabilizer, Roca.

Hard action and soft euphemisms were the weapons of the oligarchs in their fight against mounting social strife. Two of the favorite analogies they employed in defense of limited suffrage compared the electoral privilege with a loaded gun or a valuable watch, neither of which could be entrusted to a child until he had been trained and had matured.[3] Typical also was the verbiage in President Pellegrini's message to congress in the black month of May 1891, when, after more than a year of political and economic upheaval, affairs were worse rather than better. Said the president: "The most complete tranquillity reigns in all the country . . . The local authorities revolve harmoniously in their respective attributes . . . The occasional presence of troops of the line in one or another province meanwhile has served to avoid or prevent sterile and disgraceful

[2] Luis V. Somni, *La revolución del 90* (Buenos Aires, 1948), pp. 177–185, 196, 201–204, 221–234.

[3] Américo Palma, "Democracia argentina," *Revista Nacional*, 2a. sér., t. 15, Jan. 1, 1892, p. 47.

conflicts, yet without depreciation of any liberty . . . The only extraordinary measure that the Executive Power has been obliged to adopt consists in the declaration of the state of siege in the Federal Capital."[4] Of the same nature was President Luis Saenz Peña's explanation of the prolongation of the state of siege after the 1893 revolution: "The state of siege is maintained in the entire republic not so much for fear of a new uprising as to assure the tranquillity of the people."[5]

La Prensa wrote on the last day of Pellegrini's term (Oct. 12, 1892) that he was delivering the republic to his successor in the same condition as he had received it from his predecessor. In the short run this may have been correct. But Pellegrini was no Juárez. His financial acts, unproductive as they seemed at the moment, saved the oligarchy's Argentina for another two decades. Despite opposition, Pellegrini held firm to Europe, except for his brief flirtation with the United States. The consolidated moratorium-loan which he arranged with the Bank of England-Rothschild consortium was for a time violently attacked by persons within as well as outside the president's class, but it was what England wanted and it was the surest route back to international good standing. Without foreign capital and markets the oligarchy could not continue to live in the style to which it had become accustomed in the eighties. Pellegrini knew this: he was not only president of Argentina, he was president of the Unión Provincial, the organization of estancieros of the province of Buenos Aires. Some years after the crash, Pellegrini told with his usual frankness the story of his action in the 1890 crisis. In a speech to the senate he said: "When I became President . . . it was my belief that the credit of the nation was superior to any sacrifice . . . In the midst of the government's financial suffering, when resources to pay even salaries were lacking, I sent the last peso to England to cover the coupons of our debt."[6]

Control of political activity was becoming more difficult than control of the economy. The Unión Cívica Radical, led after

[4] *Pellegrini, 1846–1906: Obras* (5 vols.; Buenos Aires, 1941), IV, 163–164.
[5] Ismael Bucich Escobar, *Historia de los presidentes argentinos* (Buenos Aires, 1934), p. 314.
[6] *Pellegrini*, IV, 76–77.

1895 by Hipólyto Yrigoyen, began its long fight for electoral freedom, mixing tactics of occasional revolt with the strategy of civic non-participation, refusing to enter electoral contests even when permitted. There was the Socialist Party, formed in 1894–1896, tiny but well led. There were anarchists. Strikes, almost unknown before 1890, became increasingly numerous and extensive after that date as the demands of the European immigrants began to find outlets in action. There was violence in the streets and in the basement meeting places where the socialists battled the anarchists and both fought the police and the firemen, the latter carrying Mausers as part of their standard gear. [7]

Despite resistance, the political machinery of the government continued to win victories. Roca gained the presidency easily in 1898. There was little opposition within the governing class to the way affairs were conducted. Only an unusual leader such as E. S. Zeballos raised his voice against his peers. This inhumanly active man was forty-six years old at the turn of the century—a newer, Yankee-type breed of Argentine compared, for instance, to the Europeanized Cané. Zeballos had been foreign minister twice before he was forty, and would hold that office a third time. In addition, he did an enormous amount of writing; ranging from archaeology to United States constitutional law; was editor of *La Prensa* for many years; founded and edited all his life the *Revista de Derecho, Historia y Letras*; and was an estanciero and, from 1888 to 1894, president of the Sociedad Rural. The quiet gray suits in which he habitually dressed and the white carnation boutonniere he sported belied his fiery temper. He minced no words when he wrote, a few weeks after the election of the great Roca: "The national, provincial, and municipal administrations are rotten. Political life does not exist. Organized parties have disappeared. The federal provinces are so only nominally; an unmasked unitarism absorbs and humiliates them." [8]

It would appear that the country was no better off in 1900

[7] Jacinto Oddone, *Gremialismo proletario argentino* (Buenos Aires, 1949), p. 39; Enrique Dickmann, *Recuerdos de un militante socialista* (Buenos Aires, 1949), pp. 62–80, 89–91.

[8] E. S. Zeballos, "Roca," *Revista de Derecho, Historia y Letras*, año I, t. 2, Nov. 1898, p. 162.

than in 1890. Yet social and political antagonisms may look larger to a succeeding generation than they do to the people who live through them. Argentina, as the present century began, entered an era that has gained a name, a title evoking for the upper class nostalgic memories of gas lights and billowing dresses, discreet swims at Mar del Plata and strolls around the shady park in Adrogué where, an hour's carriage drive from the city, the well-to-do could shed some of the formalism of winter society for a picnic, with the men, perhaps, in shirt-sleeves, but not without vest and tie. These things were part of Argentina's *novecientos*—the "nineteen hundreds"—her post-poned gay nineties, her halcyon decade or so before the troubles of the world began to touch her shores.

In 1900, Buenos Aires was cosmopolitan but liked to believe it was criollo. The provinces hoped that they were not. In many ways Argentina was not far removed from 1880. But the people were more conscious of Argentina—the Argentina born around 1880. Nationalism—a new nationalism—was stirring among the mixed millions of immigrants and natives.

A blend of mellow and acerb flavors the era. Zeballos and Groussac were the awesome critics of thought, but there was another who was a critic of action, and more beloved. "Fray Mocho" (José A. Alvarez) was a multi-dialect Mr. Dooley, cheering the porteños with droll stories of gauchos and of immigrants, provoking them to anger or to laughter in his periodical *Caras y Caretas (Faces and Masks)*. In politics the cast was old and experienced. The audience might long for fresh lines, and even for fresh faces, but it acknowledged polished performances. Fray Mocho put it well: "Here in Buenos Aires there's only one gringo and that's Doctor Pellegrini, see? Just like there's only one Don Bartolo [Mitre], and no more Rocas than Julio, whom his friends call 'The Fox' in private, to show that the man can pluck a cock without making him crow, and then make him believe that the feathers will be out in time for Carnival Sunday." [9]

[9] Gastón Federico Tobal, *Evocaciones porteñas* (Buenos Aires, 1947), pp. 233–234; Elvira Aldao de Díaz, *Recuerdos dispersos* (Buenos Aires, 1933), pp. 255–261; Fray Mocho [José S. Alvarez], *Cuentos de Fray Mocho* (Buenos Aires, 1943), p. 89.

In the cafes *truco* was played long and vehemently; in the barrios, or sections of the city away from the center, cockfights were the favorite sport. Sunday was reserved for the horse races. A few negro washerwomen still bustled along the streets with their bundled work balanced on their heads. No one paid them heed; far more interesting to the porteños were the four huge, bejewelled Sengalese who passed through the city on their way inland to labor in the new sugar mills of Tucumán. Racial resentment openly expressed was almost unknown, and foreign names popped up in strange places, such as that of Doctor Daniel Donovan, who was chief of police of Buenos Aires.

Mansions of magnificent proportions were being constructed along Avenida Alvear; the exterior of the city water works was done in imported porcelain tiles; the greatest public mansion of all, the edifice of the National Congress, was rising against the evening sun at the head of the Avenida de Mayo.

Most of the people lived in *conventillos*, oblong human warrens of one or two stories of one-room apartments opening on long, dank patios; a family that was more fortunate moved farther out to a tiny house crowded against other tiny houses, each with a bit of greenery in front, a high wall on each side, and Moorish crenellations all over.

In 1900 the city was big (815,680 persons) and growing, tough and gaudy. Argentina had no extradition treaties and Buenos Aires was a haven for criminals from many lands. Prostitutes patrolled the streets in impressive numbers; in the music halls the tango was beginning to be heard, and knife fights were common. Calle Florida got its first electric lights in 1900; in the same year the last of the conventillos on the street of fashion was closed down, "for reasons of hygiene, safety, and public order." Away from the city, in the *campo*, the peón's life was pretty much as it had always been, hard and dirty. Entertainment was limited to what the crossroads store or the local market day could provide.

The large newspapers and reviews fed the cosmopolitan interests of their readers in Buenos Aires. A typical newspaper page might be given over to a lecture by Rubén Darío, a discussion of what was wrong with the nation's schools, and a treatise, with sketches, of a proposed canal through the Alps. Europe was still the most attractive place in the world to most porteños. If one was of the upper class, he hoped to go there soon again; if one was of the lower classes, he perhaps had just come from there. In Europe an Argentine leader could in one evening banquet with the Duke and Duchess of Clevant at the Palace of the Legion of Honor, hear a recital by Sully Prud-homme, a concert by artists of the Opéra Comique, and mono-logues by Coquelin (Cadet). And what could Buenos Aires, or New York City, for that matter, offer to compare with the pleasure of dining at the Carlton at the height of the season, with the Prince of Wales and his ten guests at the next table?[10]

Sometimes the Argentines heard comments from abroad which they did not enjoy. Cecil Rhodes, for example, told the Yankees to take control of Latin America and give the bar-barians "a white man's government." But more wounding than threats to Argentine self-esteem was neglect. Argentines could not understand that the United States was not following their every act with admiration. Zeballos knew that such was not the case, but still he wrote: "What wounds my *amor propio* is pre-cisely that [the United States] are not preoccupied with us, either much or little . . . The Americans concern themselves with South America with a mortifying, paternal air . . . They consider themselves the natural protectors of these countries."[11]

There were still Argentine leaders who looked to the United States. When Luis María Drago was preparing Argentine rail-road legislation he repeatedly invoked United States precedent, just as the previous generation had done in shaping much of the nation's law.[12] The government itself requested and received an exposition of United States law on anarchism. Articles appeared in leading journals on such subjects as the status of women in the

[10] Carlos Pellegrini to Ernesto Pellegrini, Feb. 27, Dec. 17, 1900, *Pellegrini*, II, 565, 567.

[11] Rhodes in the New York *Herald*, Feb. 12, 1899, quoted in "Los americanos en Sur América," *Revista de Derecho, Historia y Letras*, año I, t. 3, May 1899, p. 452; E. S. Zeballos, "La Puna," *Revista de Derecho, Historia y Letras*, año I, t. 3, June, 1899, pp. 632–639. See also E. S. Zeballos, "Civil Wars in South America," *North American Review*, 159:153 (August 1894).

[12] Luis María Drago, "Los ferrocarriles," *Revista de Derecho, Historia y Letras*, año I, t. 2, Nov. 1898, pp. 79–87.

United States, always a matter of interest to the more patriarchal Argentines.[13]

The *Revista de Derecho, Historia y Letras*, founded by Zeballos at the end of the nineties was, if not pro-American, at least willing to learn from the United States. In contrast was another important journal of the day. The *Revista Nacional* serialized V. G. Quesada's pseudonymous and bitterly anti-United States book, *Los Estados Unidos y la América del Sur*, introducing the first installment with the comment that the time had come to drop "the eternal cliché . . . of 'our brothers of the north.' "

Quesada, a leader of the Argentine aristocracy, had been ambassador to the United States for six years prior to 1891. During part of that period he also served as ambassador to Mexico. He considered it his mission to alert the Mexicans against their neighbor to the north, and wrote that the United States was seeking to annex both Mexico and Canada and to dominate the hemisphere. He claimed that the First Pan American Conference had been convoked to close the markets of Spanish America to European products. He attacked the slums, the divorce rate, and the avarice of the United States, while praising the country's free press, philanthropy, and mechanical efficiency.[14]

In this division of attitude Quesada resembled many Argentines before and since who savagely criticize aspects of United States society, then turn about and admire the elements which are most similar to their own traits or ambitions. Paul Groussac revealed this same outlook when he wrote from Chicago to his friend García Merou that the Americans were barbarians, with a destiny comparable to that of the people who destroyed Rome, but that they were admirable in their energy and material accomplishments.[15]

[13] Despatch no. 93, Argentine legation, Washington, July 30, 1894, reprinted in the *Revista de Derecho, Historia y Letras*, año I, t. 2, Jan. 1899, pp. 449–456, and Feb. 1899, pp. 639–644; Felipe Senillosa, "La crisis social," *Revista de Derecho, Historia y Letras*, año I, t. 3, May 1899, pp. 53–64.

[14] *Revista Nacional*, 2a. sér., t. 16, Oct. 1, 1892, note, pp. 271–272; Domingo de Pantoja [Vicente G. Quesada], *Los Estados y la América del Sur; los Yanquees pintados por sí mismos* (Buenos Aires, 1893), pp. 5, 7.

[15] Paul Groussac to M. García Merou, Sept. 15, 1893, Biblioteca Nacional, 8345–2; Paul Groussac, *Del Plata al Niágara* (Buenos Aires, 1897), p. xiii.

No matter how they regarded the United States, Argentines vigorously assured each other that Argentina was superior to the rest of Latin America. Occasionally this impression was supported by a distinguished North American, as when Secretary of State Gresham remarked that Argentina had a predominant role to play in Latin America in the future, and *La Prensa* (Oct. 16, 1893) expanded the comment in a long editorial which claimed for Argentina "a great civilizing mission in the New World."

Perhaps Argentines emphasized their achievements and their future so resolutely because the rest of the world seemed convinced that it was superior to Latin America, and because the Argentines themselves had reservations about their capacities. It was rare to find an Argentine who stated his country's faults. One who did was Zeballos, who created his *Revista* with the purpose of helping to overcome the lack of justice, the political backwardness, and the tendencies toward easy hatreds, negligence, and the use of force which he believed to be powerful among Argentines and other Latin Americans.[16]

Pride in Argentina was never lacking, but it was often mixed with bitter doubts. One of these doubts concerned the quality of the people, their ethnic composition. The turn of the century saw the beginning of a new national feeling, but it also witnessed an increasing flood of foreigners and this just at the time when the so-called Anglo-Saxons dominated the earth. Was there a connection, Argentines asked themselves, between blood and national achievement, as some Europeans claimed? A member of one important Argentine family made a large reputation as a sociologist with a book in which he laid the blame for Argentine and Latin American evils at the door of the mixture of blood.[17] Another popular book of the day was Ayarragaray's *La anarquía argentina y el caudillismo* (1904), a study of instability and authoritarianism in earlier years from an ethnic-psychological viewpoint.

Another writer distinguished between Latin Americans and

[16] *Revista de Derecho, Historia y Letras,* año I, t. 1, May 1898, pp. 5–7.
[17] Carlos O. Bunge, *Nuestra América; ensayo de psicología social* (Buenos Aires, 1903).

Anglo-Saxons. "We," he wrote, "rise much higher in idealism and descend much lower in the passions of life." Out of Spanish American individualism and pursuit of the ideal, he continued, have come monstrous deformations of society; yet in the future there is much promise for the race.[18] Another periodical (*El Economista*, July 2, 9, 16, 23, 1898) reprinted from the *Edinburgh Review* four long articles entitled "The Superiority of the Anglo-Saxons."

In general, however, influential Argentine periodicals rejected the thesis of racial inferiority, at least so far as it concerned Argentina.[19] But there were other aspects of inferiority which gave concern. One of these was the question of the causes of the political instability of Latin America compared to the stability of other regions. Here the racial issue popped up again with analysis of the relative work capacity of the various races, as the national groups in Argentina were called, compared to the output in England and the United States, the circular theory being that lack of productivity made for political unrest, or incapacity for strong government.

There was a stigma of inferiority attached by some Argentines to one of their main characteristics—the imitativeness of their culture—imitation of North American political forms, of French intellectual forms, of English and French manners. This condition made the Argentines sensitive still to the words "South American." As *La Prensa* (Sept. 2, 1896) put it, "South America," when uttered by the Yankees, smacked of "prideful compassion." Never mind, the paper went on: "This powerful land is destined to undertake in the southern continent a democratic and humanitarian mission as great as that of the country of Washington."

This was not, however, to be undertaken in cooperation with the United States and the other nations of the hemisphere. Pan Americanism, to the government, the press, and the leaders of Argentina was nearly non-existent at the opening of the

[18] J.Abasolo,"Temperamento político de los pueblos hispano-americanos. Como hallarle una expansión saludable," *Revista Nacional*, año XX, t. 39, Jan.–Feb. 1905, pp. 13–26.

[19] An example is Felipe Senillosa, "Anglo-Sajones y Latinos," *Revista de Derecho, Historia y Letras*, año II, t. 6, April 1900, pp. 227–233.

twentieth century. As though by the conviction that this particular door to inter-American cooperation had been slammed shut by Saenz Peña and Quintana at the First Pan American Conference, the idea and the name were ignored in Buenos Aires for more than a decade after the Washington meeting.

Commerce with the United States continued to be attractive, however, if our political influence was not. Trade was good, and getting better, not only with Europe, but with the United States. United States shipments to Argentina were worth $9,563,510 in 1899, $11,558,237 in 1900, and $11,537,668 in 1901. Argentine exports to the United States were valued at $5,112,561 in 1899, $8,114,304 in 1900, and $8,065,318 in 1901.[20]

It was at this time, a decade after the first Pan American meeting, when Argentina was beginning to savor the good years of novecientos and the excitement of growing nationalism, which was stimulated by the luxury of an armament race with Chile, that proposals for a second Pan American conference came from the United States. The desuetude into which the Pan American movement (if it can be called that) had lapsed after the Washington conference would in likelihood not have provided sufficient incentive for a second meeting had it not been for the existence of the International Bureau of the American Republics which, according to the agreement made at the First Conference, was to be maintained for ten year periods. It was to this fact that President McKinley referred in his annual message to congress on December 5, 1899. In February 1900, Secretary of State Hay sent a circular to the diplomatic representatives of the Latin American states in Washington proposing a second conference in one of the capital cities other than Washington. Soon after, Hay suggested Mexico City to the Mexican ambassador as a suitable meeting place.[21]

On April 14, 1900, tenth anniversary of its establishment, the executive committee of the International Bureau met and decided upon itself as the proper agency to draw up the conference

[20] *Statistical Abstract of the United States, 1906* (Washington, 1907), p. 217.
[21] A. Curtis Wilgus, "The Second International American Conference at Mexico City," *The Hispanic American Historical Review*, 11:29–40, 44–48 (February 1931).

agenda. The Argentine minister was not present. When the committee next met, in May, the Argentine representative, Dr. Eduardo Wilde, who had long been one of Roca's intimate assistants in the government, was on hand. A tentative program was prepared, embracing (1) points studied by the previous conference which the new conference might decide to reconsider, (2) arbitration, (3) an Inter-American Claims Court, (4) measures to improve commerce and communications, (5) reorganization of the International Bureau of American Republics. The executive committee referred coldly to its progenitor, the First Conference, as of "some importance," chiefly because it had created "better harmony" among the American states.

The conference site was selected in June, all present voting for Mexico City but Peru and Argentina, who voted for Buenos Aires. The conference invitation was shortly after issued by Mexico. Argentina accepted in September 1900.[22]

The significance of the program of the Second Conference lay in its omissions. The central issues of the First Conference—the bold customs union plan, the project of a common coin—had disappeared, along with the other proposals which implied a strong regional association. In their places were generalized topics. Pan Americanism had matured in ten years, although it had not grown.

Not Argentina alone, but also Chile, placed obstacles in the way of the conference. Fear that the disputed results of her victorious War of the Pacific might be brought under the scrutiny of the assembled hemisphere by vanquished Bolivia and Peru and by Argentina, with whom Chile was still embroiled in near hostilities over their common frontier, led the Chilean government to protest that the program was "too ample," especially the "vague" points concerning arbitration and a court of claims. A four-cornered tug of war ensued. The United States Government, attempting to placate Chile, hinted to the Mexican government that the conference program might be

---

[22] Archive of the Pan American Union. Minutes of the Executive Committee of the International Bureau of American Republics, II, pp. 182–185, 199–210, 223–231; *Segunda Conferencia Internacional Americana, México, 1901–1902* . . . (México, 1901), pp. 3–7.

altered. The Mexican foreign minister replied that it would be impossible to modify the program because the invitations had been issued; he went on to say that if a change were made, he feared that Argentina, Bolivia, and Peru might vacillate over attending the meeting. The fact was that the Argentine government had cabled to the Mexican foreign office, stating that any change in the announced program would result in her refusal to attend.

The result was a compromise. A variation of the conference agenda was produced at a meeting of the executive committee in May 1901. Chile apparently believed that the new wording was less vague than the former version; Argentina apparently was satisfied that it was sufficiently broad to accomplish her ends.[23]

The United States delegation to the assembly was selected. The chairman was former Senator Henry Gassaway Davis, aging but hale, who had been a delegate to the First Conference and then had labored hard in the infertile vineyard of the Pan American Railway. Two lesser-known delegates were Volney Foster, a businessman and Republican Party leader, and Charles M. Pepper, a newspaperman later active in Latin American affairs for the United States government. Neither man played any part in the conference. John Barrett was a delegate, his missions in Argentina (1903–1904) and Panama (1904–1905) and his tenure as Director General of the Pan American Union (1907–1920) still ahead of him; his time as minister to Siam from 1894 to 1898 presumably of modest value in dealing with Latin America's problems. The United States delegate most expert in Latin American affairs was William I. Buchanan, minister to Argentina from 1894 to 1899 and director of the Buffalo Pan American Exposition in 1901. Buchanan became the *de facto* head of the American group.

Argentina sent three delegates to Mexico. The leader of the group was Antonio Bermejo, professor of international law at the University of Buenos Aires, former minister of justice, congressman, and senator, and later chief justice of the Argentine

---

[23] Minutes of the Executive Committee, II, pp. 309–319; SCIA, pp. 13–21, 350; *La Conferencia Internacional de México. Antecedentes* . . . (México, 1902), p. 36.

supreme court. Equal to Bermejo in ability was the second member of the delegation, the minister to the United States, Martín García Merou, who had begun his literary-diplomatic career as a secretary of his fellow porteño Miguel Cané and whose career was ended by death at the age of forty-three when he was minister to Germany. His intelligent appreciation of the United States is set down in his *Estudios Americanos* (1900). The third delegate was Lorenzo Anadón, president of the faculty of letters of the University of Buenos Aires, senator, later minister of finance and minister to Chile, as well as a director of banks and other corporations.[24]

The strength of the Argentine delegation was not so much a testimony to the Pan American conference as it was to Argentina's desire to keep one eye on Chile and the other on the United States. The conference was viewed with distaste by Argentina. William E. Curtis, who had been a center of controversy at the First Conference, was one object of criticism. Zeballos, who had known the Director of the Bureau of American Republics while minister in Washington, attacked the conference and Curtis, claiming that the latter had persuaded McKinley to call the meeting to "throw dust in the eyes of the inhabitants of the new world while presenting the United States as exercising a species of hegemony over these . . . negligent nations."[25]

Zeballos and other Argentines were principally concerned with the effect which the conference might have on the South American balance of power, which was in dangerous equilibrium at the moment between Argentina and Chile. Each suspected the other of intent to use the conference for its own purposes. The Argentines were anxious that the meeting consider existing disputes, under the heading of arbitration. Argentina and Peru considered the results of the War of the Pacific an existing dispute. This attitude was carried to the point where

[24] *Dictionary of American Biography* (21 vols.; New York, 1928–1944); *National Cyclopaedia of American Biography* (I–, New York, 1893–); Enrique Udaondo, *Diccionario biográfico argentino* (Buenos Aires, 1938); William B. Parker, *Argentines of Today* (2 vols.; Buenos Aires and New York, 1920).

[25] E. S. Zeballos, "El Congreso Pan-Americana," *Revista de Derecho, Historia y Letras*, año IV, t. 11, Nov. 1901, p. 144.

the Argentine chargé in Washington was instructed by Minister García Merou from Mexico City to inform John Hay that "the Conference will prove a failure should the United States fail to employ legitimate influence on behalf of obligatory arbitration." [26]

The same attitude was reflected by the journals of opinion. Long before the conference *La Prensa* (May 18, 25, 31, 1901) editorialized that Argentina should abandon the meeting if Chile succeeded in excluding arbitration from the program. Earlier, *La Nación* (Oct. 28, 1900) attached the success of Pan Americanism to arbitration. The influence of Paul Groussac was publicly brought to bear on his friend, García Merou, in a letter given to the press in which the Franco-Argentine critic castigated the United States and described Pan Americanism as "continental cohabitation." Groussac referred to the failure of 1890 and to "the customs union plan [which] was shattered by the eloquence of our friend Sáenz." Argentina, the writer continued, could derive nothing from the conference, but must protect weaker nations against conquerors. [27]

Theodore Roosevelt and Henry Cabot Lodge were criticized by *La Prensa* (May 27, 28, 30, 1901) for their aggressive defense of the Monroe Doctrine at the opening of the Buffalo Pan American Exposition. Up to the middle of July of the year of the conference, the public did not know whether or not Argentina would attend, and the press printed a multitude of versions of the reasons behind the meeting, none of them favorable to the United States.

The struggle against attending the conference was carried on in the Argentine congress. There the issue rested on the appropriation of funds for the delegation to Mexico. The more nationalistic representatives interpellated Foreign Minister Alcorta about the instructions which the Argentine delegation

[26] Merou [*sic*] to Del Viso, Nov. 22, 1901, The National Archives of the United States, Notes Between the Argentine Government and the United States, Vol. 5.

[27] Groussac to García Merou, letter of Jan. 5, 1901, printed in *El Diario*, Jan. 8, 1901. Also reprinted in the same paper on May 1, 1928 at the time of the Fifth Pan American Conference. See Juan Canter, *Contribución a la bibliografía de Paul Groussac* (Buenos Aires, 1930), pp. 256–257.

would receive. This incursion of the usually complaisant legislature upon the executive was caused by concern that the administration might weaken its insistence upon compulsory arbitration. One congressman opposed spending time and money on a "literary tourney," "a puerile demonstration" which would irk Europe, where Argentina owed money. The funds were finally voted, sixty-two to nine.[28]

Meanwhile, in Washington, the secretary of state was preparing instructions for the United States delegation. The delegates received their instructions from President Roosevelt on Oct. 8, 1901. A theory of United States policy toward Latin America was brilliantly stated in that document, probably for the first time:

The end toward which the proposed conference is directed is the promotion of the mutual prosperity of the American Republics, and of harmony between them . . . The chief interest of the United States in relation to the other Republics upon the American continent is the safety and permanence of the political system which underlies their and our existence as nations—the system of free government by the people . . , It should therefore be the effort of this commission to impress upon the representatives of our sister Republics that we desire, above all, their material prosperity and their political security, and that we entertain toward them no sentiments but those of friendship and fraternity. The method by which this result may be best accomplished is not, however, that of direct assurance, but of generous cooperation for the common good . . . It is not opportune for the delegates of the United States to assume the part of leadership in the conference . . . It is desirable that the plans and propositions of the Latin American states should be solicited, received with consideration, and brought to fruition—if this can be done in consonance with our national interests, and without offense to other powers . . . Nothing is of greater importance from a political point of view than that the United States should be understood to be the friend of all the Latin American Republics and the enemy of none . . . With reference to questions of a commercial and industrial character, it is important to lay stress upon the growing desire in the United States to secure the largest mutuality of interest and to avoid

[28] Congreso Nacional, *Diario de sesiones de la Cámara de Diputados*, Aug. 21, 1901, pp. 536–540, 543–550, 552–554.

even the semblance of an attempt to obtain unfair advantages for ourselves. The true interest of our people lies in helping the Latin American countries with our more advanced industries and our characteristic forms of energy to expand into strong and flourishing communities, and not in seeking to aggrandize ourselves at their expense . . . If the influence of the United States spreads southward, it will be a pacific, not a hostile influence . . . Whatever advantages the extension of trade has to offer are of necessity reciprocal. By opening a wider market to our productions, our sister republics will greatly extend their own . . . The policy of our government is well and clearly expressed in the memorable address of our lamented President, delivered in Buffalo, in which he said: "We must not repose in fancied security that we can forever sell everything and buy little or nothing . . . Reciprocity is the natural outgrowth of our wonderful industrial development."

Specific instructions followed: to support voluntary arbitration and the pacific settlement of disputes, but to take no cognizance of any existing controversy; to maintain strict neutrality should the Chile-Peru dispute enter the debates; and to support an international court of claims. [29]

Absent from these instructions were the categorical plans and arrogance of the United States government's preparations for the First Pan American Conference. The lesson on Latin America which Argentina had administered at that meeting was not forgotten. The caution expressed in the Hay-Roosevelt instructions may have emanated also from a new awareness of the fact that the republican character of the other American states varied considerably from that of the United States. Latin American international delegations were usually responsible solely to powerful chief executives; the United States president had the Senate with which to reckon. Latin American legislatures were in general socially homogeneous with the dominant class in the nation, and were usually obedient to the president, who was a member of that class or eager to serve it. Unlike the First Conference, the second meeting was an assembly of plenipotentiaries, another restraining factor upon the United States representation. The United States plenipotentiaries reported to

[29] *Second International Conference of American States, Message from the President of the United States . . . with Accompanying Papers . . .* (Washington, D.C., 1902), pp. 31–36.

an administration accountable ultimately to the people and to the representatives of forty-five states, who did not always vote as the federal executive might wish. At Mexico City the result of these instructions and of dawning recognition of the complexities of international, multilateral negotiation was some criticism of the North American delegates for not being "progressive" and for "not assuming that leadership which they were expected to yield . . . The position was a difficult one, especially in view of the reported aggressiveness and imperialistic tendencies of the present Chief Executive of the United States."[30]

The Second Pan American Conference convened on October 22, 1901 at the unaggressive hour of four in the afternoon. The Mexican foreign minister's welcoming speech matched the time. But the meeting was not an hour old before an incident occurred reminiscent of the First Conference. The Ecuadorean delegation presented a resolution deploring President McKinley's death, adding a reference to President Roosevelt's statement that he would follow his predecessor's policies. Argentine delegate Anadón arose to suggest elimination of the reference to Roosevelt. The resolution was accordingly modified and approved, and on this note the first day ended.[31]

Next day the chief of the Argentine mission, García Merou, was first to request the floor. He took up the matter of the strained relations between Colombia and Venezuela, calling upon the Conference to express to these countries its wish for a solution to their difficulties.

The Argentine action was significant in two ways. First, the fact that it was taken revealed that Argentina had a far wider view of the role of this Pan American conference than she had displayed at the first of those meetings. Second, it revealed Argentina as a spokesman for a group of nations, García Merou's resolution having been presented in the names of Argentina, Bolivia, Peru, Paraguay, Uruguay, and Brazil.

That Argentina in bringing up the Colombia-Venezuela

---

[30] *Actas y documentos de la Segunda Conferencia Pan-Americana. Second Pan-American Conference, Minutes and Documents* (México, 1902), p. 290; John V. Noel, *History of the Second Pan-American Conference* (Baltimore, 1902), pp. 70–72.

[31] SCIA, pp. 25–26; *Actas*, p. 18.

dispute was laying the groundwork for the assembly's consideration of the tense Chilean-Peruvian situation seems to have been
the conclusion drawn by the representatives from Chile. Walker
Martínez of that delegation immediately suggested referring the
proposal to committee. An acrimonious dispute ensued, the
conference not having had time to approve regulations for the
meeting. At last the Argentine resolution was passed by fifteen
nations, including the United States, with Chile, Venezuela,
Colombia, and Haiti abstaining. Argentina had taken the lead
in the conference.[32]

On October 25 debate began on the regulations for the conference. Argentine delegate Bermejo dominated the discussions.
He insisted on precise rules for all conference activity. He wished
the credentials of all delegates to be examined, and opposed the
employment of absentee voting. On one organizational issue
there was no dispute: the presidency of the conference went to
the head of the Mexican delegation, but not until the Colombian
delegate had moved the election of the chairman of the United
States delegation. Davis refused, not only because he could not
speak Spanish, but because of the restraints under which his
group was working. But in refusing the nomination, Davis made
an unrestrained speech. "Eighty million inhabitants of the
United States," he informed the assembly, ". . . a happy, true,
loyal, independent, and liberty-loving people . . . say to our
friends on our South that we want no further territory, but we
are firm, as firm as the Medes and the Persians, in what is known
as the Monroe Doctrine, which means that your territory is to
be protected . . . and your liberties forever guaranteed."[33]

The opportunity for conflict supposedly had been reduced by
the limited agenda of the Second Pan American Conference.
The opportunity for accomplishment was also reduced. The
committee on committees divided the work of the meeting
among eighteen committees, ranging from arbitration to general
welfare, but before the work was well begun two other matters
occupied the attention of the delegates.

[32] *Actas*, pp. 23–29, 639–641; *La conferencia internacional*, pp. 52, 55; Noel, *History*,
pp. 98–99, 102.
[33] *Actas*, pp. 31–65; SCIA, pp. 33–63.

The first was the issue of the freedom of the press. Here the United States ended by voting with Mexico and Haiti against admitting newsmen to the plenary sessions of the meeting, while Argentina, supported by Peru and Bolivia, emerged as the successful sponsors of press attendance. [34] The other matter was the special report made to the conference by the Argentine delegation at the end of November, printed simultaneously for the public in English and Spanish, and read to the conference by one of the Argentines.

The Argentines described their report as an interim balance statement on the conference and a summary of conditions in Argentina. The report to the Second Pan American Conference described Pan Americanism as a movement "governed by vague sentiments," which could only become practical when "inspired by justice, equality, territorial integrity, and commercial relations founded upon a competition open to all." The Argentine people, the report continued, "is young and sure of its strength, although it is exempt from all ambition save that of remaining at peace with all and earnestly working out its destiny." After further tributes to the resources and virtues of their homeland the delegates declared that "whichever may be the resolutions adopted by [the conference] on arbitration and other matters of its program, said resolutions shall not affect [Argentina's] interests." [35]

Without attempting to solve the paradox of support for practical Pan Americanism and opposition to measures aimed at that end, the Argentine delegation showed again, in this report, the independence and firmness of their national policy. Each of the major issues before the assembly was discussed in the report. The first of these problems to cause a clash was the Peruvian-Chilean dispute. Here a wider issue was at stake—the whole question of intervention, which in the future would come to be a center of hemispheric politics. The Peruvians aimed at obtaining from the conference some declaration on arbitration which would amount to collective intervention on behalf of their demands for

---

[34] SCIA, pp. 53–63.
[35] *Actas*, pp. 147–148, 197. See also *Informe que la delegación de la República Argentina presentada a la Segunda Conferencia Pan-Americana* (México, 1901).

recovery of their lost southern territories. The Chileans had no intention of allowing the conference to deal with the matter. Maneuvering began. Chile succeeded in having the committee on arbitration made up of one delegate from each country. Mexico introduced a strong arbitral plan in a secret session which was held despite Argentine, Bolivian, Paraguayan, and Peruvian opposition to secrecy. Argentina demanded settlement of the dispute by compulsory arbitration, claiming that she had been the nation responsible for converting Pan Americanism into a system conciliatory in economics and pacific in politics. This, it was said, had been done by the Elizalde note of 1862. Now Argentina called upon the conference to "put its hand where the hurt is," offered its own arbitral record as testimony of its faith, and called upon that idea which had dominated Argentina's internal and foreign policy for two decades—peace. "Without peace," the Argentine declaration said, "it is a pitiful waste of time to deliberate on railroads, maritime communications routes, banks, etc., since without peace there is no production."[36]

The debates grew hotter. No matter what subject was discussed, it turned out to be arbitration. Rebuttals were rebutted until the original subject was unrecognizable. The Argentine delegates repeatedly came to the side of those engaged against Chile. The danger that the conference might break down became so real that it was agreed to strengthen the regulations to oblige speakers to stay on the point. By mid-January, with no report from the committee on arbitration, or from the subcommittee formed to speed the business, relations had become so strained that Argentina, Peru, Bolivia, Paraguay, Venezuela, and Santo Domingo refused to attend plenary sessions until the arbitration issue had been solved.

The impasse was broken outside the conference. On January 15 the delegates of Argentina, Peru, Bolivia, the United States, Costa Rica, Nicaragua, Colombia, Paraguay, Uruguay, Santo Domingo, Salvador, Guatemala, Haiti, Honduras, and Mexico informed the gathering that they had signed a protocol outside the conference recognizing the arbitral principle set down in the

[36] SCIA, pp. 48–49, 304–314; *Actas*, pp. 110, 186, 194–197.

Hague Convention on the Pacific Settlement of Disputes. Chile, isolated, introduced an identical proposal within the conference, calling for adherence to the same convention. A furious dispute ensued over the disposition of the protocol and the resolution, Chile being unwilling to have official conference recognition given to the protocol which she had not signed. Argentine delegate Bermejo revealed that at the end of December his delegation had signed with the delegates of Mexico, Guatemala, Santo Domingo, Salvador, Venezuela, Peru, Bolivia, Paraguay, and Uruguay, outside the conference, a treaty of compulsory arbitration. He could not understand why there was need for debate, since the majority of the conference had expressed their views in these two agreements. Mexico and the United States, which had supported the device of an extra-conference protocol in order to avoid a stalemate within the assembly, now found the protocol stalemated.

Buchanan at last achieved a formula which brought the matter to a peaceful conclusion. In view of the fact that Chile and Ecuador had from the outset demonstrated their sincere adherence to the Hague principle of voluntary arbitration, he proposed that the minutes of the sessions on arbitration together with the protocol should be passed to the two official depositaries of conference actions, the United States secretary of state and the Mexican foreign minister. This pleased Chile and Ecuador; Argentina had secured a compulsory arbitration agreement with a goodly number of Latin American states, as well as conference recognition of arbitration, and the conference could continue.[37]

The Conference was not all bickering. There was much leisurely and elegant entertainment provided by the Díaz regime. The United States delegates traveled from Washington on a special six-car train which contrasted with the canvas-covered prairie schooners that they saw as they passed through

[37] *Actas*, pp. 225, 333–334, 439, 443–447; SCIA, pp. 328–369. The text of the voluntary arbitration protocol may be found in James Brown Scott, ed., *The International Conferences of American States, 1889–1928* (New York, 1931), pp. 61–62, and the text of the compulsory arbitration treaty on pp. 100–104. Argentina upheld her record as champion non-ratifier by failing to ratify this agreement which she had inspired.

Indian Territory. The meetings in Mexico City were held in a wing of the national palace, luxuriously decorated with satin wall hangings, carved mahogany wainscoting, and illuminated by hundreds of light bulbs naked in their chandeliers. Away from the work of the conference, the time of the delegates was occupied with receptions, operas, poetry readings, luncheons, teas, dinners, toasts, speeches, rides, and dances. There were fireworks in the Plaza de la Constitución on opening night. There was a long trip out of town, from November 8 to November 27, to Puebla and Orizaba, although some of the delegates remained in the city to keep up with their work.

The United States delegates were not men to forget worthy causes not on the agenda. Delegate Pepper presented a resolution which even in 1901 must have appeared unduly optimistic. On behalf of the International Peace Bureau he moved that "states should, as soon as a favorable opportunity offers, declare themselves fundamentally and permanently neutral." Delegate Davis conveyed to the conference the greetings of the National Association of Agricultural Implements and Vehicle Manufacturers. Free copies of *The Book of Infants' Health* were distributed by the Americans. None of this pleased the Argentines, who were intent upon the strict functioning of the conference, insisted on a thorough review of all credentials, the reading of the minutes each day, which the United States delegation had attempted to dispense with, and opposed the transmission of the good wishes of the assembly to the new Republic of Cuba.[38]

Meanwhile, at home in Argentina the great daily newspapers were giving to the conference coverage which was a tribute to the importance of the meeting to Argentines and testimony to the high development of the news agencies serving Buenos Aires. In its issue of October 27, 1901, *La Prensa* reprinted opinions on the conference taken from four German and one Russian newspaper. *La Prensa*'s mood shifted with the issues before the conference. Dire hints of the collapse of the assembly appeared

---

[38] *Segunda Conferencia Pan-Americana, crónica social* [México, 1902?]; Noel, *History*, pp. 55–56, 65–66, 108–109; *Actas*, pp. 142, 144, 218–219, 315, 527–529; SCIA, pp. 66–68.

when the border dispute with Chile flared into new bitterness. The paper went so far as to be incorrect in its reporting when it declared in the issue of December 13 that on the following day Argentina would withdraw from the assembly, a piece of misinformation which apparently came from an excellent source, García Merou, head of the Argentine delegation and a close friend of Zeballos, editor of *La Prensa*. In the edition of January 4, 1902, *La Prensa* claimed that only the intervention of John Hay caused Argentina to remain at the Second Pan American Conference, but on January 18 expressed pleasure at the signing of the arbitration agreements. Surveying the results of the meeting on February 1, *La Prensa* stated that the two Pan American conferences had demonstrated the impossibility of any understanding between the Americas. Chile was arrogant, the United States was vacillating, and Argentina must be more careful in the future about embarking on such impractical adventures.

La Nación took a similar though less adamant position. On November 10 the paper wrote that it would be better for Argentina to withdraw from the meeting rather than to enter unwelcome quarrels or attempt to win friends through "gastronomic reconciliation" at banquets (Nov. 15). On January 13, *La Nación* attacked the United States for vacillation, discrimination among the American nations, and its "mercantilist spirit." On January 18 the arbitral pacts were hailed as defeats for Chile. And on January 31, *La Nación* also interred the still-living conference, declaring that by their nature these meetings produce only declarations of common faith. However, said the editors, we Argentines "do not doubt that we have won the respect of peoples and governments which . . . recognize that we fulfil with distinction the mission which is imposed upon us of marching at the vanguard of South American civilization."

El Diario, the evening paper, welcomed the conference on October 22 as "a Yankee invention which, to dissimulate paternity, they have put in the charge of Mexico." The familiar theme of the United States intention to evict Europe from Latin America's markets was repeated in later issues, with the opinion that Argentina would never allow herself to be drawn within the orbit of Yankee power.

El País, Carlos Pellegrini's paper which spoke for the estancieros of Buenos Aires province, stated on November 30 that the conference had failed and that Foreign Minister Alcorta "should order the return of the tourists." On December 17 *El País* also mistakenly applauded the government's decision to recall its representation. [39]

Although arbitration was the central issue of the conference in the eyes of the Argentine press, in Mexico City there remained other matters to be considered. One of these was the revived idea of a Pan American bank. The committee on the bank, headed by García Merou, recommended establishment of such an agency in New York. When the question of the method of subsidizing the institution came up, Argentine delegate Anadón described himself as a liberal in economic matters and an opponent of subsidies, but he strongly urged a great expansion of the credit relations of the United States and Latin America, pointing out that United States businessmen still demanded cash as they had at the time of the First Pan American Conference and that their banking arrangements were made through Europe. To the United States Senate, the Argentine continued, goes the blame for the failure to create a bank after the First Conference. He also attacked the "Chinese wall" first built by the McKinley tariff. Then he proposed establishing several inter-American banks instead of one, and after much bickering all the delegations present except that of Chile voted to set up banks in New York, San Francisco, New Orleans, Chicago, Buenos Aires, or other centers. This was something of an advance over the position which the Argentine delegation had taken in its report to the conference, where it was maintained that Argentine banking facilities were more than ample to carry on transactions with the United States. [40]

Another Pan American plan which at one time might have been voted most likely to succeed was revived at Mexico, but progressed no further than did the railroad which was its object.

---

[39] Wilgus, "The Second International American Conference at Mexico City," pp. 40–44, 62–68, contains an excellent review of United States, European, and other Latin American press opinion. See also Orestes Ferrara, *L'Amérique et l'Europe; la panaméricanisme et l'opinion européenne* (Paris, 1930), pp. 25–28.

[40] SCIA, pp. 83–103, 170–171; *The International Conferences*, pp. 65–66.

A resolution was passed by all the mainland states ratifying the railroad resolution of the First Conference, a new committee was appointed, and a meeting set for a year later.[41]

In another field of transportation the Argentines again demonstrated their interest in increased hemispheric trade and, at the same time, their satisfaction with Argentina's present condition. In their November report they described in glowing terms the facilities of the port of Buenos Aires and the shipping lines which could handle far more than the present volume of trade with the United States, but in January they signed a resolution calling for an investigation of port charges which were impeding maritime commerce among the Americas.[42]

In the direction of expanding trade the Conference recommended the calling of a customs convention within one year to study unification of customs practices. Here, too, the Argentine report left no doubt about that country's position. In a section entitled "Commercial Reciprocity" the Argentines decried tariff barriers in the New World, but referred at length to the Old World, whence came Argentina's immigrants and capital and "all the forms of civilization that we possess." The Argentines pointed out that the Alcorta-Buchanan trade convention of 1899 was languishing in the United States Senate. If the convention is rejected by the senate, they continued, this will have no important effect upon Argentine trade, which has so far successfully managed to ignore these beneficial reciprocity treaties "that have no reciprocity in them." After predicting that the United States would some day fall into an "unprecedented industrial crisis," the Argentines quoted McKinley's warning to his countrymen: "We ought not to have too much confidence in the visionary security of always being able to sell everything and buy little or nothing." They added: "It is to be feared that America will witness great struggles before attaining an ampler trade and a true fraternity."[43]

The Argentine delegates in another matter clearly established

[41] SCIA, pp. 104–122; *The International Conferences*, pp. 63–65.

[42] SCIA, p. 239; *Actas*, pp. 156–160; *The International Conferences*, pp. 156–160.

[43] *Actas*, pp. 162–170, 296–302; SCIA, pp. 123–130; *The International Conferences*, pp. 66–68.

8

the special position of their nation in Latin America. The committee on international law was charged with defining the rights of aliens residing in the American states. The vigorous report of this committee, which was headed by Bermejo, struck out against diplomatic interventions by nations on behalf of their citizens and their citizens' property in foreign lands, calling for equal judicial protection for foreigners and citizens. He advocated the doctrine of *jus soli*, repeatedly emphasizing that Europe was dealing with civilized nations in America. The United States delegation announced that it would abstain from debating or voting on the report. The convention of the rights of aliens, which provided for the equality of foreigners and nationals before the law of the signatory nations, was signed by all the nations at the meeting with the exception of the United States and Haiti, which abstained from voting, and Brazil and Venezuela, which had withdrawn from the conference. It was ultimately ratified by Bolivia, Colombia, Ecuador, Guatemala, Honduras, Nicaragua, and El Salvador.[44]

The Conference entered more deeply into the realm of international law when Bermejo strongly advocated the compulsory arbitration of pecuniary claims through the Hague Permanent Court, without a maximum upon the amount claimed. Buchanan insisted upon fixing a limit, and carried his proposal against the votes of Argentina, Bolivia, Haiti, and Santo Domingo. But the effort of the United States and Mexican delegations to tie the resolution on claims to adherence by the Latin American nations to the 1899 Hague Convention on Arbitration precipitated a fiery attack by the most active Argentine delegate. He termed this an unacceptable imposition upon the Latin American states, for only the United States and Mexico were Hague signatories. Buchanan sought to sooth the Argentine emissary by assuring the Conference that the United States hoped to see each one of the American republics represented at the Hague. But the inferior position of the other states rankled

---

[44] A related treaty on extradition followed a similar course through the conference, with the inconspicuous United States position the object of Argentine criticism. See *Actas*, pp. 233–235, 538–540, 554; SCIA, pp. 271–283, 182–214; *The International Conferences*, pp. 83–88, 90–91.

and they succeeded in modifying the offending article so as to eliminate reference to the special position of Mexico and the United States. The resulting treaty of arbitration of pecuniary claims was signed on January 30, 1902 by all the nations at the conference, and was later ratified by Colombia, Costa Rica, Ecuador, Guatemala, Honduras, Mexico, Peru, Salvador, and the United States.[45]

Three days earlier all the delegates present at the conference signed the treaty on patents and trademarks—all but the United States. By this treaty equality of patent and trademark protection was agreed to among the signatories. Yet the issue was not an easy one to bring to agreement despite its limited scope. The difficulty was one that was intrinsic to the composition of the conference: how to coordinate diverse national laws and practices into a single acceptable formula.

The Argentine delegation claimed that no patent convention was necessary because the American states, particularly Argentina, provided by their laws all needed protection for foreign and domestic patents. Bermejo was in fact perhaps seeking to avoid an agreement that would make registration of a patent or trademark effective among the American states, thus limiting the need for national registration which, despite some law on the subject, was a farce in Argentina. The treaty, finally signed by all the delegations except Brazil, Venezuela, and the United States, provided for the equality of the citizens of each signatory state with the citizens of the other signatories in this matter.[46]

One act of the Conference that won unanimous approval was the reorganization of the International Bureau of American Republics. The assembly endorsed the changes which had been made in the Bureau in the late nineties, including the establishment of a governing board headed by the United States secretary of state and composed of the Latin American diplomatic representatives in Washington. An administrative and financial reorganization of the Bureau was also prescribed by the Mexico

[45] *Actas*, pp. 112–118, 123–127, 556–557, 567–575, 583–584; SCIA, pp. 295–304; *The International Conferences*, pp. 104–105.
[46] *Actas*, pp. 177–178; SCIA, pp. 159–180; *The International Conferences*, pp. 76–79.

Conference, and the Columbus Memorial Library was established. The life of the Bureau was set at ten years from the conference adjournment. Argentina strongly supported these steps, and opposed a Chilean motion that would have weakened the Bureau. [47]

Argentina showed disinterest, however, in formalizing the Pan American conference system. The committee on future conferences recommended to the assembly that they be convened at five year intervals. Although he was a member of this committee, Argentine delegate Anadón did not sign the report. On the assembly floor he explained his position, stating that there was no basis for selecting five year periods. Why not eight years? He desired to leave the matter of future meetings up to the diplomatic corps in Washington. Delegate Pepper claimed that to do so would be "vague . . . and prejudicial" to the conferences. Finally, it was decided to fix on a five year interval, and if this were impossible to let the matter be decided by the diplomats in Washington. [48] In this way the life of Pan Americanism was prolonged and regularized into a five year conference cycle which has been followed ever since except during major wars.

On January 31, 1902 the closing session of the Second Pan American Conference was held. Mexican Foreign Minister Marsical made a speech emphasizing the practical achievements of the assembly and brought the meeting to an end. [49]

The role which Argentina played at the Second Conference differed little from her part at the first; the role of the United

---

[47] *Actas*, pp. 518–521; SCIA, pp. 245–248; *The International Conferences*, pp. 92–94.

[48] SCIA, pp. 285–287; *The International Conferences*, pp. 96–97.

[49] A résumé of the minor results of the conference follows: The nations agreed to send statistics on their resources to the Bureau (SCIA, pp. 130–132); they agreed to exchange scientific and cultural publications, although here Bermejo insisted that the Brussels Exchange Convention would serve better than a Pan American system (SCIA, pp. 132–139); a convention for the protection of literary and artistic works was signed, and opened to non-American states, thanks to the Argentine delegation's efforts on behalf of Europe (SCIA, pp. 139–146); a convention on the exercise of the liberal professions was signed, after considerable dispute between the Argentine and United States delegates over their varying national practices (SCIA, pp. 218–236; *Actas*, pp. 373–375, 428); an International Sanitary Bureau was established and provision made for the first Sanitary Conference; this was one of the few conventions which Argentina did not sign (*Actas*, pp. 127–139, 576–582);

States was considerably altered. At the second meeting, as at the first, the Argentine delegates were meticulous with the rules, insistent on their policies, and firm in asserting leadership. The ill effects of the crash of the nineties had worn off; Argentina was once more strong and rich, destined to a great future in Latin America. If the Argentines showed less resistance to the agenda, this was because the agenda was different, and because Argentina intended to overlook no opportunity to use the meeting to isolate Chile.

Twelve years before, in Washington, the United States delegates had been aggressive and long-winded. At Mexico City they were modest and mediating. Their goal was to abate conflict between Argentina and Chile, to build Pan American unity, to fortify a shaky system.

In the last two decades of the nineteenth century the United States learned much about Latin America, and Argentina was one of her most effective teachers. The First Pan American Conference had set major political and economic goals, and achieved little. The Second Conference was more limited, its goals more technical in the juridical and economic fields, and the results, although modest, promised to serve as a more solid base for the future. This change meant a blunting of U.S. preponderance in Latin America, at least in open assembly, and the appearance of the only viable principle for a regional coalition of the Americas, the principle of the equality of states. It is a curious fact that this equality should have been sought by the United States in the administration of Theodore Roosevelt, who was busy elsewhere in the Americas making clear his nation's authority.

---

a resolution providing for a Coffee Congress to be held in New York for the purpose of "investigating the crisis through which that great industry is passing" was signed by all the delegations except those of Chile, Venezuela, and Brazil, which had withdrawn from the meeting (SCIA, pp. 288–289); a convention for the formation of codes of public and private international law was signed by all the countries present (SCIA, pp. 147–158).

Most of the acts of the conference were subsequently ratified by the United States and a number of the other countries. None was ratified by Argentina.

14

Two Doctrines

ARGENTINA at the Second Conference gave evidence of accepting institutionalized Pan Americanism, but it was not alone by this route that Argentine leaders sought to advance their nation's interests. Within a few months of the closing of the Mexico City meeting, events in Venezuela elicited from the Argentine government a statement of policy which achieved the stature of a "doctrine." The Drago Doctrine may be viewed as another Argentine bid for a leading part in a slowly developing hemispheric drama in which the United States, with its power and its Monroe Doctrine, had long preëmpted all the important roles.

Late in 1902, Venezuela was blockaded and bombarded by British and German naval units, later joined by those of Italy. The European powers were seeking to force payment by the Venezuelan government of debts which it owed to nationals of the blockading states. There was no nation in Latin America with larger financial ties to Europe than Argentina; there was, therefore, no country where the spectacle of armed intervention for such ends might be expected to have a deeper effect. Nor was there in Latin America any nation more willing and able than Argentina to make its position clear in such a crisis.

The Argentine government imparted its views on the Venezuelan affair to the world in a characteristically direct, if surprising, manner. A note was sent to the government of the United States. Prepared by Foreign Minister Luis M. Drago on December 29, 1902, it pointed out certain facts of life: that capitalists loaning money to a foreign state assess the risk beforehand; that it is known that a sovereign state is not unilaterally subject to executive or judicial procedure; that a state is bound to pay its debts but cannot justly be subjected to forcible debt collection; that European expansion threatens now to be directed against Latin America; that the use of force against Venezuela implies territorial occupation, which is contrary to the Monroe Doctrine; and that, while Argentina claims no special rights for Latin America against just claims justly presented, Argentina would view with great satisfaction the avowal by a great power such as the United States of the principle that "public debt gives no place for armed intervention, and less still to the material occupation of the soil of American nations by a European power." Drago closed by pointing out Argentina's redemption of her own suspended debt payments and her attachment to Europe, especially to England, an attachment that would not, however, be extended to English policy "in the improbable event that it should tend to oppress the nations of this continent."

John Hay's reply of February 17, 1903 cited President Roosevelt's declaration of December 1901, that the Monroe Doctrine gave no guarantee of protection against the "repression" by another power of a badly behaved state, so long as such repression did not take the form of acquisition of territory by a non-American power. Hay advocated arbitration of international disputes.[1]

The Argentine note was too relevant and timely to languish as half of an exchange of diplomatic opinion. It was taken up by the press and public of the Atlantic world. It became an issue at two international meetings, the Third Pan American Conference at Rio in 1906, and the Second Hague Conference in the following year. In Argentina, Drago's statement came to have a significance which was not diminished by the fact that Theodore Roosevelt did succeed in having the claims against Venezuela placed under adjudication. In the eyes of its own citizens and of the civilized world—as the phrase went—the standing of Argentina was considerably heightened. Further, Drago had endorsed the use of the Monroe Doctrine; this gave his statement added significance, for it was a time when the

[1] Luis M. Drago, *La República Argentina y el caso de Venezuela* . . . (Buenos Aires, 1903), pp. 1–12.

Monroe Doctrine was being summoned once more from its un-
stoppered bottle to assume new and frightening shapes.

Yet the Drago Doctrine, like the Monroe Doctrine, might more
properly be known by another name than that which it bears.
Issued in the name of President Roca, explicitly endorsed by him
at the beginning and later, [2] it represents his concern and that of
his class for Argentina's position with regard to Europe and the
United States. It also showed his country to be an emerging force
in the Americas. Nor was Roca the only Argentine leader to sponsor the foreign minister's note. Bartolomé Mitre, eighty-one years
of age and still a power in the land, was consulted by Drago, who
was his grandson. The foreign minister presented his statement to
this chief of the Argentine genro before he sent it, eliciting from
Mitre the opinion that the message should indeed be dispatched
because "it will do honor to you and to our government." [3]

The agitation felt by Drago, Roca, and others because of
European intervention in the New World was shared by many
Argentines. Drago later described the situation in Buenos Aires
when the aggression against Venezuela became known as one
of "hysteria." Before he evolved his own note he received advice
from all sides, including a private letter from Pellegrini, who
certainly had much experience with demanding European
creditors, in which the former president urged Drago to tell the
Venezuelans to accept Argentine funds as a deposit to be placed
in a bank in London, Berlin, or Rome, as evidence of good faith
until arbitration could decide the issue. [4] In congress—decidedly
not the place where Argentina's foreign policy was shaped—the
minor attention paid to the Venezuelan affair divided into two
views, held by those who desired a declaration of South American solidarity and those who feared to do anything that might
strain Argentina's ties with Europe. [5]

[2] H. Mabragaña, compiler, *Los mensajes* . . . (6 vols.; Buenos Aires, n.d.), VI,
47–49; Roque Saenz Peña, *Escritos y discursos*, I, *Actuación internacional* (Buenos Aires,
1914), pp. 449–456.

[3] Carlos Saavedra Lamas, *Luis María Drago. Su obra, proyecciones y trascendencia* . . .
(Buenos Aires, 1943), p. 106.

[4] República Argentina, Ministerio del Interior, *La política internacional de la
Nación Argentina* . . . (Buenos Aires, 1946), p. 506.

[5] Congreso Nacional, *Diario de sesiones de la Cámara de Diputados*, Dec. 15, 1902,
pp. 531–532.

In the first days of the intervention the press of Buenos Aires was also concerned, but uncertain of solutions. *La Prensa* (Dec. 12, 1902) expressed pained surprise at the Anglo-German policy, then (Dec. 13) appealed hesitantly to the Monroe Doctrine, hastening to add that the Latin American states had won their independence without the United States and knew how to retain it without that nation's assistance. Next day the editors had gone a step farther, declaring that instead of awaiting a declaration from the United States, the South American nations should voice their disapproval of Europe's violent action. On December 18 the Argentine government was accused by *La Prensa* of isolationism; the editors called for formation of a Latin American bloc. By December 21 the paper was so aroused over the need for solidarity that the cherished slogan coined by Saenz Peña, "America for humanity," was cast aside in an editorial entitled "South America for the South Americans."

Mitre's *La Nación*, usually less responsive to the exigencies of Argentina's international trading position and less hostile to the United States than *La Prensa*, on this issue went through a similar evolution of opinion. On December 13 the paper decried both European intervention and the Roosevelt interpretation of the Monroe Doctrine as conferring the right to intervene in a financially chaotic nation. Later (Dec. 16, 18) the paper warned of the need for United States action on behalf of Venezuela. On December 23 and 24, *La Nación* ran a long interview with the British foreign secretary, in which Lord Lansdowne disavowed improper intentions in Venezuela and praised Argentina's great progress, great future, and great friendship for England.

Pellegrini's paper, *El País*, hailed the Monroe Doctrine on December 3, called it a fiction on December 16, on December 20 called for Argentine, Brazilian, and Chilean action, and on December 26, when it was apparent that the United States was successfully employing its influence in the dispute, charged that country with the intention of setting up a protectorate in Latin America.

El Economista (Dec. 20), unlike the other papers, had a single policy: no intervention by Argentina where no Argentine economic interests were involved.

In the years following the stabilization of the Venezuelan situation, two principal effects of Argentina's role in the affair became visible. One was satisfaction with the part Argentina had played in the matter and thus on the stage of world opinion. The other was a sharpened awareness of the issues of intervention and leadership in Latin America between Argentina and the United States. The Drago note may be construed as a sign —a sort of involuntary start on the part of the Argentine leaders —of their increasing consciousness of the drawing together of remote Argentina and other areas of the earth, of the meeting of underdeveloped Latin America and still-expanding Europe, against a background of a looming United States on the move toward the south, propelled by the eruptions of Teddy Roosevelt. *La Prensa* hit the nail on the head in an editorial of March 19, 1902 entitled "Neither a U.S. Protectorate nor European Intervention."

Unflinching defence of Argentine sovereignty implied for many Argentines rejection of the Monroe Doctrine and all its works. This was not a wholly defensible position, if only because not all Argentines had taken it, including those who in the time of Rosas had looked to the United States for aid against Europe, and including the foremost Argentine authority on international law, Calvo, not to mention Drago's appeal to the doctrine in his famous note. But a more popular attitude was that taken by one leader of the Argentine oligarchy, who, when asked by Drago for an opinion on the note, supported it up to the point where the Monroe Doctrine entered. There Roque Saenz Peña dissented strongly, denying (correctly) that any Argentine government had ever adhered to that declaration, and calling for the formation by the Argentine people of a "defensive confraternity" against the "new interventionist doctrines." [6]

Yet the Drago Doctrine was not considered to be a doctrine by the man who knew it best, its author. It was, he said, not a principle of law but only a "simple expression of a political viewpoint." It was an expression that won the support of the Argentine press, however, and relieved public concern over the action Argentina should take. *La Prensa* on March 13, 16, and

[6] Saenz Peña, *Escritos*, I, 455–456.

17, 1903 supported the message and denied, as Drago himself was soon to do,[7] that Argentina had thereby in any way subordinated itself to the Monroe Doctrine. *La Nación* (March 14, 21, 22, 1903) was even more enthusiastic.

Argentines were pleased by the favorable foreign reaction. Drago included one hundred and fifty pages of foreign press comment in a book on the Venezuelan affair which he published in 1903, a study which perhaps disproved as far as the Argentine foreign minister and his doctrine were concerned James Bryce's comment that the "wisest among American Foreign Ministers, such as Mr. Hay and Mr. Root, are those who have least frequently referred to the Monroe Doctrine." The praise of the United States press had a beneficent effect in Argentina, and the American chargé reported that Drago was "elated" and the attitude of the public "friendlier" to the Yankees.[8] Argentines believed that their national voice was being heard in the world.

There was a decided difference between the two doctrines of Monroe and Drago, despite the friendly reception of the latter by the American public. The gap became wider when, in December 1904, President Roosevelt expounded his "corollary"—the idea that the United States might be obliged to act as a policeman in the more chaotic countries of Latin America. It did not take long for Argentines to note that the amended Monroe Doctrine and the Drago idea were mutually exclusive. *La Prensa* (Dec. 8, 1904) termed the Roosevelt statement "the most serious and menacing declaration against South American integrity which has come out of Washington."[9] (It should be noted, however, that *La Prensa* [Nov. 10, 1904 and March 9, 1905] continued to place before Argentine eyes the good political example of United States democracy, including the active leadership of Teddy Roosevelt.) On December 13 the paper assured its readers that their country should be considered as excluded from Roosevelt's definition of a disorganized Latin

[7] Drago, *La República Argentina*, pp. viii, ix.

[8] Ames to Hay, May 5, 1903, National Archives, Dept. of State, American States, Diplomatic Despatches, U.S. Legation Argentina, Vol. 41, No. 255.

[9] *La Prensa*, Dec. 27, 1904, March 4, April 6, 7, 17, July 20, Aug. 15, 17, 22, Oct. 24, Dec. 7, 8, 14, 1905; *La Nación*, Dec. 12, 25, 1904, Dec. 6, 1905.

American state, but that it was up to Argentina to defend the principle of sovereignty and the rights of all Latin America against the *gran garrote*—the "big stick."

La Prensa consistently attacked United States foreign policy in Latin America, professing greater fear of United States interventionism than of European imperialism. *La Nación* was less severe, but drew many similar conclusions, including the one that Argentina was not to be included in Roosevelt's backward Latin America. Both great journals were concerned by the implied inferiority of Argentina and by the implication of separation from Europe lurking within the Monroe Doctrine.

In the midst of the concern over Venezuela and the two doctrines, the United States "took" Panama. The impact of this event in Argentina was curiously at odds with the mounting fear of the United States. The press urged the Argentine government to stay out of the affair and to recognize the new republic. This was as true of *El País* (which nonetheless commented with acerbity on November 16, 1903 that "Destiny is *really* manifest now") as it was of the other important papers.[10]

The Roca administration had to decide whether or not to recognize the new state of Panama. Minister García Merou in Washington left little doubt as to what the Roosevelt administration desired in this respect; he cabled to the Argentine foreign minister urging recognition because the acting secretary of state had told him that those powers which had not recognized Panama would be considered as committing "an act of tacit reprobation and concealed hostility."[11] The foreign minister told United States Minister John Barrett, who was soon after ordered to Panama—the first United States representative there —that Argentina was disposed to recognize the new state and "entertained the most kindly feelings toward the United States, with no criticism whatever of its attitude in this crisis."[12]

One man of stature did criticize the United States–Panama transaction. Bartolomé Irigoyen, eighty-one years old, spoke in

[10] *La Prensa*, Dec. 18, 22, 1903, Jan. 4, 1904; *La Nación*, Nov. 6, 12, 18, 1903; *El Diario*, Dec. 17, 22, 1903; *El País*, Nov. 5, Dec. 13, 1903.

[11] García Merou to Terry, Dec. 29, 1903, *Memoria de Relaciones Exteriores*, 1903, pp. 4–5.

[12] Barrett to Hay, Dec. 25, 1903, Despatches, Vol. 42, No. 14.

the senate. He said that Argentina had a tradition of condemn-
ing the violation of the rights of other American republics.
International justice, he argued, should not be abandoned in
this case, and Panama should not be hastily recognized. But the
government did recognize Panama on March 3, 1904, in a spirit
which our minister described as one of the "kindliest feelings
toward the United States, and after a delay caused only by the
fact that Argentina had consulted with other South American
nations in the interests of coordinating the decisions of all."[13]

Why did Argentina become aroused over European intervention in Venezuela in 1902, yet remain calm in the face of
United States action in Panama in 1903? The differing nature
of the two incidents is the basic explanation. The Venezuelan
situation was an outright aggression which might be extended
into a general occupation on behalf of European financial
interests; in Panama there was concealment by the aggressor
behind native separatism, and a more specific end—the canal.
Then too, there was some agreement in Argentina with the
Rooseveltian thesis that the United States was acting on behalf
of "progress," and that the more turbulent Latin American
nations had to be dealt with firmly.[14] There was also the fact
that the United States possessed only a tiny economic foothold
in Argentina, while Europe held a vast beachhead. The Argentine people from time to time showed their alarm over Europe's
hold on them: they had done so in 1901 when Roca and Pellegrini proposed a consolidation of the Argentine foreign debt, to
be secured by the country's customs revenues. Public disturbances in Buenos Aires followed revelation of this plan of the
oligarchy, and it was promptly withdrawn by politically sensitive Roca, at the cost of the friendship of his old associate

[13] Congreso Nacional, *Diario de sesiones de la Cámara de Senadores*, Dec. 31, 1903,
pp. 745–749, Jan. 13, 1904, pp. 814–827; Barrett to Hay, March 3, 1904, Despatches, Vol. 42, No. 41.

[14] *La Nación* (Nov. 6, 12, 1903), while not approving United States action in
Panama, placed all blame for the affair on the "bad government" of Colombia.
La Prensa (Jan. 28, 1903), prior to the revolution, endorsed the Hay-Herrán treaty
between the United States and Colombia, which was later rejected by Colombia,
as a logical and beneficial extension of United States interests. Zeballos in his
Revista frequently presented Roosevelt as a model of civic and economic leadership.

Pellegrini.[15] Venezuela had been another instance. But what the United States did in Panama had no such implications for the ruling class in Argentina. The United States presented an increasingly attractive market to Argentine producers and exporters, and United States imports meant more business for Argentine merchants. So too, despite the possible long-run danger demonstrated by experience with Europe, was United States capital welcomed as it began to enter Argentina in small amounts in these years, although the lures of increased trade and new sources of money were mixed with fear of imperialism and interference with European commerce.

Argentina and the United States were growing nations, and their mutual trade was increasing. This was clear after 1880; it was clearer after 1900, as figures (Table 3) demonstrate.

TABLE 3. Value of Argentine trade with the United States (dollars): 1880–1906.

Year	Argentine Imports	Argentine Exports	Total
1880	1,882,841	6,214,575	8,097,416
1885	4,676,501	4,328,510	9,005,002
1895	4,456,163	7,675,270	12,131,433
1900	11,558,237	8,114,304	19,672,541
1901	11,537,668	8,065,318	19,602,986
1902	9,801,804	11,120,721	20,922,525
1903	11,437,570	9,430,278	20,867,848
1904	16,902,017	9,835,161	26,737,178
1905	25,564,056	15,354,901	40,918,957
1906	32,673,359	18,379,063	51,052,422

Source: *Statistical Abstract of the United States, 1906*, p. 217.

The flow of trade between Argentina and the United States which had prevailed through the eighties and nineties was reversed after 1900 when United States exports to Argentina outvalued the latter's exports to the United States. Not that our representatives in Buenos Aires were satisfied. Barrett in 1904

[15] José A. Terry, *Contribución a la historia financiera de la República Argentina* (Buenos Aires, 1910), p. 33.

reported nine steps which should be taken to expand commerce; none of the points, from the need for Spanish-speaking salesmen to the need for United States banks, was new. His successor, Beaupre, continued to make the worst of a good thing, listing defects in our trade machinery while claiming that nearly every article made in the United States could be sold in Argentina. Both gentlemen probably would have agreed with the fundamental, if simple, analysis of our trade made by the chief of the Bureau of Foreign and Domestic Commerce, who wrote that it was useless to urge the establishment of steamship lines and a dozen other facilities if the United States businessman was not willing to go out and sell his goods in the first place. Americans were still too busy with the home market or those within easier reach.[16]

Nor was the Argentine government after 1900 any warmer toward special Pan American trade arrangements than it had been in the past (although Argentina sent a greater quantity of official publications to the Bureau of the American Republics than did any other nation). Early in 1903 there assembled in New York a Customs Congress, as provided for at the Second Pan American Conference. The Argentine delegate was the consul-general in New York City. Acting with what must have seemed to him to be consistency with the good of his country's commerce, he introduced a resolution calling for prompt ratification of the reciprocity treaties still pending between the American states, and for preferential tariffs for hemispheric raw material imports. Two days later he resigned as a delegate, with the request that his resolution be withdrawn. His action had aroused powerful interests in Buenos Aires which opposed hemispheric preference as a betrayal of Europe.[17] The Customs Congress, incidentally, led to no governmental action.

[16] Barrett reports of Feb. 8 and 11, 1904. *U.S. Consular Reports*, No. 285, June 1904, pp. 819–823; Beaupre to Hay, Aug. 26, 1904, Despatches, Vol. 43, No. 24; undated Beaupre report, *U.S. Consular Reports*, No. 306, March 1906, p. 68; Frederic Emery, "Causes of Our Failure to Develop South American Trade," *The Annals of the American Academy of Political and Social Science*, 22:154 (July 1903).

[17] U.S. Senate, 57th Congress, 2nd Session, *Message from the President of the United States . . . Relative to the Proceedings of the First Customs Congress of the American Republics . . . January, 1903* (Washington, 1903), pp. 34, 37; *La Prensa*, Jan. 23, 24, 1903.

At the same time one could find Argentine businessmen (not estancieros) like Francisco Seeber, owner of "Las Catalinas," the vast warehouse chain in Buenos Aires, who corresponded with Elihu Root and with Argentine representatives in the United States, urging measures for the expansion of trade between the two countries, and going so far as to subsume United States "conquests" in the Caribbean under twentieth-century laws of progress.[18]

Certainly there was little danger of United States business interests on the scene dominating Argentina. Prior to the year 1903 there was no United States branch office in Argentina. In that year the United Shoe Machinery Company opened an office in Buenos Aires. The Singer Sewing Machine Company opened the second United States branch in the city in 1906. These were primarily merchandising offices, not manufacturing plants. United States capital investment in Argentina on January 1, 1899 was $3,000,000—and this seems to be a highly optimistic figure. Nearly one-quarter of this amount was in public utility shares.[19]

Indeed, the shoe was on the other foot, for Argentine competition in the grain and meat markets of Europe was beginning to be experienced by United States producers—this at the very time when the old sense of inferiority caused a lengthy debate in the Argentine senate between Cané, Pellegrini, and Figueroa Alcorta over whether or not Argentine products were of sufficient quality to be represented at the St. Louis Exposition.[20]

In another market the United States and Argentina were tangled in competition. A Brazilian decree of 1904 granted a 20 per cent tariff reduction to United States flour. Actually, the price of United States flour delivered in Brazil was so much higher than the same product from Argentina that it is doubtful if even a total remission of duty would have created a much larger market for the American product. But the Argentines,

---

[18] Francisco Seeber, *Argentina . . . Estudios comparativos* . . . (Buenos Aires, 1903), pp. 233–239, 241–245.

[19] D. M. Phelps, *Migration of Industry to South America* (New York and London, 1936), pp. 11–13; Cleona Lewis, *America's Stake in International Investments* (Washington, D.C., 1938), pp. 603, 607–608.

[20] *Senadores*, Oct. 24, 1903, pp. 589–601.

who by 1900 had completely displaced United States wheat in the Brazilian market, claimed that there was a United States-Brazilian plot against them. This charge was not borne out by trade figures, which show that, from 1903 to 1915, Brazil imported more flour from Argentina than it did from the United States, an indication of the development in Argentina of a milling industry accompanying expanding wheat production.[21]

Anti-Yankeeism was certainly no less pronounced after 1900 than in the two preceding decades, and it was perhaps more bitter. This was in part because it now had a positive side upon which to feed—*hispanismo*, sentiment for Spain. Animosity toward the United States and love for Spain could be directly related because it had been the final hard push of the Yankees that had sunk the old monarchy to its lowest depths, stripped of its last possessions in the Indies. A century had elapsed since the revolution of the colonies against the motherland; now the children could indulge in a racial-cultural myth, with curious manifestations such as the official modification, at the turn of the century, of verses in the Argentine national anthem which were deemed by Argentine leaders to be insulting to Spain.

Numerous articles in diverse periodicals attacked the United States. Yankee imperialism, according to one author, could be defeated if the Spanish American states would strengthen their ties with each other and with the motherland.[22] The United States, wrote another, controls the Caribbean and seeks to force Europe out of the Spanish American market.[23] *La Nación* (March 30, 1900) and *El Economista* (Nov. 22, 29, 1902) called for enlarged trade with Spain. Zeballos paid tribute to Spain on the ninetieth anniversary of Argentina's revolution.[24] A young Argentine, who was to be a good friend of the United States for many decades, bearded the lion in his den. Ernesto Nelson, speaking in Philadelphia before the Academy of Political and

[21] *La Prensa*, July 13, 14, 16, 27, 28, 1906; *La Nación*, July 27, 28, 31, 1906; U.S. Tariff Commission, *Reciprocity and Commercial Treaties* (Washington, D.C., 1919), pp. 285–300.

[22] A. Rodríguez del Busto, *Revista Nacional*, año 16, t. May 1901, pp. 441–453.

[23] Aquiles Vaillate, "Los Estados Unidos y la América Latina," *Estudios*, año 1, t. 2, 1902, pp. 241–269.

[24] E. S. Zeballos, "Hispania," *Revista de Derecho, Historia y Letras*, año 2, t. 6, June 1900, pp. 628–637.

Social Sciences, pointed accurately to the non-complementary economies of the United States and Argentina, the rivalry of the two countries for Europe's food markets, the impediment presented by the United States tariff, and his country's satisfaction with European capital and European trade.[25] A less temperate writer called for the confederation of all of Latin America.[26]

The most formidable antagonist of the United States in Argentina at this time, as before, was Roque Saenz Peña. This dominant figure of the Argentine upper class voiced admiration for the material power of the United States, as did many of his fellows, while challenging its acts abroad. *Norteamericanos*, the future president of his country observed, regard public law as a fiction and consequently do not believe in the principle of the equality of states. The United States, he believed, has had no interest in the political solidarity of the hemisphere; her objectives have been economic. Therefore, "the Monroe Doctrine appears to be made of rubber . . . adaptable to the exclusive interest of the interventions which the United States itself generates."

In 1905, Saenz Peña returned to the scene of his youthful military adventures. He crossed the Andes to Peru to accept promotion to the honorary rank of general in the Peruvian army in commemoration of his service in the battle of the Morro of Arica. The Argentine leader did not let this occasion of inter-American fraternization pass in mere reminiscences. His theme was the menace of Yankee imperialism, first seen, and defeated, in the form of Blaine's plan for economic mastery of Latin America. Now, he told his audience, the menace has returned, more dangerous than before because disguised as political protection. He ended his principal speech in Peru by repeating the peroration of one of the speeches he had made at the First Pan American Conference—the invocation of Europe, mentor and support of Latin America.[27]

[25] E. Nelson, "Posiciones respectivas de los Estados Unidos y de Europa en el comercio de la República Argentina," *Revista de Derecho, Historia y Letras*, año 6, t. 17, Dec. 1903, pp. 284–293.

[26] J. Abasolo, "Cómo confederar la América Latina—Cómo resistir al extranjero," *Revista Nacional*, año 21, t. 41, May and April 1906, pp. 97–102.

[27] Saenz Peña, *Escritos y discursos*, III, *Actuación nacional* (Buenos Aires, 1935), 169–170; I, *Actuación internacional*, 160–164, 393.

What Saenz Peña said was important not only because of his past achievements, but because of the future—he was gathering about him a following of men from within and beyond his own class, men who were discontented with the methods of political domination employed by the oligarchy. His was a rising star.

At the same time a star was setting, prematurely for Argentina and, perhaps, for better relations with the United States. After decades of vital leadership devoted to his country and to his class, Carlos Pellegrini was nearer to death in 1906 than his sixty years warranted.

In recent years Pellegrini's position on internal and on foreign affairs had changed considerably from what it had been in the eighties and nineties, when he was one of the most forthright and successful defenders of the political techniques and the exclusively pro-European policies of his class. After 1900, by conviction, and in part because of hostility to his old friend Roca, El Gringo advocated principles far removed from the conservatism of his earlier days. The political maneuvering, which led to the hand-picked "convention of notables" which elected Manuel Quintana president in 1902, repelled him. The first years of that administration, reactionary even by prevailing canons, seem to have stimulated the former president to accept the need for wider social and political action. Some of his new opinions may have been gained by his growing knowledge of the United States.

In 1902, Pellegrini criticized his countrymen who upheld the "continental policy," by which Argentina was mystically endowed—possibly by San Martín—with the right to take a hand in affairs on the Pacific Coast. Not what occurred beyond the Andes but what was happening along the Atlantic should interest Argentina, he wrote to Indalecio Gómez, future minister of Saenz Peña. (Roca, too, realized this, and acted always for peace with Chile, although he was Argentina's most experienced general.) At that moment Pellegrini himself did not seem to regard the United States as bordering on the Atlantic, but two years later he made a long visit to the northern republic. There he traveled widely, witnessed the national political campaign, questioned, and observed. From the United States he sent to

Argentina six long letters which were published in *La Nación*. In the first he commented that an Argentine in the United States immediately set about comparing the two countries. He expressed admiration for the triumphant creation of a free and diverse people which was the United States. He liked Yankee energy, he liked New York, he liked Washington, and the St. Louis exposition amazed him. He was too much the European-ized Argentine gentleman to appreciate "dormitorios Pull-man," but he reported with perception upon labor unions, immigration, women, and tariffs. In his final letter he com-pared United States and Argentine electoral methods, and pre-dicted that it would require a greater effort than any his genera-tion was capable of to endow the Argentine people with a similar degree of political liberty. The difference between the two countries, he wrote to his brother, is so great that "I begin [to believe] that we shall always be, more or less, *South American*." If, he wrote, some Argentine president should succeed in gain-ing political liberty for the citizenry, "posterity will honor him as it does the founders of the independence and the liberty of the Argentine people." The prediction was to come true; the time, only eight years in the future; the president, Pellegrini's life-long comrade, Saenz Peña.[28]

The grip of the oligarchy upon the electoral machinery in Argentina seemed firmer than ever. Pellegrini's awakening to reform did not result from his visit to the United States, for it was apparent prior to his trip, but his talks with Roosevelt and Gompers surely did not harden his conservatism. Long before that trip he showed some of that bitterness toward his native land which so often seems to alternate in Argentine hearts with intense pride. In 1900 he had written to Zeballos from Monte Carlo, quoting the comment of revolutionary war General Las Heras: "In the Argentine Republic the sky and the earth are admirable, but in between is detestable." In January 1904, in public speeches made before departure for North America, and again in August 1905, after his return, he denounced electoral fraud. He came to admit his error in aiding in the imposition

[28] *Pellegrini, 1846–1906: Obras* (5 vols.; Buenos Aires, 1941), pp. 359–390, 423–427, 430–504, 621.

and maintenance of the system. On May 9, 1906 he spoke in the chamber of deputies. He acknowledged the truth of the accusation made by the only Socialist deputy, Alfredo Palacios, that the majority of the national deputies had been elected by fraudulent votes. To his acknowledgment the tall leader added accusations of his own against the oligarchy; then he crossed the wide chamber and clasped the hand of Palacios.

A month later he stood again in the congress. He spoke bitterly of the theory which he and his class often advanced on behalf of preserving the political virginity of the Argentine people. Pellegrini said: "If today the shade of Del Valle were to present itself to me in this place and were to ask, 'How goes it?' I would have to confess that my evolutionary theories have failed lamentably, and that today we find ourselves worse off than ever before."[29] Five weeks later Pellegrini was dead.

It is impossible to know whether or not, had he lived, Pellegrini might not have been responsible for reform in Argentina, and a broader view of the United States. Of the three great leaders of the Generation of Eighty, Roca was committed to the internal status quo and to Europe; Saenz Peña was deeply antagonistic toward the United States, although ultimately the conqueror of electoral fraud; Pellegrini alone was beginning to display the understanding and flexibility which might have meant both internal development and a larger friendship for the United States.

He was a great man in his land, this founder of the Banco de la Nación, of the Caja de Conversión, and of the Jockey Club. His death was sharply felt by his peers. Speaking for the nation at the graveside in the Recoleta, President Figueroa Alcorta revealed, no doubt unintentionally, the extent to which the aristocracy knew itself to be weakened by this latest loss in a year of many deaths. "Ha caído el más fuerte"—"The strongest one has fallen," said the president.

In 1906 old Mitre died, a founder of the country, in its second establishment after Rosas. Bernado de Irigoyen died, as old as Mitre, and almost as wise. The president died, Quintana,

[29] *Pellegrini, 1846–1906*, II, 663–664, 666, 670–671, III, 401–409, IV, 377–388, 505–512, and Pellegrini's letter on electoral reform in *La Nación*, Nov. 27, 1902.

who had accompanied Saenz Peña to the First Pan American Conference in Washington in 1889.

The electoral laws had been relaxed a bit at the end of Roca's second term, and a Socialist had slipped through into congress. They were tightened again under Quintana, who was a gentleman who believed in authority, and whose election was the result of the rigged "Convention of Notables," but less publicly of estancia politics, for his selection was the result of conferences between Roca and other factional leaders within the oligarchy, meetings held often in the pleasant and private surroundings of one of the great estates ringing Buenos Aires. In Buenos Aires in 1904, out of a population of more than 800,000, the right to vote was held by 53,220 people.[30]

The strain on the oligarchy was beginning to show. Even in so public a place as the annual presidential messages on the state of the nation, delivered in person by the chief executive to congress, the tensions within the country were visible. Roca's message of 1903 refers to interventions and strikes, rebellion and states of siege—all deemed to be perturbations of the social order, as indeed they were, and all to be met with the force of authority, one of whose new weapons was the Law of Residence, providing for expulsion from the country of social agitators.[31]

Quintana had had deepening difficulties upon which to report in his first message to congress in May 1905; there had been disturbances in the University of Buenos Aires, a general strike, and, three months earlier, a revolution, severe if abortive. But when President Quintana stated his concept of his office it carried no hint of a different Argentina than that which he had helped to construct in the quarter of a century past. "I place myself," he told congress and the country, "above the democratic movements, to preside over them with justice."[32]

---

[30] Elvira Aldao de Díaz, *Reminiscencias sobre Aristóbulo del Valle* (Buenos Aires, 1928), pp. 144–152; Mabragaña, *Los mensajes*, VI, 74, 80.

[31] Mabragaña, *Los mensajes*, VI, 49–51.

[32] Mabragaña, *Los mensajes*, VI, 112–116.

15

A Conference and a Visit

WHATEVER their difficulties in mastering internal affairs, the oligarchy continued to preside with a steady hand over the external relations of the nation. Another test of Argentine policies toward the United States and the Pan American organization came in 1906, with the Third Conference of American states.

To many Argentines the First Conference had been a plot of the United States to establish its economic supremacy in the hemisphere; the Second Conference had been a wrestling match with wily Chile, with the United States an unneutral referee. The Third Conference was also viewed as a challenge to Argentina, this time as a plot concocted by the United States, eagerly supported by Brazil, to enmesh Argentina in the spreading net of United States hegemony, baited with the Monroe Doctrine.

The Argentine position may be considered to be in part a reaction to Theodore Roosevelt's aggressive Latin American policies. There was a more positive side to Argentina's role at the conference, however, in that country's emphasis on the universality of its own Drago Doctrine.

The two countries and the two creeds seemed sure to clash. Before the assembly convened, the basic issues, old and new, were raised in Argentina. Foreign Minister Montes de Oca requested Drago to serve as a delegate to the Rio meeting. In his letter the foreign minister stated that the Drago Doctrine must be sustained and extended by Argentina; he acknowledged that the Monroe Doctrine was a protection for the American states, but he denied that the Drago Doctrine was an extension of that statement. Friendship with the United States, he wrote, must "not impede the natural Argentine tendency to tighten the bonds with the European nations to which we owe the labor and the capital . . . that is our pride and the astonishment of the world." [1]

Drago was not impressed. He refused the invitation to serve as a delegate precisely because he believed that Argentina had accepted the Monroe Doctrine through his declaration, and by the actions of Sarmiento and Quesada when they had served as ministers to the United States. He then continued in his reply to his foreign minister to make what is probably the strongest statement of friendship for the United States that any Argentine of similar prominence has made in the twentieth century. [2]

But Drago was alone in his position. A more typical attitude among the politically influential was that of Eduardo Bidau, a delegate to the Second, Third, and Fourth Conferences. Delivering the inaugural lecture in the course in international public law at the University of Buenos Aires in April 1906, the scholar and diplomat attacked the Monroe Doctrine and United States imperialism, defended Drago's thesis, praised Argentina's material progress and her tradition of peace, and closed on a lyrical note of manifest destiny in which he joined his country to Europe, which "has sent its men, its capital, and its products" to Argentina. [3]

Nor did Quintana's successor to the presidential sash, Figueroa Alcorta, seem persuaded that any large virtue resided in Pan Americanism. In his message to congress in May 1906 (the Conference was to open in July), the president undercut the idea of hemispheric unity by pointing out that "simple reasons of location in one of the great divisions of the earth do not suffice to alter the principles of the law of peoples nor the rules of eternal commerce." [4]

Congress got the cue and proceeded to do nothing about

[1] M. A. Montes de Oca to Luis M. Drago, May 1906, *Revista de Derecho, Historia y Letras*, año 15, t. 43, Nov. 1912, pp. 315–324; White to Root, May 30, 1906, National Archives, Dept. of State, American States, U.S. Legation, Argentina, Diplomatic Despatches, Vol. 47, No. 365.

[2] República Argentina, Ministerio del Interior, *La política internacional de la Nación Argentina* . . . (Buenos Aires, 1946), pp. 498–499.

[3] Eduardo Bidau, "Las doctrinas de Monroe y Drago," *Revista de la Universidad de Buenos Aires*, V (1906), 98–110.

[4] H. Mabragaña, *Los mensajes* . . . (6 vols.; Buenos Aires, n.d.), VI, 168.

authorizing funds for the Argentine delegation to the Conference until the month in which the meeting was to be held.
There was little debate, and that was listless, except for the plea
made on the Fourth of July by old Mitre's son, Senator Emilio
Mitre, on behalf of Argentine-United States friendship and in
defense of the Monroe Doctrine. The appropriation was passed
a scant nine days prior to the departure of the Argentine delegation for Rio. [5]

One matter which irked the Argentines was the recent eleva-
tion of the ministries of Brazil and the United States in each
other's country to the rank of embassies. It was against this
background of injured pride that an incident occurred between
the Argentine and United States governments a few months
before the Conference met. An official bulletin of the Argentine
foreign ministry published, "almost textually," remarks which,
it was stated, President Roosevelt had addressed to Argentine
minister García Merou. In this version the president praised
Argentina as a great land, inhabited by a superior people. Much
attention was given in the Argentine press to this display of
partiality by the president of the United States, and unfavorable references were made to Brazil. The result was a strong
denial from Secretary of State Elihu Root. In no uncertain
terms Root told the Argentine foreign minister that President
Roosevelt had directed him "to say with all earnestness that
Señor Merou's recital is a complete distortion of the kindly
remarks [the president] made concerning the notable development of the Argentine Republic." [6]

Root's charge was of course not made public, but it may be
assumed that it circulated among the close-knit group of
leaders who ran the government. It could only have confirmed
them in their course of neglect of the Pan American movement
between conferences, and opposition to it at the meetings themselves. In the interval between the Second and Third Conferences the Argentine representatives in Washington ignored most

[5] Congreso Nacional, *Diario de sesiones de la Cámara de Senadores*, 1906, pp. 436–444.

[6] Root to Beaupre, Feb. 26, 1906, National Archives, Records of the Dept. of
State, American Affairs, Diplomatic Instructions of the Dept. of State, Vol. 18,
No. 70.

of the meetings of the executive committee of the International
Bureau of American Republics. The Argentine government
failed to pay its annual quota for the support of the Bureau for
the years 1904–1907, inclusive. In addition to the abrupt withdrawal of its delegate from the Customs Congress held in New
York in 1903, the Argentine government failed to ratify the
convention approved at the Second Conference which led to the
Pan American Sanitary Congress of 1902. Thus Argentina was
not represented at the outset of one of the most successful programs of Pan American technical cooperation. [7]

The Argentine press was as unhappy about the Third Pan
American Conference as was the administration. *La Prensa*
(Oct. 2, 1905) hailed the promised visit of Secretary Root to the
Rio meeting as an opportunity for him to eliminate the idea that
the United States was engaged in establishing an "imperialistic
protectorate" over Latin America. If the Root visit took another
course, the newspaper continued, it could cause the dissolution
of the conference. The political plans of the United States for
"South America" must be resisted, it declared on December 29,
1905; ties with Europe should be strengthened; the Monroe
Doctrine should be kept out of the Conference. Even *La Nación*
(Dec. 21, 1905 and March 28, 1906) took the same view, and in
the same words, terming the Monroe Doctrine outdated now
that Latin America (apparently meaning Argentina, Brazil, and
Chile, the only countries named) had ceased to be "South
America." Argentina is a free agent, the paper went on, trading
with the world and compromising her sovereignty with no one.
In a later issue, however, *La Nación* (May 31, 1906) warned
Argentine leaders not to "patrioteer" against the United States.

La Prensa may not have been patrioteering but it was certainly patriotic when, in the issue of March 26, 1906, the editors
declared that Argentina "has no self-interest in the next Pan
American Conference. All her internal questions are resolved;
her economic forces are unfolding . . . with enviable fortune;

[7] The Pan American Union Archive, Minutes of the Executive Committee of the
International Bureau of American Republics, III; White to Root, May 10, 1906,
National Archives, Diplomatic Despatches, U.S. Legation, Buenos Aires, Vol. 18,
No. 76; García Merou to Hay, October 3, 1902, National Archives, Diplomatic
Notes Exchanged Between the Argentine and U.S. Governments, Vol. 5.

her financial obligations are fulfilled; . . . she is sufficient unto herself and has no thought of hegemonies."

The *Revista de Derecho, Historia y Letras* joined in the attack on United States policy. One article advocated the old remedy—a Latin American alliance. Another pursued the familiar line that the United States sought to employ Pan Americanism to split Latin America and Europe, and that Argentina, destined to be the colossus of the southern continent, needed none of the Yankee organization. As timely evidence offered in support of this view, the *Revista* devoted more than one hundred pages to the Rio Conference, including the testimony of Secretary Root before a United States congressional committee to the effect that the Pan American organization provided the best means of breaking the relative isolation of Latin America from the United States, and his emphasis on the need of the United States for foreign markets for its products and capital.[8]

Meanwhile, under authority given by the Second Pan American Conference, the representatives of the American states in Washington met with the secretary of state in December, 1905 to undertake preparations for the Third Conference. Suggestions for the agenda flowed in. Peru desired unlimited discussion of arbitration. Chile wanted no discussion of arbitration. Argentina informed the governing committee that her attendance at the Conference was not certain; the note went on to explain that Argentina had not ratified many of the agreements of the First and Second Conferences because she had ratified the Montevideo Treaties of 1888 on similar subjects. Therefore, the government stated, Argentina would wish to have included in the program for the Conference measures tending to assure acceptance by the assembled states of the principles of law approved at the meetings in Montevideo, Washington, and Mexico City. The note closed with the recommendation that obligatory arbitration be included in the program.

[8] A. Sánchez, "Solidaridad Latino-Americana," *Revista de Derecho, Historia y Letras*, año 9, t. 24, April 1906, pp. 147–157; A. Gancedo, "Denuncia de los tratados de la República Argentina; Congreso Pan-Americana," *Revista de Derecho, Historia y Letras*, año 9, t. 24, May 1906, pp. 372–391; *Revista de Derecho, Historia y Letras*, año 9, t. 25, July 1906, pp. 5–121, especially pp. 71–72.

In a second note sent to the governing committee a little later, in March 1906, the Argentine government submitted that the Conference should vote favorably on the proposition that the Second Hague Conference, scheduled for 1907, include on its agenda the subject of the compulsory collection of public debts. [9]

Despite her disregard for other Pan American commitments, it seemed likely that Argentina intended to take a place at the Third Conference, as she had in the preceding gatherings. This was made clear at a meeting of the Pan American governing board in April. Despite the fact that the proposed program for the Conference was submitted to the board on this occasion, and that Portela, the Argentine minister to the United States, was a signatory of the program committee's report, the Argentine representative rose to inform his fellows that, in giving his co-operation in the preparation of the agenda, he had not restricted Argentina's liberty of action, either in the matter of attendance at the Conference or in the right to propose, at that meeting, any action which it might "deem expedient."

Robert Bacon, Assistant Secretary of State, who was presiding at the board meeting, bluntly replied that it was competent for any country to decline to attend the conference, but that he deprecated inability to accept the program unreservedly.

At the next meeting of the board Elihu Root replaced his subordinate in the chair. He referred to the situation created at the previous meeting, saying:

I think there has been some little question—some little misunder-standing—about the nature and effect of this programme. We ought to understand each other here; otherwise it is not likely we will do so at Rio. My understanding is that this programme is an enumera-tion of the subjects to be discussed at the Conference, and that no other subjects are to be discussed, unless by the prior affirmative action of the Conference itself . . . If that meets with general assent, I shall ask the Secretary to note that this statement has been generally assented to by the Board. The Secretary will please note this.

No dissent was recorded.

[9] The Pan American Union, *Extracto de las ideas de los distintos países de América con relación al programa de la Tercera Conferencia Pan-Americana* . . . (Washington, D.C., Mayo 28 de 1900), pp. 38, 45–48, 50–52.

Root also referred to another misunderstanding involving Argentina. This related to the program committee's recommendation that the Second Hague Conference be requested to discuss the extent to which force might be employed in the collection of debts. The Argentine representative had objected to the wording, on the grounds that it had the effect of admitting the validity of the use of force in such cases. Root stated that he had drafted the provision, and that he would not construe it as did the Argentines. But he drew up a new proposition, which was approved by the board. It stated that the Second Hague Conference be requested "to consider whether and if at all, to what extent the use of force for the collection of public debts is admissible."[10]

At this same meeting the program for the Third Pan American Conference was adopted. The Conference was to consider: (1) reorganization of the Bureau, (2) adherence to the principle of arbitration of American disputes, (3) extension for five years of the treaty on the arbitration of pecuniary claims signed at the Second Pan American Conference, (4) a resolution concerning the forcible collection of public debts, (5) formation of a commission of jurists to prepare codes of public and private international law, (6) a convention on naturalization, (7) development of commerce in the Americas, (8) unification of customs regulations and consular laws, (9) patent and trademark legislation, (10) sanitation regulations, (11) the Pan American Railroad, (12) copyright laws, (13) practice of the learned professions. The regulations of the conference were agreed upon also at this meeting, the hope being that in this manner the violent disagreements of the opening sessions of the First and Second Conferences might be avoided.[11]

Instructions to the United States delegation to the assembly were issued by Secretary Root in June 1906. They duplicated those of President Roosevelt to the delegates to the Second Conference because, Root said, they were "the general principles which underlie the relations of the United States to the other

[10] Minutes of the Executive Committee, III, 410–412, 452–455.

[11] Minutes of the Executive Committee, III, 453, 464–469; *Tercera Conferencia Internacional Americana, 1906. Actas, resoluciones, documentos* (Río de Janeiro, 1907), pp. 5–9.

American Republics." But Root further watered down Pan American objectives. The true function of the coming conference, he stated, was "to deal with matters of common interest which are not really subjects of controversy." From this view, he continued, it follows that the conference "is not expected to accomplish any striking or spectacular final results." The Secretary also advised the United States representatives to resist changes to the rules set up by the governing board, and attempts to bring up matters not contained in the program.[12]

The United States delegation consisted of six men. The chairman, W. I. Buchanan, had been the most active United States delegate at the preceding Conference, adding thereto the knowledge of Latin America which he had gained as minister to Argentina. Leo S. Rowe's experience in Latin America was as yet limited to work on the legal status of Puerto Rico; he was a professor of political science at the University of Pennsylvania. Paul S. Reinsch was also a professor of political science, at the University of Wisconsin. A. J. Montague had recently completed four years as governor of Virginia; he had an active interest in international as well as national affairs. Tulio Larrinaga was a Puerto Rican leader; and Van Leer Polk was a former consular official.

Of the Argentine delegates, the oldest and most experienced was José A. Terry, born in Brazil during parental exile in the time of Rosas, minister of the treasury in the administrations of Luis Saenz Peña, Roca, and Quintana, and also foreign minister in Roca's second term. Eduardo Bidau had been a delegate at the Mexico City meeting. Joaquín V. González was scholar and political leader, national deputy, former minister of the interior, minister of justice and public instruction, founder, in 1905, and president of the University of La Plata. Epifanio Portela was a career diplomat who had been minister to Brazil, Chile, and Spain.[13]

[12] *Report of the Delegates of the United States to the Third International Conference of the American States* . . . (Washington, 1907), pp. 39–40.

[13] *Dictionary of American Biography* (21 vols.; New York, 1928–1944); *National Cyclopaedia of American Biography* (I–, New York, 1893–); E. Udaondo, *Diccionario biográfico argentino* (Buenos Aires, 1938); W. B. Parker, *Argentines of Today* (2 vols.; Buenos Aires and New York, 1920).

The Third Pan American Conference was inaugurated on the evening of July 23, 1906 by the Brazilian minister of foreign affairs, Barão do Rio Branco. The building in which the Conference convened was truly named a palace—the Palace of Monroe. It had been constructed for the Brazilian exhibit at the St. Louis Exposition, then removed piece by piece to Rio de Janeiro and rebuilt on the central avenue of the city. It was given its name perhaps with the Argentines as well as the North Americans in mind.

The night of the opening session was as sparkling and alive as Rio can be. The streets and parks near the palace were brilliantly illuminated and jammed with people; the approaches to the meeting place were lined with troops.

Within the palace the eminent and bulky baron addressed the delegates with the platitudes befitting the occasion. The reign of international law, he claimed, was, happily, more and more respected in the world. He acknowledged America's debt to Europe. And he told his audience that "it is not our intent to work against anybody."

Another distinguished Brazilian diplomat, Joaquim Nabuco, first ambassador to the United States, was elected permanent president of the Conference. He assured the assembly that these meetings would never be employed "to intervene collectively" in American affairs. He outdid Root's moderation of aims when he told the delegates that "the great object of these conferences should be to express collectively what is already understood to be unanimous."[14]

These rhetorical pieces set the stage for the first working session, which was consumed by a variety of harmless but pleasurable tasks: the election of Rio Branco and Root as honorary presidents; the passage of votes honoring the memories of John Hay, Volney Foster, Bartolemé Mitre, Manuel Quintana, Carlos Pellegrini, and others.

The next matter was a proposal by Nabuco of a four-day adjournment in order to organize committees. He might have anticipated the reaction of one delegation had he studied the two preceding Conferences. Argentines Portela and Terry

[14] *Report of the Delegates,* pp. 55–58.

insisted that this was a waste of time; the other delegates followed their lead and voted that committee work begin on the next day but one.[15]

The struggle over regulations for the assembly having been avoided by action in Washington, the plenary sessions from July 26 to August 7 accomplished little except to receive congratulatory telegrams. On the latter date the committee on arbitration brought in its report. Overshadowing this issue was the impending Hague Conference to which, in contrast to the first Hague assembly, all the Latin American states had been invited. The United States delegation had been instructed to support the principle of arbitration; the Argentine government took the same position in the report which its delegation published in Rio in the first days of the meeting; the Conference committee believed in arbitration; finally, the nineteen nations at the Conference (Haiti and Venezuela did not attend) unanimously adopted the committee's recommendation that their governments should, at the Hague, work for a definite and efficacious general convention on arbitration. It was not so easy to decide on the proper manner of informing the Hague Conference of the decision. The discussions on procedure became so complicated that Argentine delegate Terry at last moved to send the question to the committee which had drafted the arbitration proposal. On August 13 the committee reported its recommendation that the Brazilian government should transmit the Rio decision to the Hague Conference, and the Conference approved.[16]

Customs, commerce, and communications provided the delegates with much to discuss. Root had instructed United States representatives to favor all practical suggestions for increasing commerce, especially the Pan American Railroad. The special report of the Argentine delegation—which described itself as a review of Argentine achievements in carrying out the recommendations of the first two Pan American Conferences, and a

[15] TCIA, pp. 55–64, 70–73.

[16] *Report of the Delegates*, pp. 40–41; *Memoria de la delegación de la República Argentina presentada a la Tercera Conferencia reunida en Río de Janeiro* (Río de Janeiro, 1906), p. 153; TCIA, pp. 132–134, 140; J. B. Scott, ed., *The International Conferences of American States, 1889–1928* . . . (New York, 1931), pp. 124–125.

few pages further on as a "demonstration . . . of the accomplishments of a young and laborious people . . . at peace with everyone, and honorably working out its destiny"—gave some figures on Argentine railroads, but went at length into statistics of trade. The figures were impressive. 1905 had been the greatest trading year in the country's history, with exports valued at 352,843,841 gold pesos and imports worth 205,154,420 gold pesos. Three-quarters of the exports were to Europe, one-quarter to the Americas. The same proportions applied to Argentine imports from those areas. Argentina traded with only nine American states; of these, five accounted for the bulk of the commerce. The report also attacked the Dingley Tariff, especially for its disastrous effect on Argentine wool exports, and reviewed the failure of the United States to ratify the Buchanan-Alcorta convention.

The Argentine delegates scarcely needed to draw the conclusion they did: that their country's trade with the Americas was modest compared to that with Europe. The Argentines listed the factors that made for strong economic ties to Europe: moderate European tariffs, good transportation, with two-way cargoes, European goods of high quality, well-packed and intended to satisfy the customer and sold by intelligent, Spanish-speaking salesmen, Argentine travel in Europe and European immigration into Argentina, and easy, ample credit. Only when similar factors should come to exist in the Americas would trade increase. Specifically, the report commented, the United States can gain an important commercial position in the Americas only when it learns more about the other countries, sends them capital, and modifies its raw material import duties.[17]

Despite Argentine aloofness in its report, the Conference passed a resolution, in which the Argentines joined, urging improvement of the American net of transportation and communication. It also approved a declaration creating a division within the Bureau of American Republics to study the much-studied problem of chaotic customs regulations.

These modest results were peacefully attained because, as the United States delegation later reported, the members of the

[17] *Report of the Delegates*, p. 44; *Memoria*, pp. 5, 7–16, 23–32, 34, 79–84.

committee on commerce early decided that "it would be unwise
to enter upon the consideration of principles affecting the commercial intercourse between the Republics," or to consider
resolutions "which might in any way tend to embarrass the freedom of action essential in order that the Republics might adjust
their commercial policy to meet their different requirements." [18]

This bland double talk was followed by a resolution urged by
the United States which provided for the study of monetary
conditions in the several American states, with an eye toward
general monetary reform. [19] Here the United States was clinging
to the remnant of the concept which had dominated the first
years of the Pan American movement—the idea of an integrated
hemispheric economy. This was now a shadow of a false hope,
and had no subsequent results.

The Pan American Railroad was also clearly dead in all but
name, and received at Rio only sufficient perfunctory support
to keep alive the permanent commission. [20]

Nor was there greater long-run success with other issues considered by the assembly. There was unanimous approval of an
agreement for protecting intellectual and industrial property,
but of the major Latin American countries only Brazil and
Chile ratified the convention. The United States and Argentina,
according to their own reports, had no intention of modifying
their practices in these areas. There the matter rested. [21]

The committee on the liberal professions also retraced familiar
ground, pointing out that nothing had been accomplished in
the field since the treaty signed at Mexico City in 1902. Confirmation of that treaty was recommended and was unanimously
given by the delegates. Neither Argentina nor the United States
intended to take the matter further domestically. [22]

A similar situation faced the Conference in the matter of

[18] TCIA, pp. 284–290, 335–338; *International Conferences*, pp. 143–144; *Report of
the Delegates*, p. 16.
[19] *Report of the Delegates*, pp. 18–19; *International Conferences*, pp. 147–148.
[20] TCIA, pp. 280–283, 455–483; *International Conferences*, pp. 142–143.
[21] *Report of the Delegates*, p. 44; *Memoria*, pp. 101–107, 109–122; TCIA, pp. 269–
275; *International Conferences*, pp. 136–140.
[22] TCIA, pp. 227–248; *International Conferences*, p. 135; *Report of the Delegates*,
pp. 22–23; *Memoria*, pp. 123–141.

arbitration of pecuniary claims. The treaty on this subject, signed at Mexico City by seventeen states, had been ratified by five, not including the sponsor, Argentina. At Rio the nineteen states present hopefully signed a convention extending the Mexico treaty until 1912.[23]

The Conference gained some new ground, perhaps because of agreement between the United States and Argentina. The program provision for action on the codification of international law was supported by Argentina, the United States, and by the other nations at Rio, all of which agreed to establish a commission of jurists to prepare the desired codes. The agreement was later ratified by Argentina and by the United States and by thirteen other American governments; the commission actually met in Rio in 1912.[24]

Two other new accomplishments were the votes to adopt the Washington Sanitary Convention of 1905, and a naturalization agreement. The latter convention, backed by Argentina and the United States, was subsequently ratified by each.[25] This convention and that for the codification of international law were two of the few Pan American agreements that Argentina has made into law.

The apparent desire among the American states to reduce the activity of the Conference to the lowest common denominator applied most obviously to what otherwise might have been the two most important and certainly most provocative subjects —the twin doctrines of Monroe and Drago.

The Monroe Doctrine had no official place on the agenda at any time, but that one nation or another—Brazil, the United States, or Argentina—might inject it into the meeting concerned the diplomats of the last two countries long before the meeting convened. Yet the United States certainly did not want the Monroe declaration discussed at Rio in 1906, and Argentina was willing to let a sleeping dog lie once she became convinced

[23] TCIA, pp. 192–194. Ultimate ratification was by Chile, Colombia, Costa Rica, Ecuador, Guatemala, Honduras, Mexico, Nicaragua, Panama, El Salvador, and the United States. See *International Conferences*, pp. 132–133.

[24] TCIA, pp. 525–536; *International Conferences*, pp. 144–146.

[25] TCIA, pp. 183–191, 275–279, 517–524; *Report of the Delegates*, pp. 15, 42, 44; *International Conferences*, pp. 131–132, 140–141.

that the Conference would not be used to formalize Monroe's statement into a Pan American policy. The only reference to the doctrine made at the Conference came when Bolivia, a loser in the War of the Pacific, attempted to make things uncomfortable for Chile by asserting that if the Monroe declaration forbade territorial conquest by European powers, it could be applied also to conquests made by American states. This extension of the doctrine anticipated by forty years the concept of inter-American mutual defense against internal as well as external aggression. However, despite brief support from Argentina, the Bolivian motion was quietly strangled in the machinery of the Conference. Nothing further was heard of Monroe.[26]

The Drago Doctrine outshone Monroe at Rio. It was part of the program but it first nearly caused Argentine defection from the Conference. The original Root formula regarding debt collection had displeased the Argentine government, which viewed the wording as permissive of forcible intervention. The foreign minister cabled to the Argentine minister in Washington authorizing him to request suspension of the Rio meeting, even if he did it alone.[27] It was after this that Root altered the phrase by inserting the words, "if at all," to satisfy Argentina.

It was Root's view, expressed to the United States delegates to the Rio meeting, that, while the Drago statement was excellent and the United States had long since renounced use of its armed forces for the collection of ordinary contract debts due to its citizens by other governments, the fact that most of the American states were debtor states might give to any stand taken at Rio in favor of the Drago declaration the appearance of a conspiracy of debtors against their European creditors. For Root the true course was to request the Second Hague Conference to consider the subject.

Events involving foreign powers in Santo Domingo were still fresh in memory when the Rio Conference convened, no doubt inspiring the delegates to enlarge their request to the Hague

[26] Beaupre to Root, Dec. 25, 1905, Despatches, Vol. 46, No. c282; White to Root, April 2 and 11, 1906, Despatches, Vol. 47, Nos. 339 and 342; TCIA, pp. 147–151, 349–353.

[27] Ernesto Quesada, "La Doctrina Drago," *Revista de la Universidad de Buenos Aires*, tomo 43 (1919), 377–378.

Conference to consider, in addition to forcible debt collection, means tending to diminish all conflicts of pecuniary origin. The Conference assured assurance by emphasizing that the Root formula by no means implied acceptance of the legitimacy of compulsory debt collection. After hearing from the Argentine delegation an "exposition" on the subject of debt collection, "to fix with clarity . . . the problem and its solution," the Third Pan American Conference unanimously voted to pass on to the Hague assembly the views of the American states on public debts. The shadow of Europe lay dark across the American conference. It was a sign of strength that any decision was taken on the issue, for some of the states were inclined to have the Conference avoid a vote. [28]

Two final subjects were dealt with at Rio, and these actions served to keep Pan Americanism alive. After some sharp disagreement, the Conference voted to continue the authority of the governing board of the international union to select the site for the next Conference; the disagreement was moderated by the expression of "warm sympathy" by the assembly for Buenos Aires as the next meeting place.

And the scope of the International Bureau of American Republics was extended at Rio. The United States delegation had been instructed to support such action because, Root said, "this institution has served a useful purpose." Other nations also favored the step. The Bureau was given power to function as the Permanent Commission of the International American Conferences, with authority to prepare proposals for Conference consideration, and to rewrite the constitution of the organization. The International Union was continued for an additional ten years. It was also voted that each country should form a domestic Pan American Commission to work for ratification of unratified Pan American agreements, and to supply data to the Washington office. [29]

Rio Branco closed the Third Conference on August 27, 1906,

[28] Report of the Delegates, pp. 12–14, 41–42; TCIA, pp. 228–230, 236; International Conferences, pp. 135–136.
[29] TCIA, pp. 157–164, 167–173, 182, 339; Report of the Delegates, pp. 23, 40; International Conferences, pp. 125–131, 146–147.

but the presiding officer, Nabuco, stated more significant thoughts on the preceding day, in his farewell. He referred to the "positive utility of these Congresses," and to the "unanimity of sentiments" which had put to rest the fears of disharmony which had preceded the assembly. The Conference, he truly said, dealt with ways of attaining objectives, not with the goals themselves. Cooperation had replaced mistrust, he maintained. He made an analogy between a tree and Pan Americanism: "Today this tree depends upon the care of each of us, but the time must come when all will depend upon it."[30]

The future would tell whether Nabuco's strong analogy was valid, or whether he spoke with the forced optimism of such occasions. One other American leader had the future in mind, and acted to make it present. Elihu Root himself went to South America and to the Rio Conference in 1906, the first United States secretary of state to make an official visit abroad while in office. If it is true, as one authority has stated, that Teddy Roosevelt and John Hay looked upon Latin Americans as "dagoes," Root gave the impression of esteeming these people. He sought to win their friendship, by creating mutual respect. Yet he agreed with the Roosevelt corollary, and he was Roosevelt's friend, associate, and emissary; his mission may also have been a calculated campaign to allay bitter distrust of the United States.

It was appropriate, and perhaps intentionally so, that Secretary Root's first port of call should have been the great harbor of the nation which was the firmest Latin American friend of the United States. When the secretary arrived in the bay of Rio de Janeiro on July 27, 1906, he was rowed ashore in the royal barge of the former emperor, amid the thundering guns of battleships. Then came the procession up the main avenue, decorated with flowers "perpetually renewed and fresh." On July 31 he addressed a special session of the Pan American Conference. He spoke of the increasing political stability of the New World, stability which was the necessary basis of democracy. He emphasized the value of cooperation among the American states. As for the United States, Root declared in a famous phrase: "We

[30] TCIA, pp. 360–366.

wish for no victories but those of peace, for no territory except our own, for no sovereignty except the sovereignty over ourselves." He spoke of the equality of states, large and small, and of the desire of the United States to "help all our friends . . . become greater and stronger together."[31]

Root departed from Rio for Buenos Aires early in August, after days filled with speeches and dinners. How much did he, and the Conference, accomplish? Something, thought delegate Leo Rowe, who one day would come to head the Pan American Union for a quarter-century: the meeting had avoided the pitfalls of the Washington and Mexico City Conferences, if only by the prearrangement in Washington of the agenda and regulations—under the watchful eye of Root, he might have added. That old standby, "mutual comprehension," he described as an important product of the assembly. Another United States delegate, Paul Reinsch, was more critical, writing that the result of the Pan American Conferences thus far "could scarcely be smaller than it is," although he seemed to agree that it was best that the United States and the other nations had been opposed to the inauguration of any sweeping policies.[32]

The American delegation was more impressed by the success of Root's visit than by that of the Conference. Further, President Roosevelt in his message to congress in the following December denied that the Monroe Doctrine implied any assumption by the United States of superiority or of a protectorate over Latin America, but, he said, an impression to that effect had been so widespread that the extraordinary measure of the Root voyage had been undertaken—successfully—to dispel the belief. Root himself, with his characteristically intelligent moderation, told the governing board of the Pan American organization that as a result of the Conference and his trip, "the people of the

[31] Philip C. Jessup, *Elihu Root* (2 vols.; New York, 1938), I, 468–469, 471, 477; A. C. Wilgus, "The Third International American Conference at Rio de Janeiro, 1906," *The Hispanic American Historical Review*, 12:434, n. 37 (November 1932); *Report of the Delegates*, pp. 63–64.

[32] L. S. Rowe, "The Significance of the Third Pan-American Conference," *The Independent*, 61:1083–1085, 1087 (Nov. 8, 1906); P. S. Reinsch, "The Third International Conference of American States," *The American Political Science Review*, 1:188, 197 (February 1907).

United States have learned more about South America in the last six months than they ever did in six times six months before."[33]

In Buenos Aires, Argentine leaders made no public report upon the Conference, or comment upon Root's visit to Brazil. The press gave extensive attention to both events. *La Nación* (Aug. 2, 1906) praised Root's speech and its rejection of unwarranted hegemony for the United States. *La Prensa* on the following day described Root's mission as an effort to quiet the antagonism aroused in Latin America by Roosevelt; it too welcomed his speech, terming it more important than the Conference because it recognized Latin American sovereignty and condemned use of the big stick. Next day the paper returned to the theme that the slightest encroachment by Root on the political or economic rights of Latin America would cause the collapse of the Conference.

La Prensa was highly critical of the results of the Rio meeting. On August 25 the paper noted that Buenos Aires had not been approved as the site of the next Conference; that arbitration had been reduced to a meaningless formula which received a "lyrical vote;" that the vote on the Drago formula had been "essentially evasive." From all this *La Prensa* concluded that Argentina had no need of Pan American conferences to realize its destiny. Two days later the paper of the Paz family termed the Conference a "deplorable failure," whose only benefit had been the opportunity which it gave to Mr. Root to know Latin America.

La Nación (Aug. 24, 27, 30) was critical, for the same reasons. The Conference had been "sterile" in its "vague and ceremonious deliberations." Yet, in the same editorial *La Nación* perhaps unknowingly revealed a dilemma facing the Argentine government with respect to the Pan American system and its own position in Latin America: the paper praised the manner in which the Conference had avoided political themes, and commended the fact that the Argentine government had gone to the meeting without pretentious plans for leadership.[34]

---

[33] *Report of the Delegates*, pp. 23–24; Minutes of the Executive Committee, IV, 5.

[34] Despite its criticism of the Conference, *La Nación* continued to be more friendly toward the United States than any other Buenos Aires paper. See the superb signed

The smaller journals of Buenos Aires followed the lead of the two important dailies, but less temperately. *El Economista* (June 16, Sept. 1, 1906) castigated the United States for a series of offenses. *El Diario* (April 5, 1906) typified its running attack on the United States with a cartoon showing a leering Uncle Sam forcing his dogs, labeled Argentina, Uruguay, and so on, to jump through a hoop. In contrast, Europe had showered on Argentina the gifts of civilization, and will "always have markets and gold" for her. Anyway, wrote the paper on August 24, the Conference had succeeded only in consigning arbitration and the Drago Doctrine to the Hague Conference as "cadavers."[35]

Despite harsh criticism of the Rio meeting and of Root's visit to Brazil, the press and public of Buenos Aires gave the Secretary a warm if nationalistic welcome when he came to Argentina. A few days prior to his arrival *La Nación* (Aug. 11) welcomed his visit for the opportunity it provided Argentines to demonstrate the wealth of their country. When Root arrived, *La Nación* (Aug. 14) welcomed him to the richest and most powerful nation in South America, where his false ideas of the degree of Latin American progress would be vanquished. *La Prensa* made the same point on the same day, commenting further that Argentina had advanced beyond the danger of imperialistic conquest and of economic seduction. Welcome to Root, future messenger of Argentine greatness!

Courtly, authoritative, conservative, Root was the kind of man the upper-class porteños admired. He possessed another quality which they esteemed: he matched their fulsome and idealistic rhetoric with his noble and flattering oratory. For Argentines, what better statement, from what higher source,

---

editorial by Emilio Mitre in the issue of August 26, 1906, in which he called attention to the fact that in Argentina the United States was singled out as "imperialistic," while the public was indifferent to the swallowing of Africa by the European powers. He also noted that in Argentina the name of Canning was exalted, the name of Rush forgotten.

[35] *El País* was generally friendly to the Conference (see issues of July 13, 20, 23, Aug. 9, 1906), until the issues of Aug. 26 and 29, which condemned the meeting as a noisy farce. The English and French newspapers of Buenos Aires consistently attacked the meeting. For a good sample of European press opinion, see Orestes Ferrara, *L'Amérique et l'Europe* . . . (Paris, 1930), pp. 28–32. Wilgus, "The Third International American Conference," pp. 438–440, gives U.S. press opinion.

than Root's declaration to the United States citizens in Buenos
Aires that, "Argentina will take some of our markets from us,
but what are they? They will be markets she is entitled to; and
with her prosperity and with right understanding . . . our commercial relations with her will more than take the place of the
markets she takes away from us." How pleasant for Argentines
to hear the secretary of state of the United States speak of the
desire of his countrymen to invest in Argentina; to hear him
praise the magnificence of Buenos Aires; to hear him deny that
he had ever made any statements regarding an alliance with
Brazil; to hear him invoke the names of San Martín and Sarmiento, and the ideals of arbitration and of peace!

At the official banquets, Root was the equal of his hosts,
whether they might be the president of the nation, or famed
Luis María Drago. The President, in welcoming Root, referred
to Argentina's inheritance of United States political forms; Root
evened the score by placing Argentina on the same plane of
success as the United States. To Drago's friendly references to
the old links between the two lands, including the Monroe
Doctrine, the Secretary replied with praise of Argentina's
energy, moral strength, and glorious future.[36]

The Buenos Aires newspapers were delighted with the visitor,
his soothing tributes, his humble yet upright attitude. But they
did not forget while he was on the premises that their own
principal mission was his enlightenment. Then, too, Root's
visit to Buenos Aires possessed, in their eyes, the virtue of offset-
ting his triumph in Rio de Janeiro.[37]

The results of Root's visit were fairly summarized by the
United States minister to Argentina, who reported back to his
chief a few weeks after the secretary's departure from Argentina. With no more than the optimism appropriate to a subordinate telling his superior of the latter's accomplishments, he
wrote: "The Monroe Doctrine and the Drago Doctrine were
harmonized; . . . the Argentine press disarmed; the Argentine
people and those of the United States made friends."[38]

[36] Elihu Root, *Latin America and the United States. Addresses by Elihu Root*, edited by
Robert Bacon and J. B. Scott (Cambridge, Mass., 1917), pp. 81–86, 92, 97–102.

[37] *La Prensa*, Aug. 16, 17, 19; *La Nación*, Aug. 15, 16, 19, 21, 1906.

[38] Beaupre to Root, Sept. 6, 1906, *Foreign Relations, 1906*, No. 411, pp. 21–25.

Much of this, for a time at least, Root accomplished—as much as one man can achieve in a few days by force of character and official position. It is true, as one historian writes, that Root did not have a "Good Neighbor policy," but he did have "a new tolerance" in dealing with Latin America.[39] Even Argentines responded.

Perhaps the important question for the future was not how much friendship the United States had purchased by the Root mission, or how much the cause of Pan Americanism had been advanced by the relatively tranquil Third Pan American Conference. Assuming some gain in each of these directions, the question became: at what price had success been purchased?

To have continued the rancorous conflict of Argentina and the United States into a third conference might have brought an end to the American organization. Yet the air of kindly accord which surrounded the Rio assembly had in fact been achieved by eliminating from the program of the Conference all fundamental approaches to inter-American issues. Pan Americanism had been reduced to its lowest common denominator, which was just where Argentina wanted it.

Officials of the government of the United States had come to learn, largely at Argentine hands, that if the Pan American aspect of the Latin American policy of the United States were to continue to operate, it had to rest on a basis of voluntary and unanimous—or nearly unanimous—cooperation. And unanimity has never been cheaply purchased in human affairs, let alone in conferences of a score of nations. The votes of the Third Conference were unanimous; the issues voted were negligible.

Yet Argentina, a principal architect of Pan American weakness, was placed by her own actions in a paradoxical position. She desired an infirm Pan American system—if there had to be one—but on issues which she deemed to be important, such as intervention, or her own leadership among Latin American states, it was desirable that there be a bulwark upon which to plant her banner.

Some might maintain that the men who controlled Argentina

[39] Richard W. Leopold, *Elihu Root and the Conservative Tradition* (Boston, 1954), p. 192.

were concerned with events in Rio and elsewhere in the hemisphere in a negative way only. A few days prior to the beginning of the Third Conference, General Julio A. Roca attended a banquet in London. Twenty years had elapsed since the ex-president, then too ex-president, had attended the Anglo-Argentine banquet at Richmond. In 1906 the names of the participants were much the same; the food as excellent; the economic statistics far more impressive. In 1906, when Lord Revelstoke—another Lord Revelstoke, but of the same Baring family—proposed the health of Roca, he was able to state that two hundred million pounds sterling, invested in Argentina, were represented at the dinner table.

16

A Centenary and a Conference

ARGENTINA was moving toward two denouements, one of certain, the other of uncertain date. The first was the centenary of the revolution of 1810; the second, the crisis of politics and society.

Between 1902 and 1910 the people of Argentina knew the state of siege five times: November 1902–January 1903, February–May 1905, October 1905–January 1906, November 1909–January 1910, May 14–September 29, 1910. There was a revolution in 1905, and a general strike in 1909. The strike followed the May Day clash of parading workers and troops in the heart of the city. Four men were killed and forty-five wounded in that encounter. The strike in turn was followed by one of those desperate acts of violence which were not uncommon in Europe at the time, and which had admirers among Argentine radicals: on November 14, 1909 the chief of police of Buenos Aires, riding in an open carriage with an aide, was blown to bits by a bomb.

Economic dissatisfactions caused some of the popular unrest. Wages and working conditions were poor, compared to the standard of existence of the upper class. But it was continuing frustration of political freedom that created a climate for increasing violence. To limit the political power of the landowning oligarchy, a power only faintly expressed by the fact that, in the Argentine senate in 1908, seven of the thirty members were *hacendados*, as were seventeen of the one hundred and twenty deputies,[1] was the aim of the Radicals, Irigoyen's party of resistance and abstention, and of the Socialists, who desired economic reforms as well as political.

[1] José N. Matienzo, *El gobierno representativo federal en la República Argentina* (Buenos Aires, 1910), p. 184.

Immigrants had a hand in the growing turmoil. By sheer weight of numbers and by alien or excessive ambitions they created difficulties for the conservatives. There was in Argentina a net addition of immigrants to the population in 1900 of 50,485, in 1905 of 138,850, in 1906 of 198,397, in 1907 of 119,861, in 1908 of 176,080, in 1909 of 140,640, and in 1910 of 208,870.[2] A few among these hordes were hardened agitators for anarcho-syndicalism. The safety of the government required measures to contain these revolutionaries. The Law of Residence of 1902 had been such an act; the Law of Social Defense, passed in the one hundredth anniversary year of the country's revolution for freedom, was another. The latter law permitted the expulsion of convicted agitators. Argentines could have pointed out that the United States had long since passed anti-anarchist laws, and that on occasion martial law had been invoked in parts of the great northern republic in the face of social disturbances.

But they were not the uprooted who led the Radical Party, or who castigated national leaders in the pages of what by now were two of the world's important newspapers. *La Prensa* maintained its grave and doctrinaire attack on the political stagnation of the country. Roca was no more immune now than he had been in 1880; to *La Prensa* (April 7, 1907) he was the "pseudo-sphinx," still manipulating silently his authority, for, and sometimes over, the economic and social lords of the land. *La Nación* (Oct. 11, 1904) adjudged Roca, although he was in his last day as president, as the leader of a group of caudillos, avaricious and conservative of the power to rule.

Roca agreed that he possessed authority. In a letter of 1908 he wrote: "I have contributed, it is clear, to the strengthening and consolidation of the nation, in my two presidencies . . . I believed that a strong national government was necessary . . . capable of maintaining the order and peace of the Republic within the constitution. If sometimes I have overstepped myself, credit me with good intentions and high aims."[3]

[2] Ernesto Tornquist and Co., Ltd., *The Economic Development of the Argentine Republic in the Last Fifty Years* (Buenos Aires, 1919), p. 15.

[3] Rudolfo Rivarola, "El Presidente Sáenz Peña y la moralidad política argentina," *Revista Argentina de Ciencias Políticas*, año 4, t. 9, núm. 49, 1914.

Undoubtedly there was necessity and value (or had been, twenty-five years earlier) in being a "civilizing *cacique* [chieftain]," as one traveler described Roca, but public morality hardly existed, and constitutional electoral rights were a farce. Aims and intentions were not reality; they passed the people by, and uneasiness about the upshot possessed many thoughtful men as Quintana succeeded Roca in 1904 and Figueroa replaced Quintana in 1906. The year approached—it would be the last year of Figueroa's inherited term—in which to celebrate the centenary. Contempt from above for the authority of the majority of Argentine citizens had its reply from below in their bitter agitation. Power through estancia politics, presidential manipulation of provincial governors and provincial legislatures, corruption of the elections in the federal capital, these were the enduring goals and methods of the oligarchy, as they had been for three decades. They were marks of the final failure of the Argentine hope for a strong federal union; they were emblems of the victory of the mighty metropolis of Buenos Aires, and of the landlords who made it their home.[4]

Many voices—and arms—were raised against this frustration of the Argentine dream. One voice grew stronger than the others—not a new one in foreign affairs, but speaking now with force and clarity on the state of the nation. Roque Saenz Peña as early as 1903 attacked major defects of national political life and, incidentally, President Roca. He hewed at the cornerstone of the defense of privilege which his own class was making, the argument that the citizenry was unprepared for democracy. He criticized Roca's eternal compromising, the depressed condition of the provinces, the haphazard transportation system, the corruption. "The civilized world," said the future president, "perceives at a distance only the externals and the apparatus of a nation constituted upon a republican basis. Argentina has, indeed, all the organs; not a single member is lacking to give it the fiction of life, but, in reality, life itself is

---

[4] Frederica Rahola, *Sangre nueva. Impresiones de un viaje a la América del Sud* (Barcelona, 1905), p. 97; Rodolfo Rivarola, *Del régimen federativo al unitario; estudio sobre la organización política de la Argentina* (Buenos Aires, 1908), pp. 55–65, 91–104, 363–367.

lacking, it is a cadaver, and the hemorrhage has been internal." [5]

Others did not view their country in these harsh terms. The centenary was at hand, the earth was rich, and pride, never a negligible force in the Argentine heart, could overlook for a while longer such defects, and rush to acclaim the material achievements of the day.

Argentine soil seemed endlessly expansive. The area under cultivation was 7,311,048 hectares in 1900, 13,081,461 in 1905, and 20,367,087 (more than forty-four million acres) in 1910. Out of this land had sprung a total foreign trade valued in 1910 at 768,423,875 gold pesos, giving to Argentines the distinction of possessing the highest per capita trade figure of any of the larger nations of the world. Railroad expansion was also greater in the decade 1901–1910 than in any other decade before or since, increasing from 16,563 kms. in 1900 to 27,994 kms. in 1910. At the annual livestock exposition of the Sociedad Rural a bull named Polikao II sold for 40,000 gold pesos, and a ram for 9,000. In 1909, Argentina became the leading grain exporting nation of the world. The value of frozen meat exported in that year was 153,500,000 gold pesos. [6]

National credit was sound; even the United States was awakening to that fact. A gloomy despatch from the chargé in Buenos Aires stated that a fifty million dollar loan which a United States group wished to float would not be seriously considered by the Argentines. He claimed that Argentine opinion was that the loan "would give the United States an influence in the country different from what would happen in the case of a loan raised in England." Nevertheless, the United States consortium—made up of J. P. Morgan, the First National Bank, and the National City Bank—was awarded in 1909 one-fifth of a ten million pound loan to be used for railroad and bank capital and for public works. [7]

[5] Roque Saenz Peña, *Escritos y discursos* (3 vols.; Buenos Aires, 1914, 1915, 1935), III: *Actuación nacional*, 169–170.

[6] Tornquist, *Economic Development*, pp. 26, 117, 140; Emilio Frers, *El progreso agrícolo de la Nación y la Sociedad Rural Argentina: reseña histórica* (Buenos Aires, 1916), p. 172; H. Mabragaña, compiler, *Los Mensajes* . . . (Buenos Aires [n.d., ?1910]), VI, 484, 488.

[7] Wilson to Root, Jan. 29, 1909, National Archives, Dept. of State, Argentina, Record Group 59, Numerical File, 1906–1910, Vol. 162, No. 76.

By 1910, United States investment in Argentina was in the neighborhood of $20,000,000, most of it in securities.[8] Its share in the Argentine market was also increasing, with machinery, hardware, chemicals, cordage, and other products representing, in 1909, 14.2 per cent of Argentina's imports, as against 13 per cent in 1904, and 10.2 per cent in 1889. However, Argentines believed they still had grounds for complaint against the United States. Argentina in fiscal 1909–1910, for example, was the third best customer of the United States in Latin America, not far behind the leaders, Mexico and Cuba. But Argentina sold the United States far less than did Mexico, Cuba, or Brazil. Nor was Argentina in as favorable a position as the other large Latin American countries with respect to the United States tariff. Up to the passage of the tariff act of 1909, only 17 per cent of Argentina's exports to the United States entered duty free, whereas for Brazil the figure was 99 per cent, Chile 99 per cent, Peru 90 per cent, and so on with other nations. Hides were returned to the free list in 1909, primarily because of pressure from Massachusetts shoe and leather interests, a fact not missed in Argentina. This caused a rise to 49 per cent of non-dutiable Argentine goods, still far below the figure for most of Latin America, although enough to warm the heart of *La Prensa* (Jan. 22, 1910), which praised the Pan Americanism of Taft and Knox and wrote that the abolition of the hide tariff was worth ten million gold pesos to the Argentine cattle industry.[9]

Argentines wanted United States products and capital; they were not as attracted by the men who might accompany those commodities. The chargé reported from Buenos Aires that he had "no doubt but that Americans are not liked here," perhaps because they were not "generally . . . such as bring much credit

---

[8] H. E. Peters, *The Foreign Debt of the Argentine Republic* (Baltimore, 1934), pp. 33–34, 76; Cleona Lewis, *America's Stake in International Investments* (Washington, D.C., 1938), pp. 603, 607–610. Estimates of the value of United States investments in Argentina at this time vary widely. One contemporary official in the State Department placed the figure at $40,000,000 (see *Proceedings of the Pan-American Commercial Conference, Feb. 13–17, 1911* [Washington, D.C., 1911], p. 84), yet Lewis, *America's Stake*, p. 609, gives a figure of only $10,000,000 for 1908.

[9] *Proceedings*, pp. 41–51, 85, 230; Ricardo Pillado, *Comentarios sobre los tratados de comercio argentino* (Buenos Aires, 1915), pp. 182, 185–188.

upon their country," and also because "the commercial relations between the two countries have not been of a nature to give the Argentines a very high idea of either American business intelligence, methods, or honor."[10]

Nonetheless, United States officials and businessmen who knew Argentina continued with success to work for an enlarged trade, as did men who were interested in all of Latin America. At the Pan American Commercial Conference, organized by John Barrett, the head of the Pan American Union, and held in Washington in 1911, Latin American officials and United States businessmen met together in a series of successful meetings in which question periods and open discussion played a large part. Here two Argentine representatives in vigorous terms challenged United States business leaders to bring their money and goods to Argentina, to the profit of all concerned.[11]

The demands of the *norteamericanos* in Buenos Aires were the same as over the years past: let us have our own ships and banks, better goods, longer credit. England is far ahead—and watch out for Germany. Some improvement was made in securing direct representation. By 1911 the General Electric Company, U.S. Steel Products, J. I. Case (agricultural implements), the Avery Plow Company, and a few others had salesmen in Buenos Aires. There was, however, no bank, and no good transportation between Argentina and the United States, and no steamers at all entering the port of Buenos Aires flying the United States flag.[12]

Desirable as United States capital was in theory, practice in at least one area was less appealing to some Argentines. The purchase of an Argentine packing plant by Swift and Company in 1907 for a brief time created resentment and fear among the estancieros and for a much longer time among Argentine and

[10] Wilson to Root, Jan. 29, 1909, Numerical File, Vol. 612, No. 76.

[11] *Proceedings*, pp. 191, 202–204.

[12] U.S. Consul General Synder's reports from Buenos Aires, *U.S. Consular Reports*, No. 321, June 1907, pp. 77–81, No. 328, Jan., 1908, pp. 18–20; *Consular Reports, Annual Series*, No. 24, "Argentina, Trade for the Year 1907" (October 1908), pp. 5, 8; *Commercial Reports, 1908*, II, 297, 299, and *1909*, p. 642; Department of Commerce and Labor, *Report on Trade Conditions in Argentina, Paraguay, and Uruguay*, by Lincoln Hutchinson (Washington, 1906), pp. 24–26, 35–38.

English packers. Scare talk of a United States beef monopoly was mixed with respect for United States efficiency and profit-making ability—Swift earned an estimated 175,000 pounds in its first year, one-half of the plant's purchase price. Within three years the Americans—another *frigorífico* was bought out in 1908 by the National Packing Company—had become the principal packers in the country. In the process they made an ally of the group which had at first mistrusted them, the estancieros. With these men on their side they had nothing to fear. When charges of monopolistic practices were pushed against the Yankees by English and Argentine packers, the national cabinet refused to take any action.

Both packers and estancieros had a great market. In 1900, Great Britain was closed to Argentine live cattle shipments because of an outbreak of the dread epizootic, *aftosa*—hoof-and-mouth disease. It was at this critical time that techniques of preparing, shipping, and marketing chilled beef were perfected, permitting regular entry of that quality product into the British market together with the established line of frozen meat. At the same moment, the reduction of available quantities of United States meat for export allowed Argentina to move more deeply into the market. In 1905, Argentine meat shipments to Great Britain exceeded those by the United States for the first time.[13]

Argentine grain shipments also increased enormously in these years. In 1904, for the first time in its history, Argentina exported more than two million tons of wheat, as well as record quantities of linseed (880,541 tons), and corn (2,469,548 tons). 1908 dwarfed 1904: 3,636,294 tons of wheat were sent abroad, and 1,055,650 tons of linseed, 1,711,804 tons of corn, and 440,041 tons of oats. In all categories but wheat these figures were customarily surpassed in the years up to 1914.[14]

Awareness of their increasing competition for Europe's markets was thus added to Argentine and United States interest in each other's markets. This interest was reflected in the attention given to the United States in the press of Buenos Aires. In

[13] S. G. Hanson, *Argentina Meat and the British Market* . . . (Stanford, California, 1938), pp. 50, 129, 144–157, 163, 176, 180.
[14] Tornquist, *Economic Development*, p. 31.

contrast to the paucity of twenty-five years earlier, Argentine papers now provided their readers with thorough coverage of events in the northern republic. But attitudes on main issues had changed little, whether in newspapers, magazines, or books. *La Nación* demanded lower United States tariffs, argued for the steamship subsidy bill then in the United States Congress, and called for an above-board investment of United States money in Argentina. The *Revista de Derecho, Historia y Letras* in 1910 printed an article by an Argentine naval officer which described United States intentions of excluding Europe from Latin America, and portrayed Messrs. Rowe, William R. Shepherd, and Barrett as spokesmen of the Blaine school of expansion. In another study the Yankees came in for the hackneyed accusation of being excessively materialistic—although their energy was praised.[15]

Brazilian-United States friendship, especially visible in reciprocal trade agreements, caused continuing criticism among Argentines, in public by the newspapers, more privately by government leaders. Foreign Minister Zeballos called the attention of Secretary Root to the impression Brazil was giving the world (so Zeballos claimed) that it had a military alliance with the United States. A year later the foreign minister was still concerned with this subject, and more favorably with the proposed ship subsidy legislation in the United States.[16]

If Argentine eyes turned more frequently toward the United States, Argentine hearts still belonged to Europe—to England, whose Canning outshone Monroe, and which always seemed able to convey to Argentines the sense that they were a great and respected people; to Germany, hailed by one Argentine intellectual as the nation that "today marches at the head of the intellectual world," now also a great market for Argentine goods, and second only to England in supplying products to Argentina; to France, always beloved because of her beauty and

---

[15] *La Nación*, Feb. 3 and June 7, 1908, Dec. 17, 1909, Dec. 29, 1910; L. Saborido, "El progreso de los Estados Unidos," *Revista de Derecho, Historia y Letras*, año 12, t. 35, Jan. 1910, pp. 42–47; V. Arreguine, "Latinos y anglo-sajones," *Estudios Sociales* (2nd ed.; Buenos Aires, 1907), p. 30.

[16] Wilson to Root, July 31, 1908, Numerical File, Vol. 928, No. 774.

wit; and to Spain, more cherished the more remote in time became the years of her imperial control.[17]

In Latin Europe in these years Argentina had a most effective spokesman in Roque Saenz Peña. Whether in Spain in 1906 to represent his country at the wedding of Alfonso XIII, or in Italy, working to increase trade by advocating official cabled reports by the Argentine government telling of economic developments at home, to be distributed to Italian and other European businessmen, the future president made Argentines and Europeans alike aware of the ties between them, and of the fact that Argentina had indeed ceased to be merely one of those "South American" places. In 1909 at an international congress at Rome, Saenz Peña bluntly informed the German representative that he expected more respect for the Argentine government than that gentleman had displayed; he went on to administer to his audience a lesson in the importance to Europe of the Argentine economy, ending with the statement that if Europe had more past, Argentina had more future, and the parting shot that Argentina "does not ask, but demands, the highest consideration."[18]

The widest European stage upon which Argentina acted before the First World War was provided in 1907 by the Second Hague Conference. Her relatively subordinate position in this fruitless assembly was nonetheless independent and well-founded. Her delegation was composed of three former foreign ministers, Saenz Peña, Luis María Drago, and Carlos Rodríguze Larreta. In the lofty realm of oratory they were the equal of the best European representatives, and equal too in learning and in judgment.

It had been through the good offices of the government of the

[17] Ernesto Quesada, *La enseñanza de la historia en las universidades alemanes* (La Plata, 1910), XIII; *La Nación*, Dec. 16, 1909, June 16, 1910; Francisco Bayón, "Solidaridad intelectual hispanoamericano," *Revista Nacional*, año 22, t. 43, May 1907, pp. 166–170; Archivo Nacional, Buenos Aires, Archivo de Victorino de la Plaza, leg. 7-5-4-4, 1907–1910; Beaupre to Root, Aug. 19, 1907, Numerical File, Vol. 490, No. 592; Beaupre to Root, Aug. 24, 1907, Numerical File, Vol. 490, No. 598.

[18] Note from Saenz Peña to Foreign Minister Zeballos, June 10, 1906, Saenz Peña, *Escritos y discursos*, I, 230, 371–372; despatch from Saenz Peña to Foreign Minister Victorino de la Plaza, Nov. 20, 1908, *ibid.*, pp. 249–255, 329–338.

United States, and as a result of the increased importance of Latin America, that the states of that area attended the conference, on a plane of equality with other states with regard to previous international agreements. Further, the United States government had secured postponement of the Hague meeting in order to avoid conflict with the Third Pan American Conference. It was also the United States which presented the Drago Doctrine to the European states, in the form of the Porter Resolution, which stated that no government should have recourse to force to collect contract debts, except when the debtor state refused arbitration, or, after arbitration, failed to submit to the award.

Thus Argentina came along behind the United States on an issue peculiarly Argentine, voted in favor of the Porter proposal, and saw it accepted by the conference. Argentina also set reservations which strengthened the position of debtor states, and which were accepted by all the Latin American states except Chile and Brazil.

The other chief issue with which Argentina was concerned at The Hague was arbitration; this convention too was originally presented by the United States delegation. Argentina thus succeeded mainly in making its voice heard in support of the actions of others. The voice once again was that of Saenz Peña, who, at the closing session, addressed the assembly. He assured Europe of Argentina's progress, and he quoted the words which he had spoken at the First Pan American Conference: "We do not lack affection or love for America; we lack mistrust and ingratitude for Europe."[19]

Another Saenz Peña sentiment was known in Europe. His watchword, "America for humanity," had caught the imagination of a generation on both sides of the Atlantic. While in Rome in 1910, as president-elect of the Argentine Republic, he was honored by a great number of Italians, who presented him with a gold medal upon which was inscribed the phrase which he had uttered in Washington twenty years earlier. And Saenz Peña knew what the practical application of the phrase within the

---

[19] J. B. Scott, *The Hague Peace Conferences of 1899 and 1907* . . . (2 vols.; Baltimore, 1909), I, 96–98, 100, 415, 417; Saenz Peña, *Escritos*, I, 242, 367–369, III, 84.

hemisphere meant: it was an antidote to the domination of the United States. Even when his friend, Eduardo Wilde, doctor, diplomat, essayist of the Generation of Eighty, wrote to him from Madrid implying that pacification by the United States of Latin American revolutions was a good practice if undertaken in conjunction with, say, Argentina or Brazil, Saenz Peña replied, "I am an opponent of the policy of intervention against sovereign states . . . The right that is adduced to avoid revolutions—will it not be invoked tomorrow to foment them? . . . The right of intervention is dangerous for all the states of South America."[20]

Whatever the nature of United States interest in Latin America, that interest was increasing. The work of the International Bureau of American Republics slowly gathered momentum, capably channeled by John Barrett, who vigorously wrote, lectured, and administered for the expansion by the United States in Latin America "not only of our moral influence but of our commercial interests."[21]

Argentina affords an interesting example of aroused American influence. In 1908, Argentine-Brazilian relations were far from friendly, and a naval armaments race began between the two neighbors. The desire of the Argentine government to place substantial warship contracts caused the State Department to instruct the United States minister in Buenos Aires to endeavor to obtain for United States companies the same opportunities as were received by manufacturers of other nations. Minister Eddy in due time presented a Swiss citizen named Mr. Robert, who was a representative of Mr. Charles M. Schwab, president of Bethlehem Steel Company, to several Argentine cabinet officers. Mr. Eddy's successor, Charles Sherrill, who apparently learned quickly that Saenz Peña was a power in Argentina, whether in or out of office, went about the business in a somewhat different manner. He reported to Washington that, while it was believed in Buenos Aires that Saenz Peña was decidedly unfriendly

---

[20] Biblioteca Nacional, MSS., Eduardo Wilde to Roque Saenz Peña, July 9, 1910, No. 16033; Saenz Peña to Wilde, July 19, 1910, No. 16034.

[21] John Barrett, *Latin America, the Land of Opportunity. A Report of Official Reports and Special Articles* (Washington, D.C., 1909), p. 3.

toward the United States, a friend of the Argentine statesman had told Sherrill that he would get Saenz Peña to make a statement of friendship for the United States.

No such statement seems to have been elicited, but Sherrill believed that he had achieved good results from a speech which he delivered to one thousand students of the University of Buenos Aires and a number of high government officials. Under the somewhat laborious if winning title, "The Pan Americanism of Henry Clay, Sarmiento, and Elihu Root," Sherrill spoke to his audience, on a date which he had selected "in the hope that the speech might by indirection have some effect in our favor upon the awarding of the battleship contracts now under consideration." [22]

Certainly, Secretary of State Philander Knox, judging by the frequency and tenor of his instructions in the Argentine armaments matter, was interested in a fruitful consummation of the negotiations. [23] And he had some reward. On September 4, 1909 the secretary of state received the following autograph letter: [24]

My dear Mr. Knox:
The following is a copy of a cablegram just received from our representative in Buenos Ayres, Argentina:

Prospects have been improved by U.S. working hard to obtain two battleships.

The industries of America, I know, highly appreciate your efforts to establish foreign relations for them, and it would be a great achievement for you, as well as America, if American manufacturers were to furnish the armor, guns, etc., and build the ships.

It is the sincere wish of all of us that your Department does not

[22] Root to Eddy, Oct. 22, 1908, Instructions, Vol. 139, No. 34 (this cable was billed by the Department of State to Flint and Company, New York, New York, in the amount of $43.28. Flint was, among his other activities, which included work for Pan Americanism, an arms manufacturer); Sherrill to Knox, July 3, 1909, Numerical File, Vol. 397, No. 15; Sherrill to Secretary of State, Oct. 8, 1909, Numerical File, Vol. 928, No. 116.

[23] See Knox cabled instructions of March 8, June 17, July 13, Aug. 17, 18, 30, Oct. 13, 19, Nov. 29, Dec. 7, all 1909, in Instructions, Vol. 139, 1070 series. See also Vol. 140 for further extensive correspondence from Buenos Aires, Washington, and London.

[24] Schwab to Knox, Sept. 4, 1909, Numerical File, Vol. 139.

relax in its efforts to help the United States get this work, aside from whichever concern may do it.

I want to contragulate you heartily on the unique position you have taken in your Department, which, to my mind, will bring you the greatest possible credit and prestige.

With every good wish,
Sincerely yours,
Charles M. Schwab

The somewhat recalcitrant Argentines gave Bethlehem Steel and the United States government a bit of a chase yet. A few days after the Schwab letter, Sherrill reported to Washington that the minister of marine had altered the bid basis on the proposed ship contract. This had upset United States bidders so much that one of them, Admiral Bowles of the Fore River Ship Building Company, departed from Buenos Aires in indignation. The minister of marine, Sherrill explained, had a "strong predilection" for the English builders. However, he continued, in this twenty million dollar contract, the United States bidders were agreed that they would have had no chance at all if it had not been for the State Department's assistance.[25]

Sherrill increased his efforts. He talked to Foreign Minister Victorino de la Plaza, conferred with the editor of *La Prensa* (who next day ran an editorial supporting Sherrill's position), parried the thrusts of an Italian arms maker, and generally dabbled in Argentine politics. On January 21, 1910 he had the pleasure of informing the State Department that the Argentine government had awarded the two battleship contracts to United States firms. On January 22, Secretary of State Knox informed the Bethlehem Steel Company and the Fore River Ship Building Company that they had received the contracts, as well as arms contracts totaling an additional one million dollars.[26]

Brazil, battleships, the United States, Europe—all were important to Argentines in the year 1910, but one thing was more

[25] Sherrill to Knox, Sept. 20, 1909, Numerical File, Vol. 140, No. 94.
[26] Sherrill to Secretary of State, Nov. 25, 1909, Numerical File, Vol. 140, No. 160; Sherrill to Knox, Jan. 21, 1910, Numerical File, Vol. 140, 1070/169; Knox telegrams of Jan. 22, 1910 to Bethlehem and Fore River companies, in Numerical File, Vol. 140, 1070/170.

important: themselves. It was centennial year. Pride and optimism were high. The focus of fervor was, as always, Buenos Aires, bigger (1,306,680 inhabitants) and richer than ever.

Much of the past endured, despite the fact that the population had doubled in two decades. The common form of larger domestic residence in the center of the city was still the two-patio house with a frontage of twenty-seven feet and a depth of two hundred and twenty-five feet, the bath and garden at the rear. But the colonial period and the nineteenth century were being destroyed. New town houses were not houses, or even mansions, but palaces, such as those of Paz, Anchorena, and Ortiz Basualdo, erected on choice plazas near the heart of the metropolis. The magnificent Teatro Colón was open now, seating 3,300 persons: one of the world's great opera houses, regularly presenting Alda and Caruso.

Calle Florida and Palermo Park were jammed with carriages and horsemen, but now an occasional Daimler added excitement to society's parade. Parties were gayer; the lists of guests published in the papers next morning longer; the family names more intertwined. Mar del Plata was beginning to look like a watering place and not a desolate fringe of rocky beach where the pampas met the ocean.

Inside the homes of the well-to-do, furnishings were in the late Victorian style, no better and no worse than those of London or New York or Boston. Plain tin bath tubs were now painted to resemble marble, the drapes were tasseled, the divans were horsehair and oak, the lampshades were fringed and bulbous, the mantels crowded with gewgaws.

The relations and the dress of men and women were also Victorian. There was a double standard, prized by at least half of those participating in its operations; but there was only one place for men to buy clothes, and that was London, and only one place for the women, and that was Paris.

The luxurious appointments of the Jockey Club on Florida grew richer as the public horse racing, which the club controlled, brought in more and more money; the wine cellar became larger and finer, Gobelin tapestries covered the walls of the foyers. The display of wealth was not limited to private clubs; the

Plaza Hotel, under construction in 1910, promised to rival the finest establishments in the world. And the insatiable public demand for news and stories of twentieth-century progress made for fatter Sunday supplements, full of articles about gyroscopic trains on high wires and tunnels under the English channel.

The president of the nation reported to congress each year in May, at the opening of the session. The diplomatic corps was present; the galleries were crowded with ladies. The words of the first executive faithfully echoed the sense of prosperity and destiny; they were words, it might be noted, remarkably similar to those employed by the president of the United States in *his* annual messages to congress.

In 1907, President Figueroa Alcorta attributed the happy condition of the nation to the *fuerzas vivas*—an Argentinism carrying all the favorable connotations of the Yankee phrase "rugged individualism." Yet the president mentioned imperfections in the administrative life of the country. By the time of his message in 1908 he was constrained to admit that the political situation was a "singular antithesis of the economic situation." The presidential message of May 1909 opened with an explicably strident note of alarm, coming as it did just after street fighting and a general strike in Buenos Aires. The message of May 1910, coming in the very anniversary month of the glorious revolution of a century earlier, listed the nation's material accomplishments, but also listed provincial disturbances and interventions by the federal government, told of the grim assassination of the chief of police at a street corner not far from the congress building, told also of strife, strikes, and states of siege, and wistfully consigned to the future the perfecting of the liberties of the Argentine people in this hundredth year of their emancipation.[27]

Visitors to the great city beside the Plata were less concerned with politics and more impressed by the externals. One American in 1907 liked the Yankee qualities of the city—its "snappy" newspapers, good streetcars (new, then), and reasonable rates. He was not so much taken by the people, whom he thought

[27] Mabragaña, *Los Mensajes*, VI, 201–203, 219–228, 244–249, 258, 319, 321, 387–394.

arrogant. A more competent American observer, Hiram Bingham, commented on the power and activity displayed in Buenos Aires, but noted the absence of American financial institutions and American merchants, in contrast to the brisk, clean-shaven Englishmen whom he saw in such numbers on the streets and who spoke of "B.A." and the "River Plate" as though they were English possessions, which, Bingham added, was not far from true.

A Spanish visitor in the centennial year wrote about the size, energy, and variety of Buenos Aires, the self-confidence and materialistic outlook of the porteños, including male vanity of dress, and the contrast between the almost psychopathic nationalism of most criollos and the indifference to patriotism of most of the immigrants. As had Bingham, the Spaniard noted the almost obsessive sense of rivalry which Argentines felt towards the United States, an attitude born as much of historical similarities of development as of economic competition. [28]

Others came to Argentina, to praise, to observe and report, to bring their own land closer to the rising South American nation. Vicente Blasco Ibáñez came in 1910 to do a massive and costly commemorative volume. A German named Schuster did the most thorough study of the country up to that time—from the point of view of German contributions to Argentina, that is. Clemenceau came in 1910 to Buenos Aires, to lecture, and later to write about what he had seen; he arrived in the middle of the Fourth Pan American Conference, which promptly lost some luster in the press. Clemenceau viewed Argentina with the hauteur of a civilized man who is the honored guest of barbarians. He noted the prosaic, flat banks of the estuary, the undistinguished skyline, remarkable only for towering grain elevators, the "intractable chauvinism" of the people, and their enormous local pride. He was impressed by the hurrying growth which pervaded the city, and the sense which the people had

[28] Albert Hale, *The South Americans: the Story of the South American Republics, their Characteristics, Progress, and Tendencies* . . . (Indianapolis, 1907), pp. 53–58, 128; Hiram Bingham, *Across South America: an Account of a Journey from Buenos Aires to Lima by Way of Potosí* . . . (Boston and New York, 1911), pp. 32, 35–36; José María Salaverria, *Tierra argentina: psicología, tipos, costumbres, valores de la República del Plata* (Madrid, 1910), pp. 12–20, 35–37, 45–69, 82–93, 223–229.

of being "new men." He did not overlook the predominance of French culture, which in Argentina, however, did not extend to freedom of speech, for Clemenceau while in Buenos Aires was forbidden by the police to lecture on socialism.[29] It was a sensitive year, this one of the centenary.

From England, too, came travelers who returned to write books, men who saw little French culture, but many pounds sterling. The well-known English historian, Martin Hume, who perhaps had not visited Argentina, wrote an introduction to a book about the place, and believed himself on safe ground when he predicted for it a destiny as one of the great nations of the world. And signs of English culture were not lacking, although possibly more visible in the country than in the city. The estancias in the "camp," as the English translated *campo*, were often replicas of English manors, although few could equal the Chapadmalal breeding farm which, with its privet hedges and lawns and ponds, looked, even to an Englishman, like a bit of Surrey or Devon.[30]

Peace, internal and external, presided over this maturing land, as it had, for the most part, during all the years of the regime of the estancieros—the powerful ones among the Generation of Eighty. The need for peace was known well by Saenz Peña, who not only understood the link between peace and prosperity, but also was contemplating the political reforms which he knew must come if either virtue were to be preserved. He loved his class: had he not spoken pridefully in Paris in 1908 of his "confidence and sincere faith in the prudence and in the tact of the men who direct my country"? Had he not said that "peace will be immovable because of the legitimate weight of great interests"?[31] But 1910 was another in a series of years of mounting tension, which could only be discharged by limiting

[29] Vicente Blasco Ibáñez, *Argentina y sus grandezas* (Madrid, 1910); Adolf N. Shuster, *Argentinien: land, volk, wirtschaftsleben und kolonisation* . . . (2 vols.; Diessen vor München, 1913); Georges Clemenceau, *Notes de voyage dans l'Amérique du Sud: Argentine, Uruguay, Brésil* (Paris, 1911), pp. 6–7, 26–29, 59–65; Sherrill to Knox, July 24, 1910, Numerical File, Vol. 1050, No. 506.

[30] W. A. Hirst, *Argentina*, introduction by Martin Hume (London, 1910), pp. xxiii, xxvii, 105, 115, 122–123, 180: W. H. Koebel, *Modern Argentina, the El Dorado of Today (with Notes on Uruguay and Chile)* (London, 1907), pp. 214–215.

[31] Saenz Peña, *Escritos*, I, 470–471.

the political power of the oligarchy—a task, perhaps, for a wise leader of that group, who would lead the rulers and the ruled to accept reform rather than revolution.

Despite occasional aggressive rumblings from some Argentine intellectuals, often newcomers such as Daniel Antokoletz and José Ingenieros, who saw in the economic and racial superiority of Argentina opportunity to play a tutelary role over South America—a "pacific imperialism," Ingenieros called it—the tone of the year of celebration was set by pride, prosperity, and peace. The poets reflected these qualities: Rubén Darío, in his *Canto a la Argentina*, Enrique Banchs, in his *Oda a los padres de la patria*, and Leopoldo Lugones, with his *Oda a los ganados y a las mieses*.

The centennial celebration was a grand affair. It had taken years of preparation by congress and special commissions. When May 1910 came, visitors from all the western world crowded into Buenos Aires. Products were displayed in specially constructed buildings; prize livestock by the thousands were paraded and judged; hotels, arches over the main avenues, the plazas—all were decorated by day and at night. Lavish commemorative volumes appeared; the newspapers were fat with reports of the grand doings. The Infanta of Spain made the Atlantic crossing to be with those celebrating the revolt against Spain; her picture, near life size, was printed on the front page of *La Prensa*, under the banner, "Salve, Isabela de Borbón." At the other end of the scale there was the founding in this year of the "Asociación Nacional de Damas Descendientes de Patriotas, Próceres y Guerreros de la Independencia Argentina." The volume of oratory unleashed at the many centennial activities may be judged from the fact that the *Revista de Derecho, Historia y Letras* began to publish selected orations in its pages in 1910; in 1915 it was still publishing an occasional speech of five years earlier, having already printed more than 2,800 pages of rhetoric. The chief provinces and cities put out albums in which not one heroic ancestor was overlooked, nor a single prize calf. Of all these albums that of the province of Buenos Aires was, of course, the most elegant, and, no doubt, the heaviest, weighing ten pounds, fourteen ounces, a remarkable assemblage of facts and figures about a province larger and richer than many of the nations of the earth. [32]

The centenary affair was not so much an homage to the men of 1810 as it was a tribute to the men of 1910. For the memory of the former and for the future of the latter it was sadly darkened by a shadow which lay across the festivities, and upon the hundred-year struggle for freedom, a darkness symbolized by the imposition of the state of siege eleven days prior to the one hundredth anniversary of May 25, 1810. But through it came the exultation of the voice of the nation, *La Prensa* (April 29, 1910), reciting the litany of Argentina's blessings: "Her culture, her patriotism, the virtues of her character, the extension and quality of her soil, the kindness of her climate, and the profound spirit of her organic institutions . . . How can a country fail that is endowed with such luck?" And on May 25, *La Nación* gave her salute: "Hail! Hail, Argentina! Thy future destiny—that glory may always be with thee while thou followest the path traced by the heroes of thy epic!"

It was ironic that, of all the events of the centenary, the most important was not any single act of commemoration of Argentine sovereignty, or any demonstration of that country's ties to Europe. It was the assembly in Buenos Aires in July and August 1910 of the Fourth Pan American Conference. But all the irony was not un-Argentine. It was a strange fate for the aggressive United States plans for Pan Americanism of twenty years earlier that this, the fourth meeting of the series, should have been converted by Argentines, on their home grounds, into something of a tribute to the Argentine nation.

The propriety of selecting Buenos Aires as the site of the next Pan American meeting had been strongly indicated by Argentine delegates at the third meeting in Rio, and only a little less strongly at Mexico City. It was, in all fairness, time for the largest national capital in the western hemisphere to be host to the other nations. Buenos Aires was therefore approved by acclamation by the governing board of the International Bureau of American Republics in 1909.

[32] *Album Argentino: libro de estudio de la Provincia de Buenos Aires, su vida, su trabajo, su progreso* . . . [n.d. or place of publication, ?Buenos Aires, 1910].

The remainder of that year was spent by the governing board in consultation with the American states over a program for the coming conference. The program was adopted by that body on November 10, 1909. The regulations were approved by the board on May 13, 1910; they were extensive, explicit, and effective, a far cry from the chaos which had prevailed because of lack of regulations at the First Conference.

The following points made up the program: (1) the organizing of the conference, (2) commemoration of the Argentine centenary and of the independence of the American republics, (3) consideration of the reports of the actions of the several governments upon previous Pan American agreements, (4) consideration of the report of the director of the Bureau, and attention to its possible reorganization, (5) a resolution expressing appreciation to Andrew Carnegie for his gift for the construction of the new building to house the activities of the American states in Washington, (6) the Pan American railroad, (7) steamship service, (8) standardizing of customs regulations and commercial statistics, (9) sanitation, (10) patents, trademarks, and copyrights, (11) continuation of pecuniary claims treaties after expiration, (12) interchange of students and professors, (13) resolution in appreciation of the Pan American Scientific Congress, Santiago, Chile, 1908, (14) plans for celebrating the opening of the Panama Canal, (15) future conferences.[33]

The Argentine government submitted no proposals for incorporation into the program. This was "to avoid all intervention that might wound susceptibilities," President Figueroa Alcorta stated.[34]

The delegation selected to represent the United States at the Buenos Aires meeting was a strong one, perhaps the most capable thus far selected. The chairman was Henry White, a career diplomat who had recently been ambassador to France, and a friend of Theodore Roosevelt. General Enoch Crowder

[33] Pan American Union Archive, Minutes of the Governing Board of the International Bureau of American Republics, IV, 401–404, V, 240–248, 335–340; J. B. Scott, ed., *The International Conferences of the American States, 1889–1928* . . . (New York, 1931), pp. 154–155.

[34] Mabragaña, *Los Mensajes*, VI, 415.

was a distinguished officer, experienced in Cuban affairs. John Bassett Moore brought to the meeting his experience as a former assistant secretary of state and his knowledge of international law. Lewis Nixon was a leading shipbuilder, designer of battleships, and prominent in New York business circles. Three professors filled places on the delegation: Paul Reinsch, professor of political science at Wisconsin, had been a delegate to the Third Conference, and to the Scientific Congress at Santiago; Bernard Moses was a historian at the University of California, and a pioneer in the colonial history of Latin America; David Kinley was a professor of economics and future president of the University of Illinois. Also a delegate was Lamar Quintero, son of a Cuban expatriate, a lawyer and journalist acquainted with Latin America.[35]

The instructions of the secretary of state specified that "Pan American policy takes first place in our diplomacy." Stress was laid on the opportunity that the conference would afford for "intellectual and sympathetic contact" among the representatives. Knox told the delegates that such subjects as would tend "to excite useless controversy" had been omitted from the program, since they might endanger the success of this and future meetings. Among such questions was arbitration; the secretary told the delegates that if this issue was raised at the conference, they were to oppose its consideration on the grounds of lack of competence of the conference to arrange a general arbitral accord. Knox stated that United States-Latin American relations were "perhaps" on a firmer footing than in the past, and that the "somewhat drastic action" which the United States government had been forced to take during the past year against the "medieval despot," Zelaya, in Central America, "would not be misconstrued by the progressive American Republics." Finally, the delegates were told to avoid prominence in the administration of the conference.[36]

[35] *Dictionary of American Biography* (21 vols.; New York, 1928–1944); *National Cyclopaedia of American Biography* (I–, New York, 1893–).

[36] Fourth International Conference of American States, *Message from the President of the United States . . . with Accompanying Papers . . .* (Washington, D.C., 1911), pp. 36–37, 42–43.

The delegates were also given a special confidential memorandum which reviewed the previous conferences and made minor suggestions for improving administrative relations between the American states. This document, probably prepared under the direction of John Barrett for the Pan American Committee of the United States, was the first formal technical assistance provided to a United States delegation to a Pan American conference. [37]

In Argentina preparations for the Conference had also got under way early. There, more interest was evinced in the possible composition of the American delegation than had ever before been shown in that subject by the Argentines. Foreign Minister De la Plaza informed the State Department that his government would be pleased to have the government of the United States select men of the quality of Mr. Roosevelt or Mr. Root to attend the Buenos Aires meeting. Enthusiasm for a successful meeting was expressed by the foreign minister and future president in another note, which instructed the traveling Argentine inspector general of consulates to influence the quarreling Central American republics, together with those of Colombia and Venezuela, to attend the conference. De la Plaza expressed the hope that its success might be no less brilliant than that of the three preceding assemblies. The inspector was also ordered to report information which he might gather about any government which attempted to obstruct the meeting. [38]

The Argentine delegation, in keeping with the high interest in the Conference, was composed of eminent gentlemen. Roque Saenz Peña had agreed to serve as a member; in the interval between his acceptance and the meeting he was elected President of Argentina, and so did not serve. The delegation chairman was Antonio Bermejo, who had filled the same position at the Second Conference, and was a cabinet officer, a professor, and a justice and chief justice of the supreme court. Eduardo

[37] The Pan American Union, Fourth International Conference of the American Republics, Buenos Aires, July 1910. Memoranda . . . (typescript; no date or place).

[38] De la Plaza to Portela, Feb. 27, 1908, Archivo Nacional, Buenos Aires, Archivo de Victorino de la Plaza, leg. 7-5-4-4, 1907–1910, conf. desp. no. 48; De la Plaza to Julio Carrié, Sept. 30, 1910, Archivo de V. de la Plaza, leg. 7-5-4-4, 1907–1910.

Bidau had also been a delegate to a Pan American conference. Epifanio Portela was just ending a four-year period as minister to the United States; he too had served at the last Pan American meeting, and at other diplomatic posts. Carlos Salas was a national deputy and future minister to England and Germany. The delegation was more than rounded out by three former foreign ministers, Estanislao S. Zeballos, Manuel Montes de Oca, and José A. Terry (who had also been a delegate to the meeting at Rio), and by Carlos Rodríguez Larreta, who became foreign minister of Argentina for the second time while the Buenos Aires conference was in progress.[39]

Not all Argentines were as eager for the success of the meeting as Foreign Minister De la Plaza. Rodríguez Larreta was decidedly opposed, although he had accepted appointment to the delegation. He advanced as his reason for opposition the claim that the Hague Conference, scheduled for 1914, would be better qualified to deal with the proposed program, although, according to the United States minister, the program had not been approved when he made this observation.[40] Another source (*La Prensa*, Sept. 8, 1909), perhaps as well informed as the American envoy, reported that Rodríguez Larreta wished to have the conference postponed because of the absence of any matter of importance to be placed before it, a view in which he was joined by fellow delegate Bermejo. Delegates Terry, Bidau, and Montes de Oca seemingly convinced Rodríguez Larreta that he should attend the assembly, pointing out that Argentina had no right to make a unilateral postponement (*La Prensa*, Sept. 9, 1909). Bidau took as positive a position toward Pan Americanism as an Argentine might be expected to assume (*La Nación*, May 25, 1910), maintaining that the Conferences had improved in quality from the First onward, insofar as they had refrained from dealing with large political and economic issues. It was good, he believed, for Argentina to contribute to this fraternity of Latin American ideals, so long as relations with Europe were not impaired.

[39] Enrique Udaondo, *Diccionario biográfico argentino* (Buenos Aires, 1938); W. B. Parker, ed., *Argentines of Today* (2 vols.; Buenos Aires and New York, 1920).

[40] Sherrill to Secretary of State, August 29, 1909, Numerical File, no. 2098/201–205, No. 74.

Other well known Argentines were no more friendly toward the Conference. José N. Matienzo, a leading political scientist, brought up the familiar theory that the Pan American idea had been Alberdi's in the first instance. Manuel Ugarte, beginning a long career as Argentina's loudest Yankee-hater, fired a good many old guns at the impending meeting, and touched off a few new ones such as his charge that the United States was attempting now to "infiltrate" Latin America. Only a few leaders, Joaquín V. González for one, expressed distress at Argentina's inactivity between Pan American conferences and regret over the feebleness of the agenda of the Fourth Conference.[41]

Argentine press opinion was not unfavorable to the meeting or to the United States. *La Prensa* (Sept. 9, 1909) wished the conference to be held, if only as a tribute to the Argentine centenary. Anyway, the paper claimed (July 9, 1910), the program was sound because it was uncontroversial. *La Prensa's* friendlier attitude may have been shaped by recent events: the United States tariff reductions of 1909; the friendly talk of Root and Barrett; the first perceptible increase of United States investment; and the more complex reason that the long-time director of *La Prensa*, the chauvinistic Zeballos, having successfully stirred up trouble with Brazil, Chile, and Bolivia during his recent tenure as foreign minister (including the forging of a diplomatic telegram to Brazil) seems to have believed that the Conference would serve to fortify Argentina's position with respect to other Latin American states. The editorial of July 31 pretty well summed up *La Prensa's* views: the delegates have come to the Conference to celebrate Argentina's centenary; they have a rare opportunity to see Argentina in its perfection—"one of the poles of culture, of power, of influence in the New World." The English words, "South America," with their derogatory implications, were now employed only by ignorant foreigners (*La Prensa*, July 13, 1910).

La Nación (July 12, 1910) also was pleased with the coming

---

[41] J. N. Matienzo, "La política americana de Alberdi," *Revista de Ciencias Políticas*, I (1910), 17–27; M. Ugarte, *Revista de Derecho, Historia y Letras*, año 12, t. 35, April 1910, pp. 496–513; Joaquín V. González, *Jurisprudencia y política* (Buenos Aires, 1914), pp. 314–325.

gathering, while acknowledging that important questions had gradually been eliminated from the Pan American meetings. *El Diario* (July 10, 1910) had not changed its views much, greeting the delegates with the pungent Spanish aphorism, "a few nuts make a lot of noise." *El Economista Argentina* (June 4, 1910) hailed the conference program for its vacuity, which would permit social amicability, the better part of Pan Americanism.

Vacuum or not, the Fourth Pan American Conference, identifiable by its crowd of dignified diplomats in dress suits, began its sessions on July 12, 1910. The First Pan American Conference had consumed six months; the Fourth took six weeks. Foreign Minister De la Plaza, who had recently been elected vice-president of the nation to take office with president-elect Saenz Peña in October, delivered the address of welcome on behalf of the nation. In his first words he described the meeting as an honor paid to Argentina. He next stated, erroneously, that Buenos Aires had been graciously designated as the site of the meeting at the Third Conference in Rio. He predicted success for the work of his audience because the program touched no interest in conflict in the Americas. The fact that so many Pan American agreements remained unratified was, he said, confirmation of the sovereignty of each state. He also derived comfort from the fact that proper guidance of Pan Americanism of late had dispelled Europe's fears that commercial and political barriers might be erected against her.[42]

Henry White gave the reply, echoing De la Plaza, and belittling the thought that Europe now feared the Pan American group. Bermejo was elected president of the assembly; he harped on the same themes, closing with the observation that at this meeting majority decisions were not binding on the minority.[43]

In the agenda the Conference had a few practical matters, but it quickly became apparent that these would be resolved not much more successfully than the problems which had been

[42] *Cuarta Conferencia Internacional Americana, 1910. Primer Tomo: Diario de Sesiones. Segundo Tomo: Anexos, Resoluciones y Convenciones* (Buenos Aires, 1911), I, 4–7.

[43] CCIA, I, 17, 19–23.

dealt with at previous Pan American gatherings. Even the frail ghost of the customs union plan of the First Conference could not be given life in Buenos Aires. It was found that the task of gathering customs information from the American states for the simple purpose of making some uniform regulations had proven an impossible feat for the Bureau. The United States delegation, despite the slight preliminary assistance of the Pan American Committee of the United States, found when it got down to business in Buenos Aires that the only information which it possessed about customs regulations in its own country was provided by a booklet fortunately in the possession of the United States consul in Buenos Aires. Coming full circle in twenty years, the delegation followed its instructions to support the recommendation made at the First Conference that the governments support uniform customs regulations and fees. This was agreeable to the other states at the Conference in Buenos Aires, all of which voted for three resolutions: (1) calling for the simplification of customs dues, (2) and of customs regulations and (3) calling for establishment of a section in the Bureau to deal with such matters—a recommendation which had also been made at the Third Conference. [44]

The conferees pursued another familiar course—steamship communications. The United States delegates were in no stronger position on this matter than they had been on the customs regulations; their instructions stated that they were to manifest an interest in the subject, but should not submit any proposals to the assembly because of the uncertainty about the action of the United States Congress on ship subsidy bills now before it. The conference decided in the end to recommend to their governments the direct negotiation of conventions for the establishment of steamer services "through state initiative"—a resolution interesting mainly as evidence of the encouragement which professed believers in free enterprise were willing to give to state intervention. [45]

[44] *Message from the President*, p. 39; CCIA, I, 356–396; *International Conferences*, pp. 194–200; David Kinley, "An Outlook on the Pan-American Conference," *The Independent*, 69:63 (Sept. 22, 1910).

[45] *Message from the President*, p. 39; CCIA, I, 266–278; *International Conferences*, pp. 186–188.

The Pan American Railroad fared even worse than its old companions. The United States delegation had no instructions on this matter; the Argentine delegation had no interest in it; and the committee which considered the subject decided that there was no point to drafting any plan for the completion of the line. The Conference adopted without debate a resolution recommending the prorogation of the Pan American Railroad Committee.[46] Thus another "practical" Pan American idea moved a step closer to extinction.

Success was achieved in the matter of patents and trademarks. The convention signed at Rio had been found by the United States Patent Office to be riddled with defects which prevented its submission to the United States Senate. Hence, a patent commissioner was sent along to Buenos Aires, and the United States delegates were told to work for a suitable convention. Such conventions, on the reciprocal protection of patents and trademarks, were unanimously approved by the Conference and were subsequently ratified by thirteen and by fourteen states, respectively. The United States ratified both, Argentina neither.[47]

Efforts for more effective sanitation in the hemisphere neither progressed nor regressed. The Conference merely voted that non-ratifying members should adopt the earlier conventions upon which they had not acted.[48]

Another success followed years of effort when a convention was signed on literary and artistic copyright and ultimately ratified by thirteen American republics, including the United States.[49] Many years later, and perhaps not without relation to the fact that Buenos Aires had in the interval become a great publishing center, Argentina ratified this agreement, one of the three which that government has ratified out of the seventeen treaties and conventions signed by its representatives at the Second, Third, and Fourth Pan American Conferences.

The Conference also adopted a resolution recommending the

[46] *Message from the President*, p. 38; CCIA, I, 178; *International Conferences*, pp., 179–180.
[47] *Message of the President*, pp. 40–41; CCIA, I, 341–345, 396–413; *International Conferences*, pp. 191–193, 201–206.
[48] *Message of the President*, p. 40; CCIA, I, 299–319; *International Conferences*, p. 189.
[49] CCIA, I, 181–247; *International Conferences*, pp. 180–183.

interchange of professors and students among the member states; and acted to keep alive the treaty on the arbitration of pecuniary claims signed at the Second Conference, and extended at Rio. The United States and ten other states ratified the new convention; Argentina did not. [50]

These were modest but real results, at least when ratified. And Argentina did not oppose action on these subjects within the Conference, nor did she resist the broadening of the Pan American system which was voted at Buenos Aires, although by her own admission she had done nothing until a year before the Fourth Conference even to initiate ratifying action on some of the Pan American agreements which she had signed at the Third Conference in 1906. The broadened Pan American system took the form of renaming the International Union of American Republics the Union of American Republics, and of altering the name of the service organization from the International Bureau of American Republics to the Pan American Union. A more extensive authority was given to the director general of the Pan American Union, and that body's functions were defined more widely. The Union was to exist for successive periods of ten years unless notice of withdrawal were given by a majority of members at least one year prior to the expiration of each decade. It was also voted to hold the Fifth Pan American Conference within five years, although there was some comment that too frequent meetings might produce an "impression of futility." [51]

The Conference was not all work. The first session was given over to commemorating Argentine political leaders who had died since the last Conference. There were greetings to France on July 14, speeches and a vote of sympathy for earthquake-stricken Chile, the reading of the replies to the messages of the first day, the reading of messages from the fine clubs of Buenos Aires—the Jockey, the Círculo de Armas, the Club del Progreso —placing their facilities at the disposal of the delegates. Occasionally the delegates took a day off from their duties, to visit the

[50] CCIA, I, 319–323, 248, 255; *International Conferences*, pp. 190–191, 183–185.

[51] CCIA, I, 163–178, 258–263; *International Conferences*, pp. 172–179, 186.

estancia of Pereyra Iraola, or to ride through the city on a special streetcar tour.

One old issue did not get into the Conference at all, and that was the Monroe Doctrine. Brazil made some pre-Conference attempts to have the meeting endorse the doctrine, but the Argentine and United States delegates sat down with the Brazilians outside the Conference and Brazil dropped its so-called "Nabuco formula."[52]

A blaze of self-congratulation and congratulation of the Argentine host illuminated the final day of the Conference. The host nation was told of its great qualities and its manifest destiny. Foreign Minister Rodríguez Larreta replied that the assembly had indeed been a great tribute to Argentina. "We can now say," he continued, "as was said in Washington, 'America for humanity,' because we are sovereign nations and the position we occupy in the world we owe to the efforts of our own arms." Then, with unprecedented friendliness, he devoted his final word to expressing gratitude to the United States of America, initiator of these continental conferences.[53]

Opinion on the results of the meeting varied little. The United States delegation in their official report commented on the unusually harmonious character of the assembly, but had no other conclusions to draw. Delegate Reinsch found the chief value of the meeting in the fact that so many states could meet together in a harmonious body. Delegate Kinley did not expect much from these meetings because their true function, he believed, was only to remove differences of detail between the nations.

The Argentine delegation in its report noted the spirit of concord which had prevailed at the meeting. Argentine opinion was pleased by the meeting. Zeballos saw as a result a drawing together of the peoples of the hemisphere. The director of the *Revista Nacional*, Carranza, praised the elimination of

[52] CCIA, I, 11, 15; Américo Lugo, *La Cuarta Conferencia Americana* (Sevilla, 1912) p. 28; A. Alvarez, "La Doctrina Monroe y la América Latina," *Revista de Ciencias Políticas*, I (1910), 613–624; *La Prensa*, July 22, 23, 25, 26, 1910; *La Nación*, July 21, 22, 23, 24, 1910; E. S. Zeballos, "Conferencia Interamericana," *Revista de Derecho, Historia y Letras*, año 13, t. 37, Dec. 1910, pp. 571–573.

[53] CCIA, II, 519–537.

controversial questions from the agenda, and the consequent harmonious deliberations. *La Prensa* (Sept. 1, 1910) described the assembly as a friendly social gathering, an education for the visitors in the destinies of Argentina, and an honor for the republic. *La Nación* (Aug. 31, 1910) was disappointed that the Conference had accomplished so little, but pointed to the friendship between the delegates that had grown up, and the chance afforded them to observe Argentine progress. *El Diario* (Aug. 27, 1910) thought that this Conference might well be the last.[54]

But *La Nación* (Sept. 2, 1910) expressed the clearest thought on the meaning of the Buenos Aires meeting. That Conference, wrote the Mitre paper, favored neither the United States nor Europe to the harm of the other. It demonstrated that Latin Americans were neither Europeans nor North Americans; they were Argentines, Brazilians, or Cubans.

[54] Memoria de Relaciones Exteriores 1910–1911, *Informe de la Delegación Argentina*, Sept. 30, 1910, pp. 79–87; Paul S. Reinsch, "The Fourth International Conference of American Republics," *The American Journal of International Law*, 4:777 (October 1910); Kinley, "An Outlook," pp. 638, 640; Zeballos quoted in Enrique Gil, *Evolución del panamericanismo: el credo de Wilson y el panamericanismo* (Buenos Aires, 1933), pp. 73, 75; Rodolfo Carranza, "IV Conferencia Panamericana," *Revista Nacional*, año 24, t. 47, 1910, pp. 3–6.

17

End of an Era

THE span of a generation of men is accounted to be somewhat over thirty years. The Generation of Eighty had had three decades of plenitude and power when the centenary was celebrated in 1910. This was the zenith. The decline began. The adoption of the Saenz Peña electoral law in 1912 curbed the political power of the conservatives; death thinned their ranks; the war in Europe disrupted the economy. 1914 was the end of an era, the end of a great generation, and the beginning of the end of a class.

The few years extending from halcyon 1910 to the crisis of 1914 saw a startling change in the fortunes of the men who had seemed immovably secure. All of the change, however, did not occur in that period. Ideas about Argentina, held by Argentines, began to alter earlier, around 1900, in the minds of a very young group of men.

These men may be called intellectuals, for they were intelligent, and they lived by their minds—in part. The litterateurs of the older generation (not yet too old in the late nineties) had not been self-consciously intellectuals. They were individuals without a common literary esprit, tied closely into the government in most cases by domestic or foreign sinecures. So it was with the Cané of *Juvenilia*, Wilde of the witty essays, and the irrepressible Mansilla, nephew of Rosas, more a Parisian dandy and *causeur* than the native of Paris ever could be. The new men were bohemian; moreover, they were bohemians who remained at home, in Buenos Aires. Most of them could not live wholly by their writing, any more than could García Merou or Cambaceres, but living in Buenos Aires around the turn of the century was not expensive—not in cafes and garrets—and a newspaper job earned a few pesos and many hours for talking and writing at the Café de Los Inmortales or elsewhere.

The nineties felt the first stirrings of a reviving, organized, or at least conscious, intellectual life, with the founding of the Ateneo, and the stimulation of Rubén Darío, leader of *modernismo*, who came to work on *La Nación*. But the Ateneo had older as well as younger men—even Mitre took an interest—and it was not until 1900 and after that a concern for social criticism, rather than for literary form alone, emerged. As one of the young men wrote, the time had come when Argentine critics forsook their international wanderings and returned to the hearth of the *patria*, which they had abandoned one imprudent day.[1]

The youths who sought to redefine Argentina had been born mostly between 1875 and 1890, reached early manhood around the centennial year, and did their work in a great arc stretching from 1900 down beyond the middle of the century. Yet they alone could not claim praise for making a new journey through their land, for it was, as always, the older generation which provided impetus—in this case given by two of the more percipient of the Generation of Eighty, who called for a fresh look at Argentine values. Carlos Pellegrini made a public appeal to Argentine youth in the pages of his paper *El País* (Jan. 2, 1900). He asked, "Where is the youth called to occupy the high command posts in a day not far away?," and complained of their indolence, seduced as they had been by the ease of living. Pellegrini's call proved its point: it fell on deaf ears. After several weeks had passed, Miguel Cané, an oligarch in politics and economics, but more flexible in literary ideas (in the eighties he had declared that it was more of a feat to get a book published in Buenos Aires than to recite a sonnet of Petrarch in the stock exchange) took up Pellegrini's challenge, to throw it again at the younger men. He singled out the uninspired and dogmatic educational system as the root of the moral atrophy; he hinted—

[1] Víctor Martínez Cuitiño, *El café de Los Inmortales* (Buenos Aires, 1949), and Roberto F. Giusti, *Momentos y aspectos de la cultura argentina* (Buenos Aires, 1954) recollect this period; the comment is by Emilio Becher, quoted in Manuel Gálvez, *Recuerdos de la vida literaria (1900–1910): amigos y maestros de mi juventud* (Buenos Aires, 1944), p. 38.

bold thought—that the prevailing positivism implied the danger of cultural suffocation by brutal opulence.

Two days after Cané's letter appeared in *La Nación* it received an answer. It was from José Luis Murature, twenty-four years old, later to be managing editor of *La Nación* and foreign minister of his country. Murature told his elders that if his own generation was receiving a bad education, it was the fault of the older men, who were the masters, but that more fatal than bad training had been the political climate, which stifled morality.

The political climate did not change, but the new men appeared in any event: Manuel Gálvez, Ricardo Rojas, Constancio Vigil, Roberto Giusti, Florencio Sánchez, Emilio Becher, José Ingenieros. A symbol of their coming, their literary manifesto, was the magazine *Ideas*, a "little" magazine and short-lived, published by Gálvez and Ricardo Olivera in 1903. Gálvez, who was to become one of Latin America's famed novelists, was the elder: he was twenty. Olivera, later faithful friend and secretary of Roque Saenz Peña, was not quite seventeen. In the first number editor Olivera attacked Buenos Aires for lacking love of things of the spirit. The universities, he continued, are sunk in scholasticism, while "our directing classes" view the manifestations of refined culture as exotic growths, unworthy of protection. Thus, the young editor wrote with a good dash of old-fashioned patriotism, Argentina as it approaches its first centenary "is not yet capable of the continental hegemony to which it was born predestined."

In the same year fundamental criticism of Argentina's social order came from an unexpected source. Lucio V. Mansilla, over seventy and more than hale and hearty, published a book entitled *En vísperas*. The first words described Argentine society as one permeated by hatred. This was followed by criticism of the essential disorganization of the governmental structure and of the absence of moral and spiritual qualities in the people. Mansilla called for an end of the oligarchy's oppression of political rights.

The Argentine capacity to hate weighed also on the mind of thirty-year-old Ernesto Nelson. Its cause: intense individualism, an excess of ego, which also took the form of sadness, or at least

of somberness, often noted by travelers in Argentina. The individual felt himself isolated from his fellows. His pride, so notice-
able in the vanity of dress of the male porteño, was always near
the surface, and with it the fear that it might be pierced. The
result was not only quickness to take offence, but quickness to
give unwarranted offence. Nelson himself had been the target
of one mean display of generalized social hostility: one day as
he leaned from the window of a slow-moving train a man in a
passing train purposefully spat in his face. There were other
indications of social malaise that made a far different picture
than one might get from the clubs and ballrooms: how mis-
fortune stirs laughter in Argentines; the cruelty to horses and
other animals; the proclivity for loud conversation, exaggerated
gestures, deprecating colloquialisms; how private influence
accomplishes everything, especially with the government official;
the seeking of prerogatives, warranted or not, and their heavy-
handed use when secured. [2]

There was other testimony to this state of affairs. One man
wrote about the deep penetration of *coima*—graft—in the society.
There were the *patotas*, gangs of *niños bienes*, or "gilded youths,"
whose pastime it was to roam the city insulting and attacking
transients. [3]

Such criticisms arose from no radical sources. The writers
were of the bourgeoisie, or wished to be, not of the proletariat;
even the bright young Socialists such as Alfredo Palacios and
Enrique Dickmann were true to their doctrine and preached
legitimate reform, not bastard violence.

All but the strongest minds were stifled by the strength and
wealth of the generation in command; and some who were not
choked lost themselves in a maze of sociological and psychological abstractions. José Ingenieros was perhaps the prime victim of his own speculations. Born in Buenos Aires of Italian par-
ents in 1877, his energy and sharpness made him a high priest
of sociology. He looked long and intelligently at Argentina's

[2] Letter E. Nelson to Carlos O. Bunge, October 1903, in *Revista de Derecho,
Historia y Letras*, año 6, t. 17, Feb. 1904, pp. 507–522.

[3] Francisco F. Bayón, "Solidaridad intelectual hispano-americano," *Revista
Nacional*, año 22, t. 43, May 1907, pp. 230–233; Juan Manuel Pinto, *Así fué Buenos
Aires. Tipos y costumbres de una época, 1900–1950* (Buenos Aires, 1954), pp. 47–52.

past and present, but his often shrewd judgments became obscured in an eclectic fog constructed of positivism, genetic and penal theories, psychology, and, finally, Marxism. When he died in the 1920's in his forty-seventh year he left a large reputation, and a number of books which could have been much more revealing and constructive.

Manuel Gálvez made a more lasting contribution to the reassessment of Argentina than did Ingenieros with his pseudosciences. This *provinciano* from Entre Ríos turned from poetry to prose at about the time of his work on *Ideas*, and proceeded to write over the years a series of novels about Argentina. His *El diario de Gabriel Quiroga* (1910) opened up the theme of the forgotten provinces and their relationship to Buenos Aires; it was a call to a reformation of the national spirit. He also turned to Spain, another neglected aspect of the Argentine heritage. His *El solar de la raza* appeals to the past for the sake of the present, summoning Argentines to avert their eyes from false nationalism based on pride in the number of tons of wheat exported and to turn to the "spiritualization of the national conscience" to redress the weight of materialism and scepticism.

If in later years Gálvez's intuitions for *hispanidad* and nationalism were to become rigid and authoritarian, they were in the beginning fresh and welcome to a people with a disturbed past and a chaotic present. This was, after all, the generation of youths to whom José Enrique Rodó made his appeal from Uruguay in his little essay, *Ariel*, published in 1900. Not only Argentines but all Latin Americans responded to the frail challenge thrown out to Caliban; a response of sentiment and of words, nothing more; but *Ariel* became an inexhaustible powder magazine at which to load the cannons of idealism for war against the greedy United States.

But how to spiritualize the Argentine conscience, torpid beneath two or three decades of rankest material success? Not, perhaps, by attacking the United States in the press, and then publishing nothing but reports of its material achievements, omitting nearly all reference to its cultural accomplishment. Not, perhaps, by the course advocated by one young scholar, which was to inculcate nationalism intensively in the schools, thus insuring a glorious future of Argentine leadership in South America—an "Argentine imperialism" which the author did not shrink from naming. Could it be done in the way Gálvez himself urged—by "preaching extravagantly" love of the patria, of the landscape, of the writers, of the great men of Argentina? This might be the route, but it seemed to narrow quickly, for Gálvez was already appealing against non-Latin immigration, against the "cosmopolitan and liberal" tendencies dominant in Argentina. [4] He was for Spain and criollo Argentina; out of this attitude strong politics would one day be made.

There was another front along which the battle cry of the younger generation was heard. That was education. One of the principal fighters was Ricardo Rojas. Born, like Gálvez, in the provinces—in Tucumán in 1882—he published in 1909 *La restauración nacionalista*, which in its title caught the new idea and in its content was a critique of the Argentine educational system. He urged Argentines to regard their past, and to show it to youth. The obsession with material progress, he wrote, was the principal impediment to a solution of the nation's intellectual crisis. He illustrated his thesis of contempt for the past and its positive side, desire for material change, by pointing to the ruthless destruction of the few historic buildings yet standing in Buenos Aires. In the time of Alberdi, Rojas wrote, it was the desert which isolated men; "today it is cosmopolitanism," which to him meant excessive devotion to Europe and to money. And a little later: "Today, upon celebrating the centenary, we feel ourselves to be a colony of the old metropolises." To Rojas, Buenos Aires was kept alien from the nation by the individual and international interests which had formed its new greatness. In colonial times the city had lived for the next ship from Spain; now it was living for the daily news from England or from France. [5]

Some of the leaders of the *generación del 80* were not unaware of the need for a "national restoration"—a welding together of creole and immigrant Argentina—or at least, of a lessened

---

[4] Manuel Gálvez, *El solar de la raza* (5th ed.; Madrid, 1920), pp. 14–18; Raúl A. Orgáz, "La orientación americanista en la enseñanza de la historia," *Revista Argentina de Ciencias Políticas*, I (1910), 783–792.

[5] Ricardo Rojas, *La restauración nacionalista* (Buenos Aires, 1909), pp. 53, 88–89.

materialism. Saenz Peña wrote to Pellegrini that he wished for a return to the time when "we were less, statistically, but more, morally." The administration of Figueroa Alcorta subsidized Rojas's trip to Europe to gather data for *La restauración*, and paid publication costs, and the specific educational remedies set down in the book were at least discussed within the government. And the system of higher education had been under fire long before Rojas made his contribution.[6]

Yet the Rojas book was important because it was written by a young man of obvious talent, whose fundamental message was a denial of an old Argentine creed: for Rojas, unlike Alberdi, to populate was *not* to govern, well.

Rojas practiced the nationalism which he preached. *La restauración* was followed in the centenary year by his *Blasón del Plata*, a fervent, mystical appeal to *argentinidad*—the knowledge of the destiny of the Argentine race, born of Indian and Spaniard, into which the immigrant must be absorbed.

Another Argentine who spoke for the new nationalism with more authority than Rojas or Gálvez was Joaquín V. González. Born in 1863 in the province of La Rioja in the Andes of the far west, González became by talent a member of the governing circle. His age placed him between the two generations. He served with the men of the Generation of Eighty as a deputy, a senator, and a cabinet minister, but intellectually he was also with the new generation, and so was his later career, as founder and head of the University of La Plata.

He wrote much, and well. He tenderly evoked his distant province in 1893 in *Mis montañas*, a rare contribution, then, to a literature which did not much value the local landscape and the people of the hinterland. In 1913 he published *El juicio del siglo*. His eyes were on the future; his judgment was on the past. He castigated the years of electoral corruption by which the few had retained power, manipulating the suffrage through justices of the peace and country *comisarios*. There were two social

---

[6] *Pellegrini: 1846–1906: Obras* (5 vols.; Buenos Aires, 1941), I, 238; Juan R. Fernández, "Reforma universitaria," *Revista de Derecho, Historia y Letras*, año 1, t. 2, Nov. 1898, pp. 88–121, and Dec. 1898, pp. 267–286; José Luis Cantilo, "El gran problema," *Revista de Derecho, Historia y Letras*, año 1, t. 2, Jan. 1899, pp. 299–307; Miguel Cané in *La Nación*, Feb. 19, 1900.

classes, he wrote, the directing class and the directed; among
the former, "some were rich, others civilized, and the rest were
obliged by impotence or interest to submit themselves to the
yoke of peace and order."

González offered political reform (which Saenz Peña was
just instituting) and education as the means of solving domestic
difficulties. In foreign affairs he urged an idealistic foreign
policy based upon justice, arbitration, and responsible leadership in southern South America, together with Brazil and Chile.[7]

The oligarchy was not the only target of criticism. Attacks
grew more bitter against the character of the Argentine people:
the "perpetual exhibition" they were making of themselves by
all their talk about their wealth; their egotism and indolence,
which permitted the immigrant to cultivate the soil, and other
foreigners to control commerce and industry. The national evil,
wrote one man, is vanity, ostentatious luxury its mark, and
Buenos Aires its center, with its gambling and other vices, as
well as political corruption.[8]

So the cause of the ethical redirection of the nation gathered
its few adherents as the new generation moved to the fore. But
the Generation of Eighty appeared to be unmoved. Indeed, the
older and the younger men had one vital area of agreement,
whatever their quarrels over domestic mores. That was their
view of Argentina's role in the hemisphere. Long the champions
of national political sovereignty and leadership, the oligarchs
found themselves upon common ground with the awakening
nationalism of the younger age. Some of the newcomers were
critical of Europe's dominance in their land; none of them was
attracted by the substitute offered by the United States, Pan
Americanism.

It was one of the younger generation, who was at the same
time of the oligarchy, who carried on most effectively the devotion of his elders to Europe, and their distrust of the United
States. Carlos Saavedra Lamas came of famous families; he

[7] Joaquín V. González, *El juicio del siglo o cién anos de historia argentia* (Buenos
Aires, 1913), pp. 200–206, 209, 267–268, 296–298.

[8] Luis V. Tamini, "Después del Centenario," *Revista de Derecho, Historia y Letras,*
año 14, t. 40, Sept. 1911, pp. 83–93; Joaquín Rubianes, *Revista Argentina de Ciencias
Políticas,* IV (1912), 634–652.

served Argentina as many of his forebears had done. Son-in-law of Roque Saenz Peña, Saavedra Lamas was to continue in foreign affairs a successful defense of the views of his father-in-law and of their class, long after the oligarchy had fallen on hard times.

In 1911, when he was thirty-two years old, Saavedra Lamas spoke on foreign policy in the chamber of deputies. The material and political conditions of North and South America were so distinct, he observed, that the application of United States policy, especially Pan Americanism, could have little meaning in the latter region. Indeed, he stated, the policy of the United States is to bar Europe economically and politically from Latin America. Argentina, the first country of that region, must direct its energy to drawing Europe closer, thus establishing a balance with the Pan Americanism of the Anglo-Saxons. [9]

Others, as had the author who had drawn an "Argentine imperialism" out of the inculcation of the new nationalism, saw more specific goals for their foreign policy. A 1912 article by an otherwise unidentified but active officer of the Argentine army urged the conquest and annexation of an unnamed neighboring state, making a neat equation between the situation in Morocco and that next door. He appealed to the idea of the survival of the fittest and to the claim, more widely used in another part of the hemisphere, that upon a strong nation lay the obligation to set straight the affairs of its less well-organized neighbors. This argument seemed to gain strength when given a historical foundation: such an annexation, it was claimed by this officer, would only be to recuperate a little of what Argentina had once possessed in the days of the viceroyalty. *La Prensa* (April 27, 1914) took up the cry of the lost viceregal lands, cast away by Argentine pacificism and tolerance, the paper editorialized, with little historical truth. A well-known writer went further, seeing Argentina as "the initiator of the great political solutions which are needed by humanity." [10]

[9] Congreso Nacional, *Diario de sesiones de la Cámara de Diputados*, June 11, 1911, pp. 409–430.
[10] "Marreucos, la Tripolitana y una república sudamericana," *Revista de Derecho, Historia y Letras*, año 14, t. 41, Jan. 1912, pp. 66–72; A. Pallejá, "La hora actual de la política argentina," *Revista de Derecho, Historia y Letras*, año 14, t. 41, Jan. 1912, pp. 41–51.

In part such paeans to Argentina may have resulted from the emotional release brought on by the beginning of the healing of one deep-rooted internal ill. In 1911 and 1912 the executive branch of the government presented to the legislature, and that body finally approved, a series of statutes which have ever since been known as the Saenz Peña law. The law provided for secret, compulsory suffrage for males over eighteen years of age, and for the incomplete list, which gave to minority parties representation in proportion to the number of votes won at the polls. This comprehensive reform was intended to stamp out the curse of electoral corruption. It was a victory for Hipólito Yrigoyen and his Radical party; it meant the end of the political domination by the oligarchy.

It was a great victory for Saenz Peña, an aristocrat with the rare aristocratic trait of *noblesse oblige*, a man also endowed with enough common sense and political experience to see the danger in postponing longer the settlement of the accounts of the ruling class with the bulk of the electorate.

Two men may also be singled out of the group within the dominant class who imposed upon themselves the difficult and bitter task of obtaining legislative approval of the electoral proposals, men who, like Saenz Peña, represented, near its end, the best of the liberal tradition within the aristocracy.

Victorino de la Plaza, corpulent and cosmopolitan, resident in England during all the middle years of his life, where he represented his country in the financial transactions between Buenos Aires and London, is the forgotten man in the history of the coming of democracy to Argentina. As vice-president he succeeded Saenz Peña in office and saw to the execution of the law which in 1916 put the Radical candidate, Yrigoyen, in the Casa Rosada, the presidential mansion. De la Plaza was faithful to the obligations of law, rather than to the demands of his class, at a time when the operation of the electoral law was in peril, following the death of its initiator.

Indalecio Gómez, the "last provincial *hidalgo*," ambassador to Berlin, then minister of the interior in the cabinet of his friend, Saenz Peña, was charged by him with the task of securing the passage of the reform law through a hostile legislature.

Gómez was a tall, unsmiling person with a positive dislike for the multitude; for most individuals, too, as is made clear by his custom of addressing another person not as "usted," and most certainly not as "tu," but as "el señor." Yet he served the people well, bearing the blunt of the struggle for enactment, then seeing to the proper enforcement of the law in the first congressional elections in April 1912, which also resulted in a Radical victory.

The Saenz Peña law was not merely a good law; scores of good laws lay celibate upon Argentine statute books. It was the diligence, the personal authority, the honor with which the law was conceived and bred into the lives and hearts of the Argentine people that gave it goodness. It was a matter of courage, which Saenz Peña possessed. He saw the futility of the political oppression practiced by his peers; he met with Yrigoyen, to bring the Radicals up from underground; he commanded the trust of men as far apart as the local ward heeler and Indalecio Gómez.

As president he revealed his strength in other matters; he had the courage, in 1913, to veto a bill calling for the expenditure of four hundred thousand pesos for a celebration of the centenary of the Argentine flag, and to veto it on the grounds of economy. He criticized the Jockey Club for attempting to hold races on working days, and refused to legalize such contests.

In his first inaugural speech, delivered before congress on October 12, 1912, he laid down the precepts upon which he intended to administer his office. He also gave his views on foreign affairs; these were the views of his class and of most Argentines. He could take pride in the fact that in stating them he was in accord with much of his nation's history, and that he was at the same time reviewing much of his own past work, back to the Montevideo Conference of 1888 and the First Pan American Conference. He told his audience:

My international policy is known to you. It will be friendship for Europe and fraternity for America. I share in the Pan American concept, so far as it signifies unassailable respect for the sovereignty, concord, and friendship of the states of the continent, without exclusion of the reciprocal relations which are called for by our economic development. It is not suitable for Argentine policy to be either privately American or exclusively European ... We have created an international situation with respect to Europe, incorporating ourselves in its mentality ... deliberating in happy communion on the united destiny of the great human family.[11]

Argentine views of themselves and of the United States after 1910 show pride and optimism as in the preceding decades, but somewhat mellowed, not only by the sentiment of genuine national accomplishment, but also by the beginning of a sense of disillusionment creeping into the minds and hearts of the more thoughtful, who realized that a difficult road lay ahead to the self-promised utopia where Argentina would achieve its grand destiny.

At the end of 1911, *La Prensa* (Dec. 28) reviewed recent relations with the United States and found them good, or improved, at any rate. The Pan American Conferences of 1906 and 1910 and the visits and words of leading United States representatives had tranquilized Latin American opinion, which had been aroused by the excessive interpretation of the Monroe Doctrine. That doctrine would soon be a thing of the past, *La Prensa* continued, and Argentina had had the most prominent place in the movement to establish Latin American sovereignty, as was acknowledged by the press and officials of the United States, which recognized Argentina as the United States of the south. In internal affairs, *La Prensa* (Oct. 16, 1912) continued to urge the perfecting of institutions not only for the felicity of the nation but so that no shadow of suspicion about Argentine stability and cooperativeness might cross the minds of the "kings of capital."

New writers and old kept to many of the well-worn lasts of the past three decades, but there were signs of change. Ernesto Quesada, less assured than he had been a quarter of a century earlier, wrote that Argentina's days of glory would be postponed only a little while longer, until the educational and political systems should be properly organized; meanwhile, the nation's "manifest destiny" rested on keeping peace and developing commercial relations with all the world, especially with Europe, and on abstention from mixing in the affairs of others.

[11] Saenz Peña, *Escritos y discursos*, II, 215–216, 260–264; I, 42–43.

Young Enrique Gil, studying in the United States, which he learned to esteem without sacrificing an ounce of love for Argentina, also believed in the manifest destiny of his land, and was convinced that an Argentine race was emerging, with its own ideals and temperament. Another scholar urged the assertion of the moral hegemony which was Argentina's due in Latin America, by developing stronger economic and cultural ties with the other Latin American nations.

Leopoldo Lugones, individualistic poet and prose writer, writing in 1914 in the *Revue Sud-Américaine,* which he had founded in Paris, contributed a penetrating and surprisingly friendly assessment of Pan Americanism, pointing out that the world was on the threshold of war, in danger of splitting into power regions, and that the Pan American world should seek true unity, with Argentina in the lead, abandoning her egotism and indifference toward Pan Americanism, and adopting the Monroe Doctrine.[12]

Argentina was a long way from adopting the Monroe Doctrine, but there can be little doubt that hostility toward the United States was easing. Perhaps the most important factor behind this melioration was the increasing trade between the two countries, and this despite the fact that in 1913, 70 per cent of Argentina's foreign trade was with Europe. Imports from the United States were $56,515,107 in 1911, $66,242,864 in 1912, and $70,457,225 in 1913; exports to the United States in the same years amounted to $24,685,655, $32,632,786, and $23,728,409, the drop in the last figure caused by crop failures. Argentina's total exports rose in value year by year up to World War I, reaching $500,985,551 in 1913; imports that year had a value of $478,859,145. The United Kingdom was still far and away the leader in Argentine trade, doing twice as much business as the nearest competitor, Germany. The United States was Argentina's third most important supplier, after England

---

[12] E. Quesada, "La evolución social argentina," *Revista Argentina de Ciencias Políticas,* II (1911), 631–656; Enrique Gil, "Roosevelt," *Revista Argentina de Ciencias Políticas,* VIII (1914), 424–430; Isidoro Ruíz Moreno, "Propaganda argentina en América," *Revista Argentina de Ciencias Políticas,* IV (1912), 35–53; Leopold Lugones, "Le panaméricanisme: sa force et sa formule," *Revue Sud-Américaine,* I (Jan. 1914), 31–40.

and Germany, but lagged behind those two nations, and behind France and Belgium, as a purchaser of Argentine exports. Meat products accounted for 38.7 per cent of the value of Argentine exports in 1913, agricultural products for 58.1 per cent, and forest and other products for 3.2 per cent.[13]

Perhaps the most significant aspect of the enlarged trade between the United States and Argentina was the fact that part of it consisted of meat exports from the latter to the former. The United States tariff of 1913 had favorable results on Argentine imports, in particular through the removal of duties on meat imports. Argentine meat could be landed at the port of New York as cheaply as comparable grades of United States meat could be brought from the West. In 1914, 65,390 tons of meat were imported by the northern republic from its southern competitor. This amount was one-sixth of Argentina's meat exports. Included among these shipments in 1914 was the first direct shipment of Argentina's contribution to the delight of the gourmet—chilled beef.[14]

In the other direction, United States investment in Argentina was increasing. By the end of 1914, United States citizens seem to have held $25.7 millions of Argentine securities. The figure should be compared to that for British investment. In 1913, the British had invested in Argentina the sum of £357,750,661. Of this amount, £81,582,186 was in government bonds, £276,158,475 in "economic enterprises," chiefly railroads, which accounted for £215,001,961. The annual return of the total investment averaged 4.9 per cent. British investment in Argentina was 60 per cent greater than that in Brazil, the Latin American state in which was invested the next largest amount of British capital.[15]

The growth of commercial and financial ties between Argentina and the United States pleased the former. A recurrent

[13] U.S. Dept. of Commerce, *The Economic Position of Argentina During the War* (Misc. series, No. 88; Washington, D.C., 1920), pp. 86, 88, 96, 106.

[14] S. G. Hanson, *Argentine Meat and the British Market* . . . (Stanford, Calif., 1938), p. 180.

[15] C. Lewis, *America's Stake in International Investments* (Washington, D.C., 1938), p. 655; J. F. Rippy, "British Investments in Latin America, End of 1913," *The Journal of Modern History*, 19:226.

theme in Argentina was that United States competition with England would be beneficial. Unique was the advocate of this point of view who also was sufficiently far-sighted to tell his countrymen to invest their own capital in their own economy, in order to reduce foreign control, to acquire their railroads, and to develop industry in order to reduce imports.[16] Well-worn complaints against the Americans were still common, but even *El Economista* (Nov. 29, 1913) hailed the new United States tariff.

Increasing United States trade and investment was not wholly unplanned. A United States branch bank was finally established in Buenos Aires in 1914. The National City Bank of New York had begun studying the employment of capital in Latin America as early as 1911. The decision to open South American branches was reached in June 1914, after passage of the Federal Reserve Act, which authorized for the first time the establishment in foreign countries of branches of United States banks holding a national charter. The Buenos Aires office of the National City Bank was the first foreign branch of a national United States bank.

The National City representative, R. O. Bailey, landed in the Argentine capital on August 2, 1914—one of the more timely arrivals in financial history. The bank opened for business on November 10, 1914 at No. 321 Calle Rivadavia.

The president of National City, F. A. Vanderlip, was convinced of the "extraordinary awakening of interest in the subject of trade between the United States and South America." Bailey, the Buenos Aires manager, was enthusiastic—and dramatic— when he cabled the home office: "North America's commercial invasion of the Argentine has begun." More soberly he went on to tell of previous United States indifference and arrogance toward the Argentine market, and of the need for mature adaption by United States interest to a nation whose "business respiration has been through Europe." Competition was cutthroat, he reported. Banks were extending long credits based on speculative faith in Argentina's wealth; local merchants who had

---

[16] Manuel A. Michel, "Política económica argentina," *Revista de Derecho, Historia y Letras*, año 15, t. 43, Nov. 1912, pp. 360–368.

taken American goods sometimes hid them in their cellars in order to dry up competition; and some old-time American businessmen in Buenos Aires were resentful of the newcomers who would profit by their hard-won experience. But the government, he concluded, smiles upon everything that looks like investment capital.[17]

There were other indications of closer ties between the two countries. In May 1914 the United States raised its mission in Argentina to the rank of an embassy, and the Argentine government reciprocated. The action of the United States was belatedly pleasing to Argentina; the same exchange had taken place between the United States and Brazil some years earlier. In the Argentine senate the act was welcomed by Joaquín González and by Foreign Minister Murature as evidence of their country's importance. It was noted that the United States had taken the initiative in the matter.[18]

A few months earlier a delegation of businessmen from the Boston (Massachusetts) Chamber of Commerce had visited Argentina, receiving extensive attention in the press.

Several months later, in September 1914, the Argentine senate approved an arbitration treaty which had been negotiated in the names of the respective foreign ministers of the United States and Argentina, William Jennings Bryan and Rómulo Naón. In the course of his speech presenting the favorable recommendation of the senate, González made some comments about "South America" that reflected the change in attitude which had occurred within a generation. "When one speaks today of America," he said, "one speaks of a whole America. It is a conquest of civilization that one understands that the two great divisions of this continent are meant when 'America' is mentioned." As for Pan Americanism, the senator stated that now no one mistrusted the reach of the word: Pan Americanism means the unity of all interests and the preservation of the autonomy of each, under international law. However,

[17] F. A. Vanderlip, "Opportunities," *The Americas*, 1:3–4, 15 (November 1914); R. O. Bailey, "The First Effects of the European War," *The Americas*, 1:14–19 (November 1914). *The Americas* was the house journal of the National City.

[18] Congreso Nacional, *Diario de sesiones de la Cámara de Diputados*, June 3, 1914, pp. 75–76.

this was "on the basis of the most absolute, sincere, and frank solidarity with civilized Europe, to which we owe our very culture and existence." In a telling and important analogy, González went on to say that Argentina in fact had attempted to realize the precepts of George Washington's "Farewell Address": to remain free of dangerous alliances, to conserve its own best interest, yet never to exclude cooperation with nations of similar policies. In his peroration, the Argentine professor, writer, university president and statesman told his senatorial audience that the "Yankee peril" had passed; the Monroe Doctrine had run its course; a new president, who was also a philosopher, was in the White House; and the Pan American system was in steady decline.

Foreign Minister Murature appeared in the senate chamber to support ratification of the treaty. He made a significant definition of the Argentine view of the United States. Relations between the two countries, he stated, could evolve in a friendly and *parallel* manner. The treaty was unanimously ratified.[19]

The two leading newspapers of Buenos Aires were moderately pleased with warmer relations with the most powerful nation of the hemisphere. *La Nación* (Jan. 22, 1911) praised Ambassador Sherrill—but in the next sentence criticized the Americans for being wrapped in contemplation of their own greatness. *La Prensa* (March 25, 1914) became enthusiastic (for *La Prensa*) about increasing Argentine meat and grain shipments to the United States, and paid tribute to those Americans who had brought the new Pan Americanism into being—Buchanan, Barrett, Root, Sherrill, and Roosevelt.

Roosevelt's name on the list is not surprising. There was awareness of the fact that he had distinguished between Central and South America in the latter part of his tenure of the presidency, and that he had initiated, or at least encouraged, the "good neighbor" talk of Root and other assistants. Then too, out of office he was less formidable than in the White House. Finally, in his wisdom and energy, Roosevelt saw fit to visit Buenos Aires in 1913. He won a host of admirers. The porteños

[19] Congreso Nacional, *Diario de sesiones de la Cámara de Senadores*, Sept. 19, 1914, pp. 368–391.

admired his vitality and forthrightness. With the big stick home
in the closet, he received ovations wherever he went. Even Julio
Roca turned out to honor the visitor, and a cameraman caught
them in an impressive photograph, two men of obvious talent
and authority, top-hatted, grave, their heads close together in
conversation. The University gave him an honorary degree.
E. S. Zeballos, something of a Roosevelt himself, presided at the
occasion. The former foreign minister's theme was that what
the United States might do in the Caribbean was one thing;
what it might do in Argentina another. Argentina, said Zeballos,
has "concluded its civilizing evolution, and is a respected
country." (Mr. Roosevelt applauded this statement with enthusiasm, the notes tell us.) The former president applauded
insistently when Zeballos went on to state that the Monroe
Doctrine was no longer necessary for the protection of Argentina. For Pan Americanism, the Argentine leader voiced the
usual broad reservations: it was a fine movement, but vague,
premature, and ideal. How could Argentina be interested in
Latin American countries which were located farther away than
Hamburg or Geneva? But, he concluded, "we cultivate a
theoretic Pan Americanism . . . We wish to be kindly to all the
Americas . . . But we cannot cultivate this sentiment by destroying the bonds that unite us with Europe."

In his speeches in Buenos Aires, Roosevelt struck the most
melodious chords. It is not intended, he told his eager listeners,
that the Monroe Doctrine should apply to Argentina; Europe's
importance to that country is fully appreciated; the American
states are sovereign and equal.[20] *La Prensa* (Nov. 14, 1913) was
so delighted that it proclaimed that the two opposing phrases,
"America for the Americans," and "America for humanity,"
could now be united in one: "the America of the Americans for
themselves and for humanity." The other papers were equally
impressed, one of them (*La Razón*, Nov. 4, 1913) calling the
American leader the most popular man in the world. Even in

[20] "Theodore Roosevelt y la política internacional americana," *Revista de
Derecho, Historia y Letras*, año 16, t. 46, Dec. 1913, pp. 565–568, 572–573. Upon his
return home Roosevelt published articles in *The Outlook*, in 1914, in which he
excluded the strong and stable nations of Latin America from the purview of the
Monroe Doctrine.

advertisements Roosevelt's image was invoked with good humor: one full page advertisement (*Caras y Caretas*, June 1914) showed Teddy with his teeth bared and his arms raised threateningly above his head; below, in large letters, ran the caption— "I AM THE ENEMY," and below that, in small type, the words, ". . . of all alcoholic beverages"; at the bottom, in very large type were the words Fernet-Branca.

Part of Roosevelt's new popularity may be explained as a by-product of the recent change in administration in the United States and President Wilson's avowal of a new attitude toward Latin America, a policy which met little favor in Argentina. Secretary of State Knox said his farewell to the governing board of the Pan American Union in February 1913. He used the opportunity to deny to his assembled colleagues that the United States was "asserting and abusing a claim of primacy in our Western councils." "If in the working of God's will," he continued, "it has been given to us to exert influence upon our congeners of Pan Americanism, it has ever been our steadfast purpose to use that influence rightly and benignly in the direction of the independence, the stability, and the prosperity of all your countries."[21]

Wilson took up where Knox left off, perhaps with more idealism for the good ends which the outgoing secretary so strongly endorsed, but with little better results. In a statement made on March 11, 1913, Wilson implied a policy of non-recognition to be applied to Latin American governments which were not democratic and orderly. *La Prensa* (March 14, 1913) criticized the president's criteria as a grave danger to Latin America, putting its editorial finger on the center of the question by calling the policy "essentially offensive," and injurious to sovereignty. Wilson, the paper commented, must have been thinking of countries near the United States when he made his statement. It was this kind of reaction to which the American representative referred when he reported to the State Department that the policy had received a cold reception in Argentina.[22]

[21] The Pan American Union Archive, Minutes of the Governing Board of the Pan American Union, V, 373-374.

[22] Lorillard to Bryan, March 17, 1913, Dept. of State, Argentina, Numerical File, No. 157, 710.11/124.

In October 1913 Wilson made a speech at Mobile renouncing aggressive intent toward Latin America. Unfortunately, this policy announcement perished in embryo, killed by the crisis in United States-Mexican affairs born of the revolution in the latter country. Argentine opinion was alarmed. *La Prensa* (Oct. 21, 1913) called for absolute non-intervention by the United States, and linked the success of Pan Americanism to that position. The Mobile speech received no favorable notice. Wilson's interference in Mexico was called bumbling and offensive to Europe by *La Nación* (Nov. 26, 1913).

Announcement by the government of Argentina, on March 11, 1914, of its policy of non-intervention in Mexico was welcomed by the newspapers, which then went on somewhat paradoxically to applaud the report that Argentina would be asked to share in mediating the crisis.

With the occupation of Vera Cruz on April 21, 1914 by United States forces, the Argentine press became bitterly critical of the Yankees. Scare headlines, maps of theoretical battlefields, sketches of port installations, lengthy editorials, all dinned into Argentine minds the belief that the United States was a savage aggressor, launching a full-scale war. The Argentine government was officially neutral, but public opinion was not.[23]

Then the atmosphere was cleared, perhaps in the only way that would have satisfied Argentina. Leo Rowe, prominent in Pan American affairs, on April 4 had stated that while it was the duty of the United States to insist on the reestablishment of order in Mexico, that end should be accomplished by securing the joint mediation of Argentina, Brazil, and Chile. On April 25 the three countries offered their services, which Wilson promptly accepted. *La Nación* (April 26) hailed Argentina's participation as evidence of her emergence from isolation—her first positive step as a South American power since the action by Drago. *La Prensa* (April 28) claimed that the request to mediate was testimony to the "serious inspiration given to the Pan American movement in recent years by Latin America."

The mediation conference arrived at a settlement on June 24, 1914. *La Prensa* (June 27) lauded the protocol as a triumph of

[23] Lorillard to Bryan, April 22, 1914, Numerical File, 812.00/1630.

true Pan Americanism over a continental scandal, and the first occasion that the United States had subordinated its interests to those of the other Pan American states. *La Nación* (June 26) hailed the example of peace given by the United States. *El Diario* (June 26) welcomed the victory of non-intervention. *La Razón* (June 25) wrote of the "triumph of Argentine mediation," perhaps because the Argentine ambassador to the United States had been presiding officer of the conference.

The mediation was clearly popular in Argentina. It was an inter-American, if not a Pan American success. As a Colombian diplomat pointed out in an Argentine magazine, twenty years earlier the Latin American countries would not have dreamed of offering mediation to the United States, nor the United States of accepting it. Argentine Ambassador Naón in Washington called it a demonstration of Pan American solidarity. Foreign Minister Murature regarded it as an event of signal transcendence for the history of Pan American policy, although he wanted it understood that, contrary to some opinion, the original idea of mediation did not come from the United States. He did not state where the idea had originated. [24]

In these first months of 1914 Argentina needed a spur to national morale. It was perhaps symbolic of the history of the Generation of Eighty that one of their last achievements should have been in the field of foreign affairs, where the oligarchy had always been tenacious and successful in defence of its own interests, which, in this field, had usually been those of the nation. Certainly in domestic affairs the outlook was gloomy. Politically the Saenz Peña law was being fulfilled, with the expected dismal results for the conservatives and their once invincible electoral machine. In elections in 1912 and 1913 not only the Radicals but the Socialists won numerous offices, and

---

[24] Leo S. Rowe, "The Scope and Limits of Our Obligations toward Mexico," in "International Relations of the United States," *The Annals of the American Academy of Political and Social Science*, 54:229, 233 (July 1914); República Argentina, *La política internacional de la Nación Argentina* . . . (Buenos Aires, 1946), pp. 343–351; R. Ancízar, "La mediación del ABC," *Revista Argentina de Ciencias Políticas*, VIII (1914), 360; Enrique Gil, *La evolución del panamericanismo: el credo de Wilson y el panamericanismo* (Buenos Aires, 1933), pp. 389–391; República Argentina, *Memoria de Relaciones Exteriores, 1913–1914*, pp. v–x; Lorillard to Bryan, July 7, 1914, Numerical File, 812.00/12712.

the prospect for continuation of conservative control of the presidency in the election of 1916 was dim indeed. The loss of that bastion would mean the loss of much of the political power of the class.

To the political misery of the upper class was added economic woe, for the class and for the nation. 1913 was a year of crop failures. To make matters worse, Europe began to tighten its money belt, alarmed by the threat of a war and concerned, with respect to Argentina, about over-investment there. Internal credit was vastly inflated, property was at an all-time high, speculation was taking on the desperate optimism of 1889.

Poor crops and a shortage of new money quickly brought an end to the great boom. Values fell, mortgages were called, bankruptcies multiplied.[25] As the first months of 1914 passed, it became clear that Argentina was in economic difficulties, all the more frightening because they resembled those of a quarter of a century earlier. There was the same focus on grain production for export, and on railroad construction, the same need for a steady flow of foreign money to keep the credit structure swelling, the same men, in many cases, in command of the land, the banks, and the distribution net.

The newspapers, even the best of them, sounded the same hopeful notes of twenty-five years before. *La Nación* in its fat New Year's Day edition of 1914 wrote: "The year which has just transpired has been favorable from all points of view . . . Europe and the United States should continue thinking seriously about employing large amounts of capital in this part of the world. On all sides one sees railroads in construction or in plan, ports opened, production growing, and confidence in the future reborn." *El Economista Argentina* (March 7, 14, June 13, 1914) described the economic situation as one of mere "disequilibrium," which the "fuerzas vivas" would rectify.

Certainly foreign trade was running at a high rate, totaling more than one billion dollars in 1913, of which nearly one hundred million was with the United States, over seventy million in imports from that country, and twenty-three million

---

[25] Carlos Soares, *Economía y finanzas de la Nación Argentina 1903–1916* (3 vols.; Buenos Aires, 1916–1932), I, 9–10, 34–38.

in exports to it. In the face of such impressive statistics it was hard to believe that the danger signals meant more than a squall. The argument was commonly heard that a bad government or bad financing might disturb the economic order for a time, but that cattlemen and farmers were not gamblers, and their work on the rich earth would make all well again.

The earth was undeniably fruitful, but it was not so clear that the cattlemen and farmers (and this meant big cattlemen and big farmers) were not gamblers. The pattern of landholding of the upper class was altering in these first years of the twentieth century, just as was their political control. Large holdings, or latifundios, still dominated (Table 4), but changes were occurring, and the great estates were shrinking, perhaps in part

TABLE 4. Landholdings in Argentina and in the province of Buenos Aires in 1914.

Area (hectáreas)*	Argentina		Buenos Aires	
	Number of owners	Total area of holdings (hectáreas)*	Number of owners	Total area of holdings (hectáreas)*
Over 25,001	506	28,959,853	32	1,277,555
10,001–25,000	1,566	25,397,126	198	3,021,894
5,001–10,000	3,161	25,254,982	541	4,003,507
1,001–5,000	19,998	47,952,890	3,972	8,453,097
501–1,000	13,825	9,645,336	4,638	3,218,700
101–500	86,685	19,848,907	27,425	6,334,187
51–100	45,364	3,479,210	12,930	978,033
26–50	34,662	1,337,910	8,799	333,099
Under 26	100,836	964,410	20,133	222,167

Source: República Argentina *Tercera Censo* (10 vols.; Buenos Aires, 1916–19), V; *Explotaciones agropecuarios* (Buenos Aires, 1919), p. 3.

* 1 hectárea = 2.471 acres.

because of speculation and mismanagement, in part because of inheritance laws and for other reasons. In the province of Buenos Aires, richest of all, there had been in the year 1901, 486 owners each possessing more than 10,000 hectares of land. In 1904, there were 418 such persons. In 1914, there were 230. And this

11

was not as a result of merging of holdings, for less acreage was included in the total in each case.[26]

The reduction in the number of great landlords implied basic alterations in the social, economic, and political status of the oligarchy. The change, in itself, was not, of course, a necessary indication of weakness in the organization of production, nor did it necessarily bear relation to the depression of 1913–1914. But defects in the production system did exist, defects intrinsic to the economic system under which the Generation of Eighty had become wealthy.

There was a growing proclivity for absenteeism among the landowners, and inattention to improved agricultural techniques, including the use of fertilizer. There was scarcely any independent small or middle-sized farmer class. When agriculture had become remunerative the landowners, who were pastoralists, did not farm their holdings themselves. They leased their land to tenants, men who in most instances were immigrants without knowledge of sound techniques and without experience in local conditions. These men were seldom provided with adequate tools, or able to acquire them. Being tenants of men trained by their history and by desire to hold onto their property, it was usually impossible for a tenant to become an owner. Hence, there was no incentive of stability. Production was for export, consequently diversification was ignored—to the pathetic extent that many a tenant of large acreage did not bother to have an adequate vegetable plot or livestock for his own sustenance. There was no interest in permanent improvements on the part of owners or tenants. Dwellings were apt to be mud huts. This form of land tenure and its derived methods of production were workable during the boom of 1880–1914, under an expanding economy and a restricted social order. Around the latter date it began to appear that for crops and for people it was a wasteful system.

It is revealing and not uncharacteristic that the most effective contemporary criticism of this state of affairs was made not by

[26] República Argentina, Ministerio de Agricultura, *Informes y estudios de la Dirección de Economía Rural y Estadística* (2nd ed.; 2 vols.; Buenos Aires, 1916), I, 319–320 ff.; II, 37.

an Argentine, but by an Englishman experienced in Argentine agriculture. H. Gibson summarized the situation: "We have called into existence an unsettled and inefficient rural population; we have given it a task beyond its strength; we have saddled it with a disproportionate army of intermediaries; we have built railways, contracted debts, mortgaged the very land lent to it, all upon its prospective productivity, and we have succeeded at least temporarily in disabling it."[27]

The economic storm, which might or might not have blown away, became a hurricane, but not for reasons within Argentine power to control. On August 1, 1914, World War I began. The effect in Argentina, coming on top of a delicate situation, was immediate and drastic. In Buenos Aires, on August 2, a week's banking holiday was proclaimed by the national government. This was followed on August 8 by a one-month private debt moratorium. On August 12 gold export was taken over by the government. The volume of shipping plummeted down, reflecting the collapse of both imports and exports.[28]

The ruling class shook under the blast. But the future did not appear to be hopeless. *La Nación* noted on August 1 that Argentina's meat and grain were elements as decisive as military power or financial force, and that they would have to be purchased at a good price. By August 7 the paper was using phrases such as "shortage prices," "the next crop may be double in value," and, "the economic outlook of the Republic in the face of this universal conflagration could not be more agreeable." *La Prensa* wrote on August 5: "We are thinking only of our situation and of our resources, and of how to save ourselves from the universal shipwreck, so that in doing so we may serve Europe itself, for we are now a factor in human affairs, a directing force in civilization."

In 1880 young President Roca had mapped out the course for the future, under signposts reading "Peace" and "Order."

[27] Herbert Gibson, *The Land We Live On* (Buenos Aires, 1914), pp. 14, 15–18, 23–24, 37–40; José Ingenieros, *Sociología argentina* (Madrid, 1913), pp. 84–87; U.S. Dept. of Commerce, *South America as an Export Field*, by Otto Wilson (Washington, 1914), pp. 35–36; Carl Taylor, *Rural Life in Argentina* (Baton Rouge, 1948), pp. 169–173, 190–206.

[28] Soares, *Economía*, I, 12–30.

Thirty-three years later the other great leader of Roca's generation, Saenz Peña, also delivered an inaugural address to congress: "Señores Senadores; Señores Diutados: The Republic is
in peace. No cloud obscures the horizon; no conflict threatens
to interrupt the harmony of our growing greatness . . . It is a
fact that the citizens vote, incomes increase, foreign commerce
reaches figures unprecedented in the history of our economy . . .
We enjoy the respect of nations . . . Peace . . . and wealth; such
is the picture to which the facts bear witness."

In the next year, 1914, as the war came to the old world—
that world which had done so much to make their nation strong
—Julio Argentino Roca and Roque Saenz Peña died. Saenz
Peña died in mid-term of his six years as president, on August 9.
He was sixty-three years old, his massive frame wasted of its
weight by the diabetes which had stricken him more than a year
earlier. He spoke what may serve as his own epitaph when,
shortly before his death, thinking of his class, and then of the
people for whom he had made possible the right to vote in
freedom, he said, "I have lost almost all my friends, but I have
governed for the Republic."

Roca died on October 19, seventy-one years of age, the
warrior who had brought peace first with a sword to the
pampas, then to the people by political means. He was weary
at the end, and heartsick over the passing of what he called his
"old regime," but he was realistic, as always, and resigned to
the turbulent, democratic future which he saw for his loved land.

A little earlier, another distinctive figure of the Generation
of Eighty had died, older in years than most of the other prominent figures of the generation, but still their dandy. Lucio V.
Mansilla had always carried matters to extremes: where others
of his class had spent much time in Europe, he spent almost all
of his later life there. And he was a bit extreme when he died,
for he succumbed in Paris in 1913. The men of the Generation
of Eighty liked Europe well enough, but they died in Argentina.

Their view of Argentina, their visions, their solutions, were
less attractive now, less noble and less useful, despite Saenz
Peña's last appeal to peace and wealth. They had had their
day, and it had been a great one. Under them Argentina became

rich—and also dependent. Their domestic policies and their foreign policies were tied to those factors—wealth, and dependency. But, if they lost something of economic freedom, they believed that they had preserved and advanced the cause of their political sovereignty, and that of all Latin America. Against the United States and Pan Americanism they had placed their growing strength.

Somewhat similar in national history and attitudes, Yankees and Argentines were similar also in facets of national and individual temperament—in their pride, optimism, aggressive independence, in their regard for material achievement and its reward. Both people were, in short, Americans, each ready to uphold its position in the hemisphere. The Pan American Conferences brought them together in not-too-happy collaboration. Each, to the other, seemed isolationist, proud, even arrogant, and the problems which arose out of their attempts to sell to each other added to the tensions between them.

Yet the Argentines made out a definition of Pan Americanism, just as the Yankees did, and, while their paths often diverged, they did not permanently divide. This was the glory of the Generation of Eighty: that in a short time it made a new Argentina, and gave it a place in Europe and in America.

Index

Harvard Historical Studies

(Early titles now out of print are omitted)

51. *Frank Edgar Bailey*. British Policy and the Turkish Reform Movement. 1942.

52. *John Black Sirich*. The Revolutionary Committees in the Departments of France. 1943.

53. *Henry Frederick Schwarz*. The Imperial Privy Council in the Seventeenth Century. 1943.

54. *Aaron Ignatius Abell*. Urban Impact on American Protestantism. 1943.

55. *Holden Furber*. John Company at Work. 1948.

56. *Walter Howe*. The Mining Guild of New Spain and Its Tribunal General, 1770–1821. 1949.

57. *John Howes Gleason*. The Genesis of Russophobia in Great Britain. 1950.

58. *Charles Coulston Gillispie*. Genesis and Geology: A Study in the Relations of Scientific Thought, Natural Theology, and Social Opinion in Great Britain, 1790–1850. 1951.

59. *Richard Humphrey*. Georges Sorel, Prophet without Honor: A Study in Anti-Intellectualism, 1951.

60. *Robert G. L. Waite*. Vanguard of Nazism: The Free Corps Movement in Postwar Germany, 1918–1923. 1952.

61. *Nicholas V. Riasanovsky*. Russia and the West in the Teaching of the Slavophiles. 1952.

62. *John King Fairbank*. Trade and Diplomacy on the China Coast: The Opening of the Treaty Ports, 1842–1854. Vol. I, text.

63. *John King Fairbank*. Trade and Diplomacy on the China Coast. Vol. II, reference material. 1953.

64. *Franklin L. Ford*. Robe and Sword: The Regrouping of the French Aristocracy after Louis XIV. 1953.

65. *Carl E. Schorske*. German Social Democracy, 1905–1917. The Development of the Great Schism. 1955.

66. *Wallace Evan Davies*. Patriotism on Parade: The Story of Veterans' and Hereditary Organizations in America, 1783–1900. 1955.

67. *Harold Schwartz*. Samuel Gridley Howe: Social Reformer, 1801–1876. 1956.

68. *Bryce D. Lyon*. From Fief to Indenture: The Transition from Feudal to Non-Feudal Contract in Western Europe. 1957.

69. *Stanley J. Stein*. Vassouras: A Brazilian Coffee County, 1850–1900. 1957.

70. *Thomas F. McGann*. Argentina, the United States, and the Inter-American System, 1880–1914. 1957.